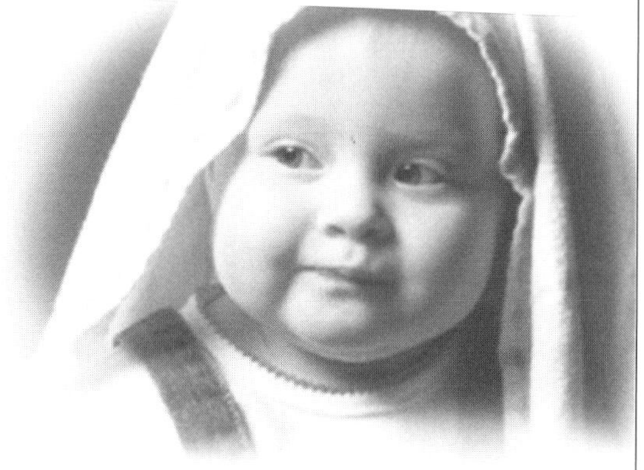

Working to be...

the BEST rural hospital in the country.

***Consistently Ranked Nationally** As A Top Hospital...*

Sunnyside Community Hospital offers "big city" health care services in a small community environment. With a team of highly skilled professionals utilizing state-of-the-are technology, it is comforting to know a trip out of town is unnecessary to obtain quality health care. Our commitment to building healthy communities extends to 24 hours a day, 7 days a week, 365 days a year. All of us at Sunnyside Community Hospital take seriously our mission of providing quality health care to meet the needs of all Lower Valley residents.

We are a community of compassionate nurturing professionals committed to improving your health...

We are the hospital building your future.

Committed to the Lower Yakima Valley for over half a century.

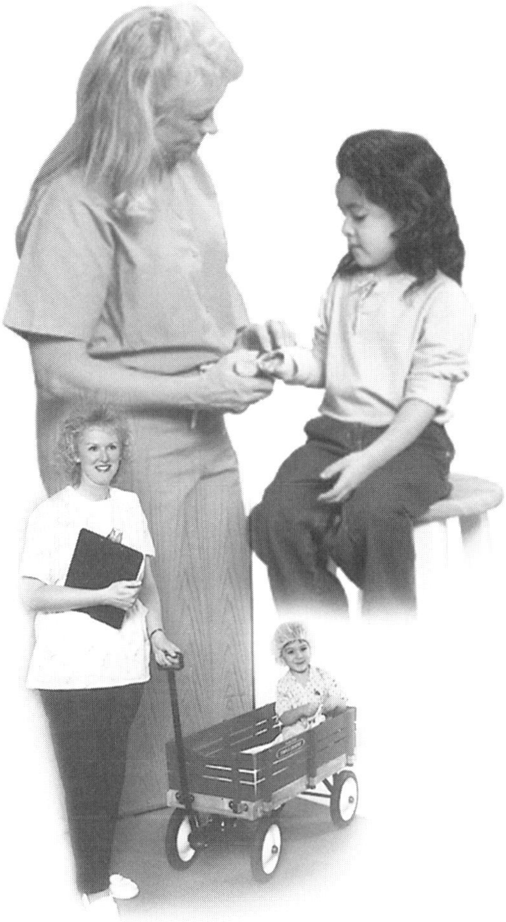

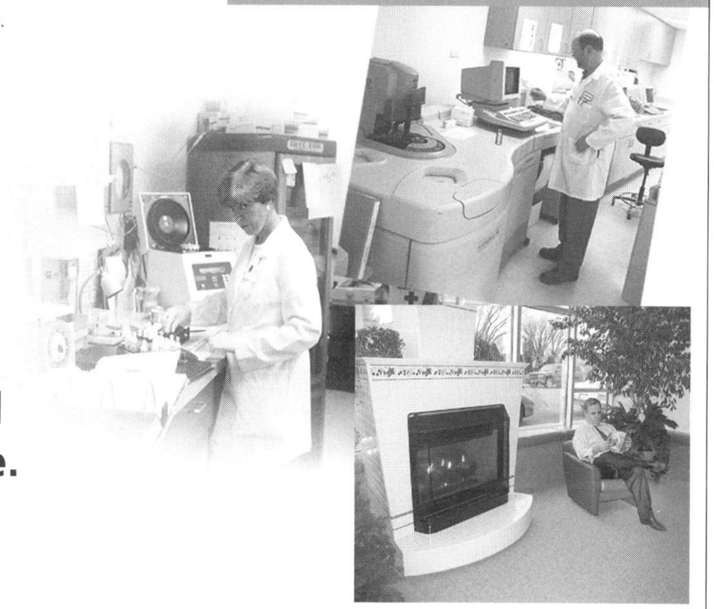

Sunnyside
COMMUNITY HOSPITAL

www.sunnysidehospital.com • 10th & Tacoma • 837-1500

MW01697895

DAILY SUN NEWS
'TODAY'S LOCAL NEWS TODAY'

600 S. 6th St. • P.O. Box 878
Sunnyside, Washington 98944
509.837.4500
www.sunnyside.net

PROUDLY serving the Lower Valley for more than 100 years from Sunnyside

We're Proud To Be Your Community Newspaper And We Thank You For Your Support Over The Years.

We Have Served The Public And Community's Interests With Honesty And A Constant Goal Of Objectivity.

We Will Never Lose Sight Of The Trust You Have Placed In Us.

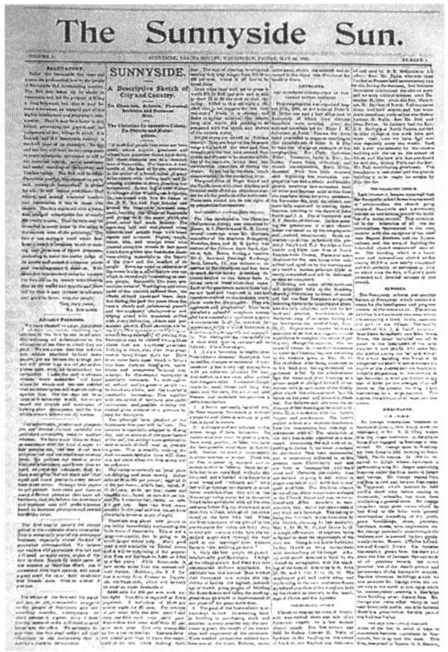
The Sunnyside Sun.

SUNNYSIDE

A Descriptive Sketch of City and Country.

1ST ISSUE – MAY 24, 1901

PROUD SPONSOR OF *"A PICTORIAL HISTORY OF SUNNYSIDE, WASHINGTON"*

A Pictorial History of Sunnyside, Washington

VOLUME ONE

FOREWORD

History is a fascinating thing. So often we go about our daily lives not realizing who has tread the same path in years past. Where streets were once lined with horse drawn wagons and buggies there are high-powered automobiles and 4x4 trucks cruising town. Where a family eked out a living growing enough food on their small plot of land to feed a family of 10 a "Mart" now stands.

This pictorial book of the Sunnyside area is not meant to be a comprehensive history of this area, rather a compilation of many of the photographs available from the Sunnyside Museum and other sources. History is not an exact science, but it does give us a chance to look back and see what life might have been like at the turn of the 20th Century. How people dressed, what they did for recreation and how many of the present-day names of buildings and roads may have come about. You may find that the building you grew up to know as a pharmacy first got its start as a bank or livery stable, or areas that were considered in the country then, are now just a part of an ever-growing eastern Washington community.

Photos, in a wonderful way, allow us to gain a sense of the area. This book is but a snapshot of the history of Sunnyside through many different images. These images would not have made it to print without the support of many businesses and individuals in our community. I'd like to thank John Saras and the Sunnyside Museum for the many fine photographs and information. Also thanks go to the Sunnyside Valley Irrigation District, Les Amundson, Al Heffron and Airport Ranches for their contribution of photographs. Also a special thanks to Monty Johnson and Julia Hart for their help writing chapter introductions.

Others who deserve recognition are the many page sponsors in the book. Without their partnership in this endeavor, this book would not have been possible. Special thanks go to Airport Ranches, Benton Rural Electric, City of Sunnyside, Port of Sunnyside, Mountain States Const., Newhouse Family, Pacific Power, Smith Funeral Home, Speck Motors, Sunnyside Community Hospital, Sunnyside School District, Sunnyside Valley Irrigation District and Van de Graaf Ranches.

I hope you find this book enjoyable and it provides you with a flavor of years past. If you should have photographs or written history of the area, I encourage you to share them with the museum. Who knows, there may be another book worth of photographs in attics and family scrapbooks throughout the town. It may be your photos will be a part of a *Pictorial History of Sunnyside, Washington, Volume Two.*

Tim Graff
Publisher, *Sunnyside Daily Sun News*

Copyright© 2002 • ISBN: 1-891395-96-3
All rights reserved. No part of this book may be reproduced, stored in a retrieval system or transmitted in any form or by any means, electronic, mechanical, photocopying, recording or otherwise, without prior written permission of the copyright owner or the publisher.
Published by Pediment Publishing, a division of The Pediment Group, Inc. Vancouver, Washington. Printed in Canada

TABLE OF CONTENTS

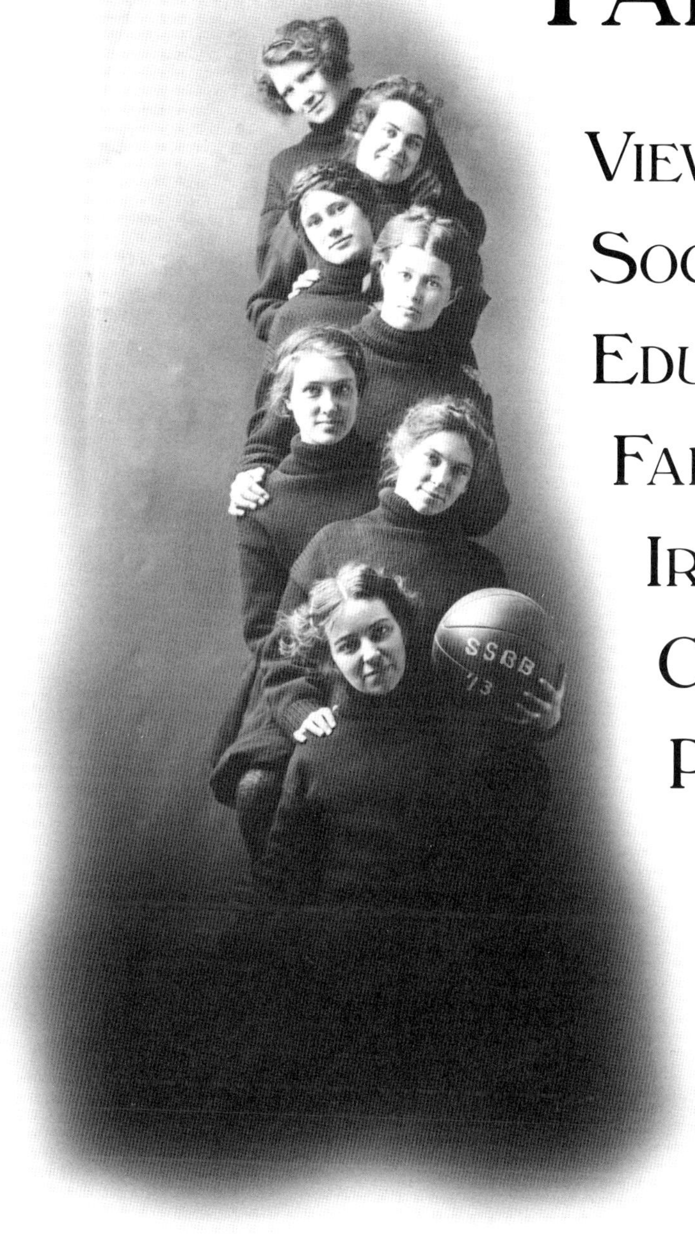

VIEWS

In the 1860s the land that would become Sunnyside was part of Ben Snipe's vast cattle kingdom. By the early 1880s the cattle were gone—replaced by sagebrush, rattlesnakes, coyotes and jack rabbits. Walter Granger came in 1889 and built the Sunnyside Canal giving life to the fertile, but dry Yakima Valley.

Granger plotted the Sunnyside town site and in 1893 William H. Cline built a general store and became the town's first resident. Sunnyside prospered, but success was fleeting. An economic depression nearly wiped the town from the map.

Sunnyside was revived in the late 1890s after Stephen J. Harrison, Harvey M. Lichty and Christian Rowland chose the town as the site to start their Christian Cooperative Colony. Soon people were trickling into Sunnyside determined to build a Christian community. Their spirits were tried, but those hardy pioneers prevailed and laid the foundations for the vibrant, multicultural community Sunnyside is today.

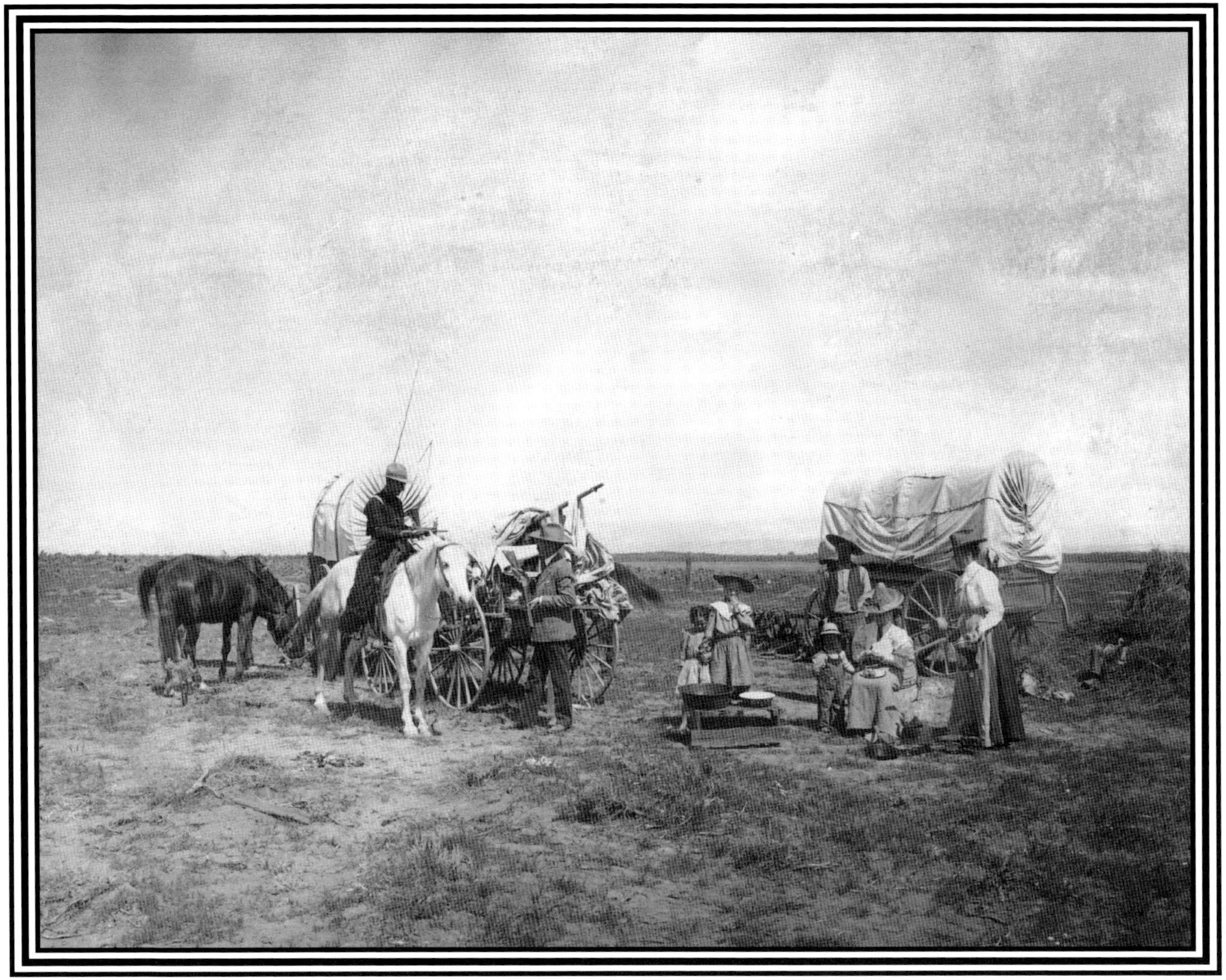

Depiction of early settlers in Sunnyside, circa 1890s.

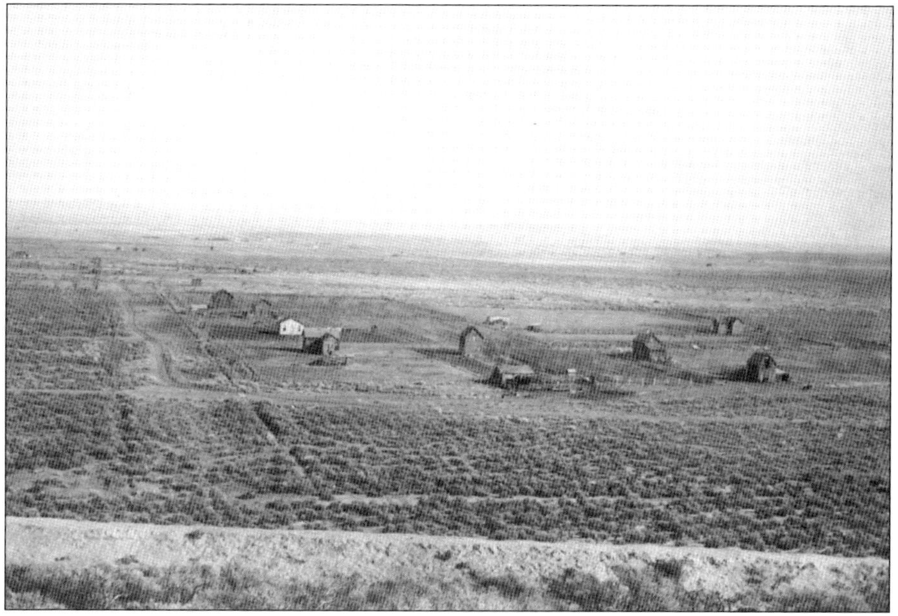

Looking north from atop Harrison Hill.

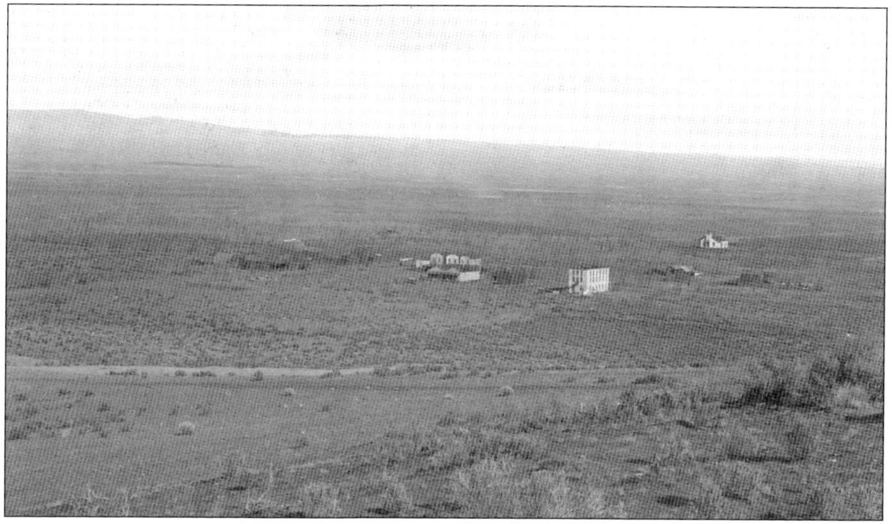

An early view of Sunnyside, circa 1899. Cline's Store, the first mercantile established and first building in Sunnyside (unpainted) left center.The white building in the distance is the Emerson one-room school.The three-story white building is the vacant Sunnyside Hotel which was located on the northwest corner of 6th St. and Franklin Ave.

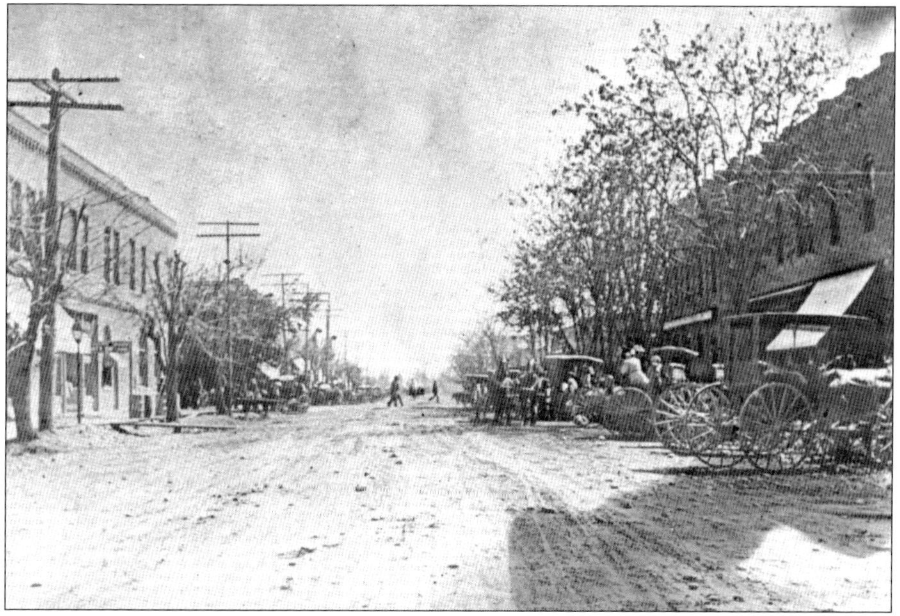

Looking south on 6th Street, early 1900s.

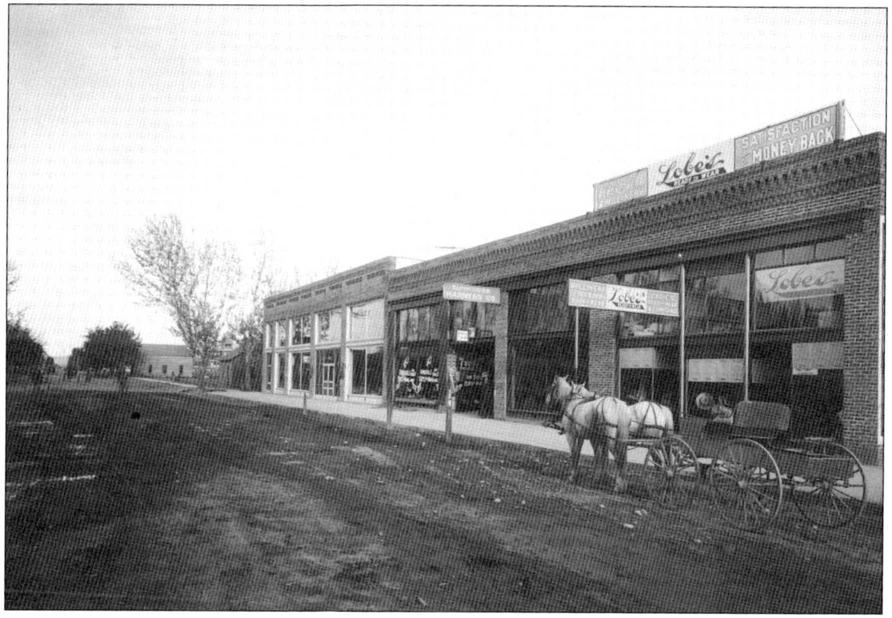

Mayhew Avenue looking east which later became known as Edison Avenue, early 1900s.

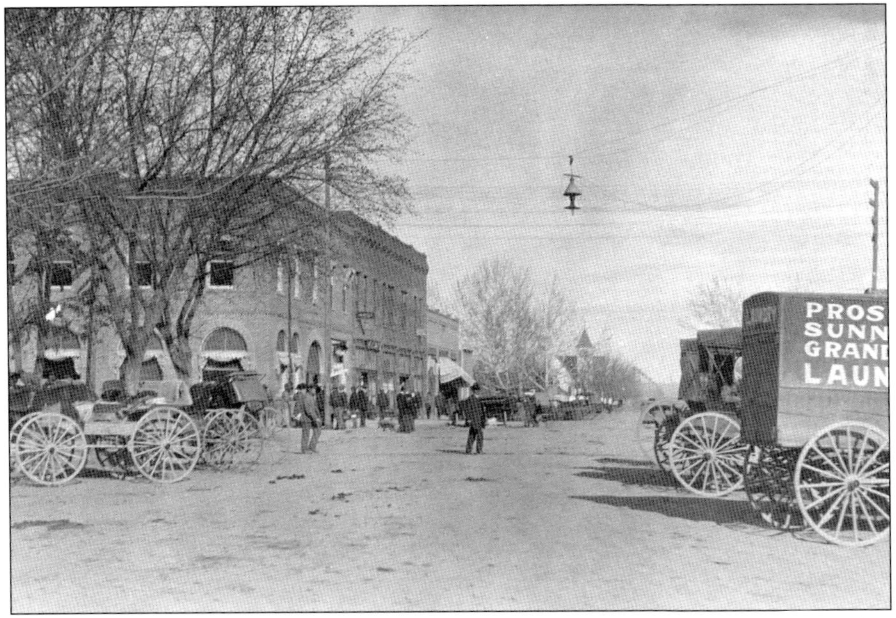

A view of 6th Street and Edison Avenue looking east, circa 1910. The Methodist Church can be seen in the distance.

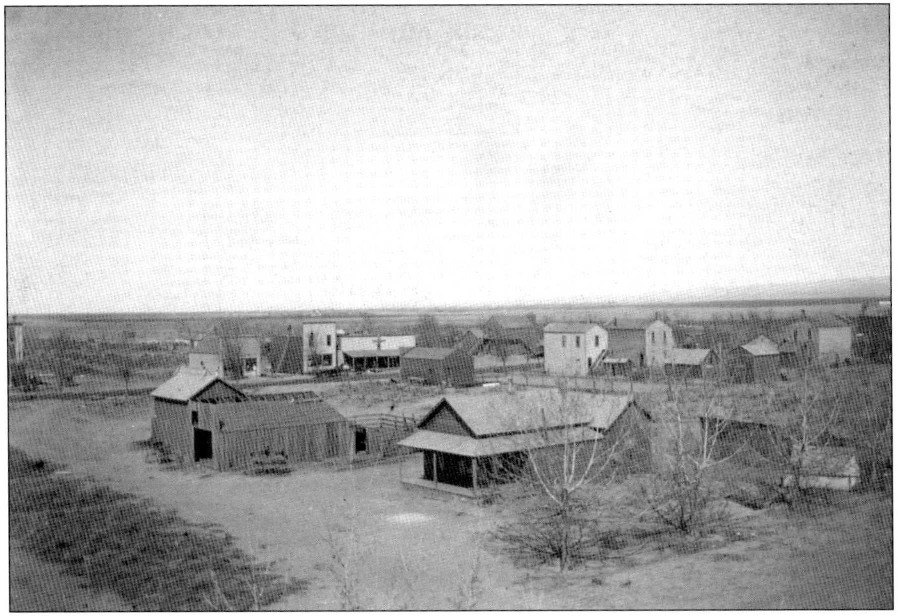

A view of Sunnyside looking northwest from the Federated Church located at 8th Street and Franklin Avenue, circa 1901.

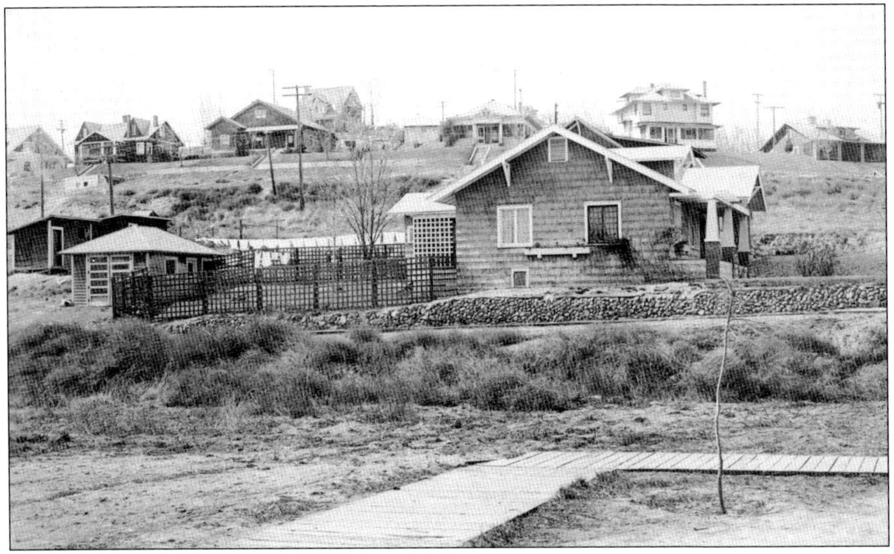

Grandview Heights residential area in the early 1900s. The seven homes at the top of the hill were residences belonging to the (from left to right); Schaders, Nealans, McKnights, McCredies, Georges, Rowlands, and Garins. The boardwalk is where the present-day Ben Snipes Park resides.

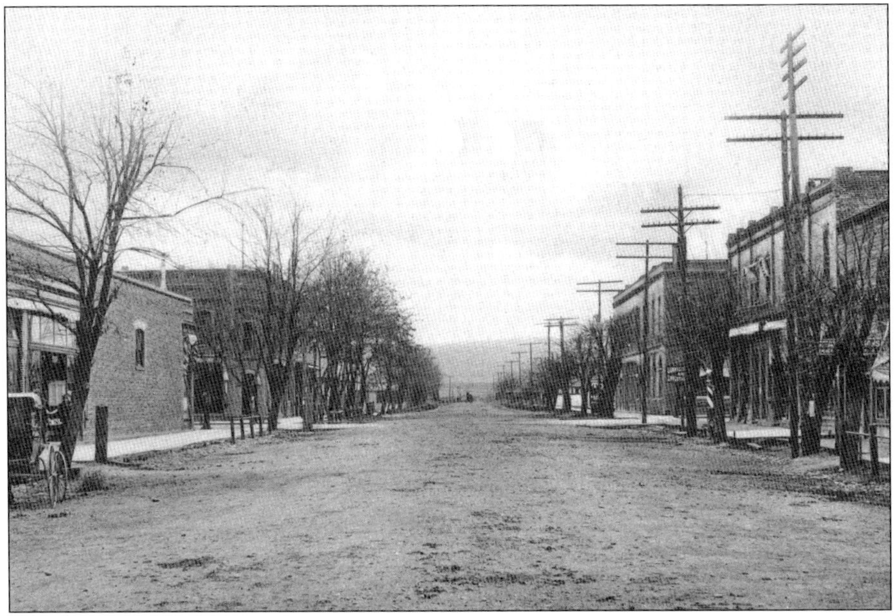

Looking north on Main Street, circa 1909.

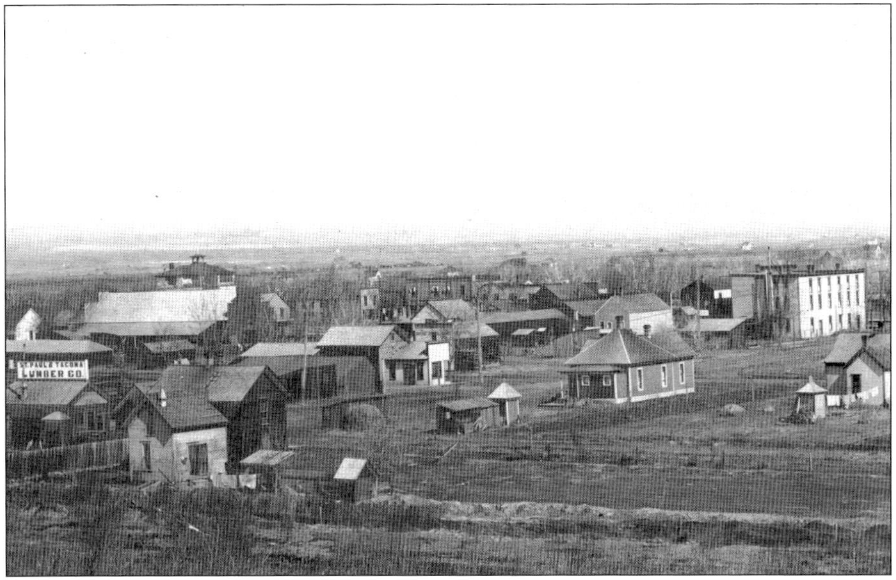

A view of Sunnyside from the hill looking northeast, circa 1905. The Sunnyside Hotel is the large three story building on the right. The hotel was located on the corner of 6th Street and Franklin Avenue.

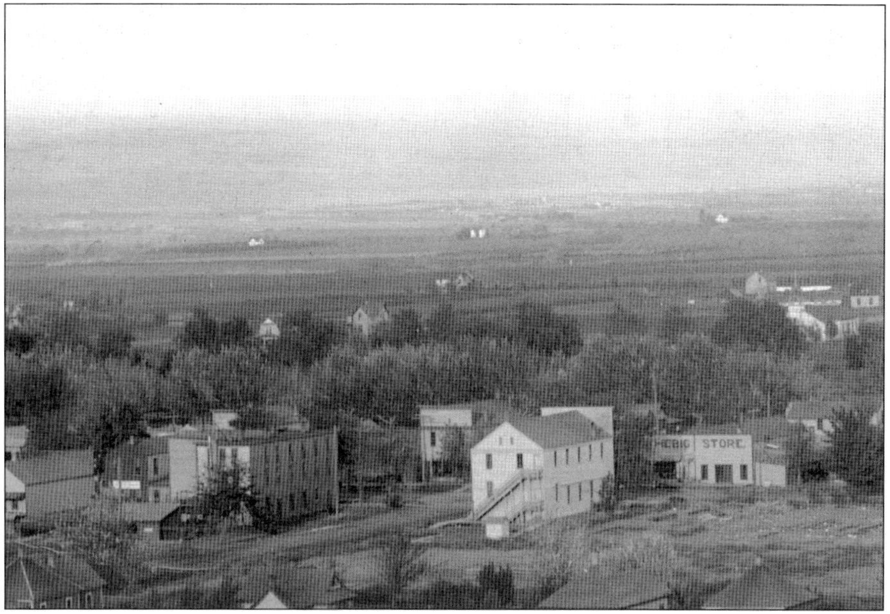

Looking east from atop Harrison Hill, circa 1907. The Sunnyside Hotel is seen on the left with the Opera House across the street.

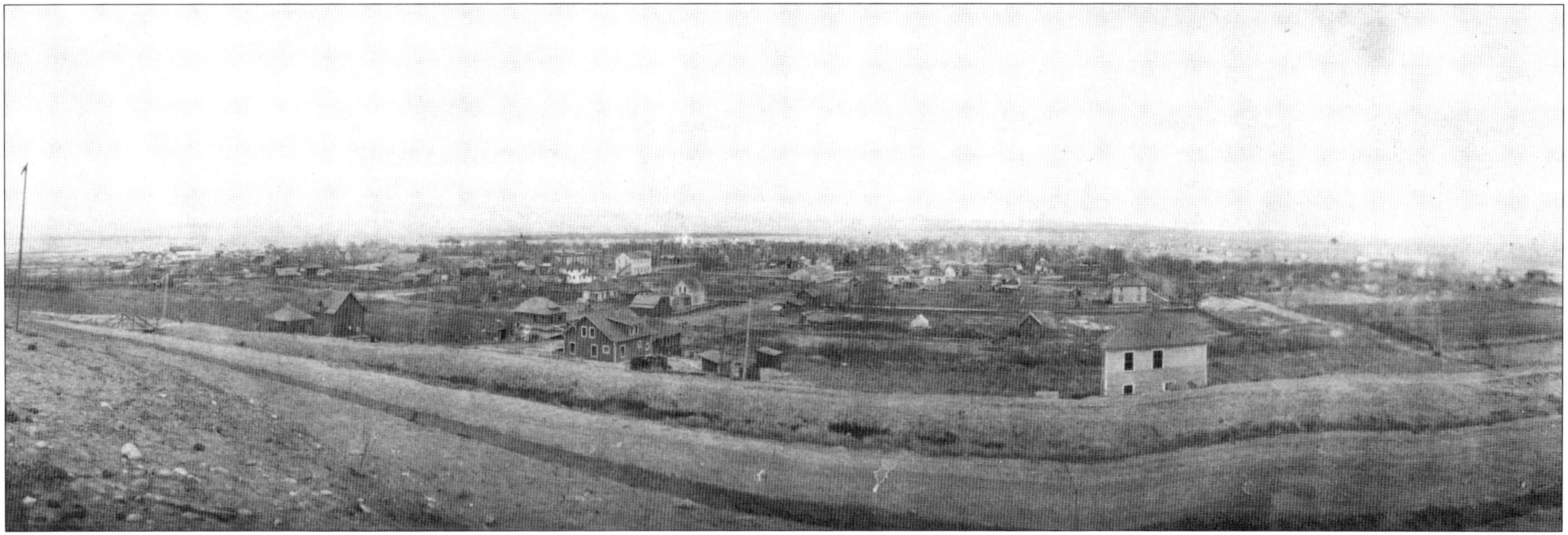

Panoramic view of Sunnyside from the present day Crescent Avenue looking east, 1908. Note the Sunnyside Canal in the foreground.

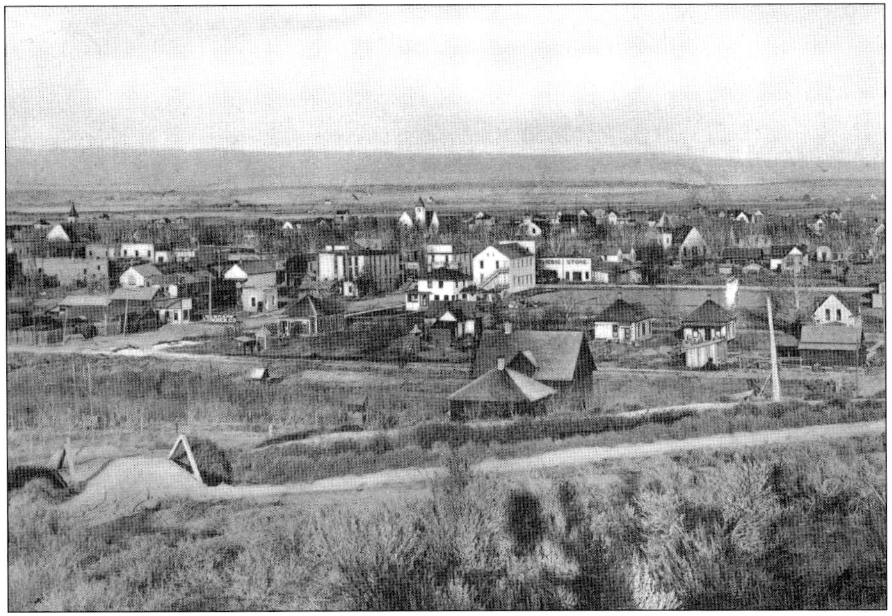

A birds' eye view of Sunnyside, 1908. One of the many taken from Harrison Hill.

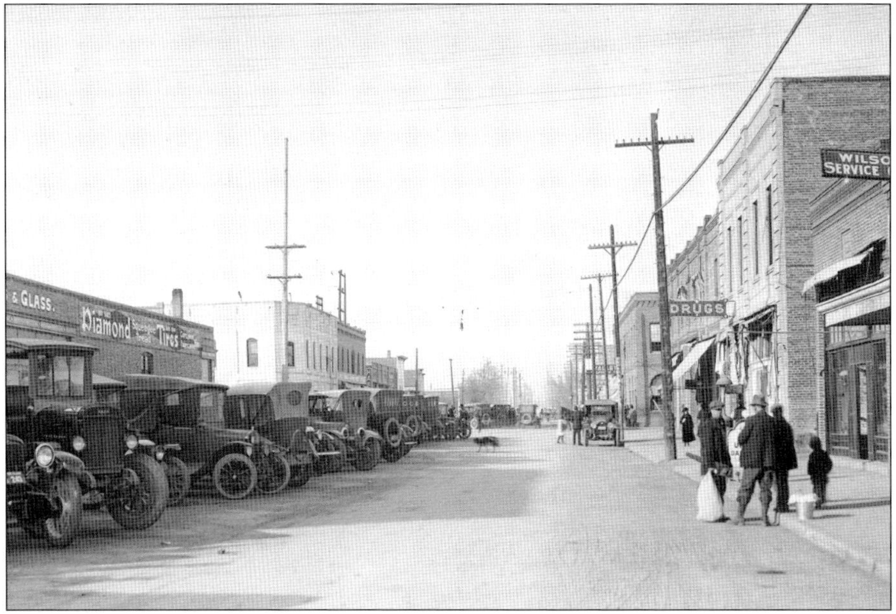

Looking north on 6th Street towards the intersection of 6th Street and Edison Avenue, Sunnyside, circa 1910.

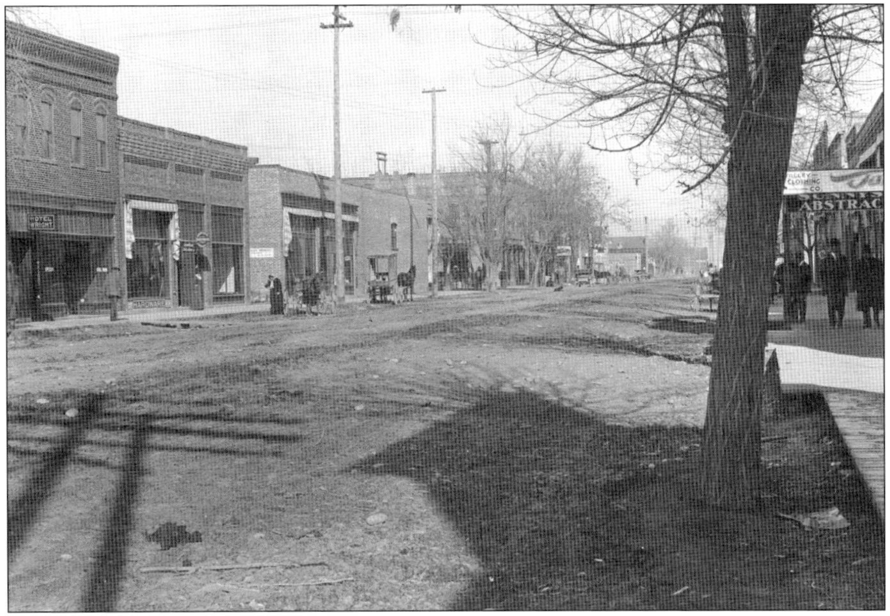

Street Scene in Sunnyside, 1910. Note the boardwalk in the foreground.

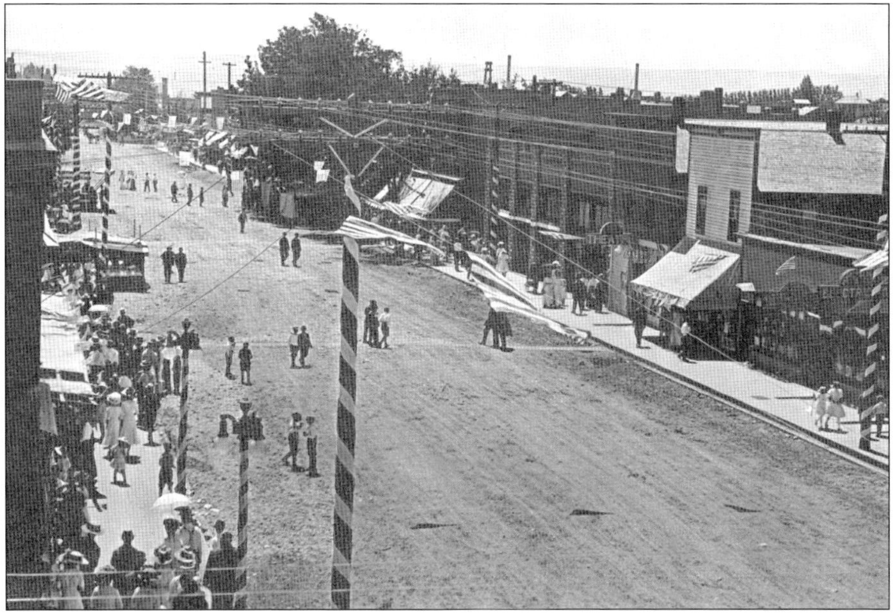

Looking south down 6th Street, circa 1910.

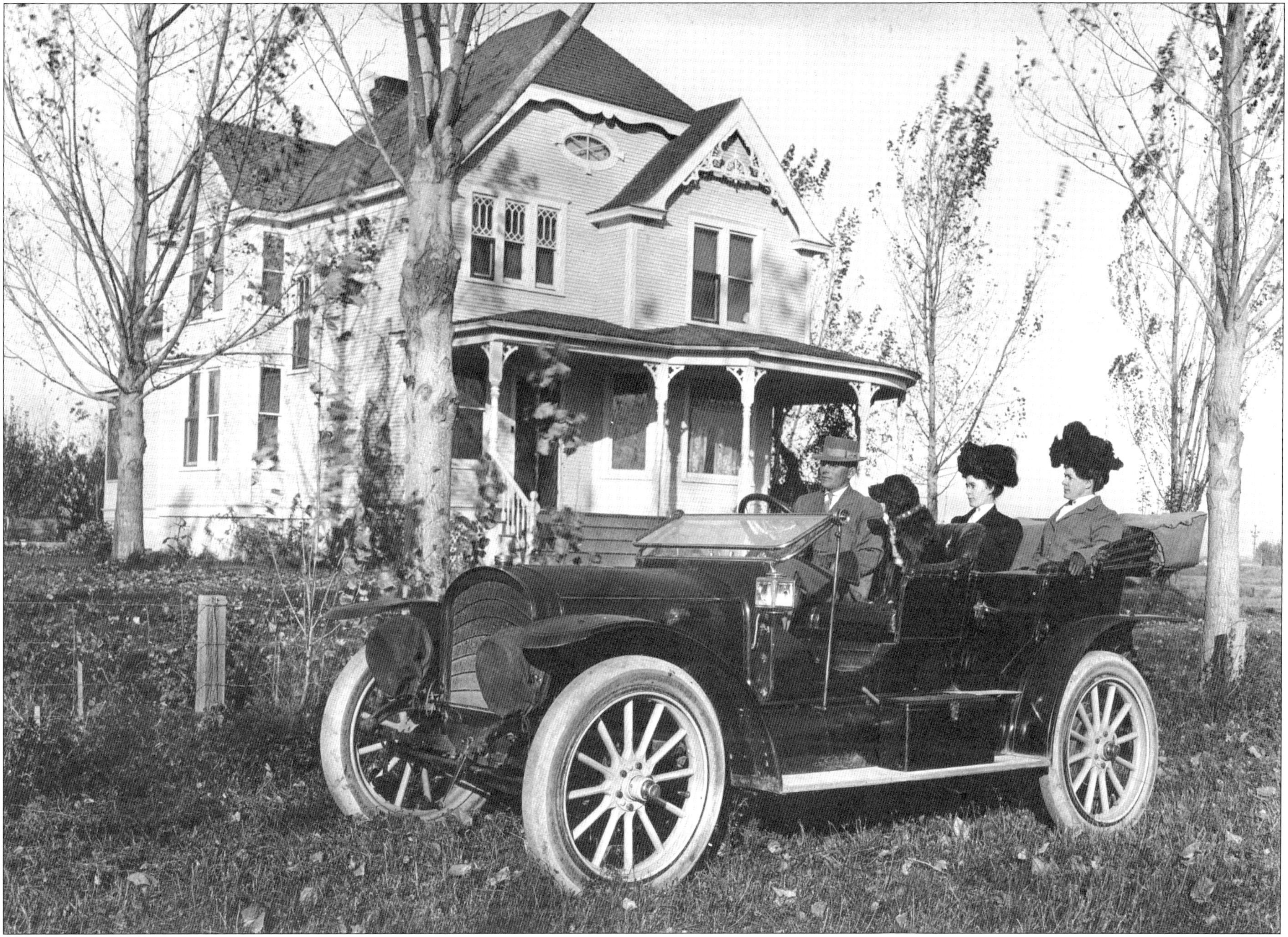

Williams House on Warehouse Avenue, early 1900s.

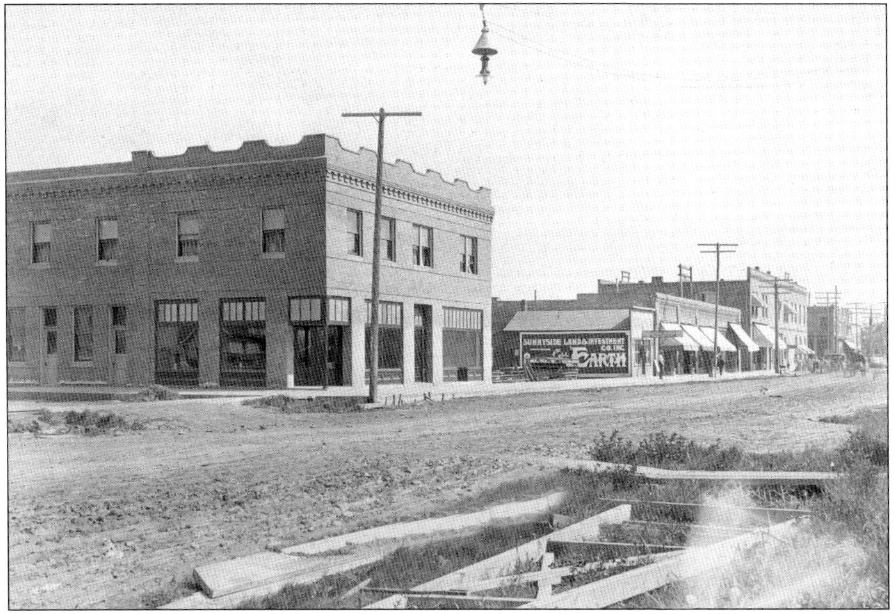

Looking south on Sixth, circa 1905.

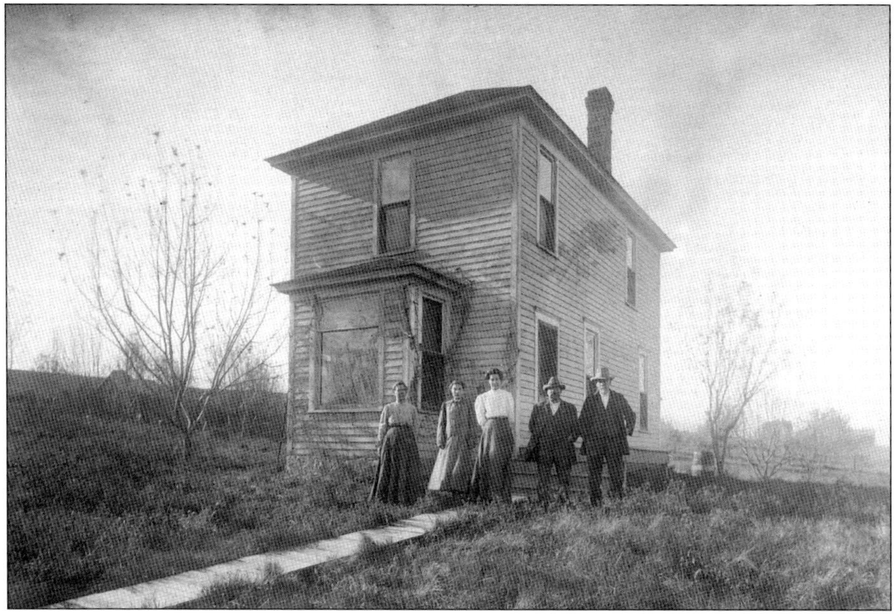
The William Harne residence at West Edison and First streets, circa 1905.

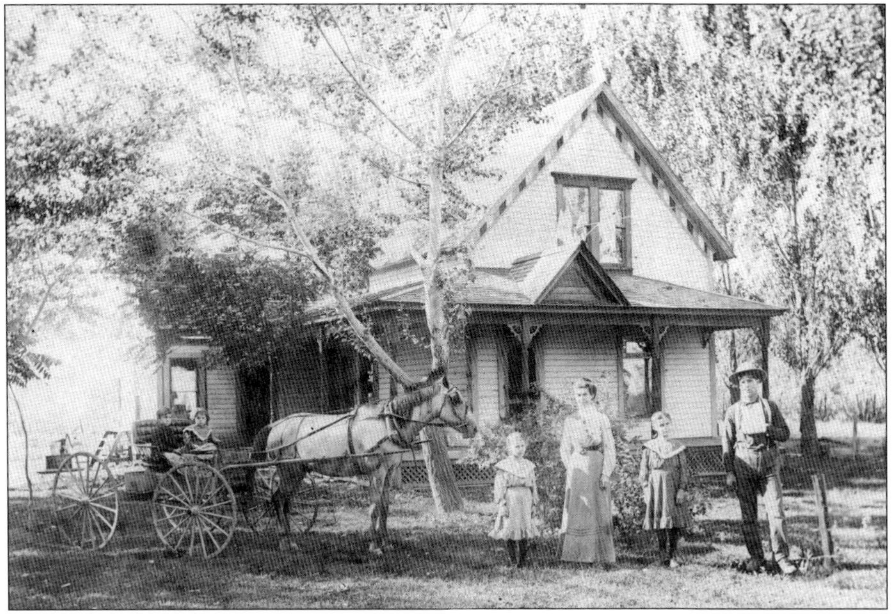
The George Matheson residence, 1905.

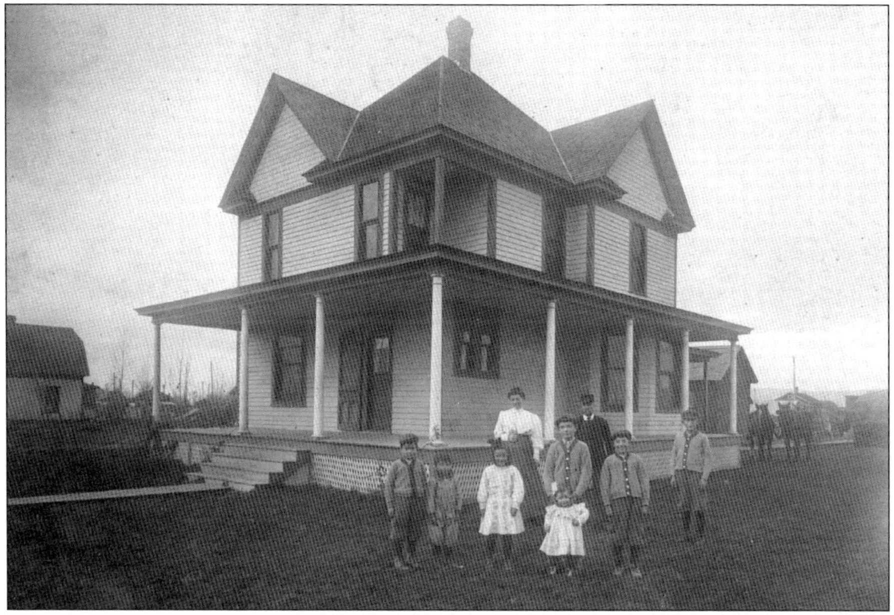
The Dougherty residence, circa 1909.

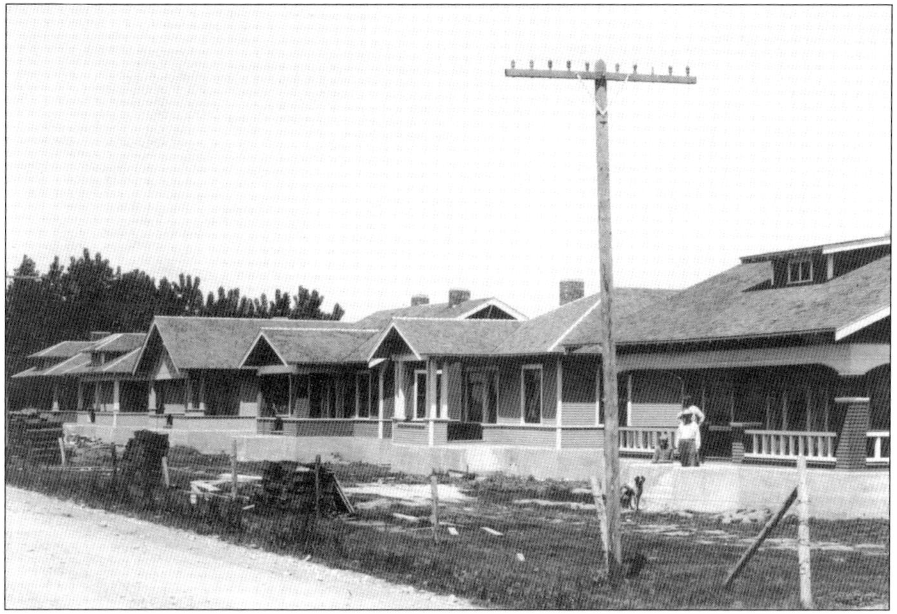

"Sugar Row" Homes built for U&I Sugar Factory officers and workers at Sunnyside factory in 1919.

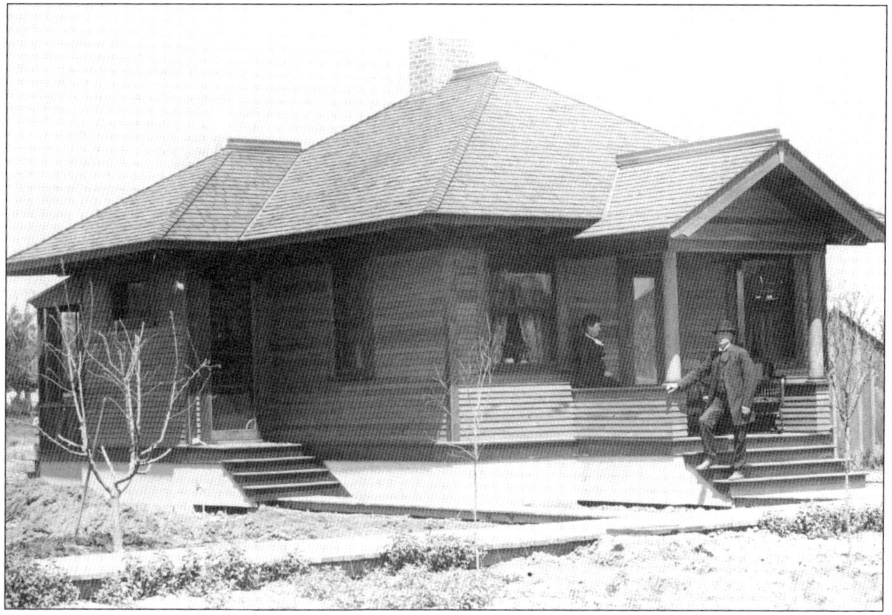

E. H. Ragland residence, circa 1915.

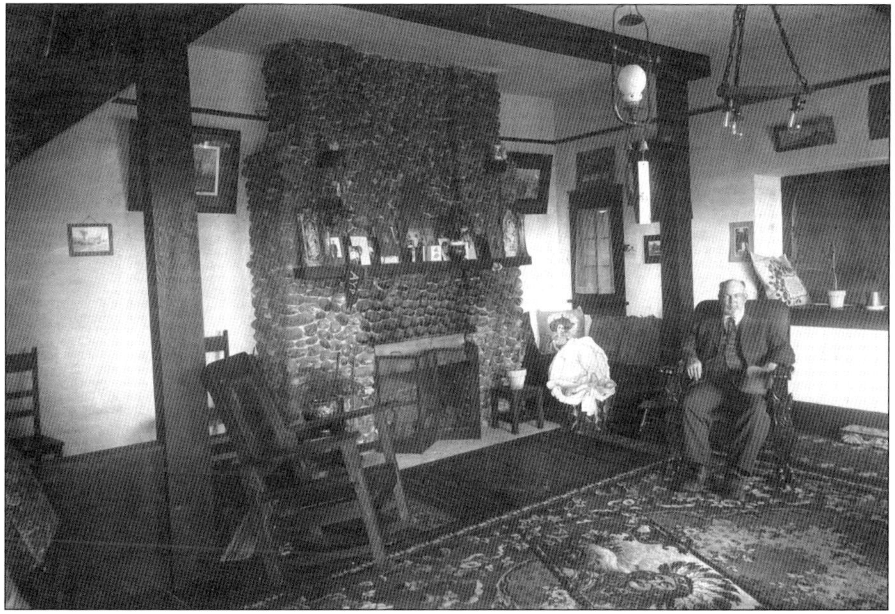

Living room of the home of Dr. F. C. Jones at the end of 6th Street in Sunnyside.

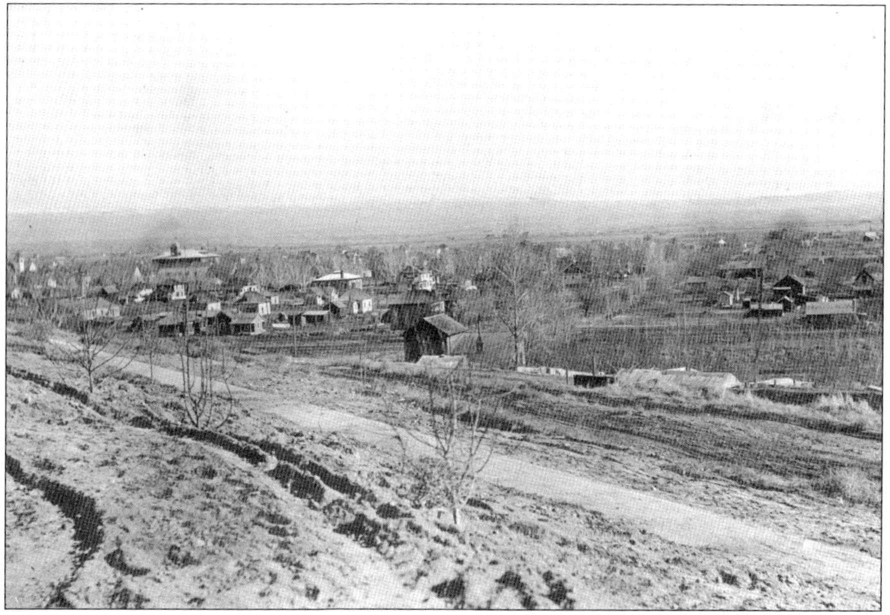

A view of Sunnyside from Harrison Hill, circa 1913.

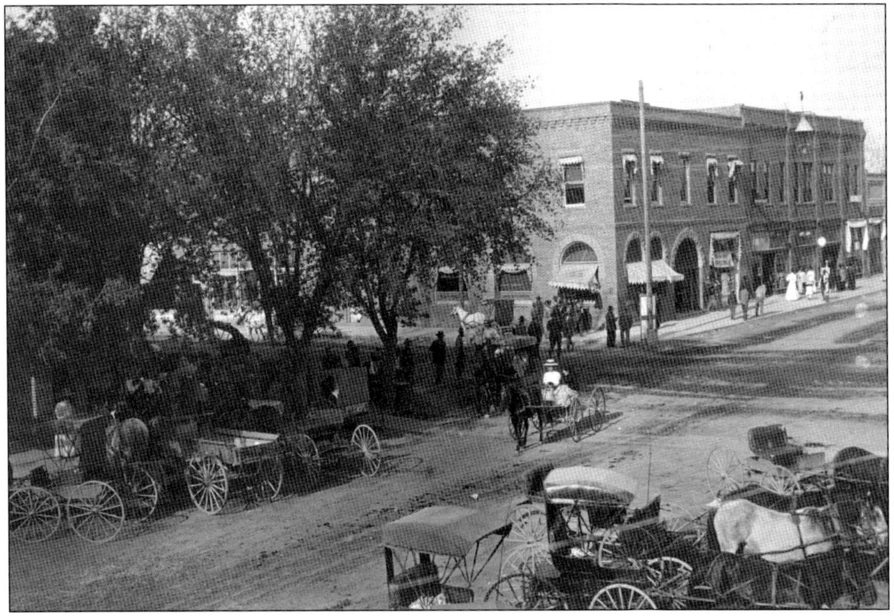

Looking east at the corner of 6th Street and Edison Avenue, circa 1900.

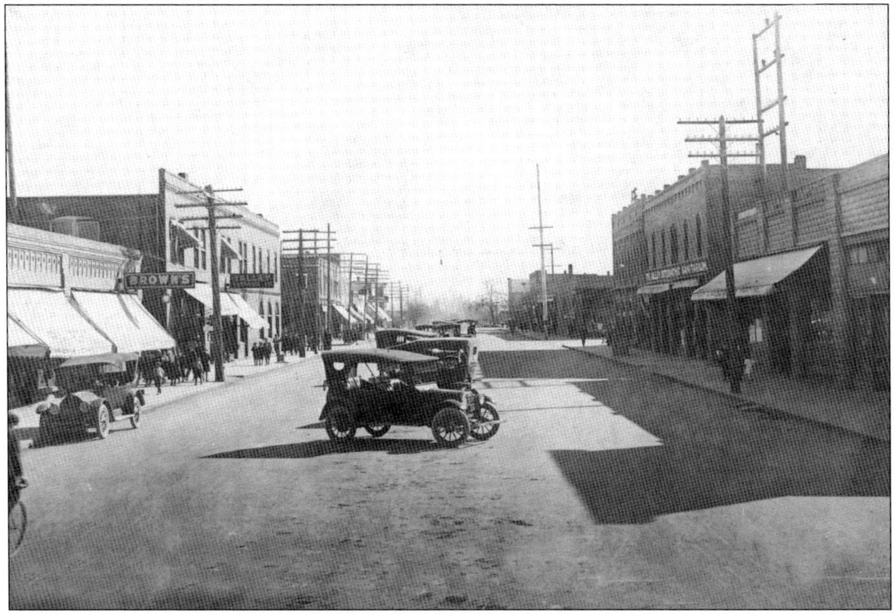

A view of 6th street looking south, circa 1918.

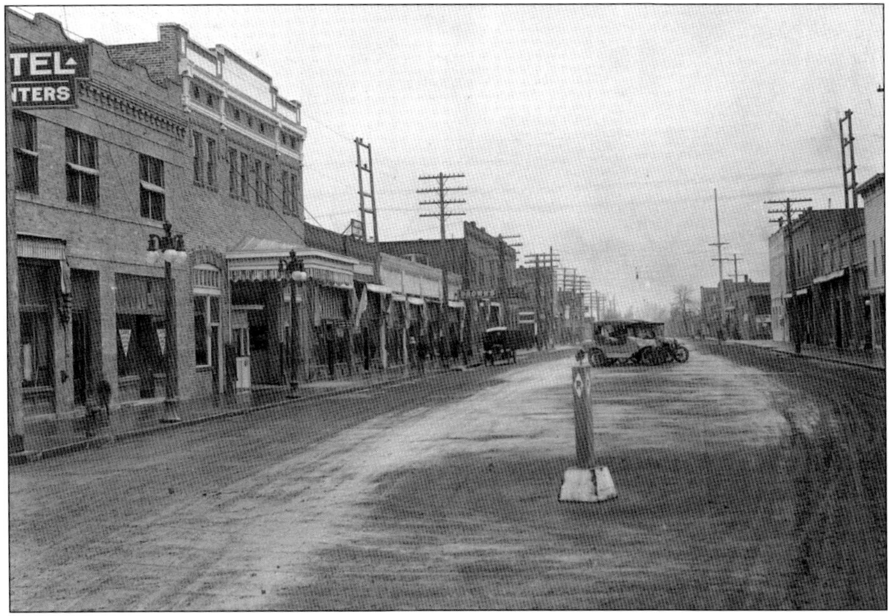

Looking south from Decatur Street down Sixth Street, circa 1919. Note the Planters Hotel on the left with the Liberty Theatre next to it.

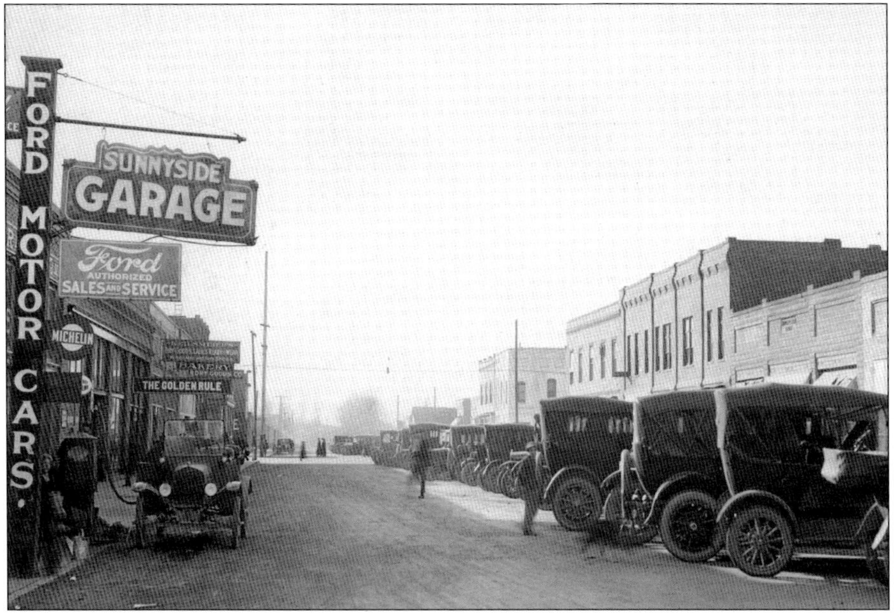

Edison Avenue looking west towards 6th Street in Sunnyside, 1920s.

SOCIETY

From the earliest days of Sunnyside's history, the community's social life centered around church attendance and related activities. As the community grew, high school drama clubs presented stage plays and city-wide variety shows, such as those presented by the Sunnyside Rotary Club, were only rivaled by the occasional appearance of a visiting chautauqua.

But it was church attendance that was the main form of social life in early Sunnyside, leading to the Christian Cooperative Colony becoming known as the Holy City.

With the formation of the Federation Church at the turn of the century, the faithful, representing Presbyterian, Baptist, Methodist, Christian-Congregational churches and the Progressive Church of the Brethren, all met in one building at the corner of Seventh Street and Franklin Avenue for several years. As new settlers made Sunnyside their home, each of the religions broke off to build their own church.

The Sunnyside Rotary Club, founded in 1925, started its annual minstrel show featuring the pillars of the community dressed in black face as a fund-raiser for the club. The minstrel shows gradually were transformed into an event called "Ladies Night" and eventually disappeared during the mid-1950s.

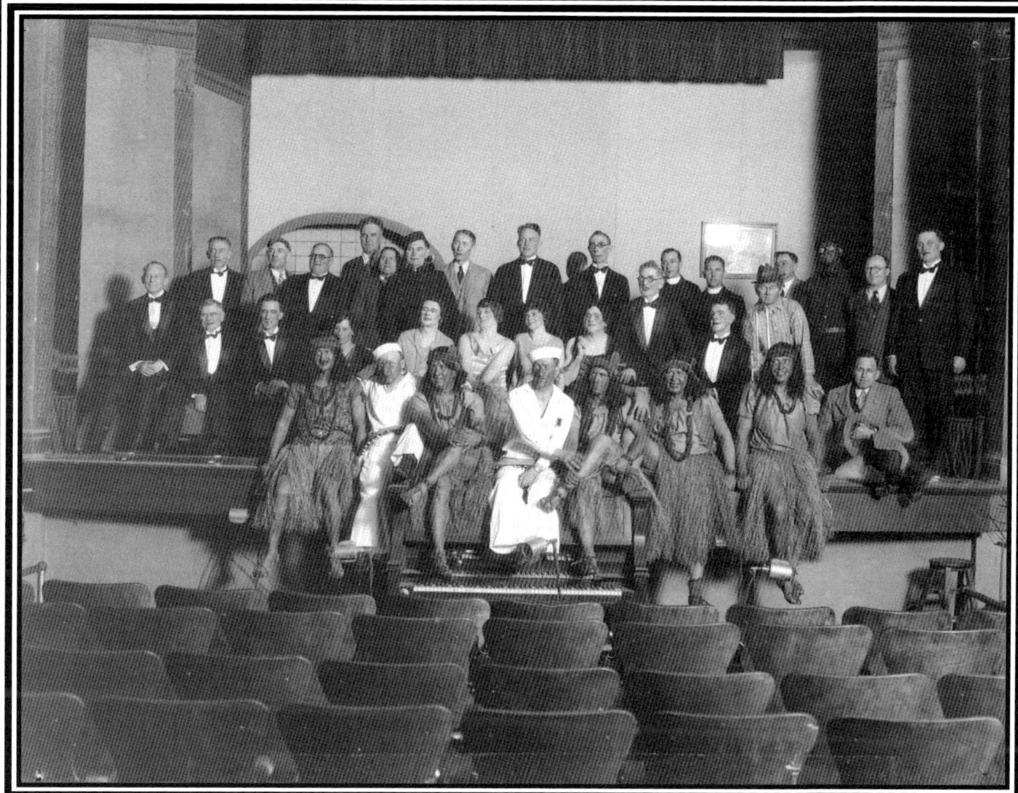

Rotary show, February 1930.

Sunnyside's list of civic groups included the establishment of such fraternal organizations as the Masons, Odd Fellows, Knights Templar, as well as women's groups, such as the Eastern Star, Rebekahs and the Woman's Club, which was responsible for the founding of Central Park, all catered to Sunnyside citizens' need to do more than farm and sit around the house by candlelight.

Sunnyside boasted a plethora of civic minded clubs including the Commercial Club, which was the forerunner of the Chamber of Commerce, the Outlook Club, the Bachelor's Club, the Riverside Club and the Daughters of the American Revolution chapter.

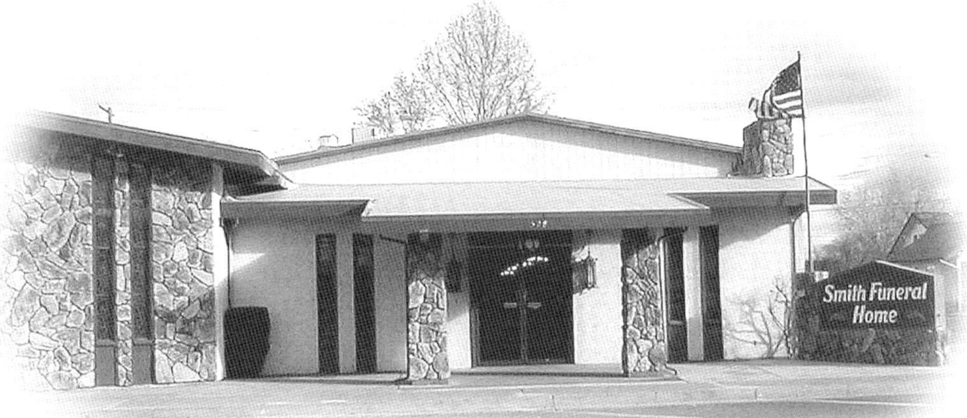

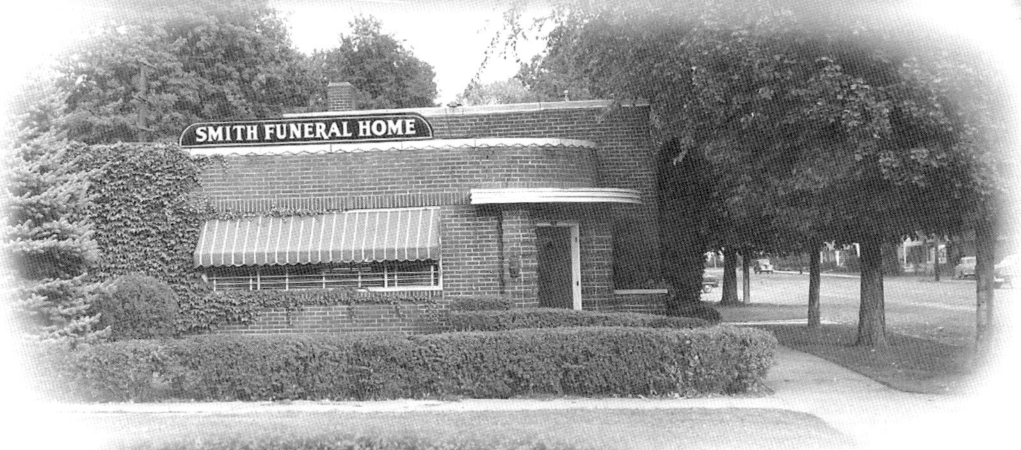

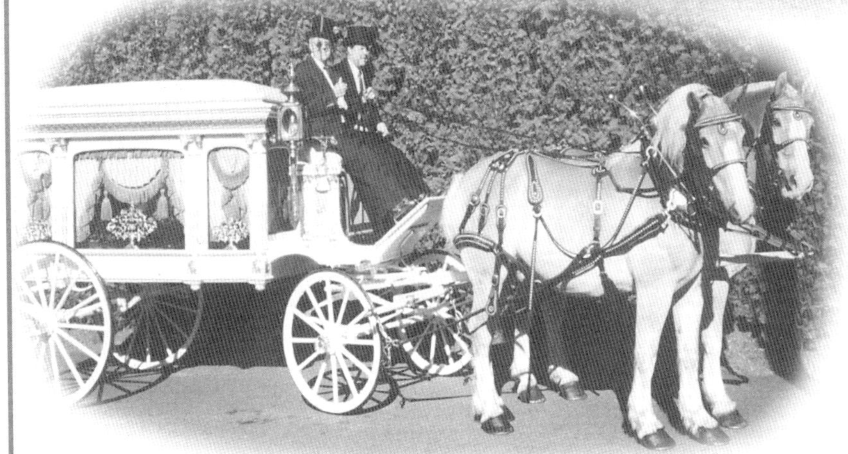

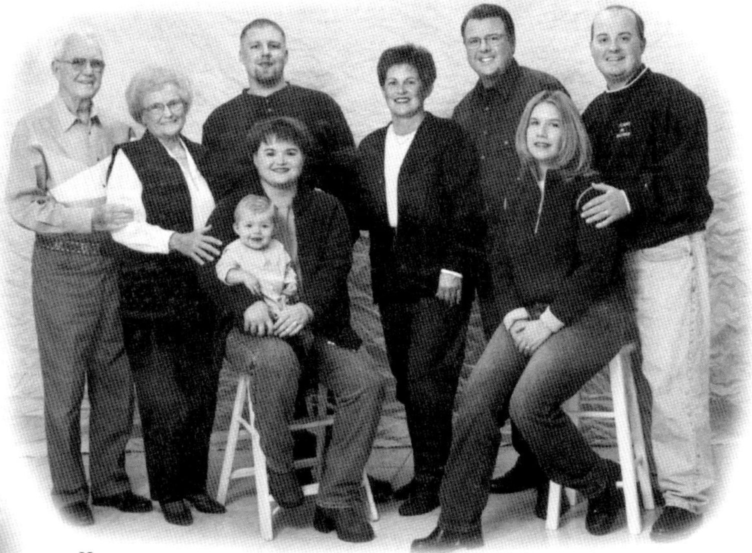

Hap, Kathryne   Zane, Heather, Madison   Carolyn, Greg   Rebecca, Grant

SMITH
FUNERAL HOMES

◆ ◆ ◆

Family Owned and Operated
Since 1951

◆ ◆ ◆

528 S. 8th St.,
Sunnyside, Washington
1-509-837-4962

512 E. 4th St.,
Grandview, Washington
1-509-882-3386

One of the first churches in town was called the Federated Church. This photo was taken in 1901 when it was home to the Presbyterian, Congregational, Christian, Baptist and Progressive Brethren churches. It sat on the corner of 7th Street and Franklin Avenue where the present-day Grace Brethren Church now stands.

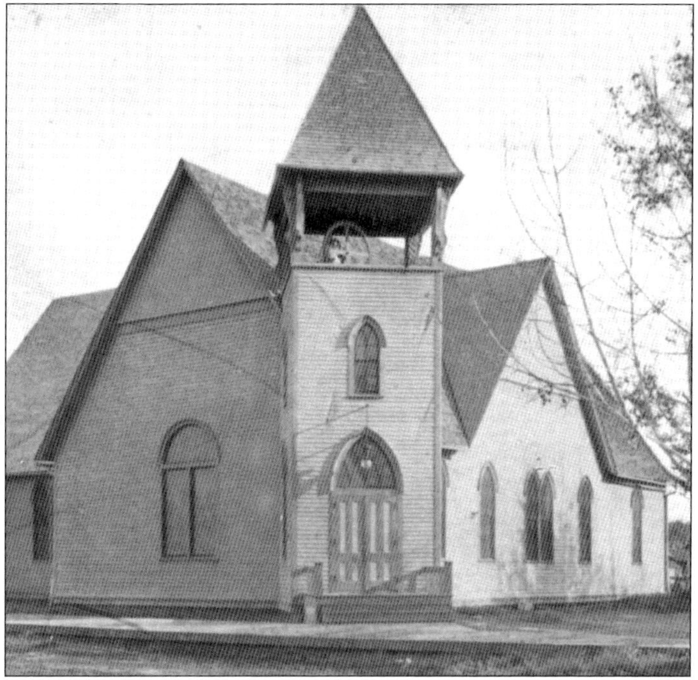

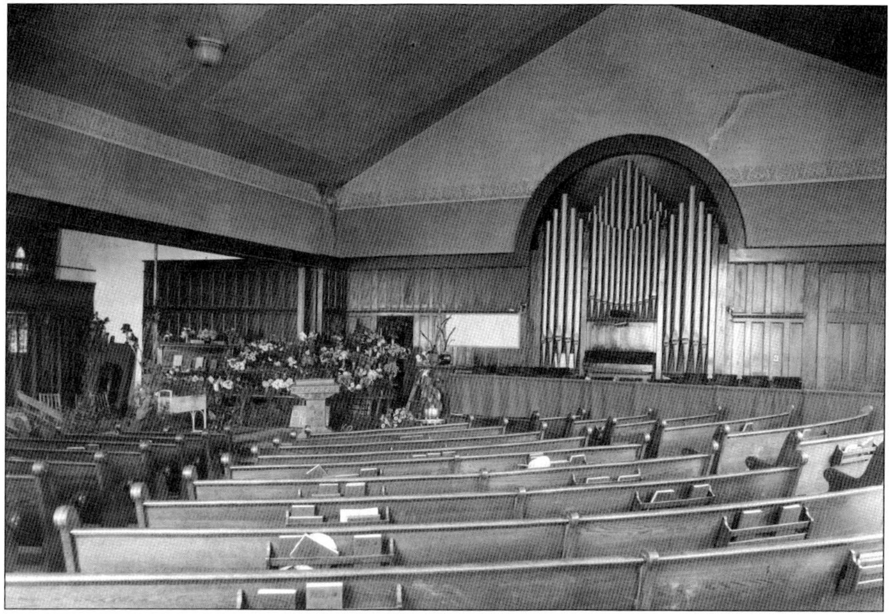

Interior of the Old Brethren Church in Sunnyside, early 1900s.

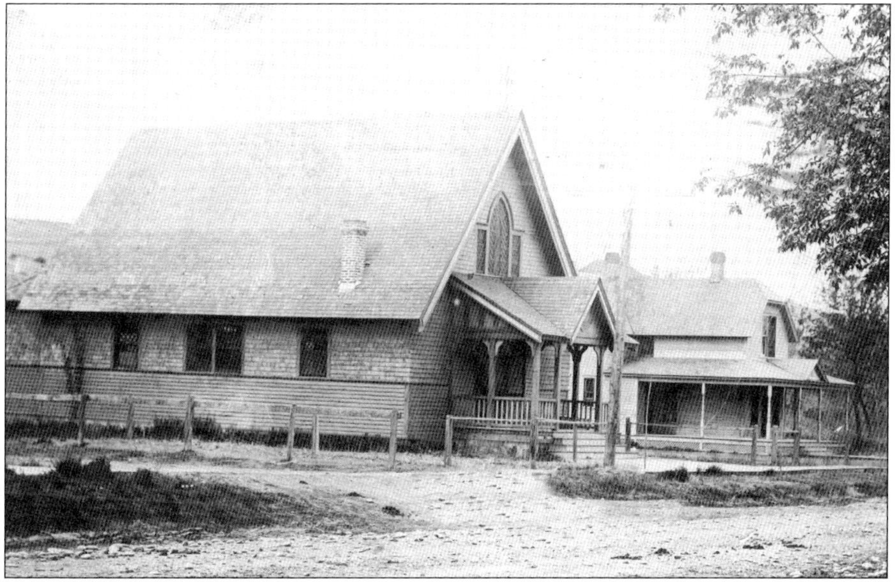

Episcopal Church, Sunnyside, 1901. This photo was taken right after construction was completed.

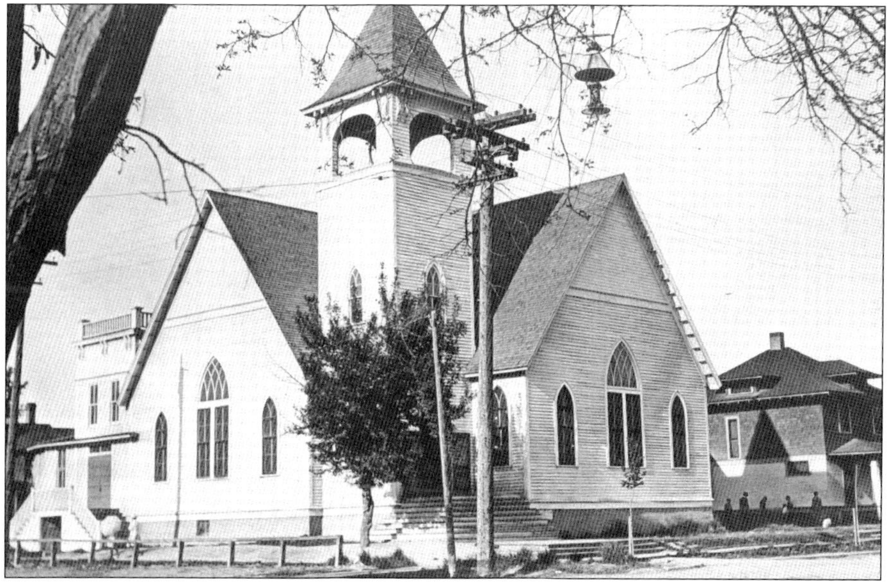

Methodist Church of Sunnyside, circa 1914.

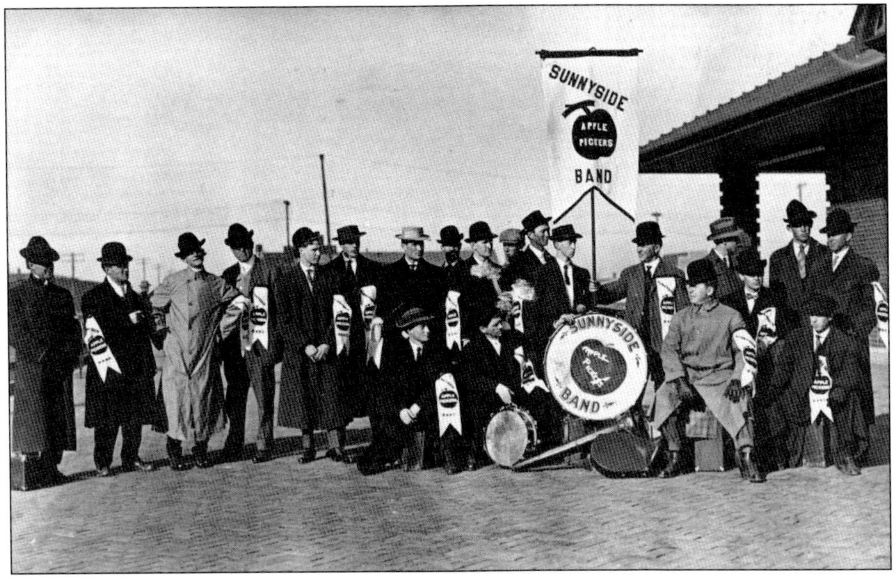

Sunnyside Apple Pickers Band awaiting a train for the ride home from a Toppenish engagement.

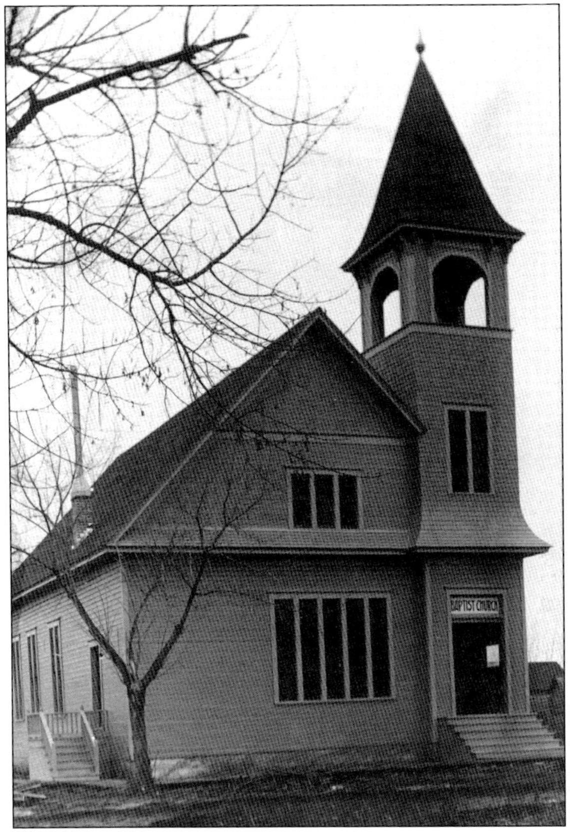

Sunnyside Baptist Church. It was built in 1907, and was located at the corner of 8th Street and Decatur Avenue.

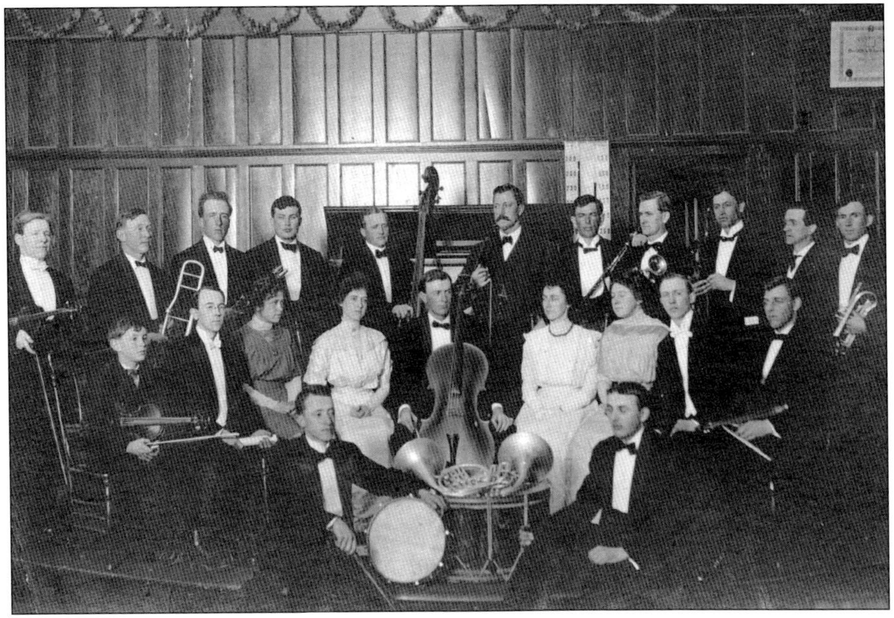

Clarion Concert Club, organized 1905.

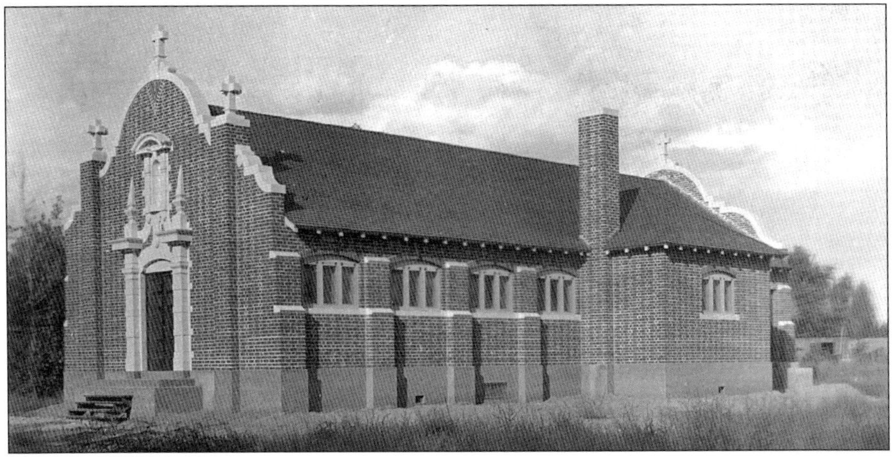

Sunnyside Catholic Church was built in 1925. Parts of the original structure make up part of today's church.

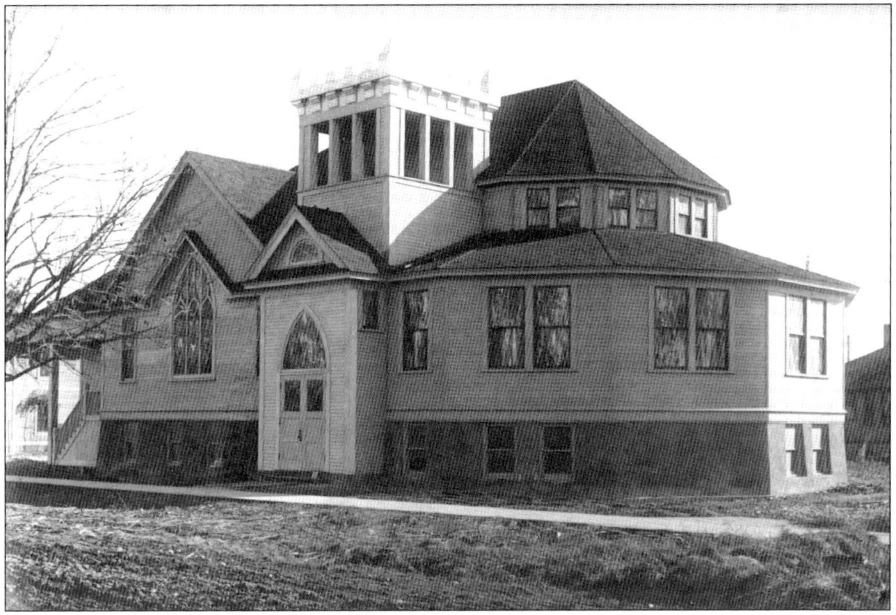
Presbyterian Church was built in 1912 and was located on the southeast corner of 8th and Edison Avenue.

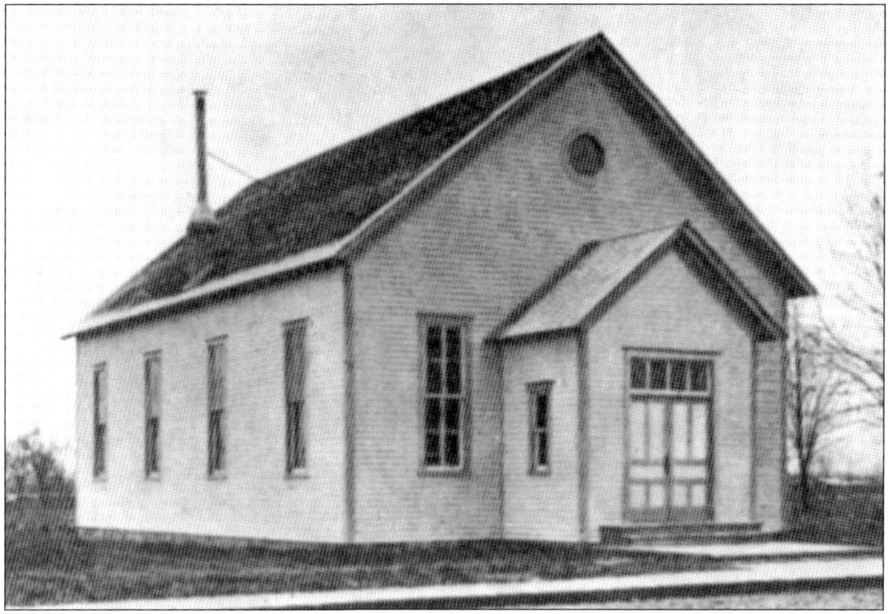
German Baptist Brethren (Dunkard) Church located on the southeast corner of 8th Street and Franklin Avenue.

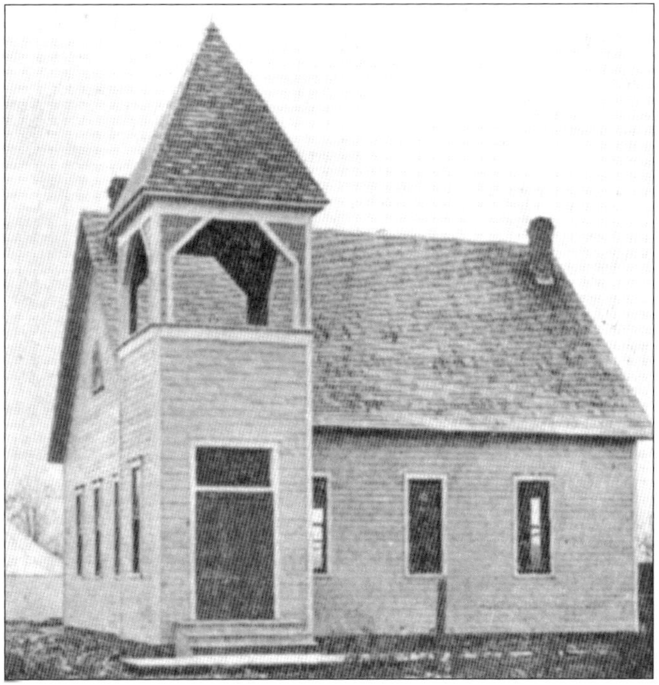
Free Methodist Church was built in 1902 and was located on the northwest corner of 9th and Franklin Avenue.

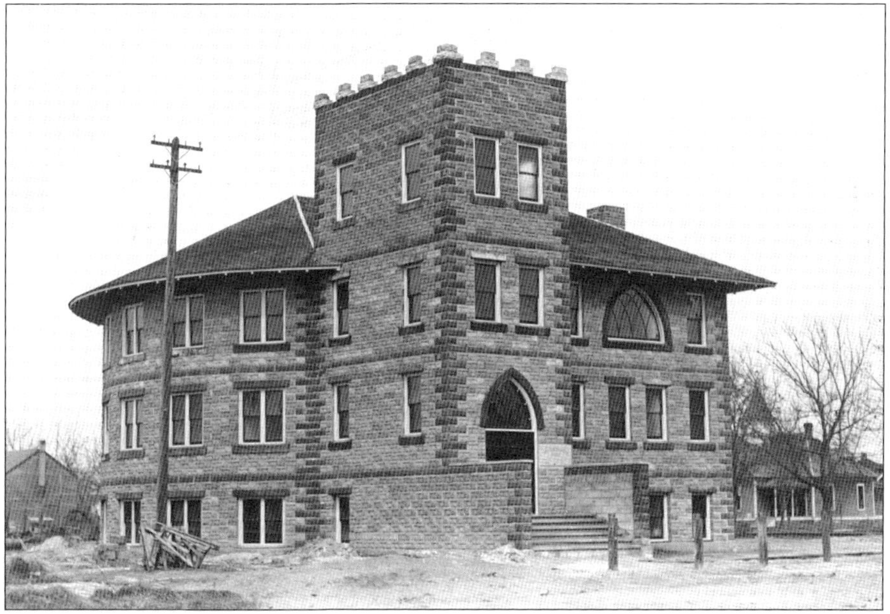
Congregational Church, dedicated on March 24, 1912 located on the north side of Franklin Avenue between 7th and 8th streets.

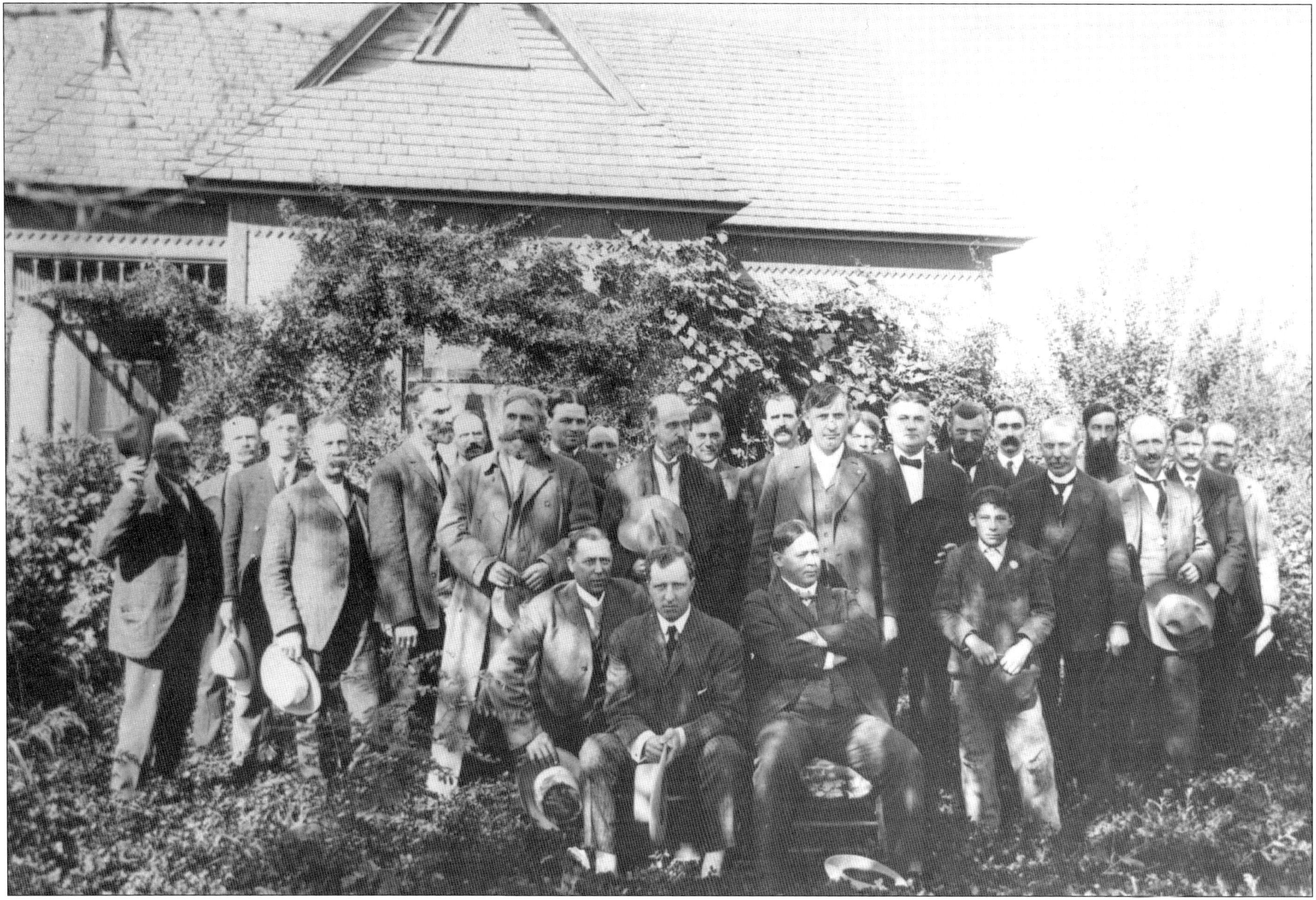

The first Commercial Club entertaining Governor Albert Mead and party and Project Engineer Walter N. Granger in 1905. Front row from left: Lew Reese, two unidentified members of the Governor's party and young Frank Harrison. Standing from left: J.B. Sheller, T.C. Williams, Roy Lichty, H.M. Lichty, Rev. A.H. Lyons, Rev. Hedges, Walter N. Granger, William Heinz, Sam Keifer, S.J. Harrison, unidentified, Frank Moody, Governor Mead (white shirt with no tie), Emmette Taylor, unidentified, J.B. George, Mayor W.B. Bridgman, E.F. Blaine, J.B. Early, R.G. Page, James Henderson and George Barnes. The photo was taken on the front lawn of the Lannin home.

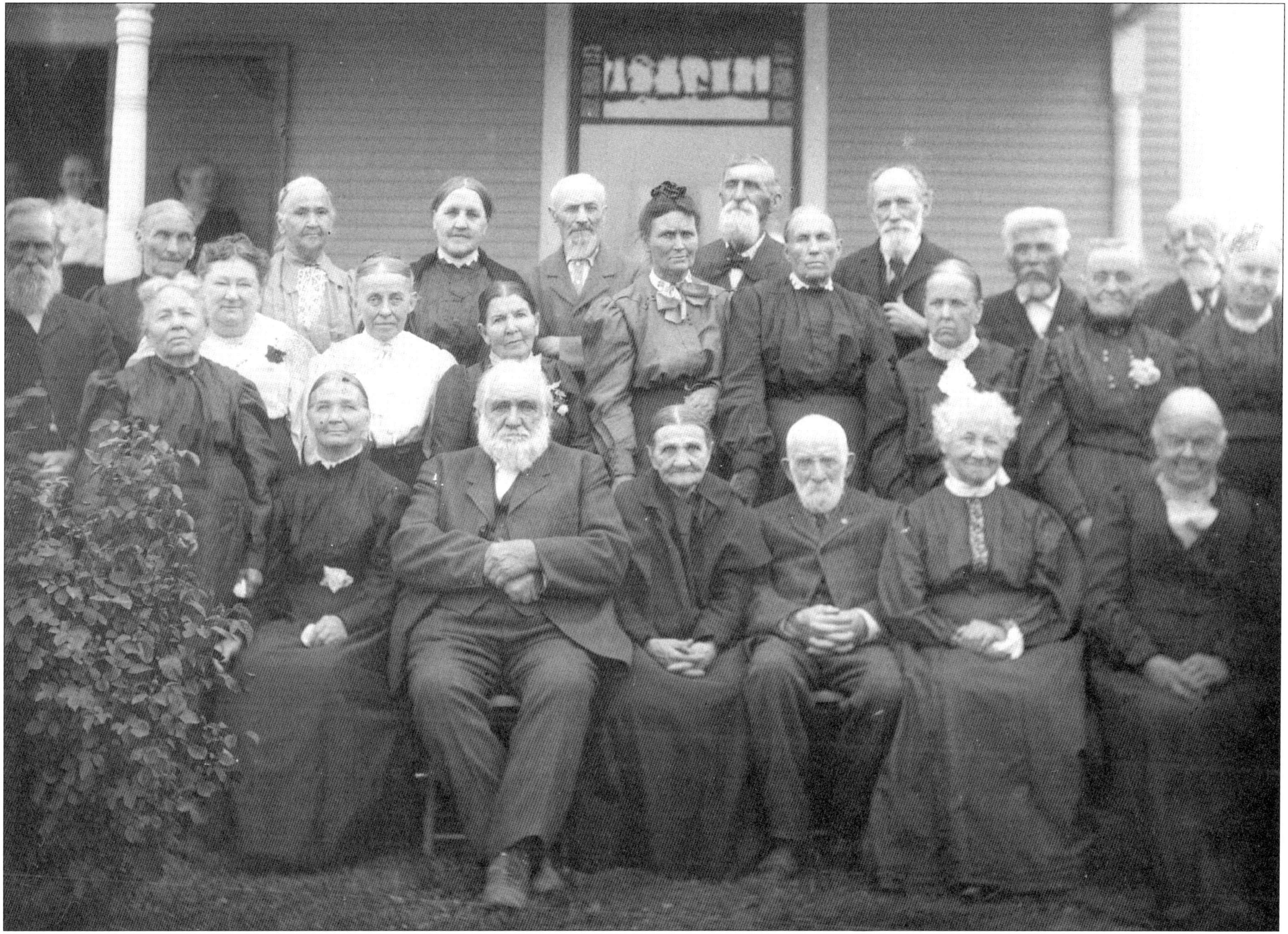

Susset tea party given by the Women's Relief Corps, circa 1907.

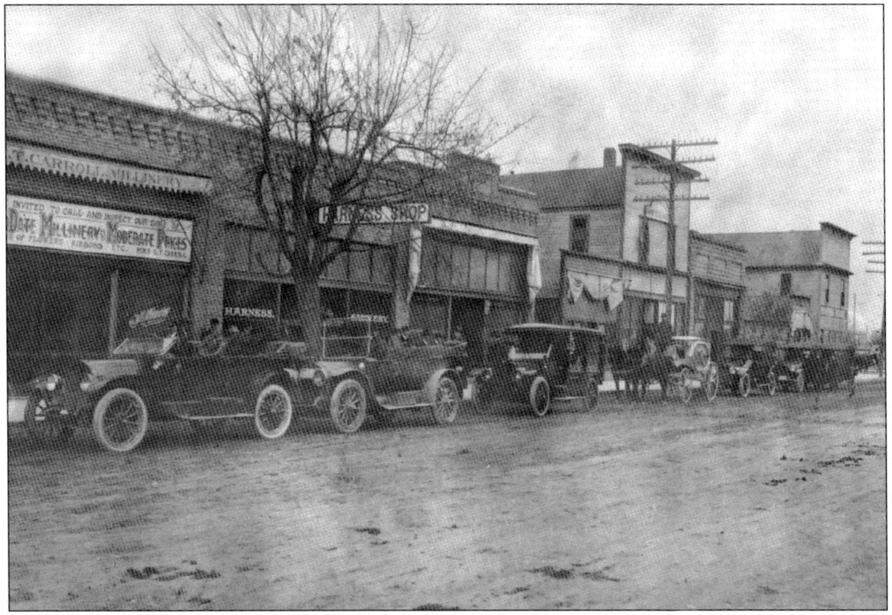

Funeral procession of the Forman brothers who were killed at a train crossing. The procession is traveling South on Sixth Street, circa 1919.

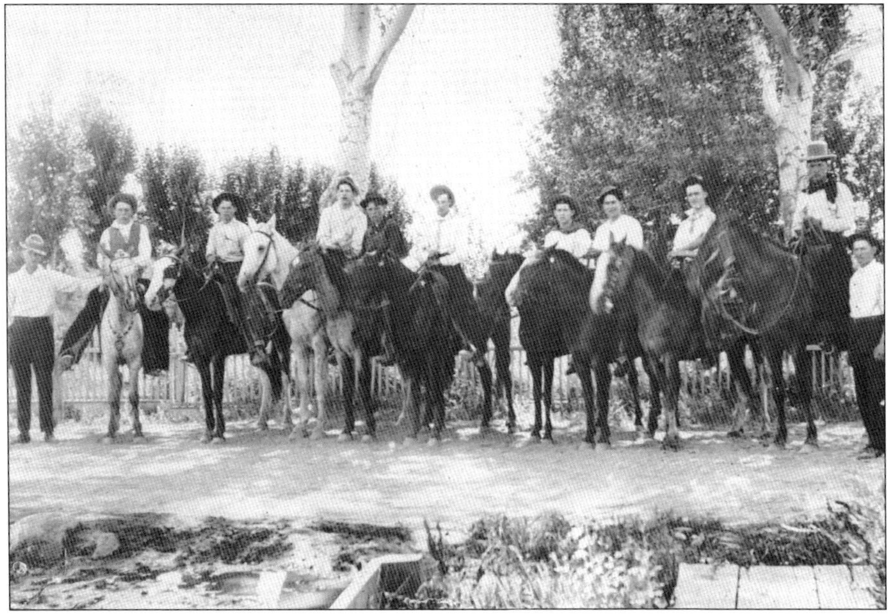

Sunnyside Busters riding club.

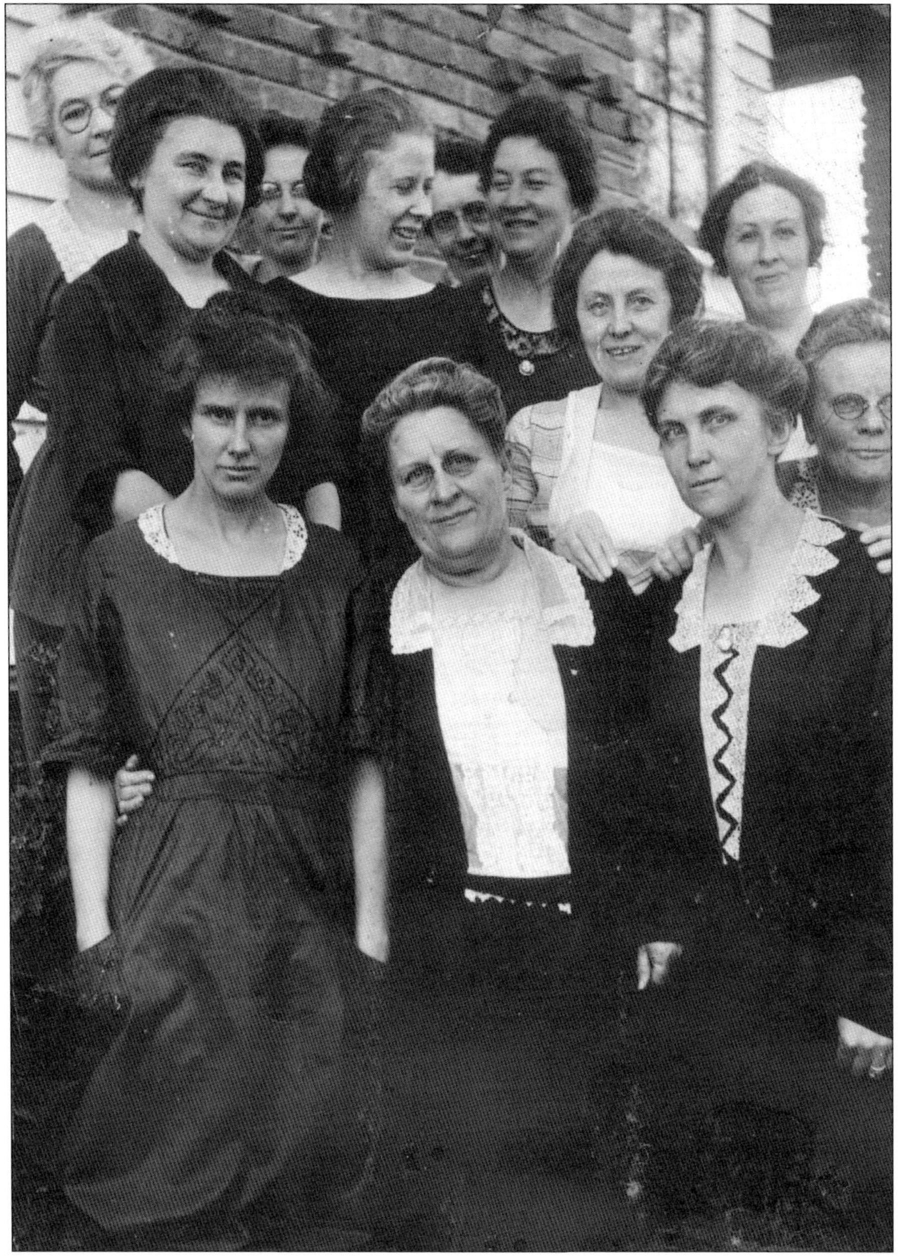

Pioneer Bridge Club. From left, front row, Elsie Tallman, Jane Langford and Catherine Amundson. Second row, Jess Hall, Alice Lichty, Charlotte Gochnour, Janet Snider and Minnie Webber. Third row, Helen Campbell, Ruth Fordyce, Alice Fleming and Zoe Langford.

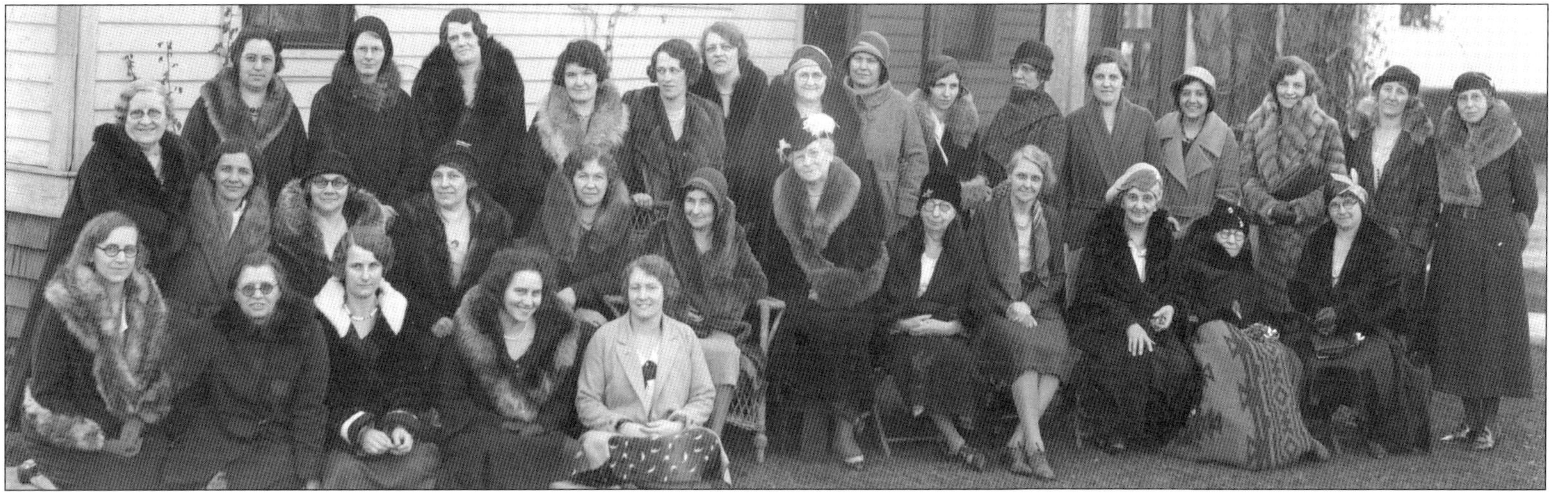

Sunnyside Women's Club 25th anniversary meeting at the home of Mrs. W. A. Funk, March 11, 1932. Left to right, standing, Mrs. C. H. Langford, Mrs. Fred Berry, Mrs. Gordon Anderson, Mrs. Crawford, Mrs. Bess Rinehold, Mrs. A. D. Whitnack, Mrs. Hallie Webber, Mrs. D. N. Wood, Mrs. Ed Nelson, Mrs. J. L. Lutz, Mrs. E. H. Ragland, Mrs. Gerald Schreiner, Mrs. Norton Mitchell, Mrs. Ray Sprague, Mrs. M. D. Scroggs and Mrs. Charlotte Jones. Sitting, Mrs. Robert Hall, Mrs. Albert Amundson, Mrs. O. W. Hoffman, Mrs. Lloyd H. Miller, Mrs. Thad Hall, Mrs. R. C. McCredie, Mrs. W. A. Funk, Mrs. W. E. Fordyce(president), Mrs. S. J. Harrison, Mrs. G. W. Reese, and Mrs. Roscoe Sheller. Kneeling, Mrs. F. L. Sinock, Miss Ella Woodin, Mrs. Paul Wise, Mrs. Dorothy Ellis and Mrs. F. D. Mack.

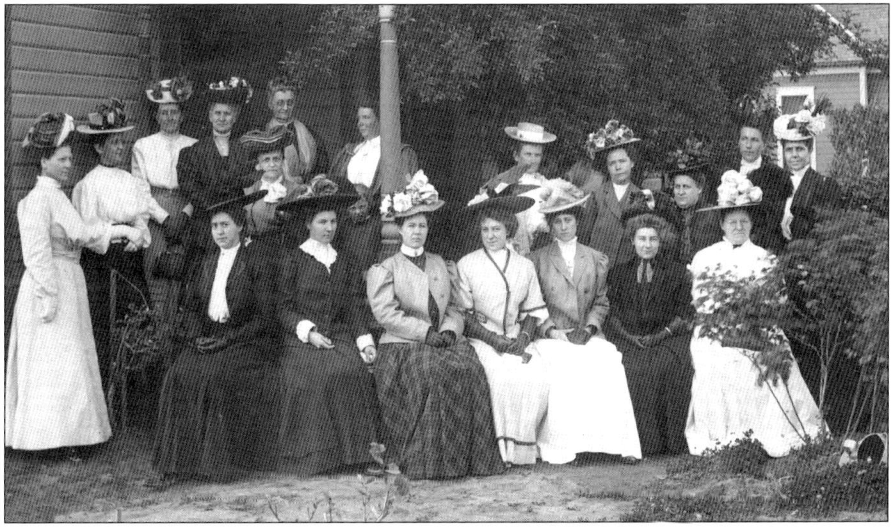

Sunnyside Women's Club, 1908. Left to right, seated, Mrs. Ray Andrews, Mrs. Woodin, Mrs. H. L. Miller, Mrs. O. Skiles, Dr. Delta Rowland, Mrs. Jess Hall, and Mrs. L. L. Higgins. Standing, Mrs. R. C. McCredie, Mrs. S. J. Harrison, Mrs. McLean, Mrs. Campbell, Mrs. Barnes, Mrs. Ren Ferrell, Mrs. Tinker, Mrs. Walker, Mrs. Langford, Mrs. Burgess, Mrs. Cline.

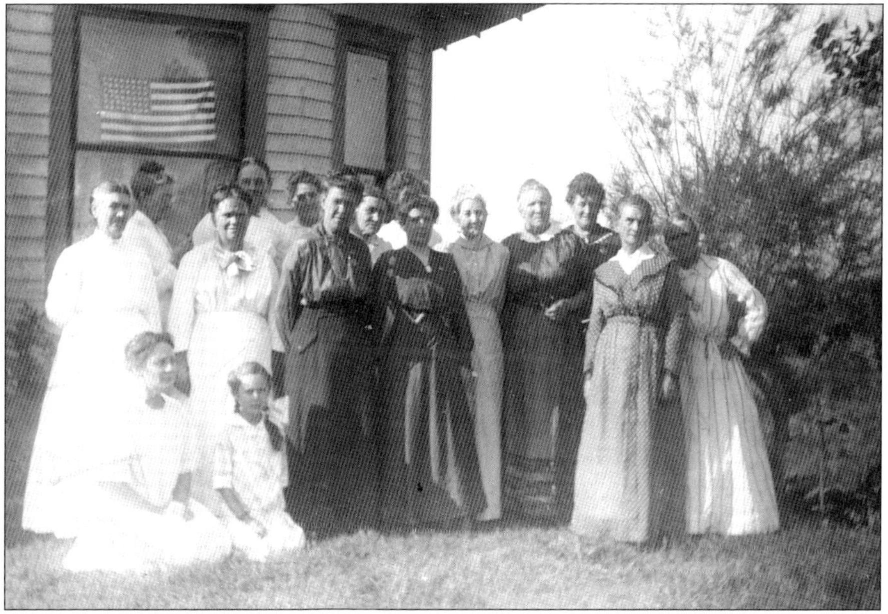

Women's Relief Corps at the home of Mrs. Earl Myers on Edison Avenue, circa 1916.

Serving Sunnyside in Education Since 1894

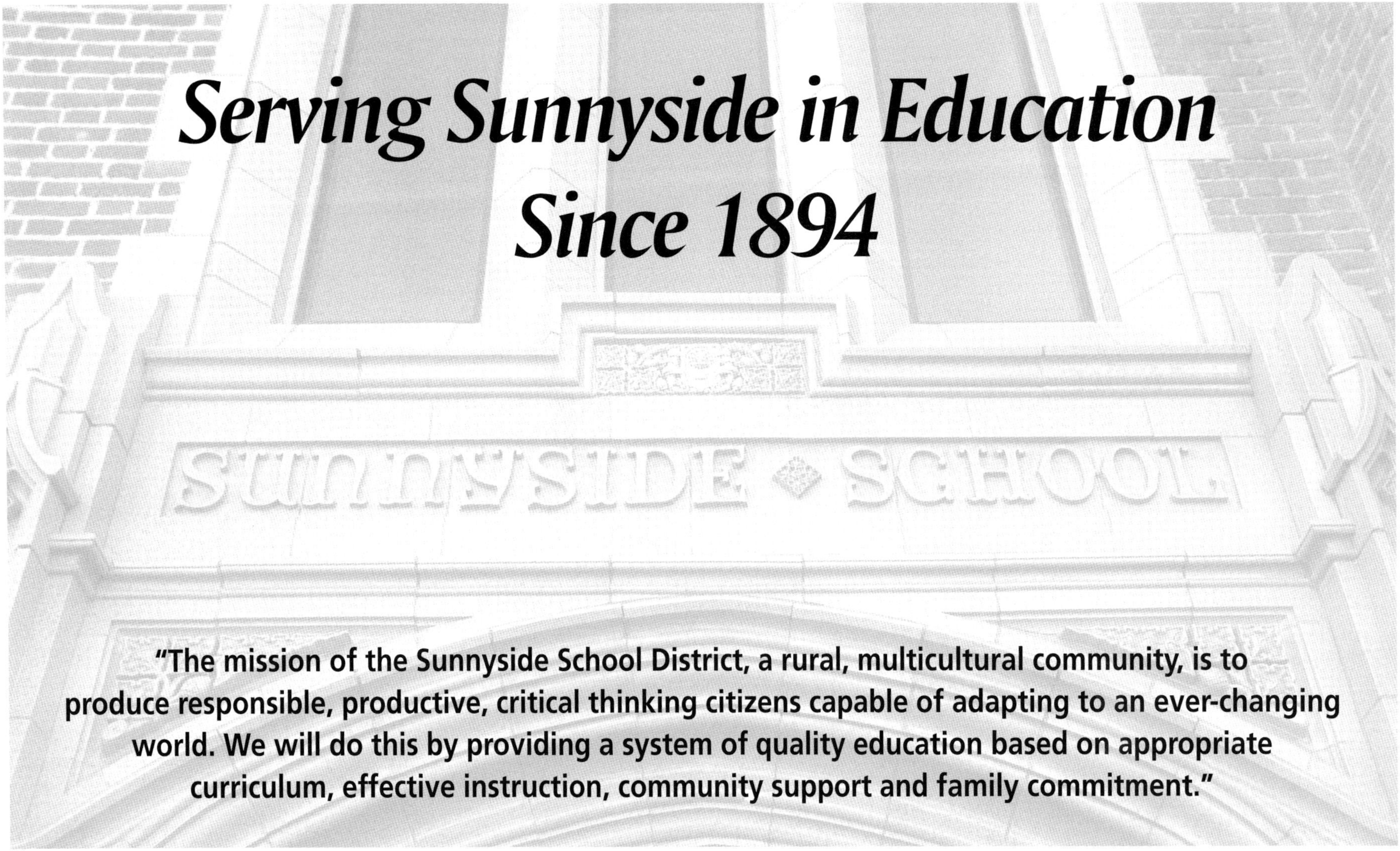

"The mission of the Sunnyside School District, a rural, multicultural community, is to produce responsible, productive, critical thinking citizens capable of adapting to an ever-changing world. We will do this by providing a system of quality education based on appropriate curriculum, effective instruction, community support and family commitment."

SUNNYSIDE
SCHOOL DISTRICT
Where Education Shines

EDUCATION

When Sunnyside historian Roscoe Sheller's family arrived in Sunnyside in the late 1890s, a school had already been established and much to his chagrin, his mother enrolled him right away. He attended one of the many one- and two-room school houses that scattered the Sunnyside countryside much of the first half of the last century. By most records, the Waneta School on Wanita Road was among the first schools to be opened in rural Sunnyside. It was reportedly a one-room shack and its school board was made up entirely of Black American patrons.

Sheller attended Emerson School, which opened in 1894 at the corner of Ninth Street and East Edison Avenue. Emerson School had the distinction of being the first painted building in Sunnyside. The building doubled as a church and town meeting hall. The first Washington School was also built in 1894 on Factory Road. It wasn't until 1903, that the community was large enough to consider building a high school. The first Sunnyside High School was opened in the fall of 1905 and was named Denny Blaine, after two men of the Washington Irrigation Company, who had donated the land for the school. By the start of school that year, the combined enrollment of Denny Blaine, Emerson and Washington schools was 345, according to early school records. By 1911, the community was already in need of a new high school building which was completed later that same year.

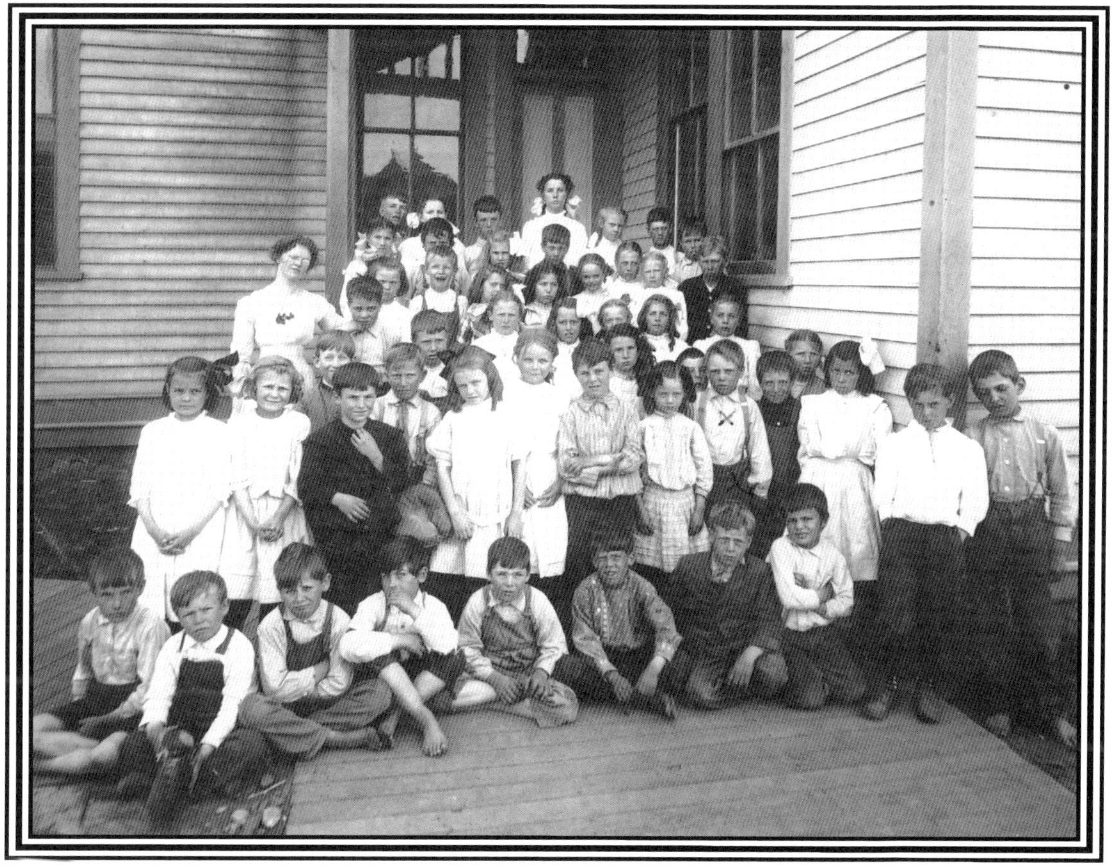

Emerson School 3rd grade class, 1909.

The Sunnyside School District eventually consolidated the smaller districts of Riverside, Wendell Phillips, Wheatland, Outlook and Green Valley schools.

From the beginning, sports played an active part in the education of Sunnyside children. By 1907, the high school could boast several championship teams. The students also proved their dramatic prowess on the stage, presenting numerous plays.

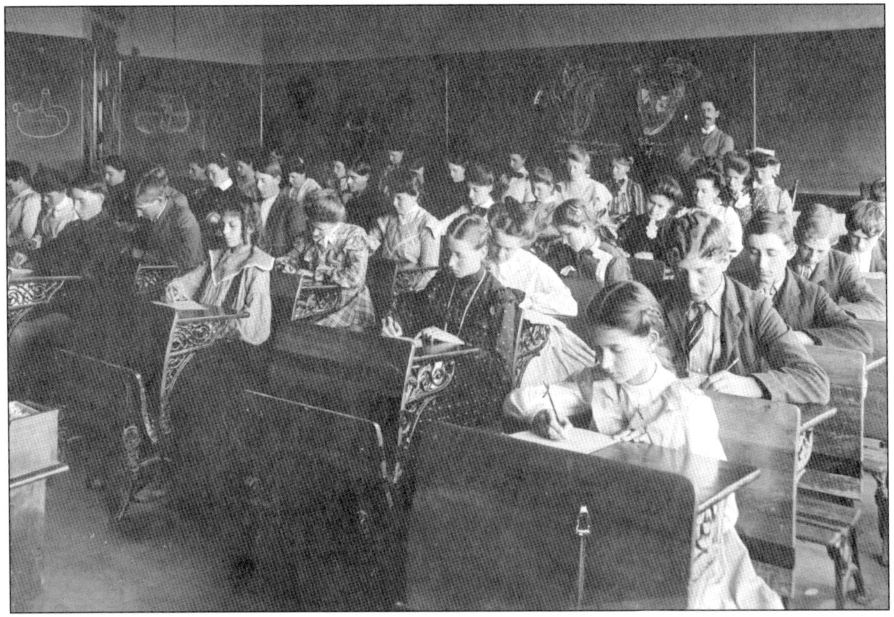

Sunnyside 8th grade class at Denny Blaine School in 1904. Professor E. McDouglass was the teacher.

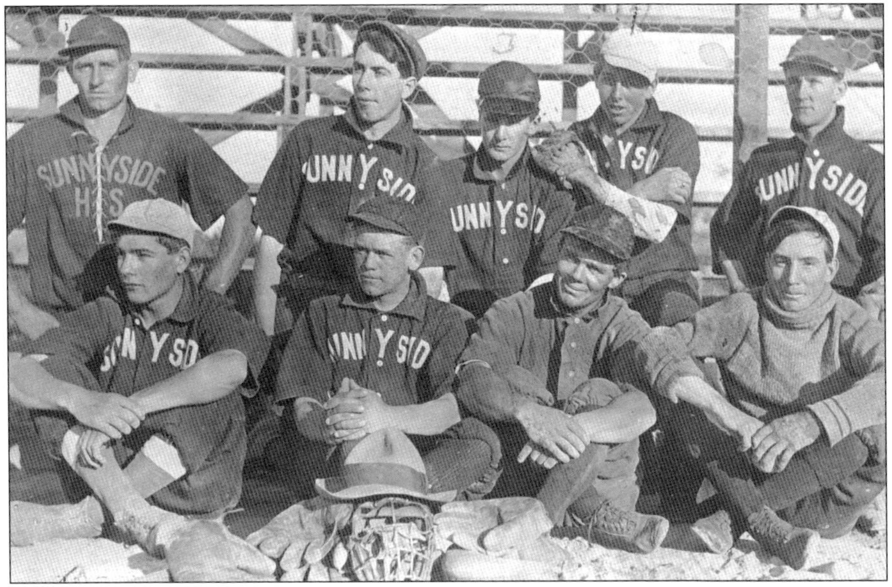

Sunnyside High School baseball team, valley champions, 1909. Front row from left: Kenneth King, Lee Johnston, M. Yeager and Glen Campbell. Back from left: John Ball, Rosey Mahaffey, Perry Johnston, Frank Greer and Delmar Gregory.

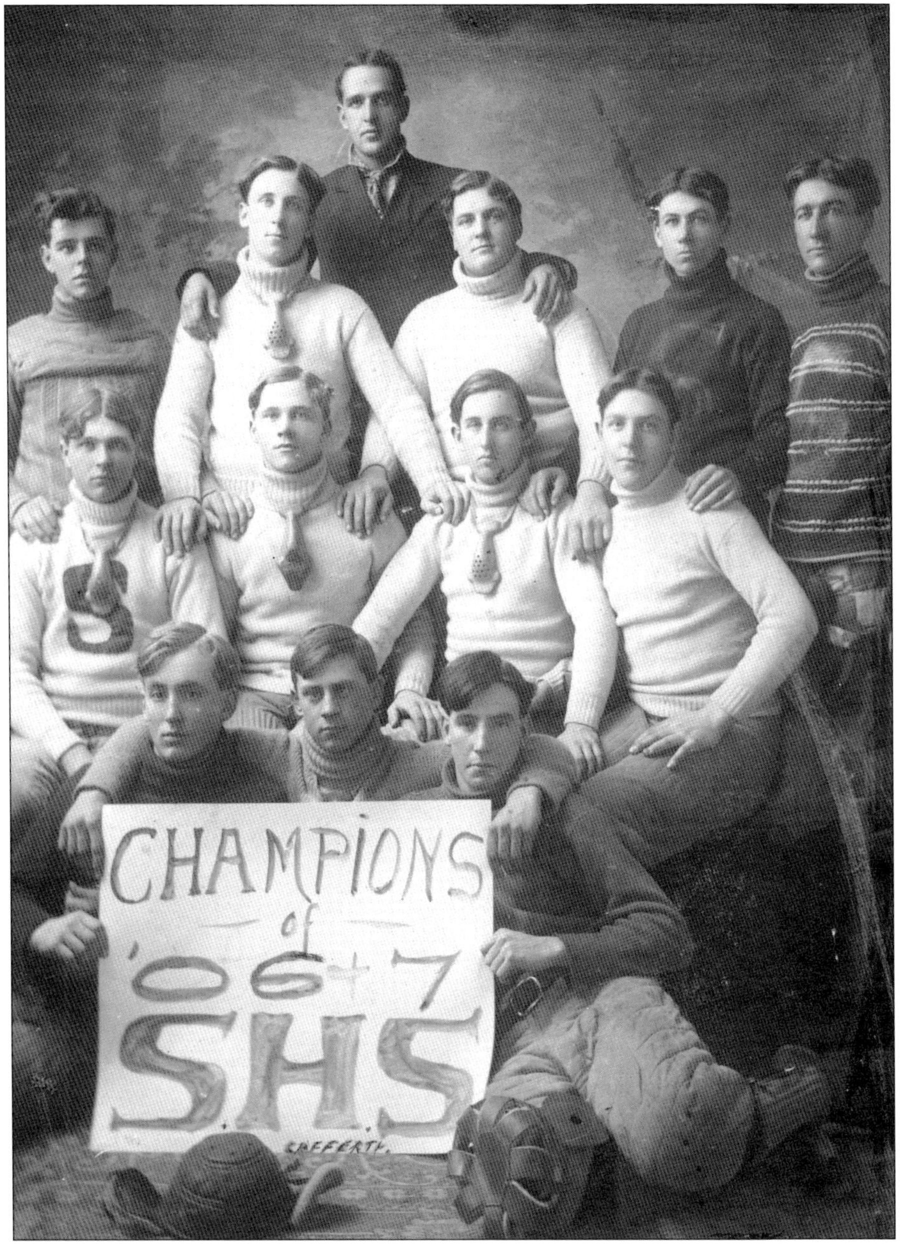

Sunnyside High School football team, valley champions, 1907. Pictured font from left; Wilfred Searle, Chester Ferson and Glen Campbell. Second row from left: Albert Rush, Alva McClain, Lybb Shanafelt and Ed Lichty. Back row from left: John King, Guy Lichty, coach Jim Scoon, Roscoe Sheller, Wilfred Stewart and Homer Gregory.

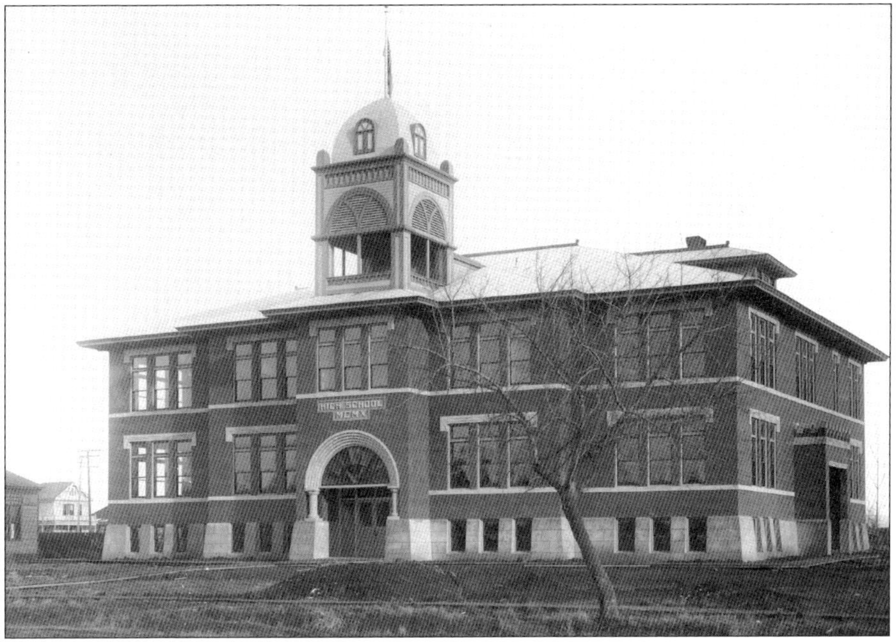

Sunnyside High School was constructed by H.A. Glaze of Pullman, Washington. The building was dedicated on January 4, 1911. It burned on March 20, 1933 and classes were forced to meet in three churches. It was extensively remodeled with additions being added on both ends and reopened in the fall of 1934. The original cost in 1910 was $30,500.

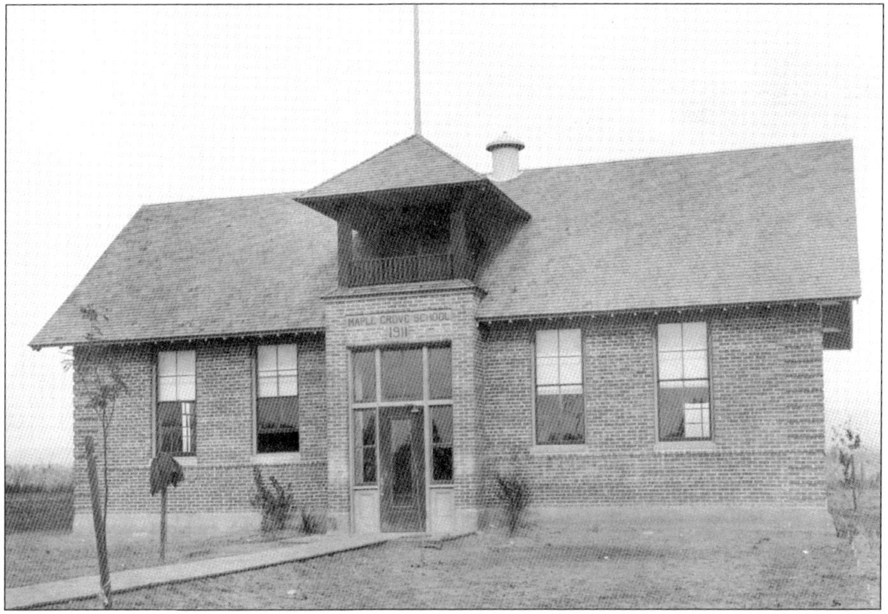

Maple Grove School, a ward school in the Sunnyside District, circa 1911. Building still stands at the Northeast corner of Maple Grove and Van Belle Roads.

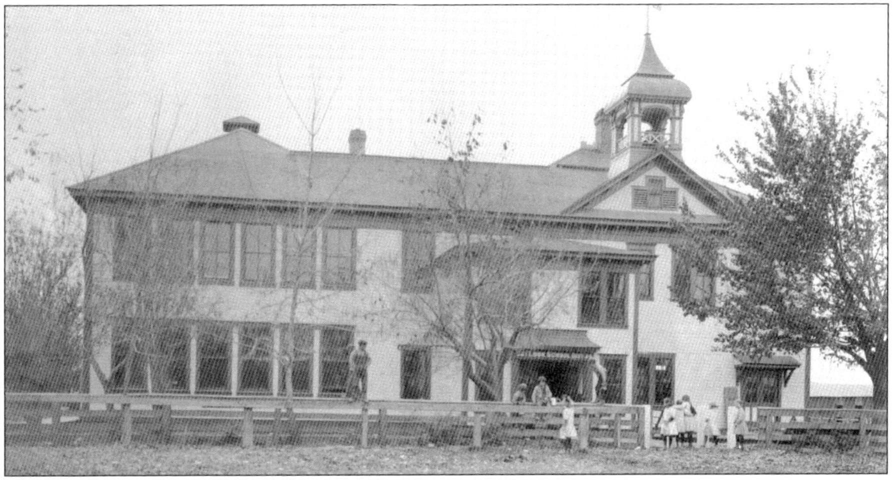

Outlook High School, located five miles west of Sunnyside on Van Belle Road at the present-day Outlook Elementary School location, circa 1911.

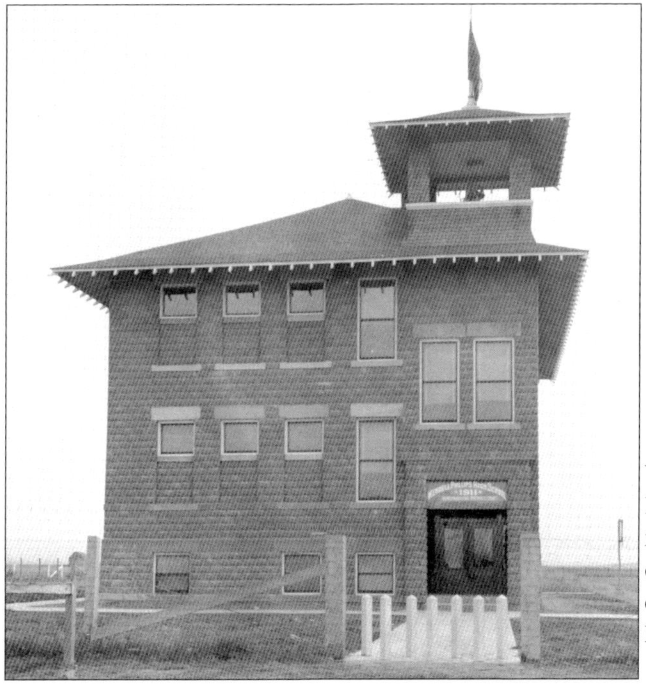

Wendell Phillips High School located four miles southwest of Sunnyside on the east side of Wendell Phillips Road, circa 1911.

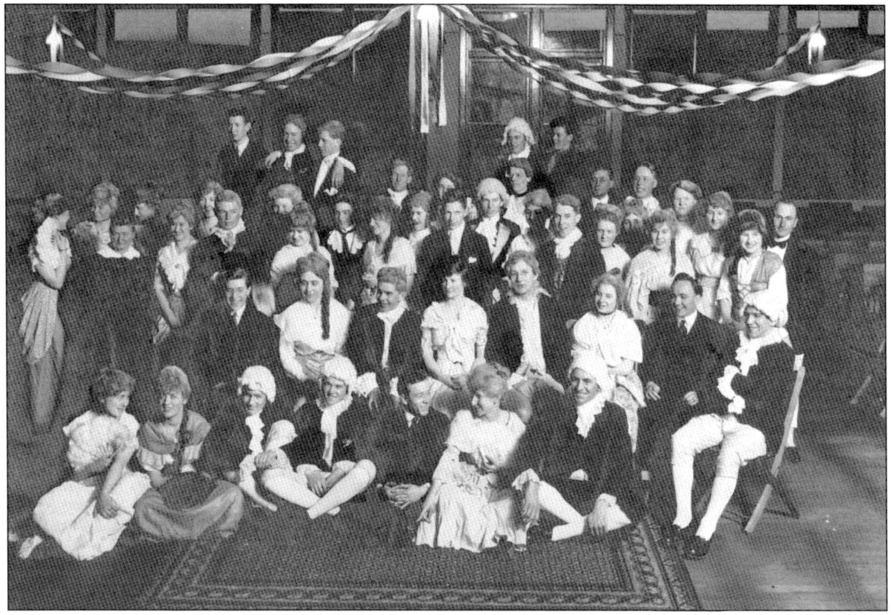

Sunnyside High School function, circa 1917.

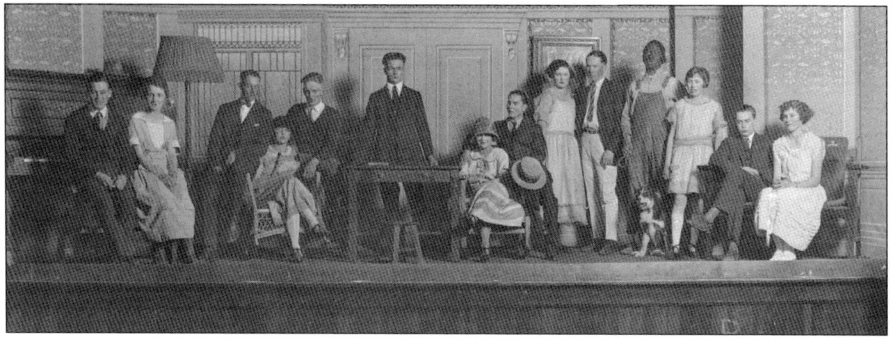

Sunnyside High School play, circa 1924.

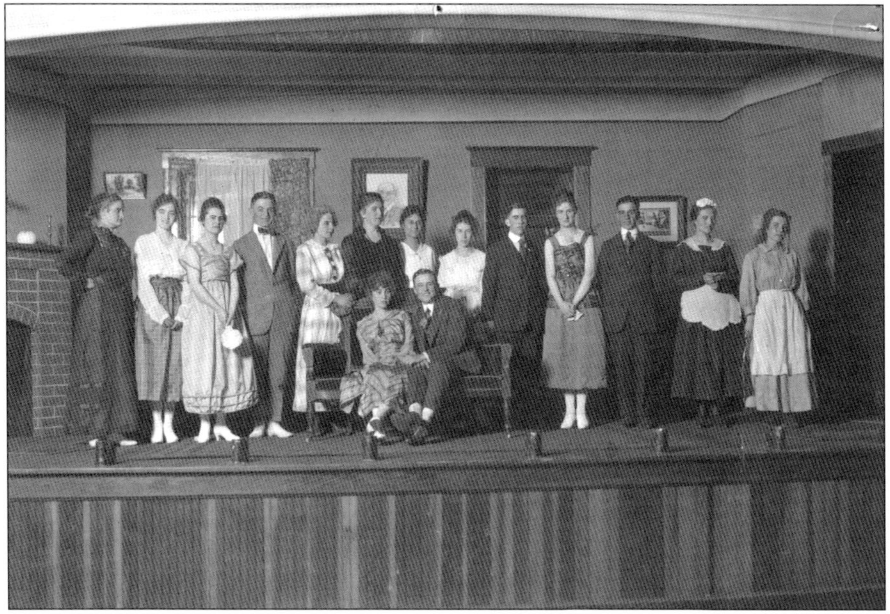

Senior Play, Sunnyside High School, 1918.

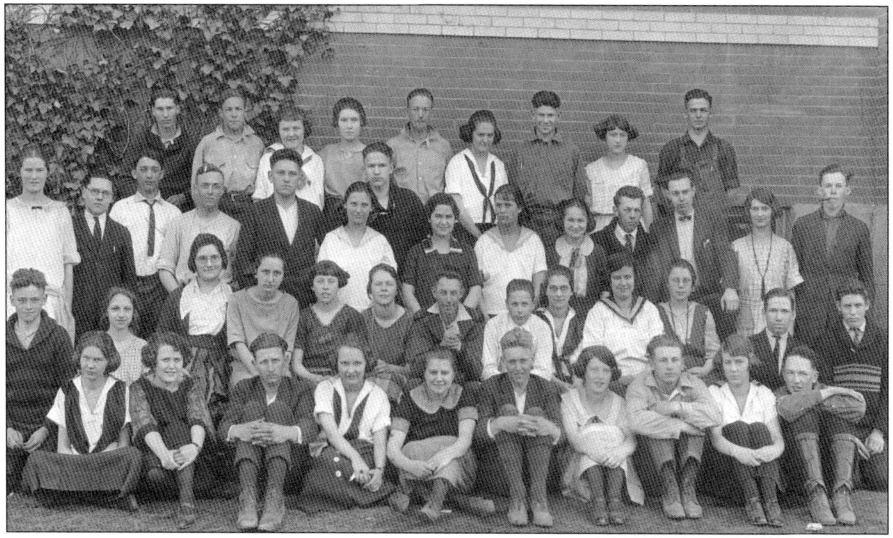

Sunnyside High School sophomore class of 1923. The class included: Forest Amundson, Riley Antles, Clarence Backer, Harold Bagley, Howard Bagley, Eugene Bishop, Walter Christian, Albert Clark, George Cloud, Lee Colby, Herbert Collins, Glenn Cosper, Vern Cowell, Bert Cushney, Preb Dow, Porter Griswold, Lyle Heffron, Durward Hohenshelt, Edward Kendrick, Claude Mauzy, Kay Olsen, Carl Phillips, Walter Phillips, John Stobie, Walter Strom, Manley Sackett, Marshal Search, Virgil Seay, Kenneth Smith, Victor Smith, Leonard Vetter, Clyde Broden, Don McEdwards, John Stump, Hessie Allen, Thelma Allen, Allie Amundson, Grace Baker, Jessie Bennington, Olga Bennington, Ruth Ferrell, Grace Rollinger, Luella Griswold, Anna Hagerman, Ethel Heffron, Alma Jeffries, Louise Kassebaum, Orpha Kostenbader, Irene Lampkin, Edith Leach, Freda Lempke, Frances Lichty, Grace McKibben, Alma Mitchel, Zada Padgham, Valla Parfitt, Verna Parfitt, Lousia Peck, Marie Piepgrass, Verna Swaney, Jessie Fry, Violet Carnes and Zola Sithwick.

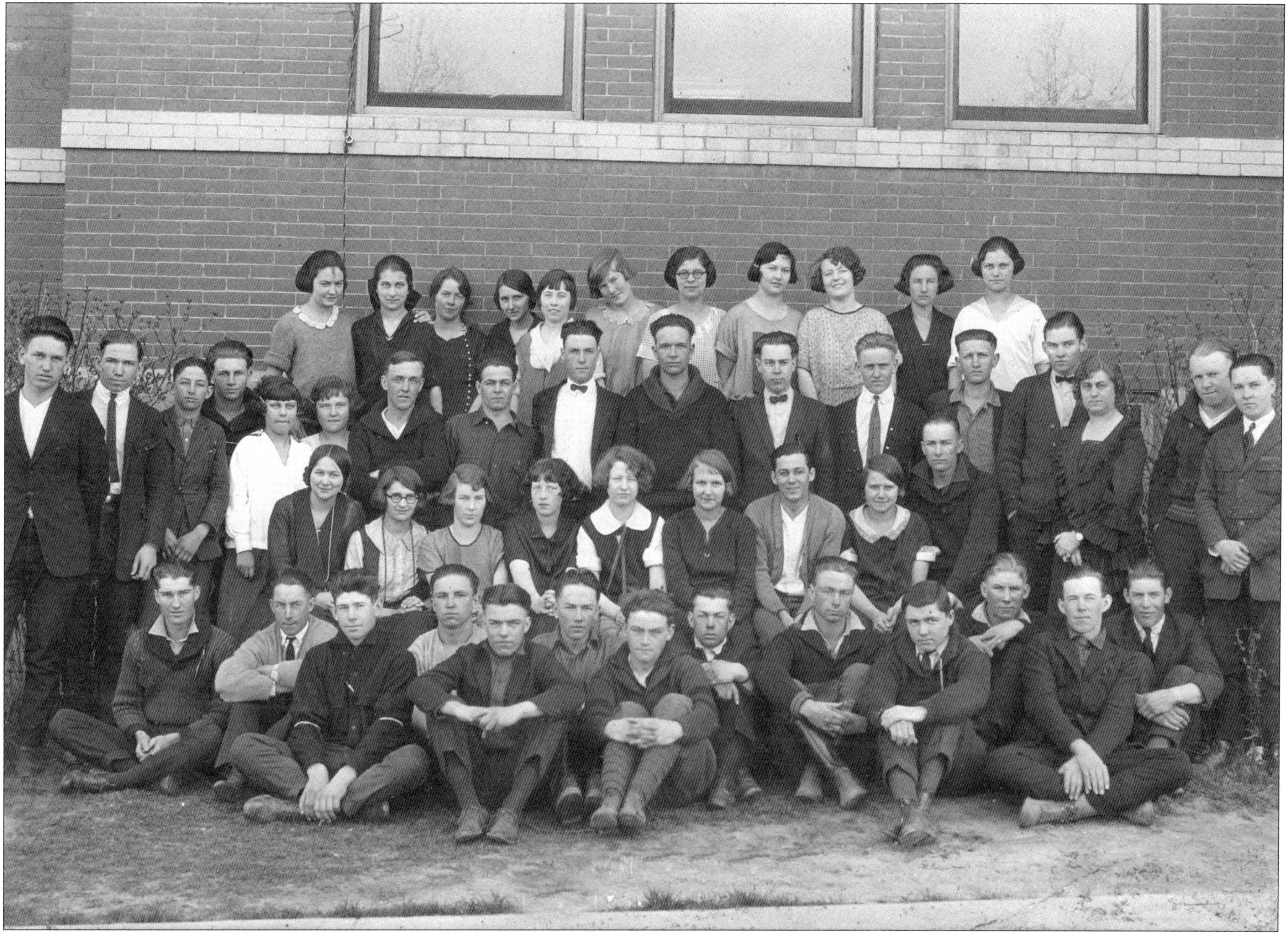

Sunnyside High School freshman class of 1921.

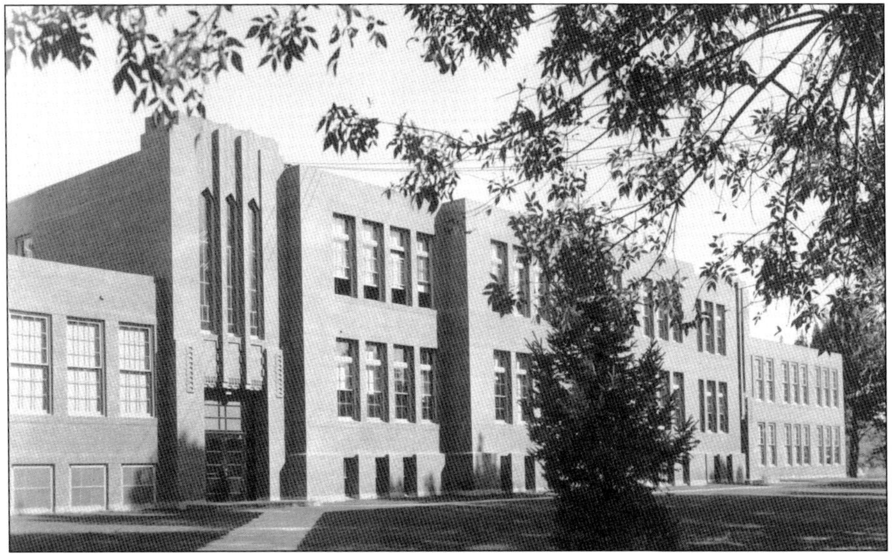

The new Sunnyside High School (later to become Chief Kamiakin) which was completed in the Spring of 1934. Located on the corner of 9th Street and Edison Avenue. It occupied the entire block where the present day hospital, Chief Kamiakin office building and Banner Bank now stand. Picture taken Sept. 10, 1934

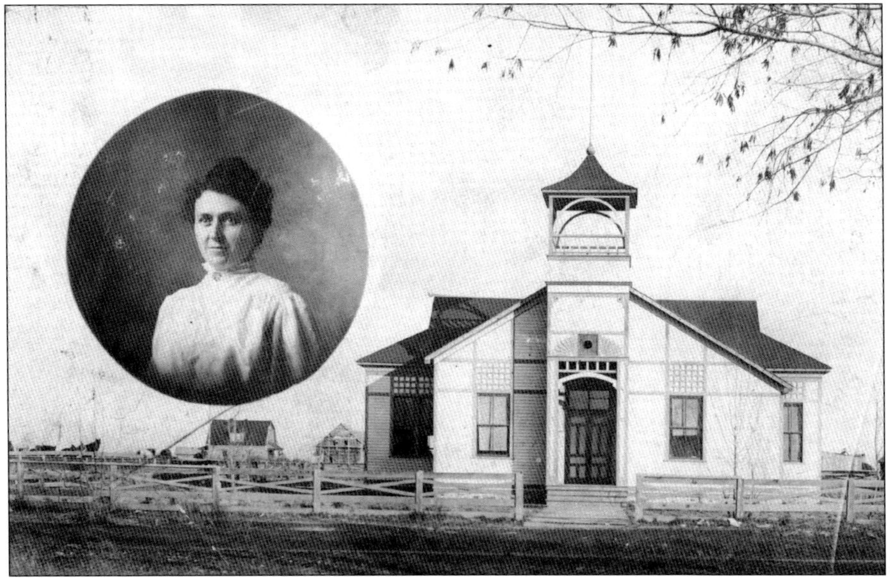

Emerson School, circa 1907. This was the first grade school in Sunnyside. Teacher shown is Miss Satterwhite. The school was located on the southeast corner of 9th Street and Edison Avenue.

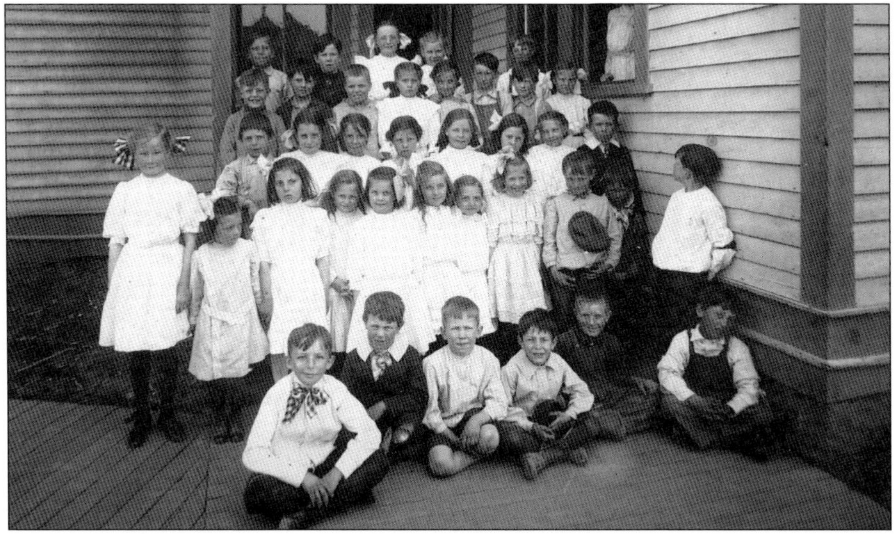

Emerson School, 1905. First row from left: Helen Morgan, Helen Robinson, Hazel Owens, Harry Minkler, Walter Cordield, Stanley Randolph, Ralph Shafer and Russel McLean. Second row from left: Alice Barnes, Ruth McClain, Bessie Eddy, Henrietta Knight, George Lowe, Lyndall Hoover, unidentified, Carl Middleton, unidentified, Laura Martin, Mary Eyraud, Gladys Yoder and Clifford Mauvis. Third row from left: Ester Malmberg, Bernice Henderson, Alberta Patrick and Ruth Stevens. Back row from left: Clifford Carr, John Stackhouse, Lloyd Merrill, Clyde Jory, George Minnick, Peter Eyraud, George Barrens, ____ Chambers, Erastus Burrus, Edna Fosket, Willie Summers, Clayton Asselstine and Frank Lyal.

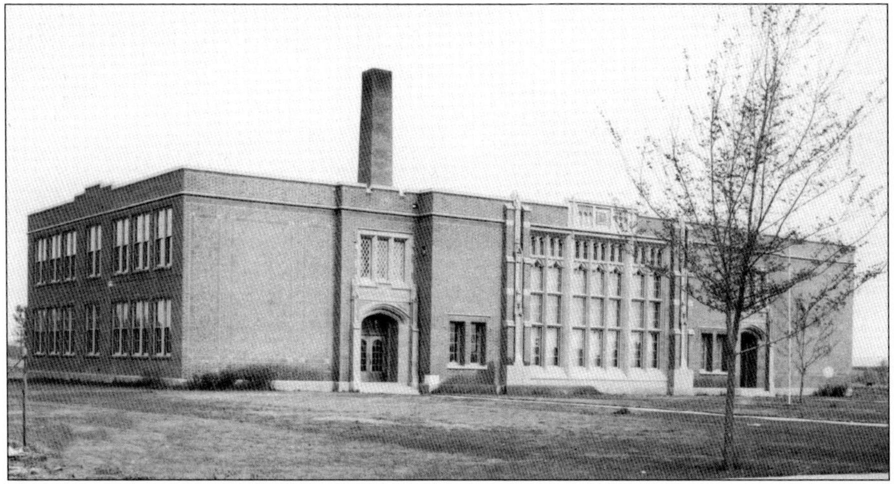

Lincoln School, opened in 1927. The building still stands at the corner of 6th and Lincoln.

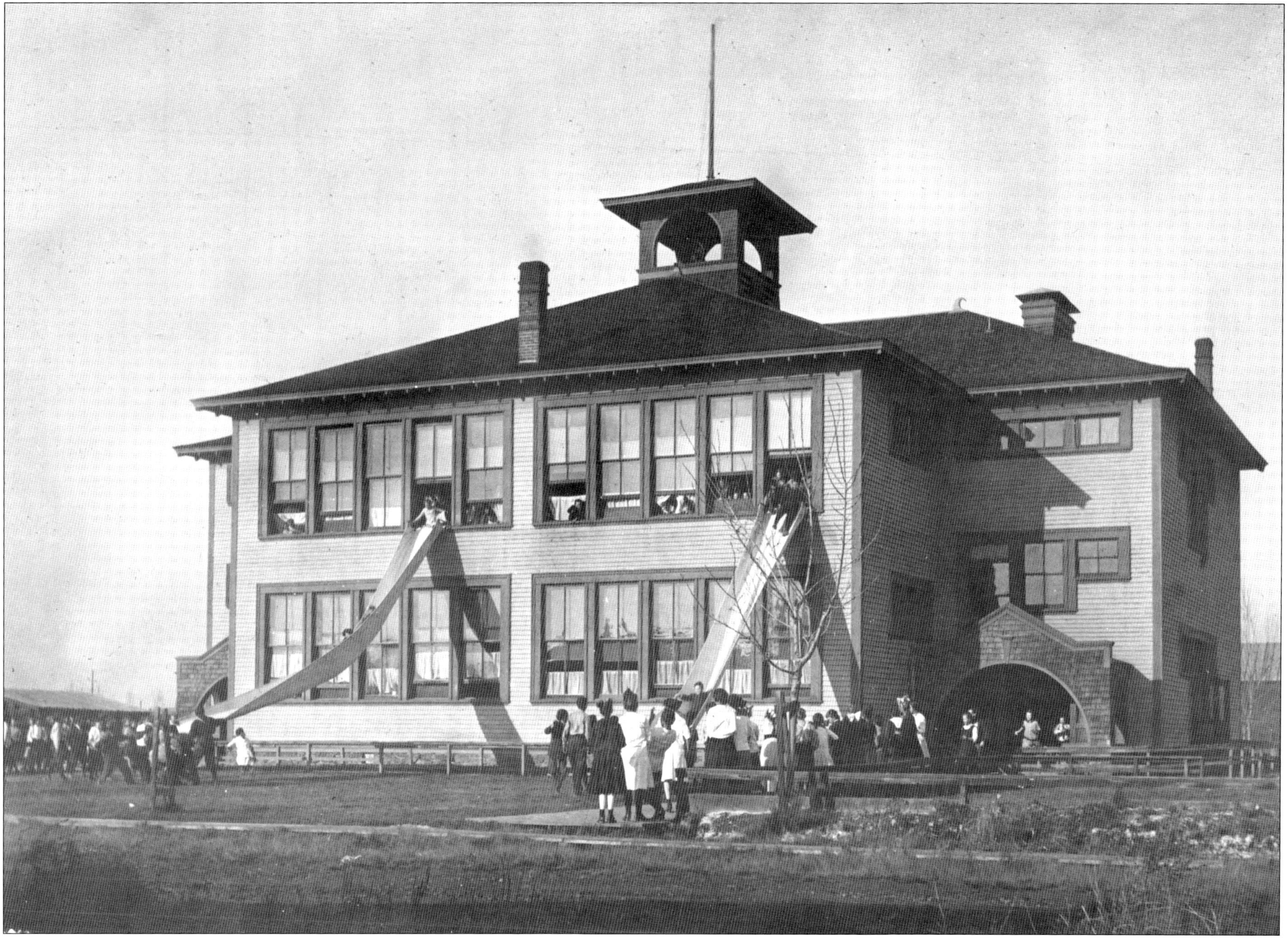

A fire drill at Denny Blaine School, circa 1910. Later they constructed metal tube style fire escapes on both ends of the building. The school was located on 9th Street and Custer Avenue.

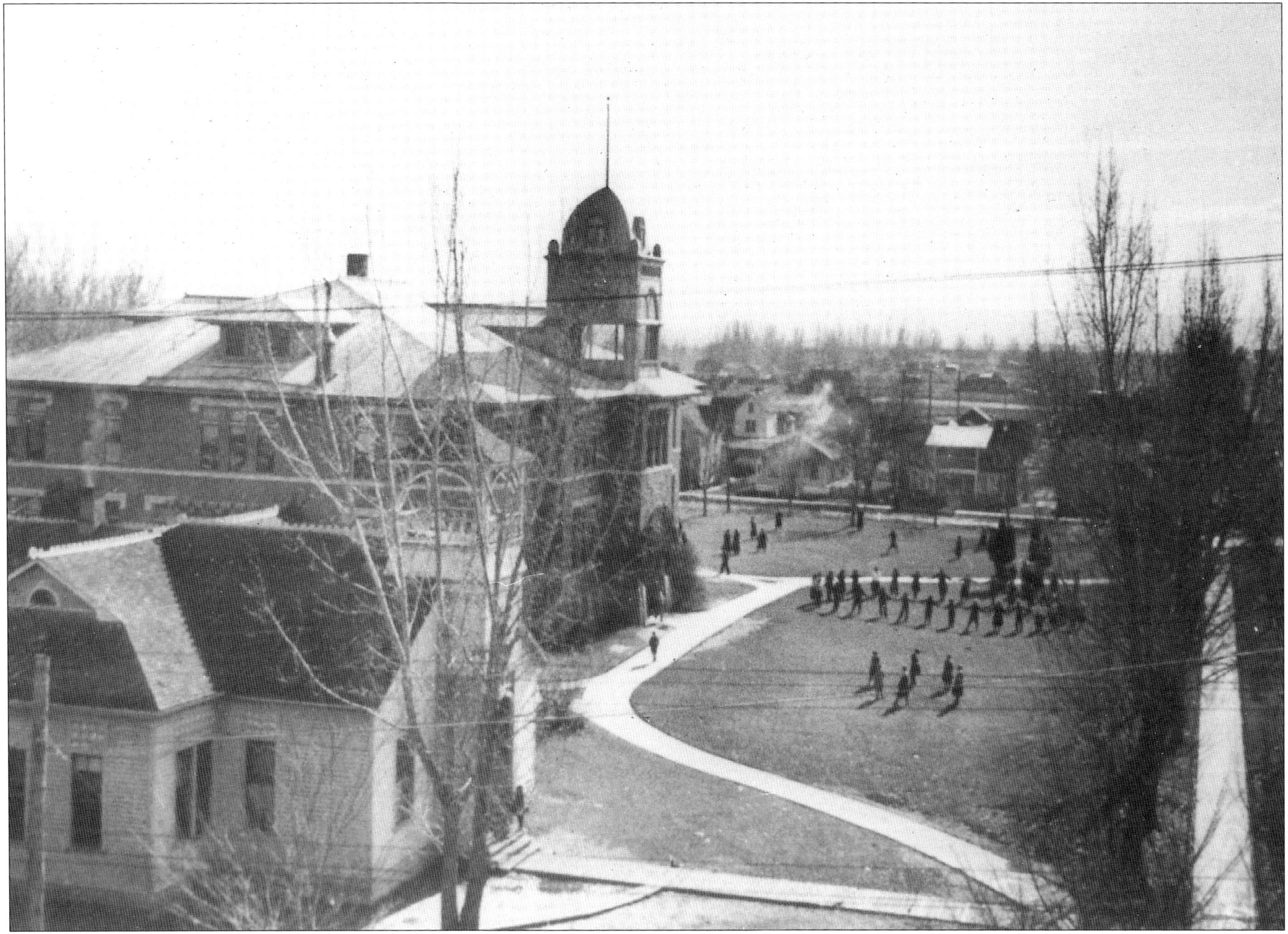

Emerson School in the foreground and the new high school in the background. Photo take from the United Methodist Church belfry, circa 1920.

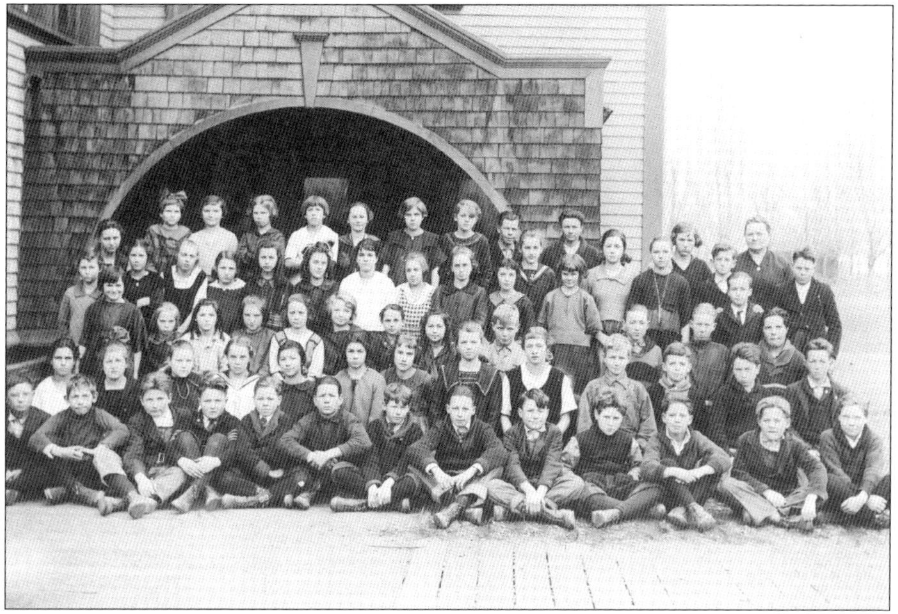

Denny Blaine Elementary School Sixth grade class, circa 1920. The teachers were Mrs. Brown and Mr. Masters.

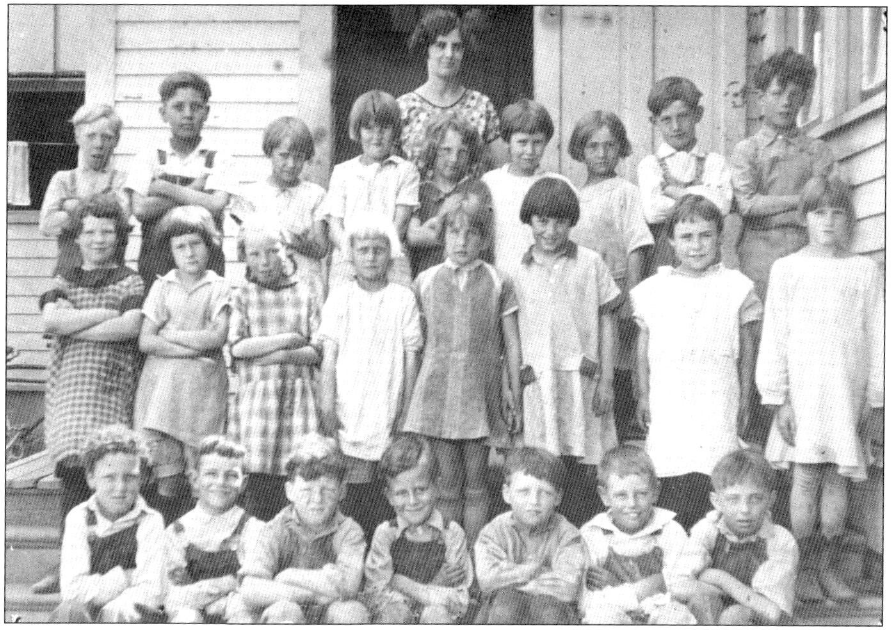

Washington School class of Margaret Eckles, 1926. The school was located of Factory Road east of Sunnyside. Pictured are front from left: Irving Dow, John Warnock, Lawrence Schilperoort, Frank Roark, Clarence Schilperoort, Charles Greet and Laurel Carlyle. Second row from left: Lillian Schilperoort, Louise Swaney, Lola Mattingly, Leona Knap, Bernice Simmons, Florence Ferson, Viola Lyons and Frances Allen. Back row from left: Elmer Mattingly, Norma Carlyle, Eloise Ferson, Grace Holt, Helen Helman, Iris Lyons, Berdena Padgham Leonard Coon and Norman Coon.

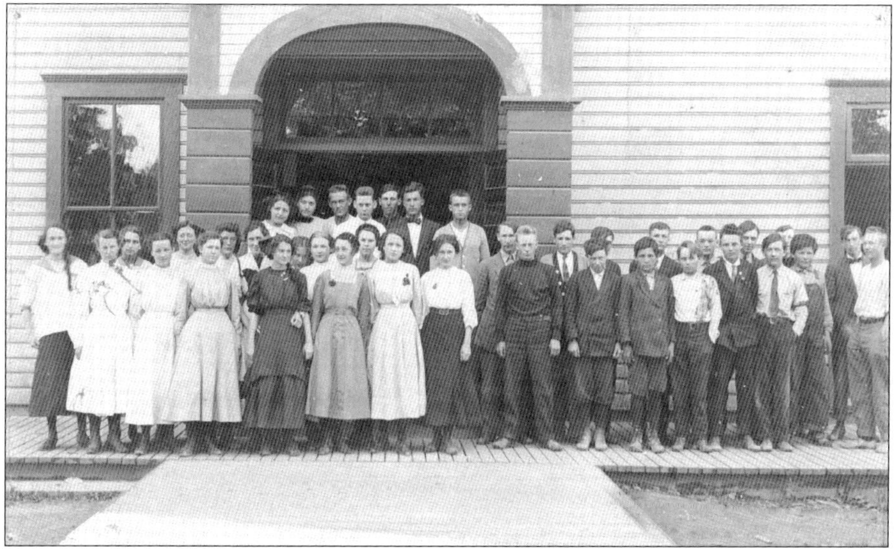

Outlook High School, 1912.

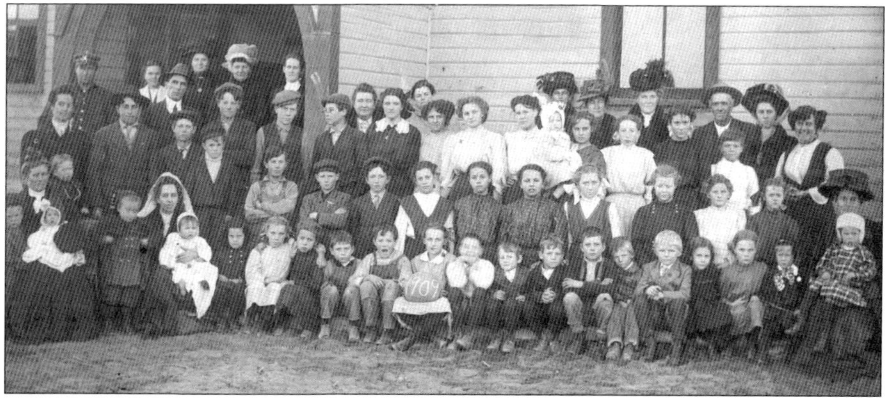

Riverside School students and faculty in 1909. The school was located on the west side of South Emerald Road. It opened in 1902.

FARM & RANCH

Writing in the May 25, 1911, edition of the Sunnyside Sun, Stephen J. Harrison, one of the founders of the Christian Cooperative Colony, stated, "The people who were in the country in 1898 and those who added to the community in the next six years underwent a grilling in privation that they will never forget."

Home for most settlers was a one-room shack or tent. Plumbing and electricity did not exist. Most people did not even have a well; instead, they stored drinking water in a cistern, which was filled with irrigation water filtered through a burlap sack.

The first task for farmers was clearing the land of sagebrush, which was everywhere and grew to great size. Clearing 40 or 80 acres was no easy task. Next, the ground was plowed. Putting in a hard day's work, a farmer could finish two or three acres. Before planting, the land had to be scraped to level out hills and rises. This was essential for proper irrigation.

Once the planting was complete, the farmer had to battle the soil and wind. The soil, which the pioneers referred to as blowsand, was rich but very fine. It contained almost no humus, so the slightest gust of wind was enough to pick it up. Dust storms were a frequent occurrence. If the soil was not constantly kept wet, the wind would blow away the first few inches of soil along with the seed requiring the farmer to replant.

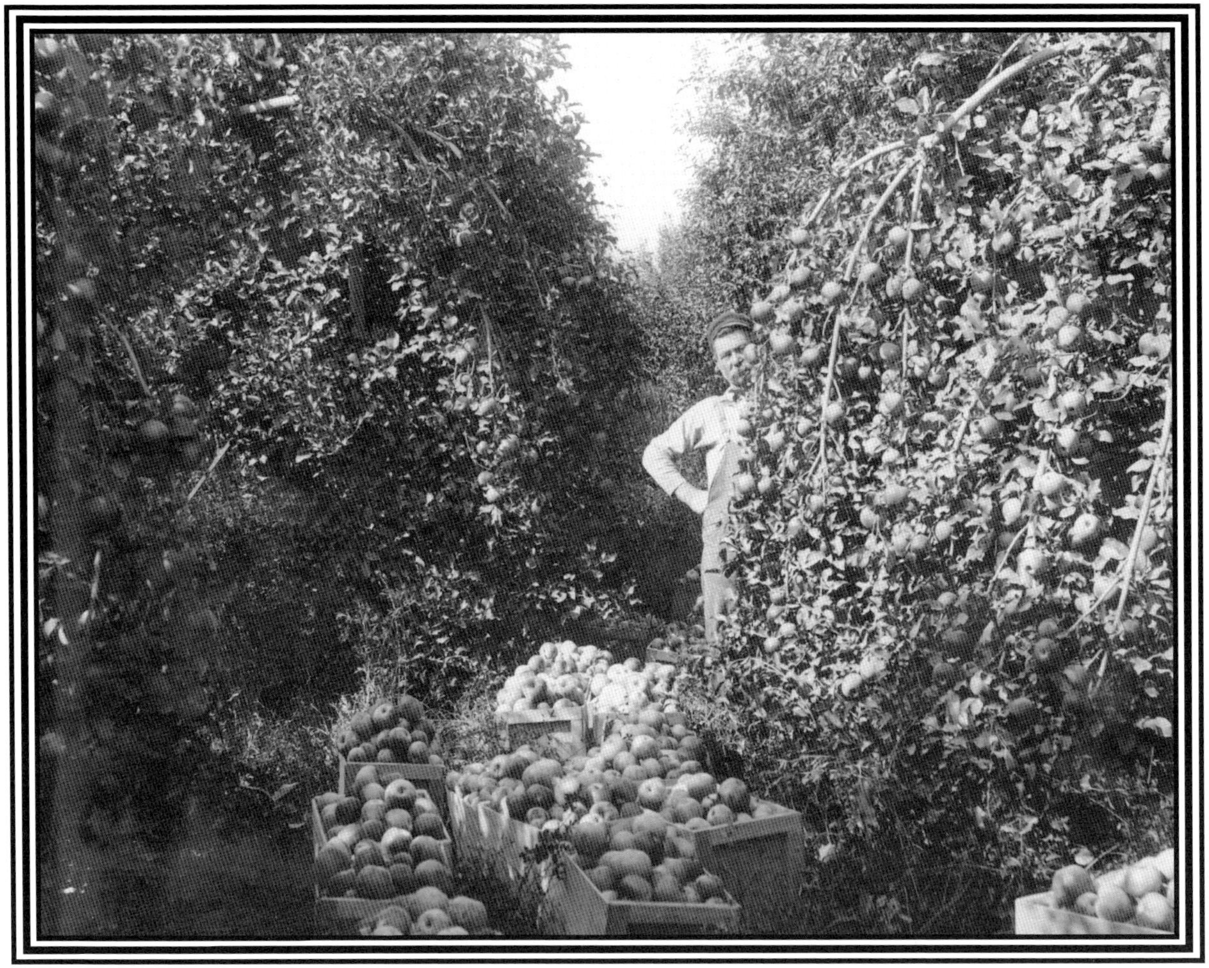

Apple orchard near Sunnyside, circa 1920.

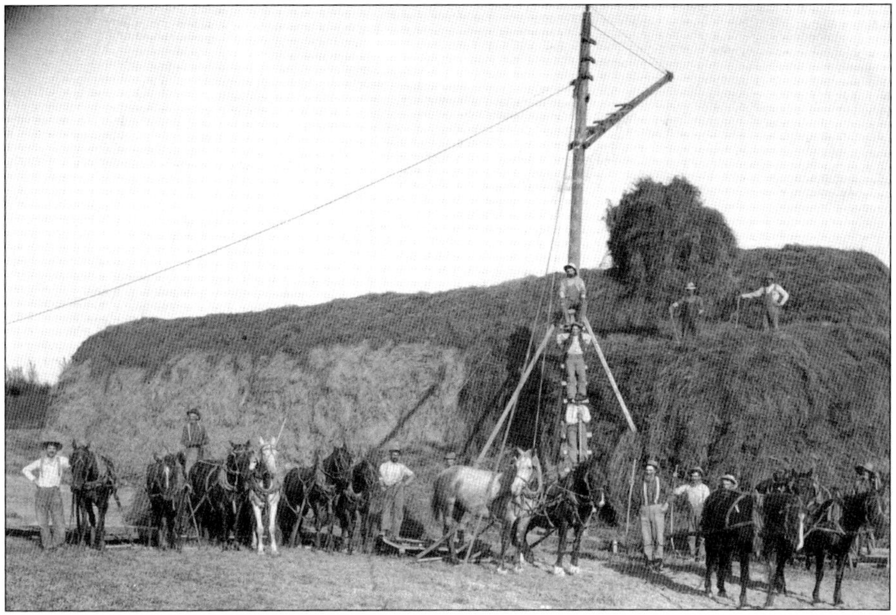
Stacking hay on a farm near Sunnyside.

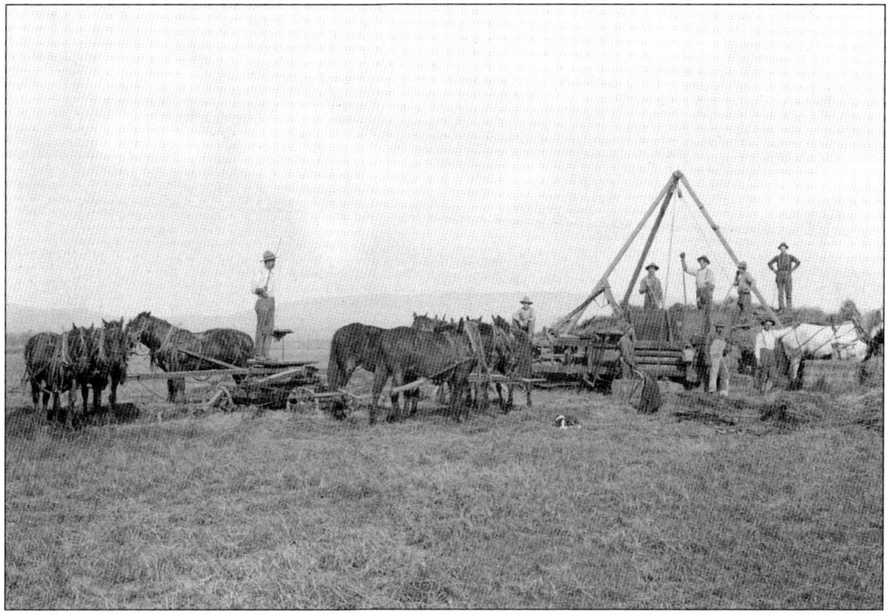
Hay harvesting in the early 1900s.

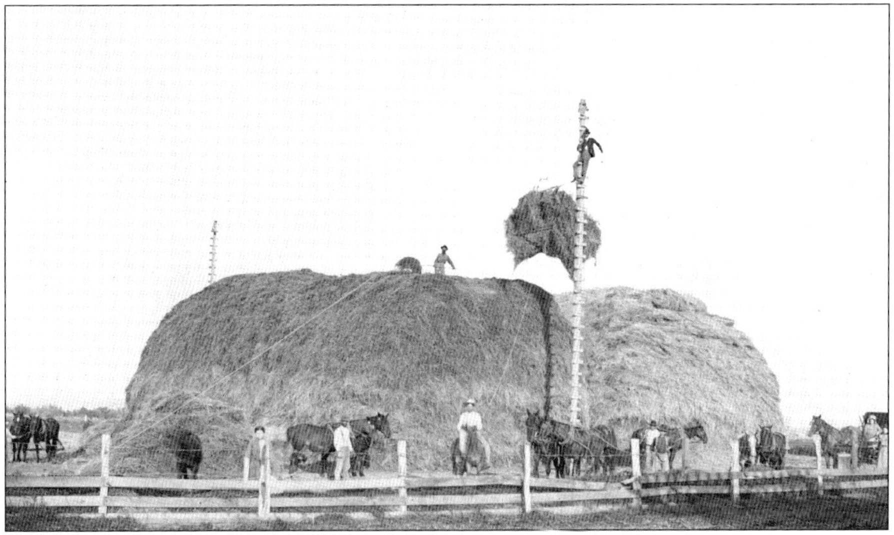
S. J. Harrison haying crew, circa 1904.

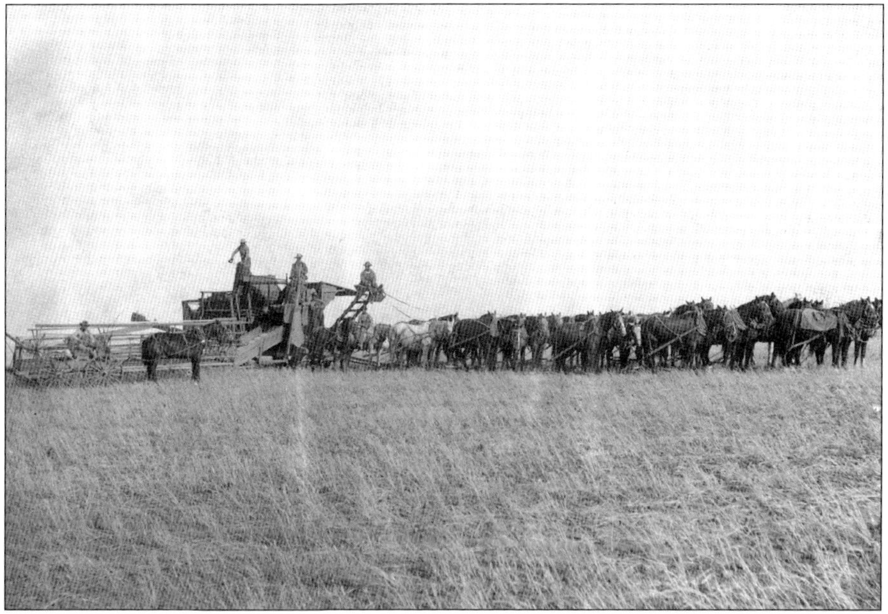
Harvesting hay in the early 1900s.

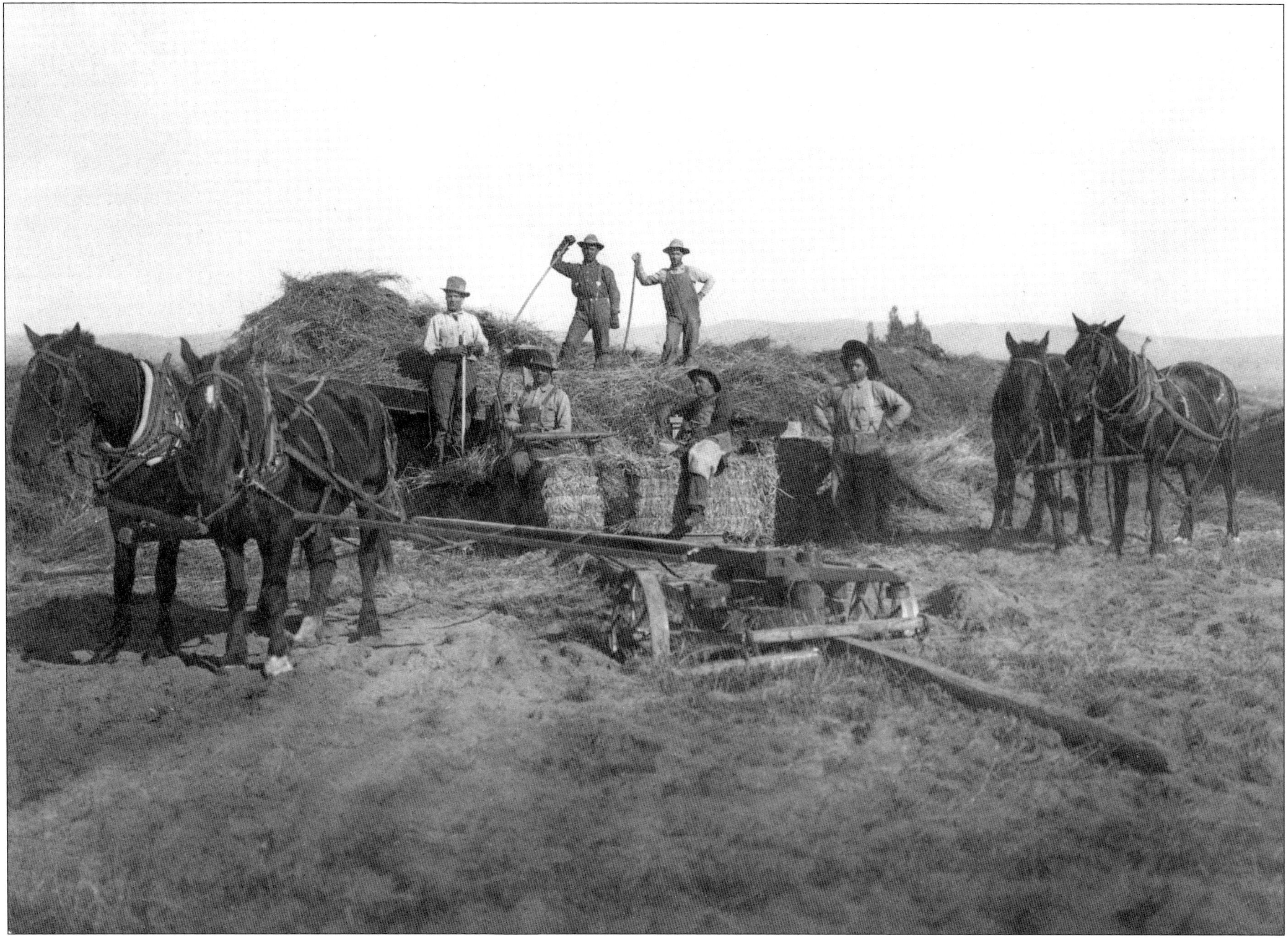

Baling hay in Outlook, early 1900s.

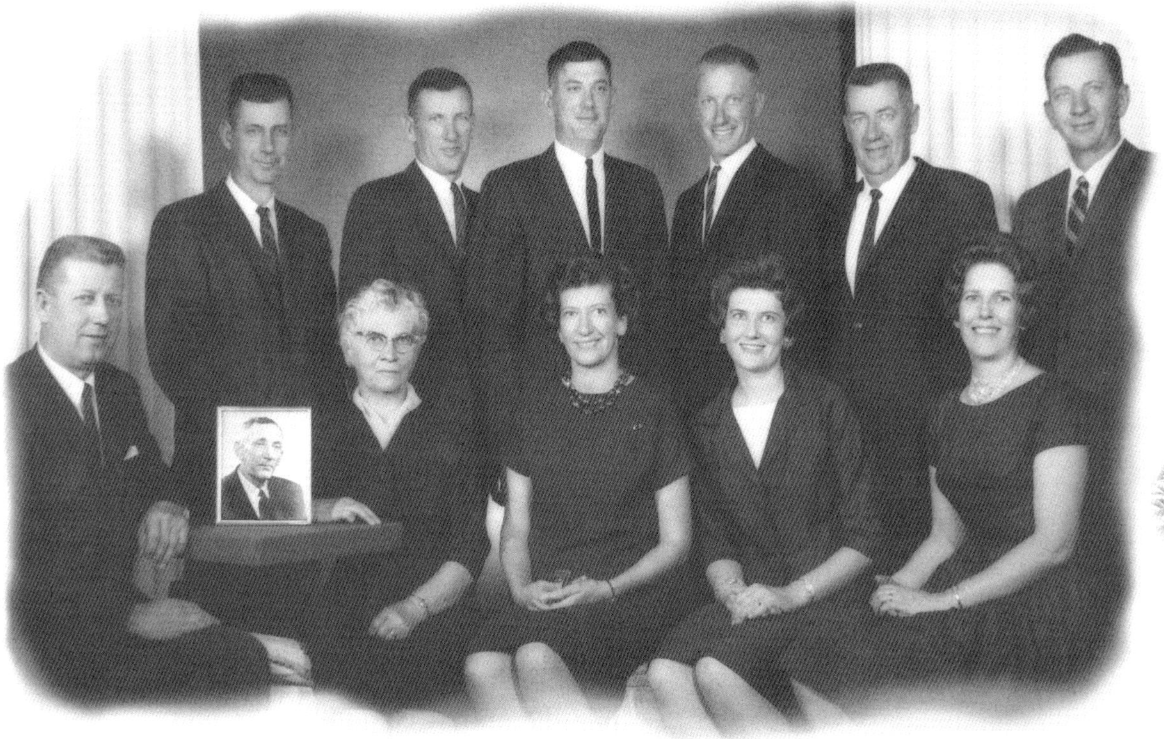

The Newhouse Family. Seated, left to right: Alfred R. Newhouse (1923 -), John Newhouse-photograph (1886 - 1950), Tina Bos Newhouse (1895 - 1973), Ellen Danley (1922 -), Maryjane Swynenburg (1934 -) and Betty Bechtold (1929 - 2001). Standing, left to right: David L. Newhouse (1926 - 1997), John E. Newhouse (1932 -), Albert R. Newhouse (1936 - 1981), Wayne R. Newhouse (1941 -), Melvin J. Newhouse (1918 - 1999) and Irving R. Newhouse (1920 - 2001).

NEWHOUSE FAMILY

John Newhouse and Tina Bos, immigrants from Holland, were married in Mabton, Washington in 1916. They made their home and started the original dairy in the Green Valley area of Sunnyside. Here they raised seven sons and three daughters, all of whom attended Wendell Phillips School before going into Sunnyside High School.

The Newhouse Dairy is the oldest continuously family-owned and operated dairy in the Yakima Valley. Over the years the family farm has grown and the generations have diversified their farming ventures, raising hops, grapes, fruit, many other varied crops, services and of course milk.

Church, community and a strong work ethic are values that have been passed down through the generations of the Newhouse family. The Newhouse families, whether they still live here or wherever life has taken them, are proud of their roots in the Yakima Valley.

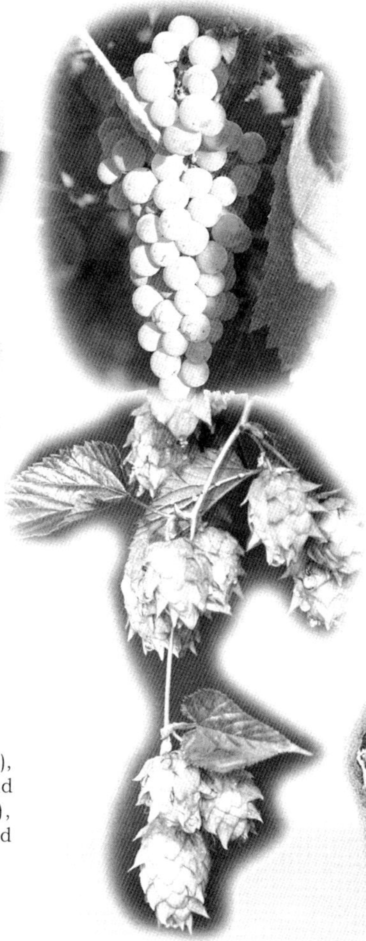

Newhouse Farms

Bittersweet Ranches

Emerald Ranches

Gilbert & Sylvia Newhouse

Irving Newhouse & Sons

Newhouse Dairy

Upland Farms

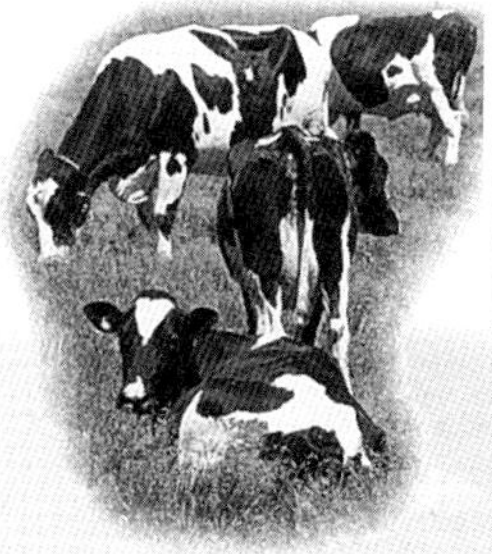

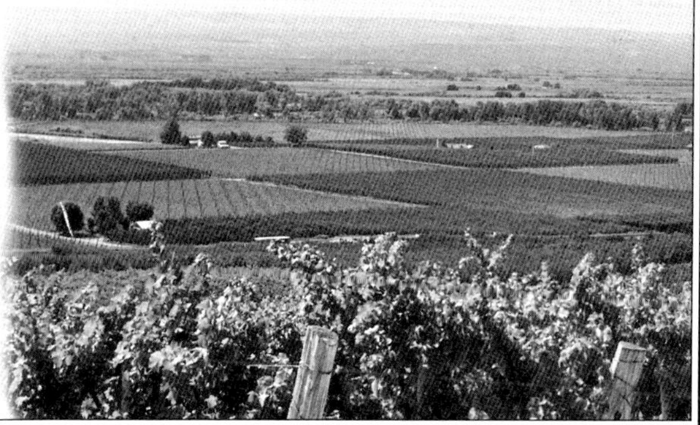

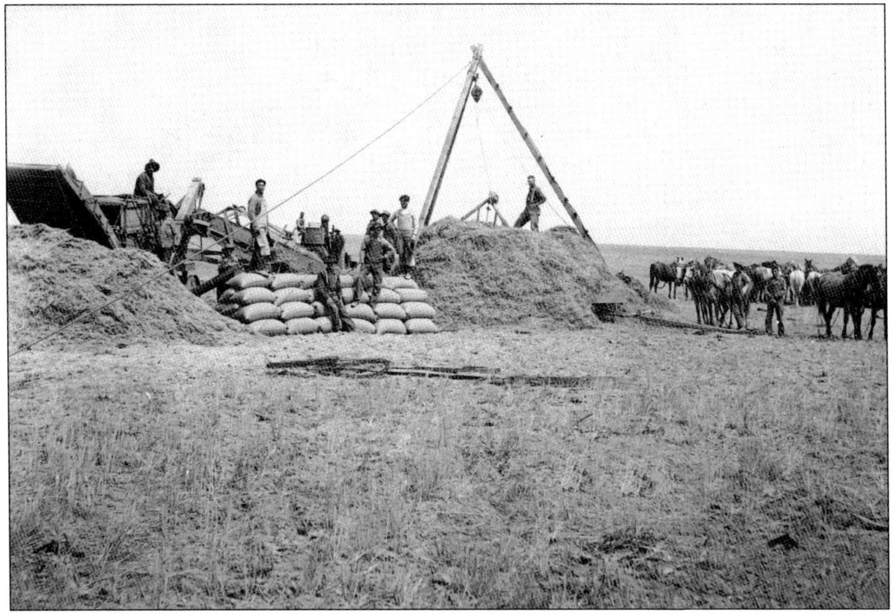

Early harvesting operation using the stationary machine powered by the steam tractor.

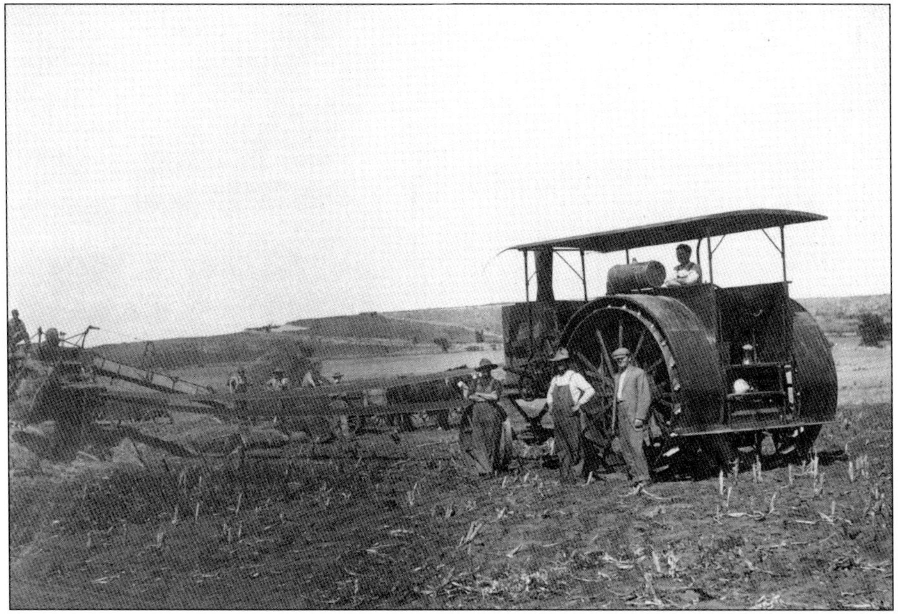

Early threshing equipment.

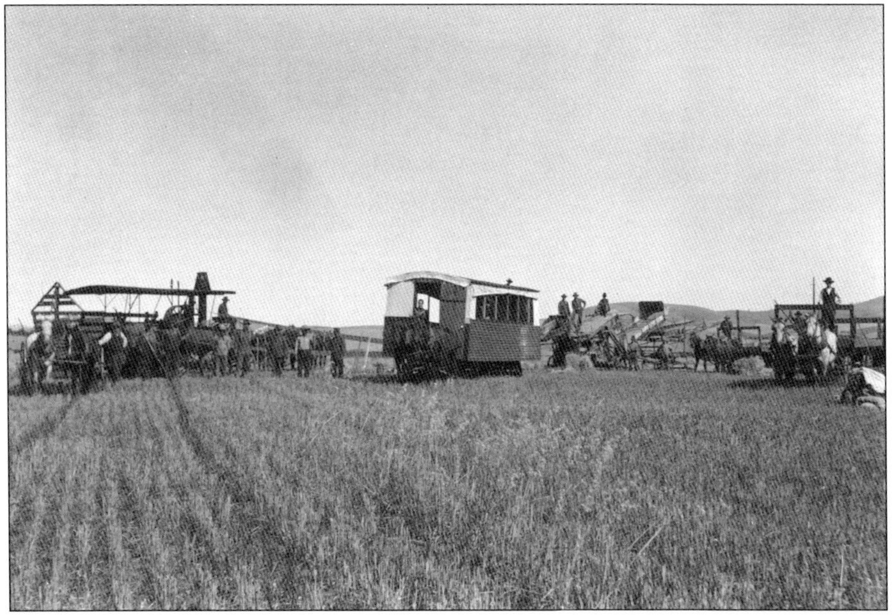

Horse-drawn wheat harvesting in the early 1900s.

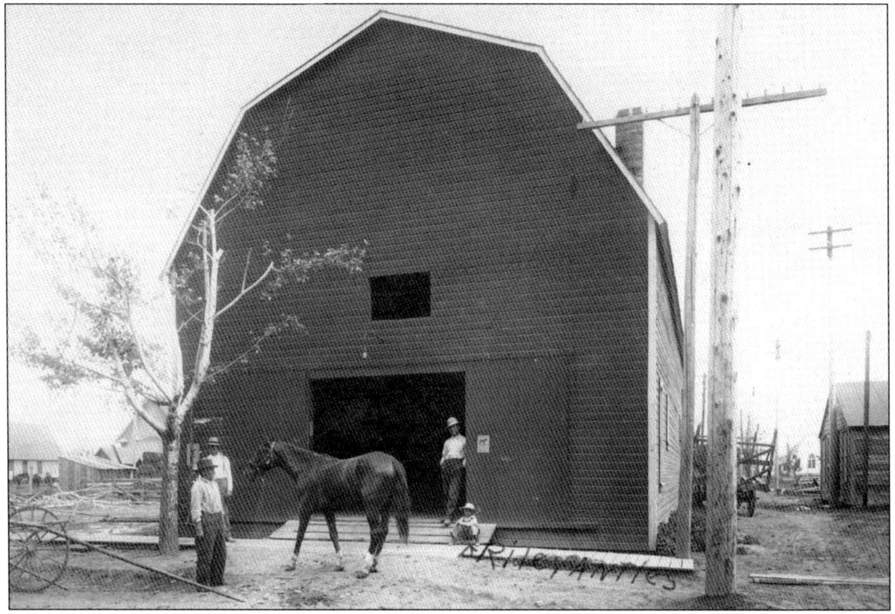

Antles O K Barn, located on the east side of 7th Street between Edison and Decatur Avenue, 1909.

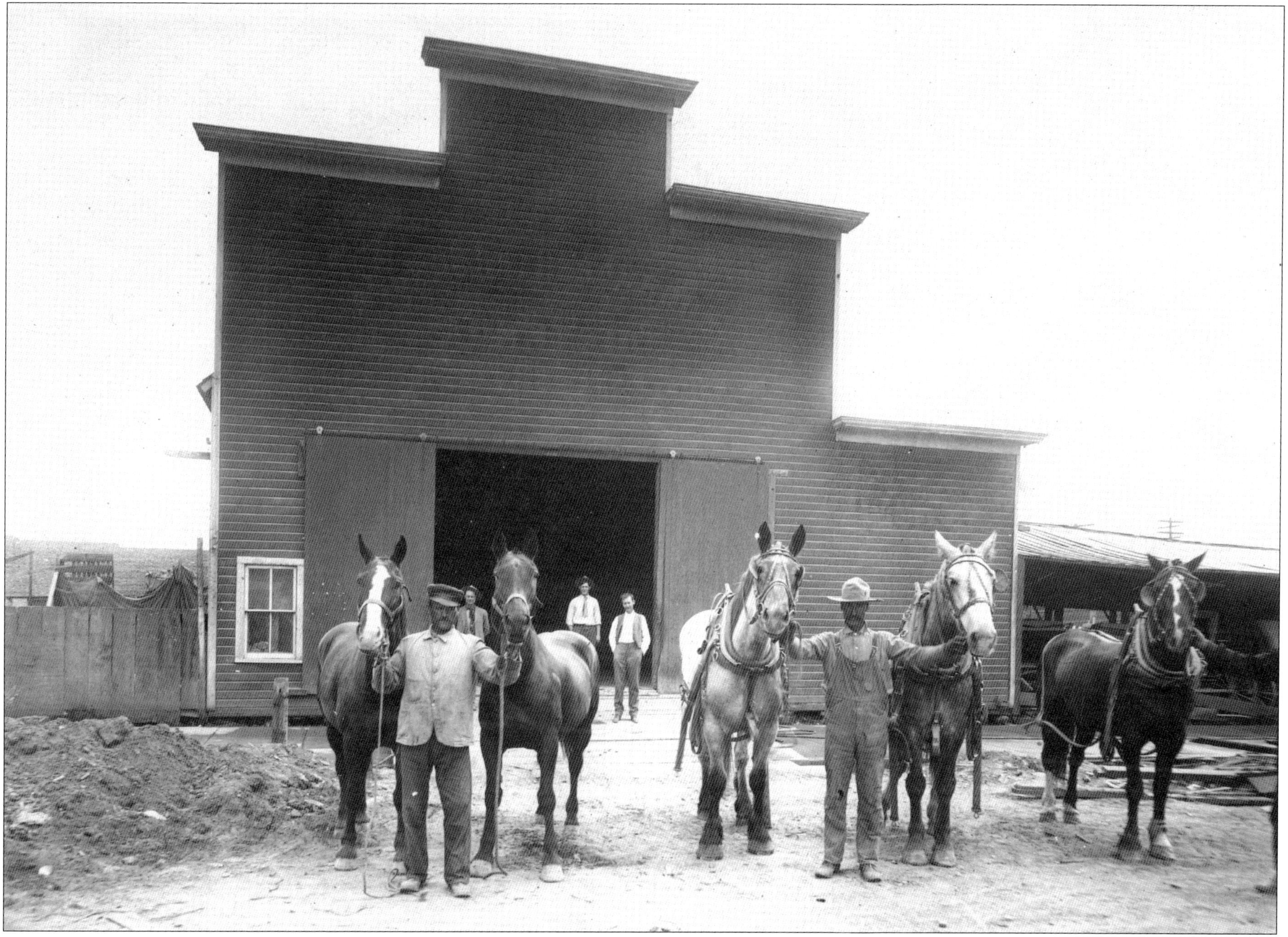

Horses in front of the Sunnyside livery stable in 1906 which was located on the south side of Edison Avenue between 5th and 6th streets. Two of the men pictured in the background are Fred Emery and Harvey Matheson.

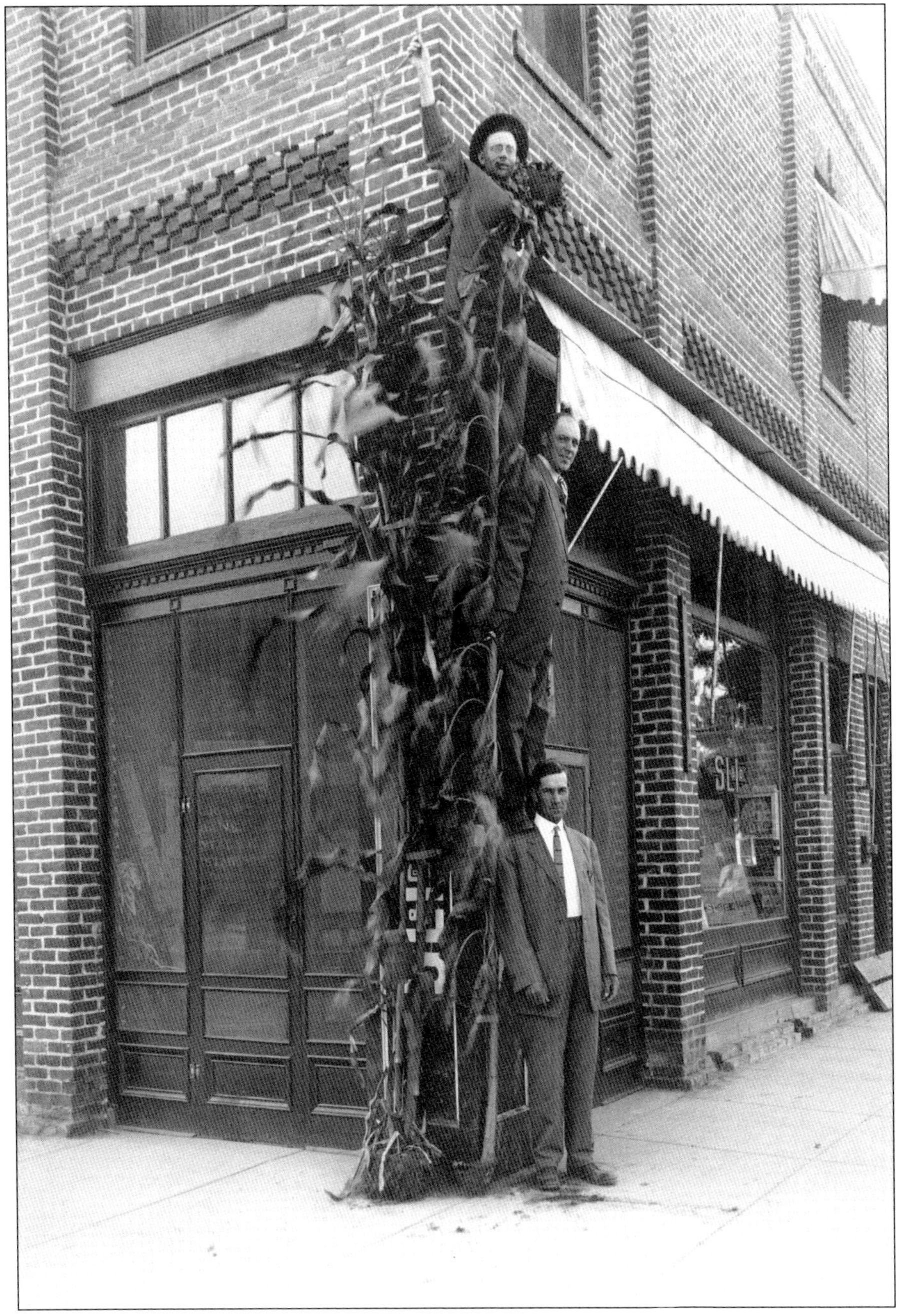

W. H. Harrison, H. Lloyd Miller and A. G. Fleming stand beside corn to show it's height in front of the S.L.I. Building on 6th Street and Edison Ave., circa 1908.

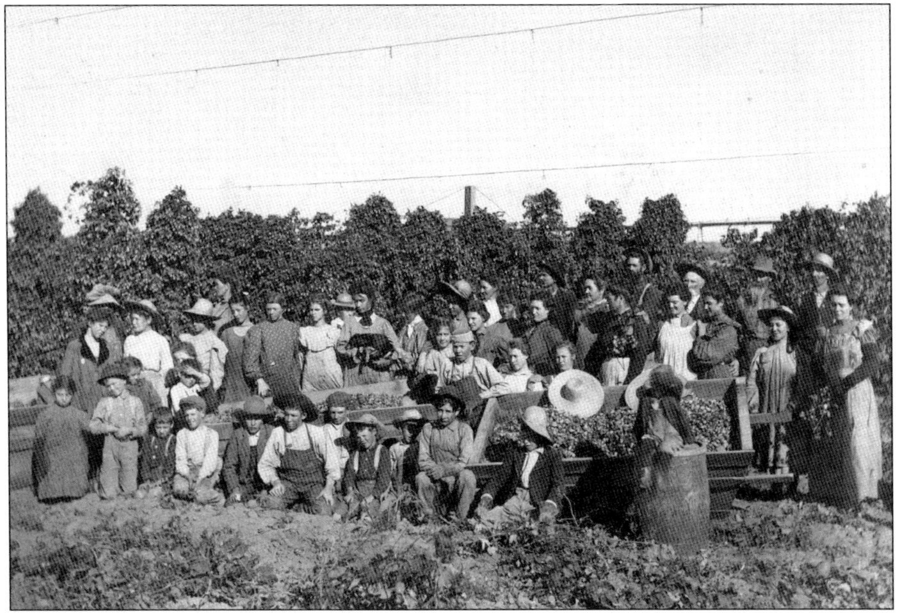

Hop picking crew in the early 1900s.

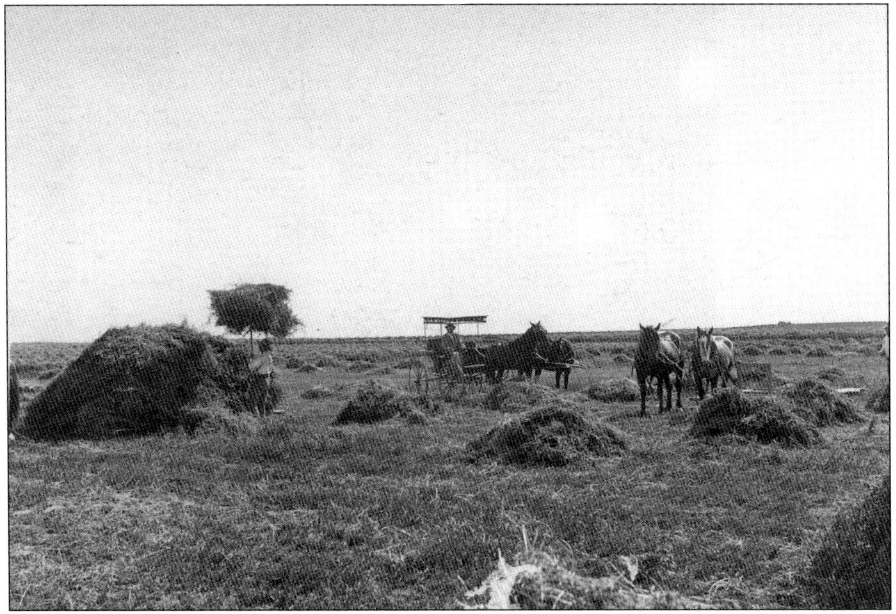

Early ranch scene. W. H. Harrison is on the left. A. G. Fleming is in the buggy.

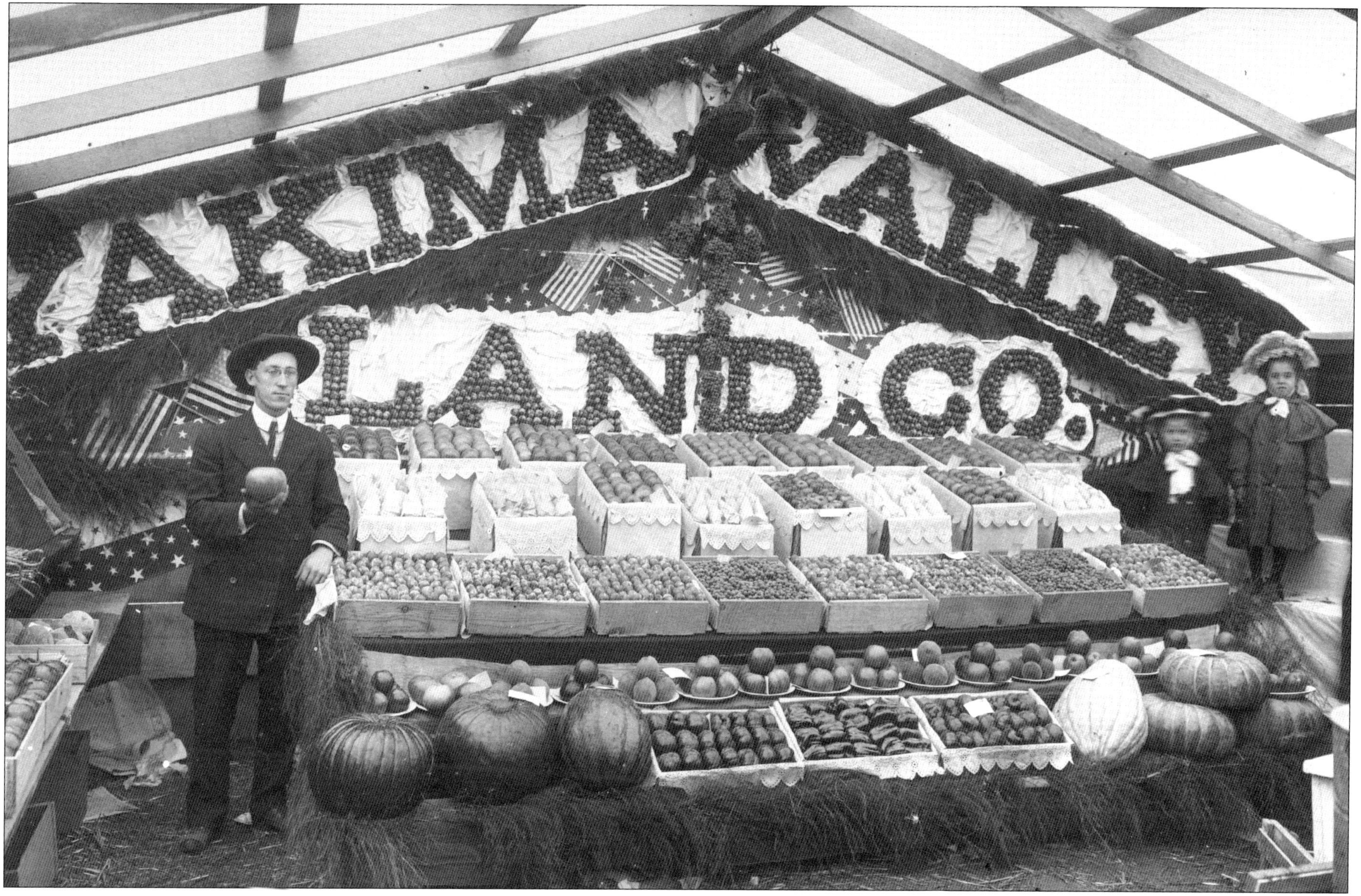

Agricultural display by the Yakima Valley Land Co. in the early 1900s.

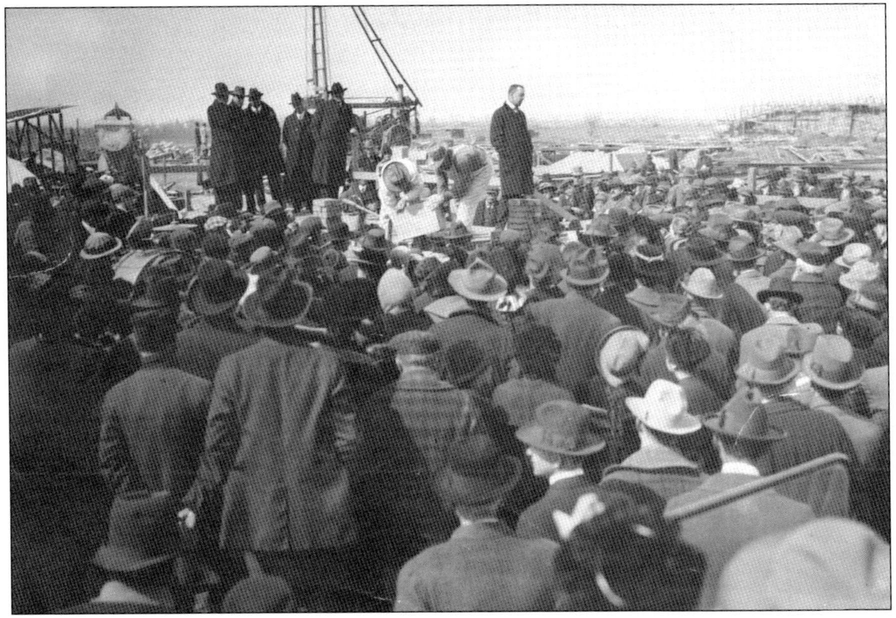

The dedication of the U&I Sugar Beet Factory, 1918.

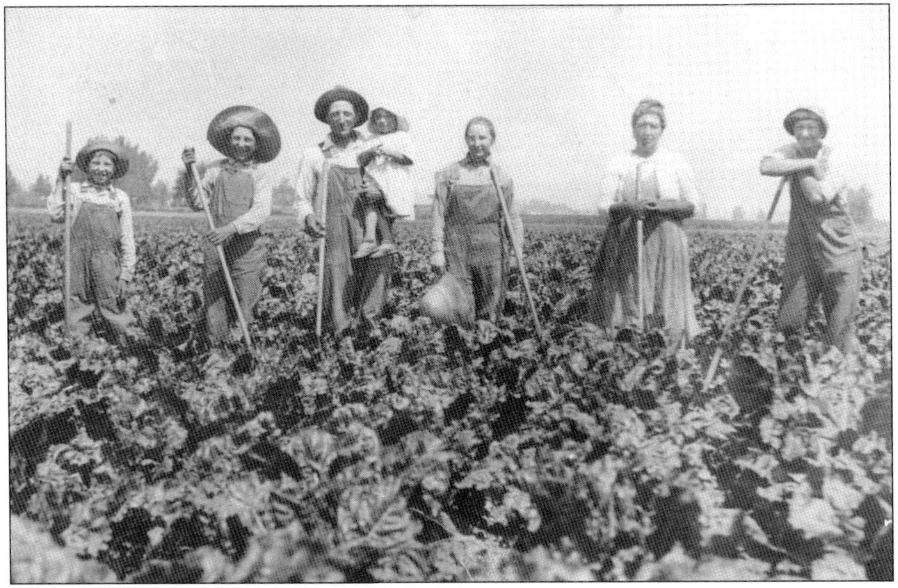

The Jacob Roth family working sugar beets near Sunnyside, circa 1920. From left, Reinhold "Kye," Fred, Jacob holding Caroline, Kate, Catherina Magdalena, and Conrad "Cal."

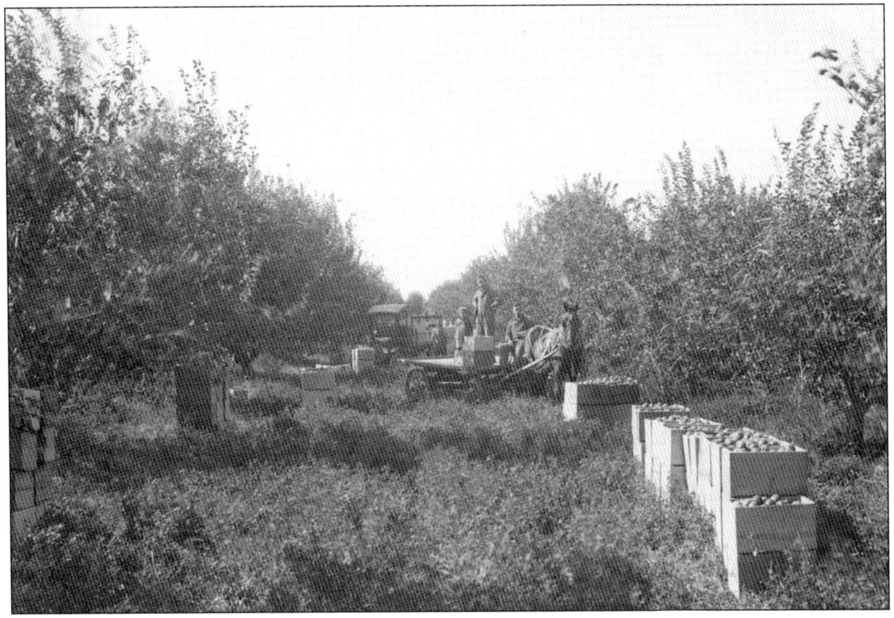

Harvesting apples in the early 1920s.

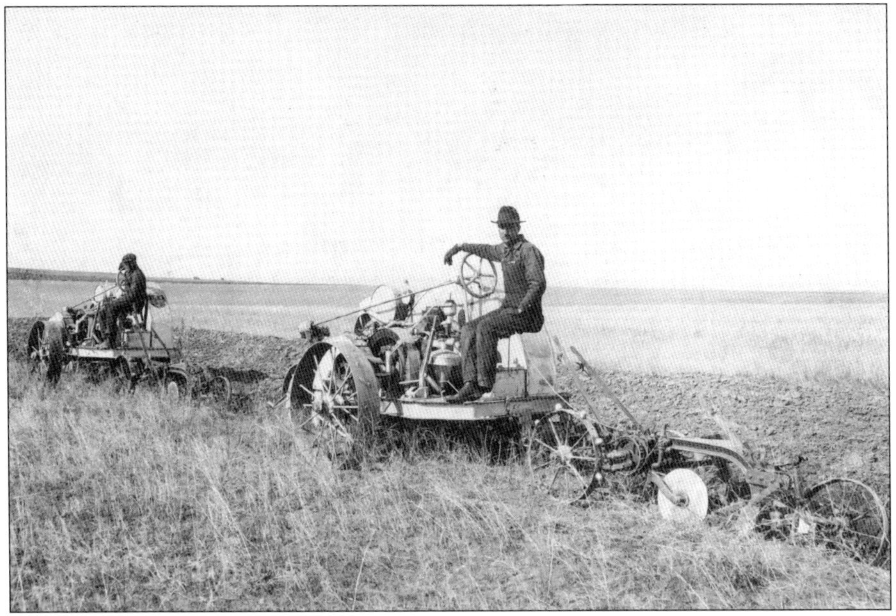

Early tractor-powered plowing operation.

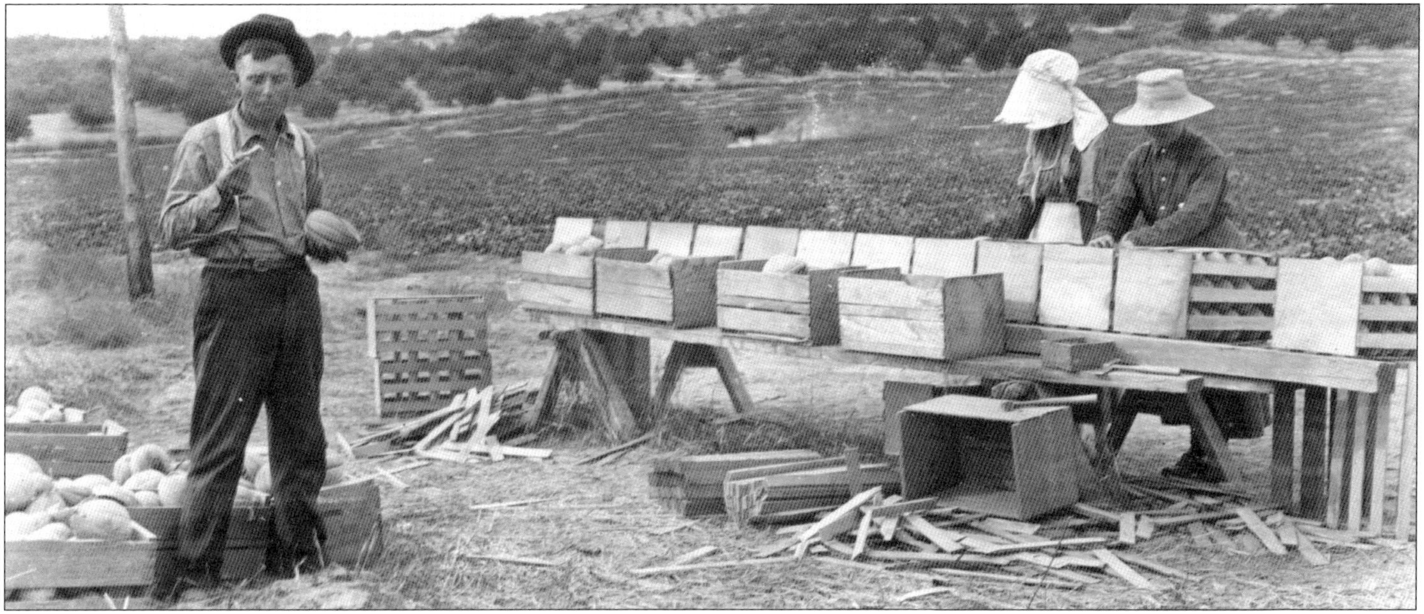

Packing Cantaloupes near Sunnyside.

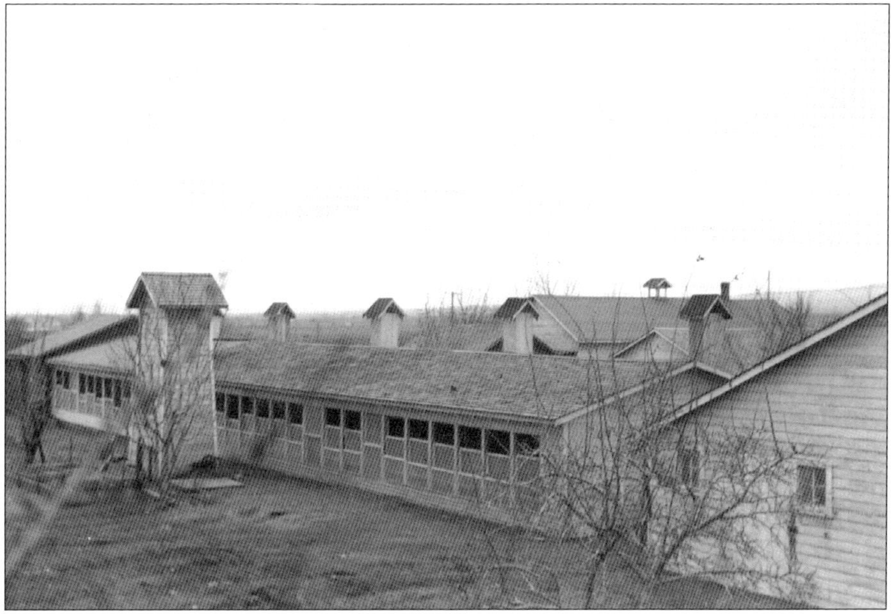

Neil Bridgman poultry ranch east of Sunnyside on Van Belle Rd. in 1931.

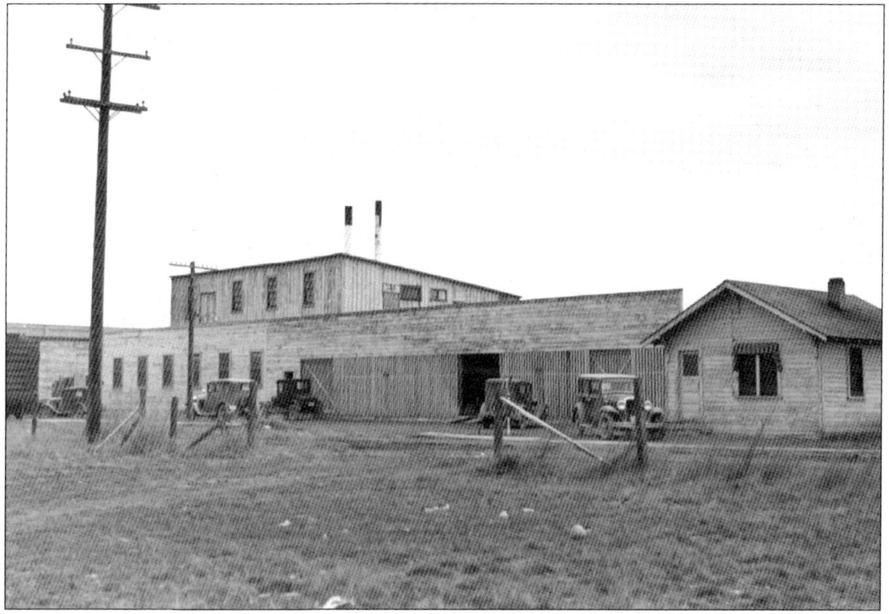

Evaporated Fruits, Inc. Sunnyside Canning Plant in 1931.

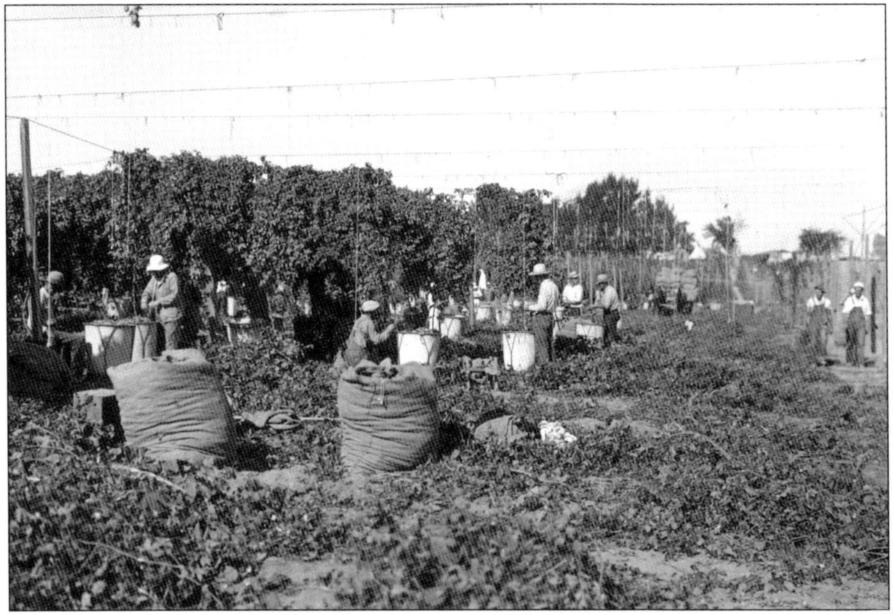

Picking and hauling hops near Granger, September 13, 1932.

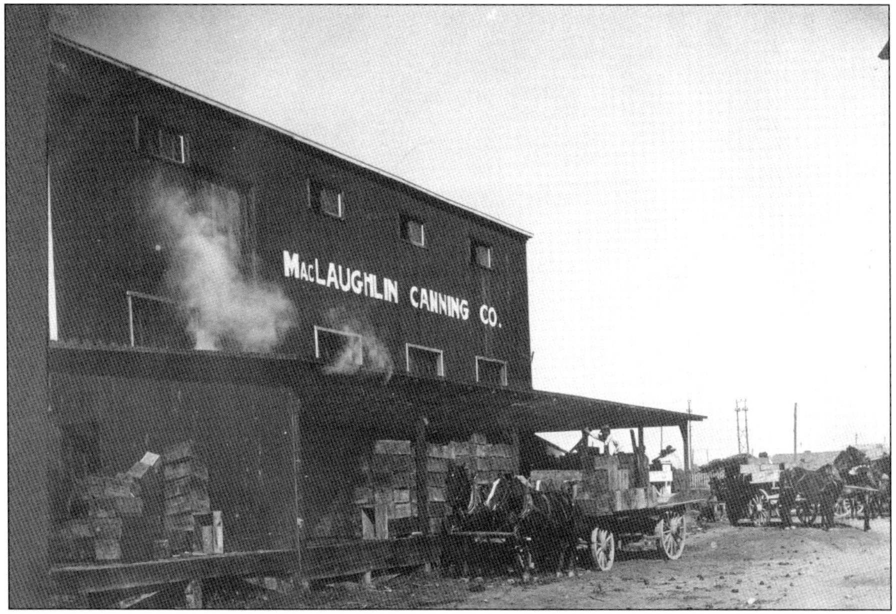

MacLaughlin Canning Company tomato cannery in Sunnyside. Photo taken Sept. 14, 1916.

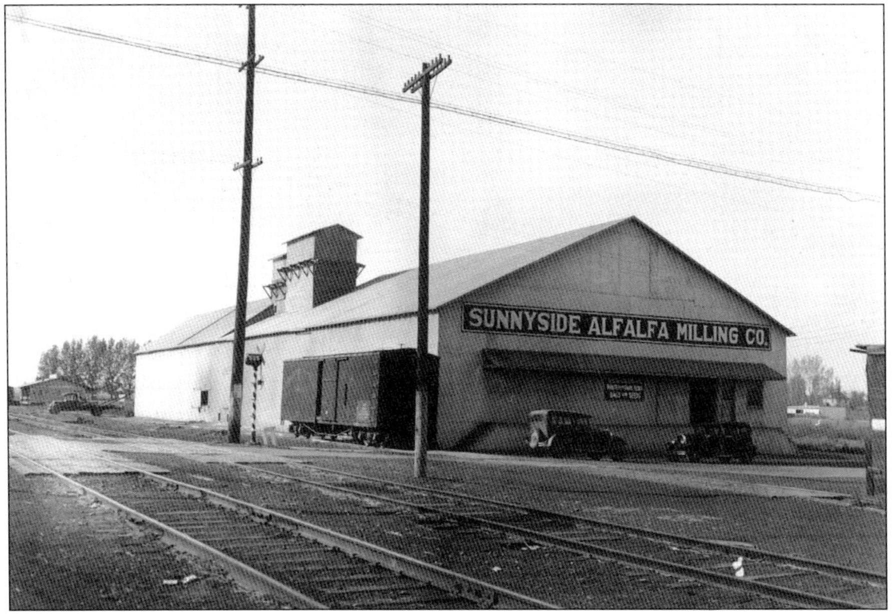

Sunnyside Alfalfa Milling Co. which offered Poultry and Dairy Feeds, 1932.

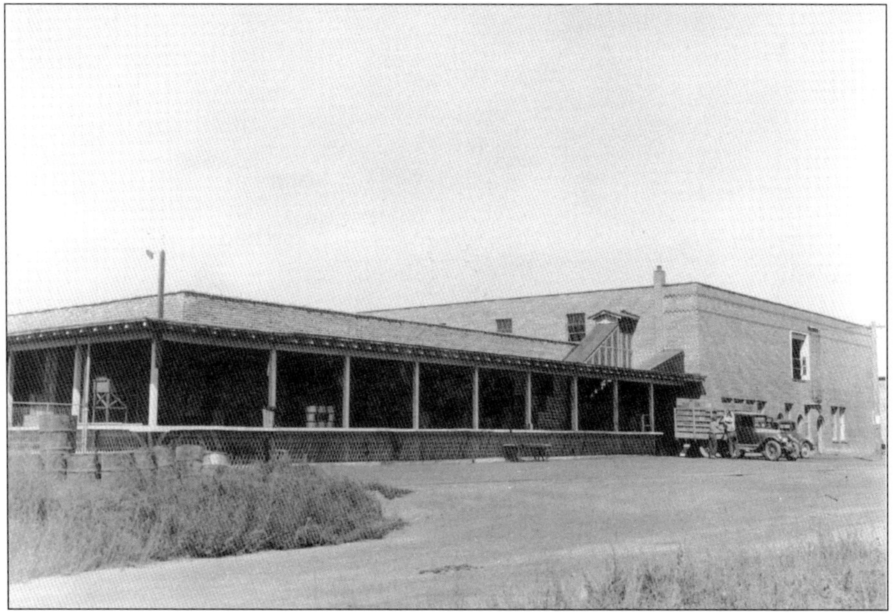

Yakima Fruit Growers Association Warehouse in Sunnyside, 1932.

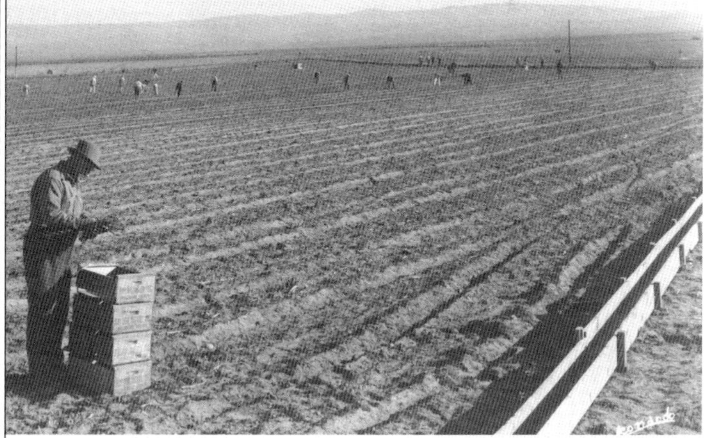

Airport Ranch has a long distinguished agricultural history in the Yakima Valley. It's origins go back to 1942 when Olympic Air Transport began using the site as an air training station for South American pilots. Later on, the site became a primary training station for the Army and the Navy. H. Lloyd Miller, the founder of Airport Ranches, had leased the ground to the government for the duration of the war. In 1946, when World War II had concluded, H. Lloyd Miller purchased the buildings constructed by the government and began farming the area surrounding the air base.

At first, Miller's only crop was hay. By 1950, Miller had begun to diversify and was raising potatoes, onions, and alfalfa in addition to 1000 head of cattle. However, over the years more profitable crops like sugar beets and mint became staple crops on the farm. Over the last 25 years, Airport Ranch has begun focusing on its core crops of wine grapes, concord grapes, and asparagus.

H. Lloyd Miller will always be known as the "Father of the Roza" for convincing President Franklin Roosevelt of the significance of developing the Roza Irrigation District in the 1930s. His efforts brought much needed irrigation water to thousands of acres in the Yakima Valley.

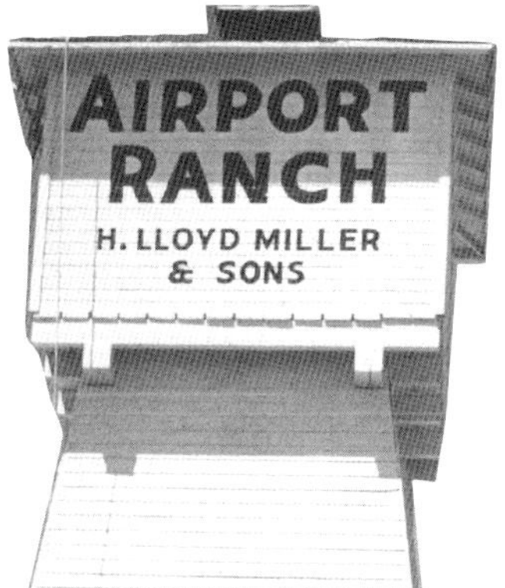

Airport Ranches, Inc.

P.O. Box 59
Sunnyside, WA 98944
509-837-2424 or 837-2401

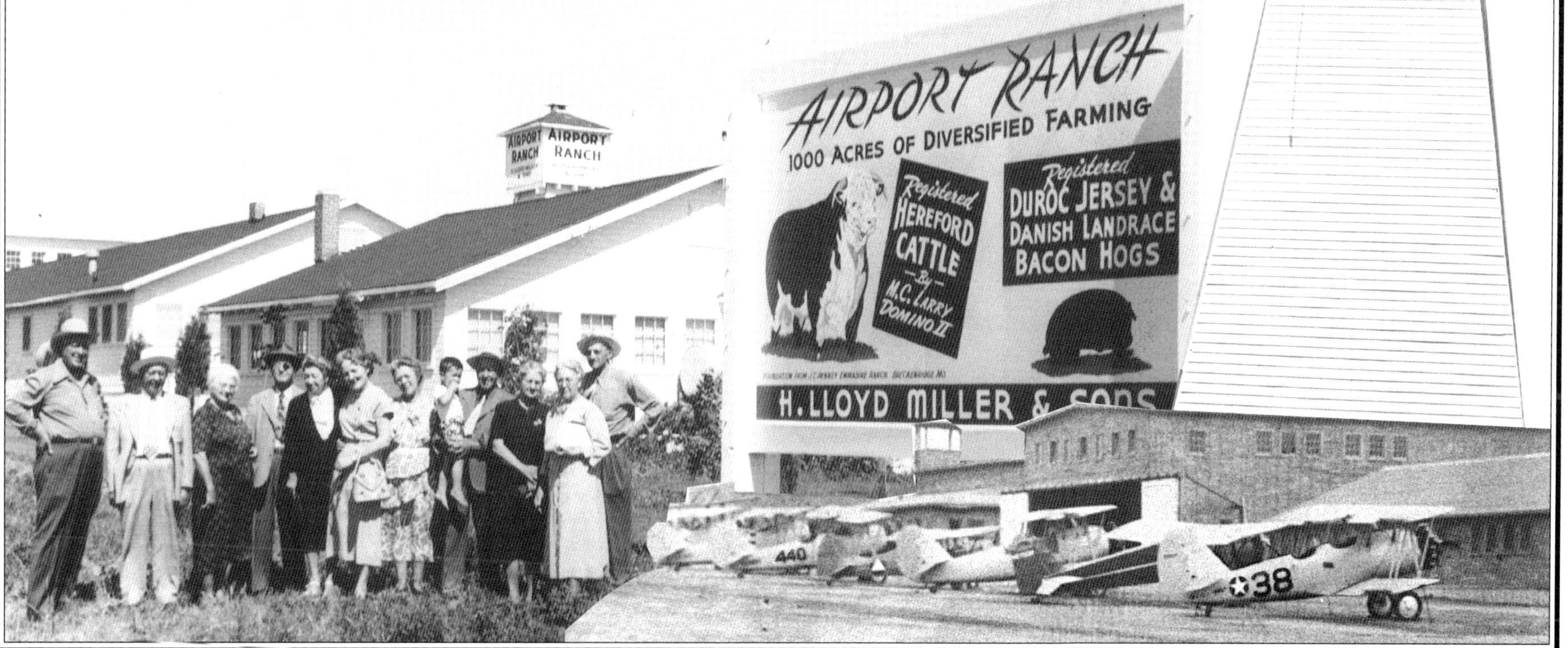

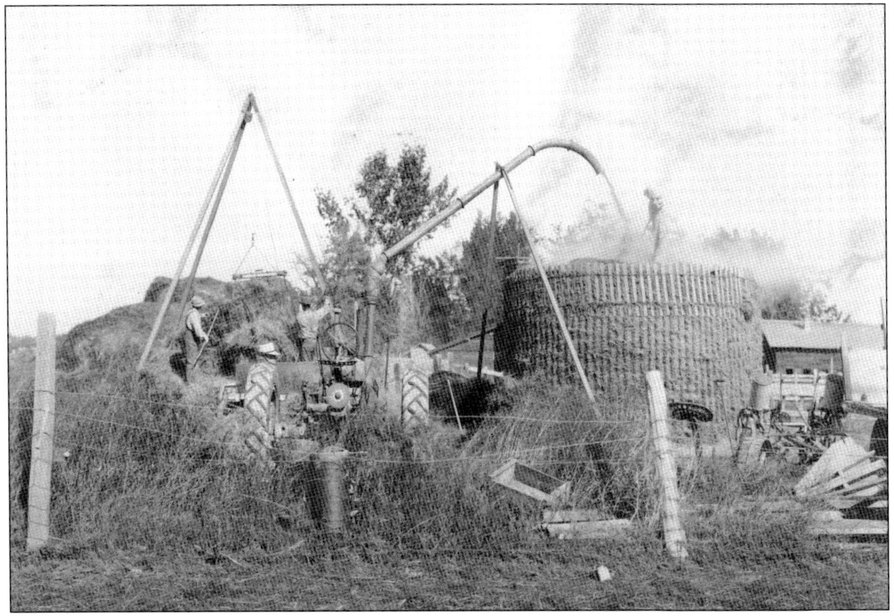

Chopping Alfalfa Hay on the E.N. Roady Ranch near Outlook. October 5, 1940.

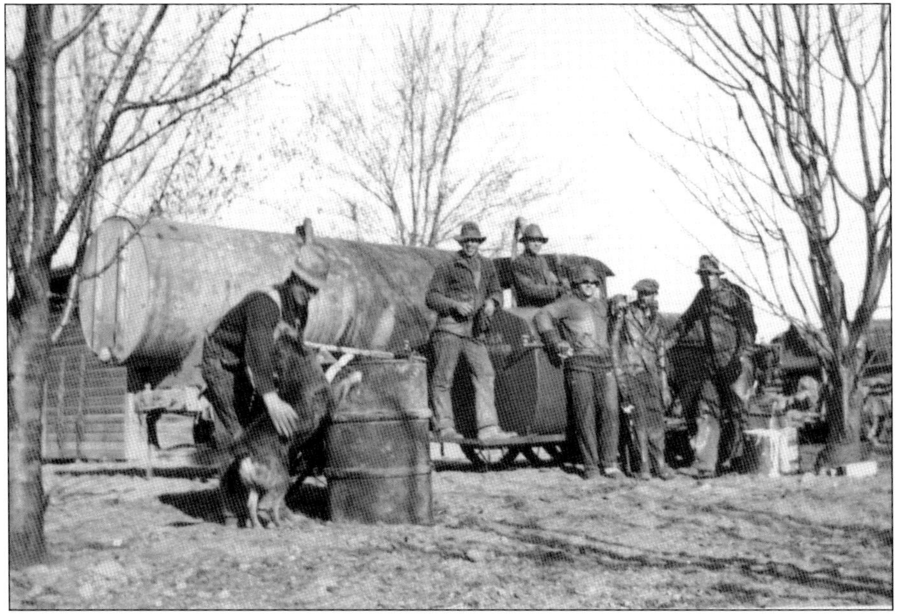

Workers preparing to spray orchards in the 1930s.

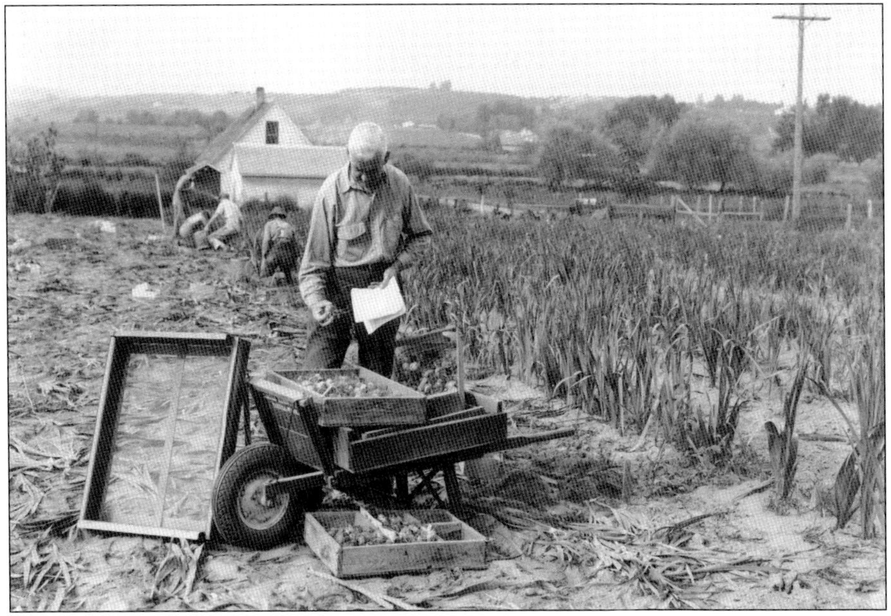

J.T. Robertson, President of the Washington Gladiolas Society, sorting bulbs on one of his tracts near Sunnyside. Oct. 12, 1940.

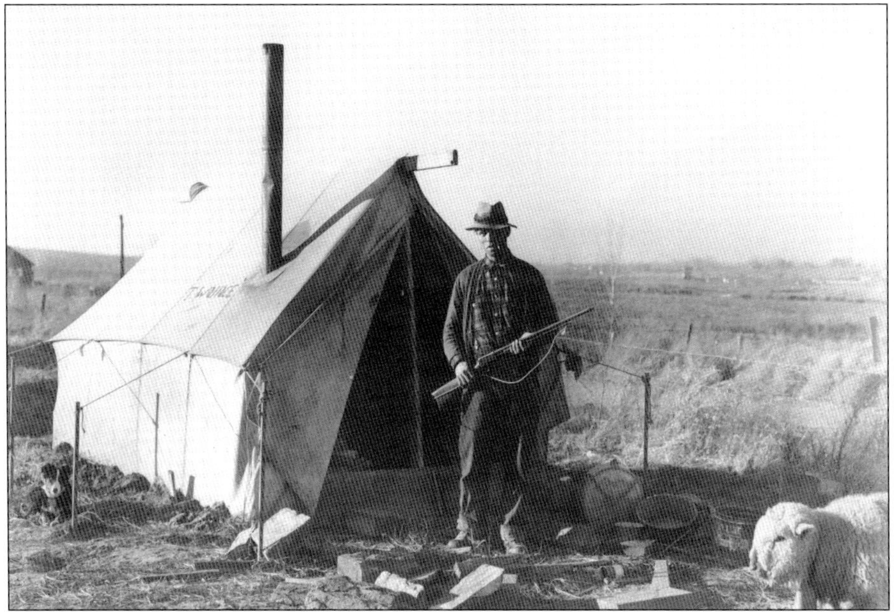

Sheepherder in charge of range sheep pasturing on sugar beet tops near Sunnyside. Dec. 9, 1940.

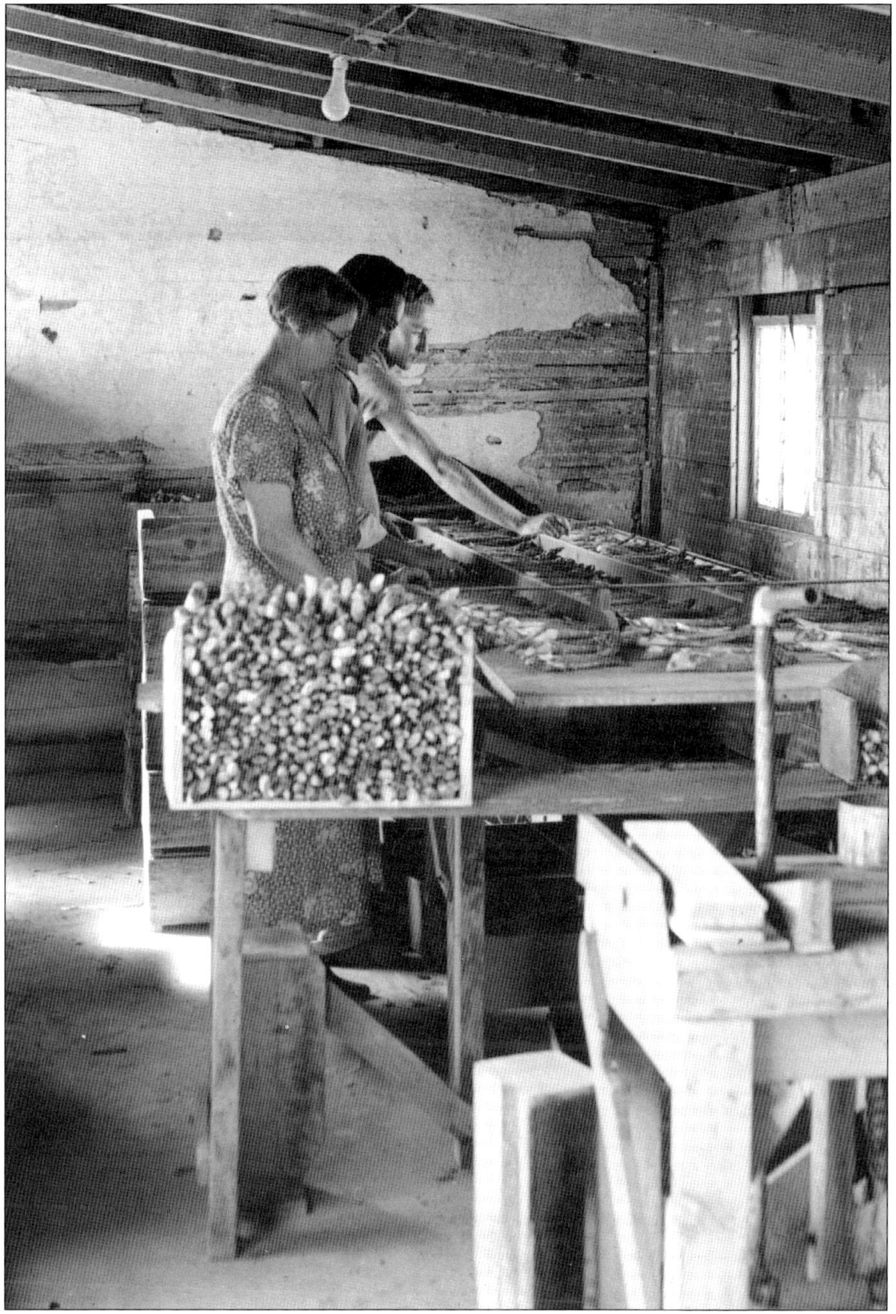

Early asparagus packing operation.

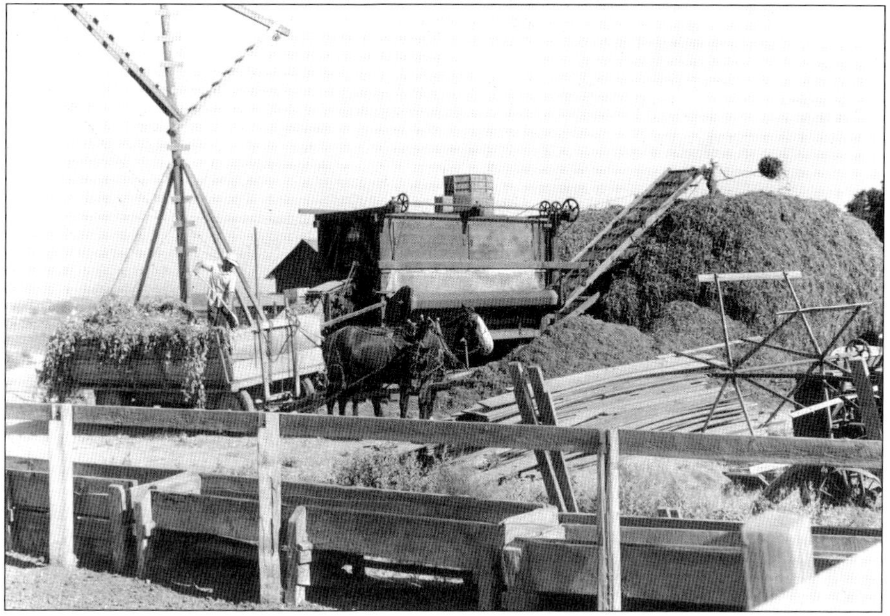

Green pea viner in operation on the T.J. Schilperoort farm near Sunnyside. The yield was 2 ton of shelled peas and 5 ton of vines per acre. Circa 1940.

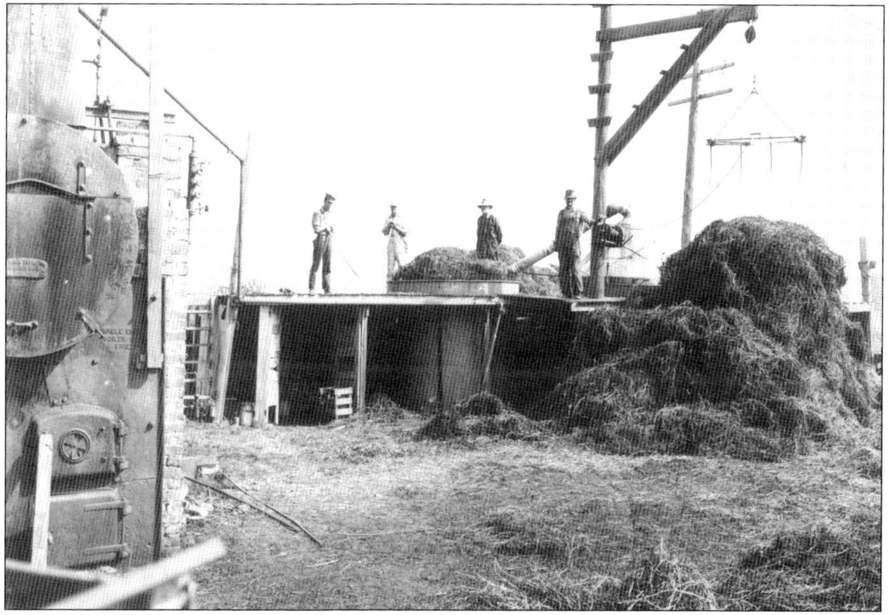

Distilling mint at the Sunnyside Plant. Photo shows mint in the hopper prior to distilling. Photo taken Sept. 11, 1940.

Sunnyside Valley Irrigation District

Leaders in conservation & water quality

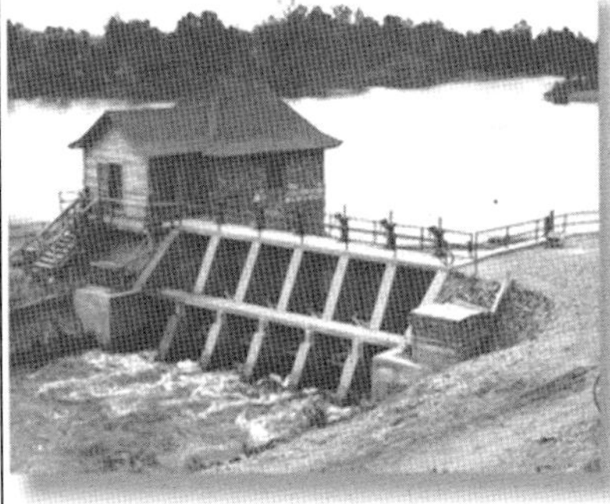
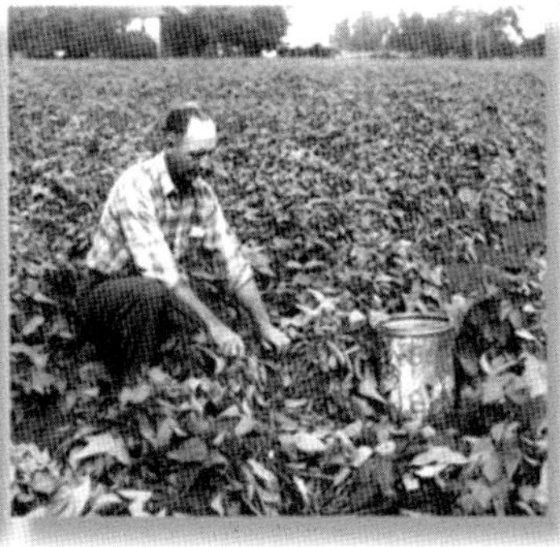
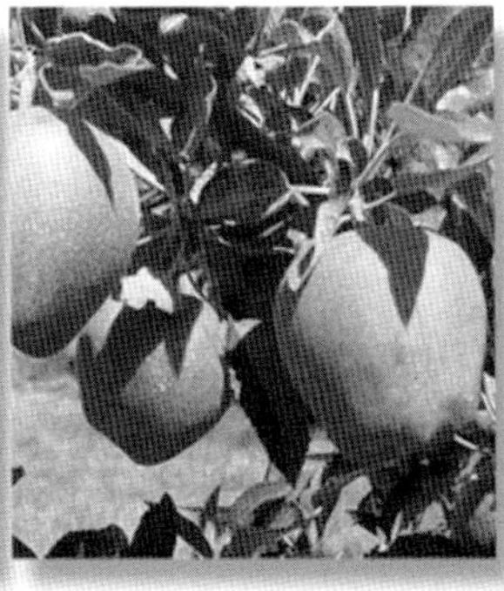
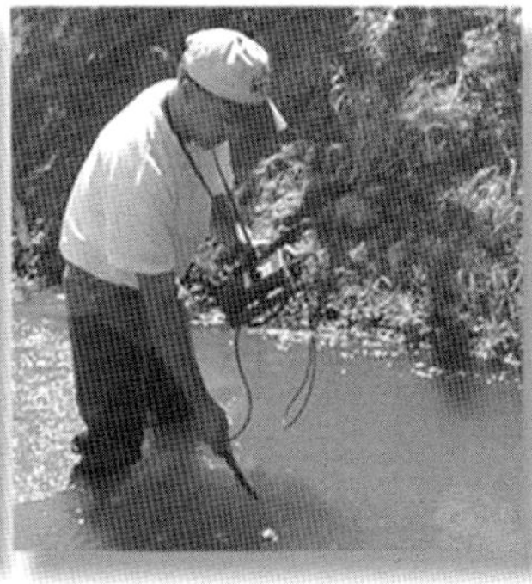
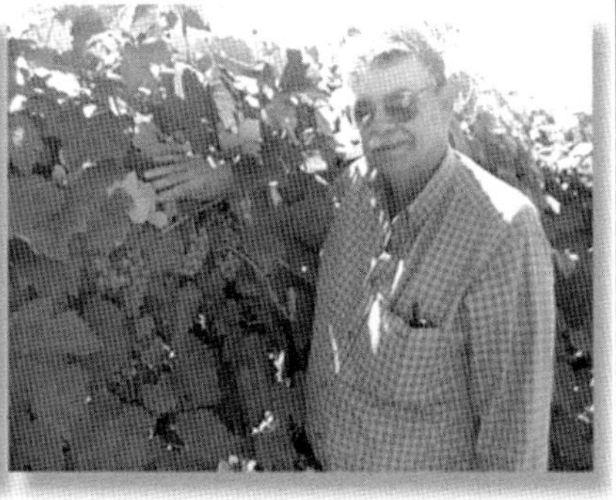

The Sunnyside Canal has supplied Lower Yakima Valley farms with irrigation water since 1892, transforming a desert into one of the Nation's most productive agricultural regions.

A leader in water conservation and water quality enhancement, Sunnyside Valley Irrigation District continues to build upon the ambitious foundation our predecessors forged over a century ago.

In commemoration of Sunnyside's innovative and industrious history, the Sunnyside Valley Irrigation District is proud to sponsor the *Pictorial History of Sunnyside, Washington.*

www.svid.org

IRRIGATION

The importance of irrigation to the Yakima Valley cannot be overstated, for it is irrigation that has made this desert valley bloom. Before irrigation the valley floor was covered with 4-5 foot tall sagebrush and home to little more than rattlesnakes, jackrabbits, and coyotes. The land was considered to be worthless.

The Northern Pacific Railroad, which owned about half the valley, realized that the valley was capable of producing bountiful crops if water could be made available. Building a canal would accomplish this and attract farmers. The railroad could then sell its once worthless land at a good price and profit by shipping the farmers' produce to market.

With those goals in mind, the railroad hired Walter Granger in 1889 to construct the Sunnyside Canal. Digging commenced just below The Gap in the spring of 1891 and reached the area that would become Sunnyside in 1893. At that point Granger plotted out the future town.

Despite many difficulties and changes in the canal's ownership, Granger oversaw the construction and management of the canal until 1910 when he retired. At one point he owned one third of the canal company's stock. Economic hard times and misappropriation of funds by a business partner would wipe out Granger's investment. Through it all Granger continued to manage the canal, and more than any other man made possible the valley we know today.

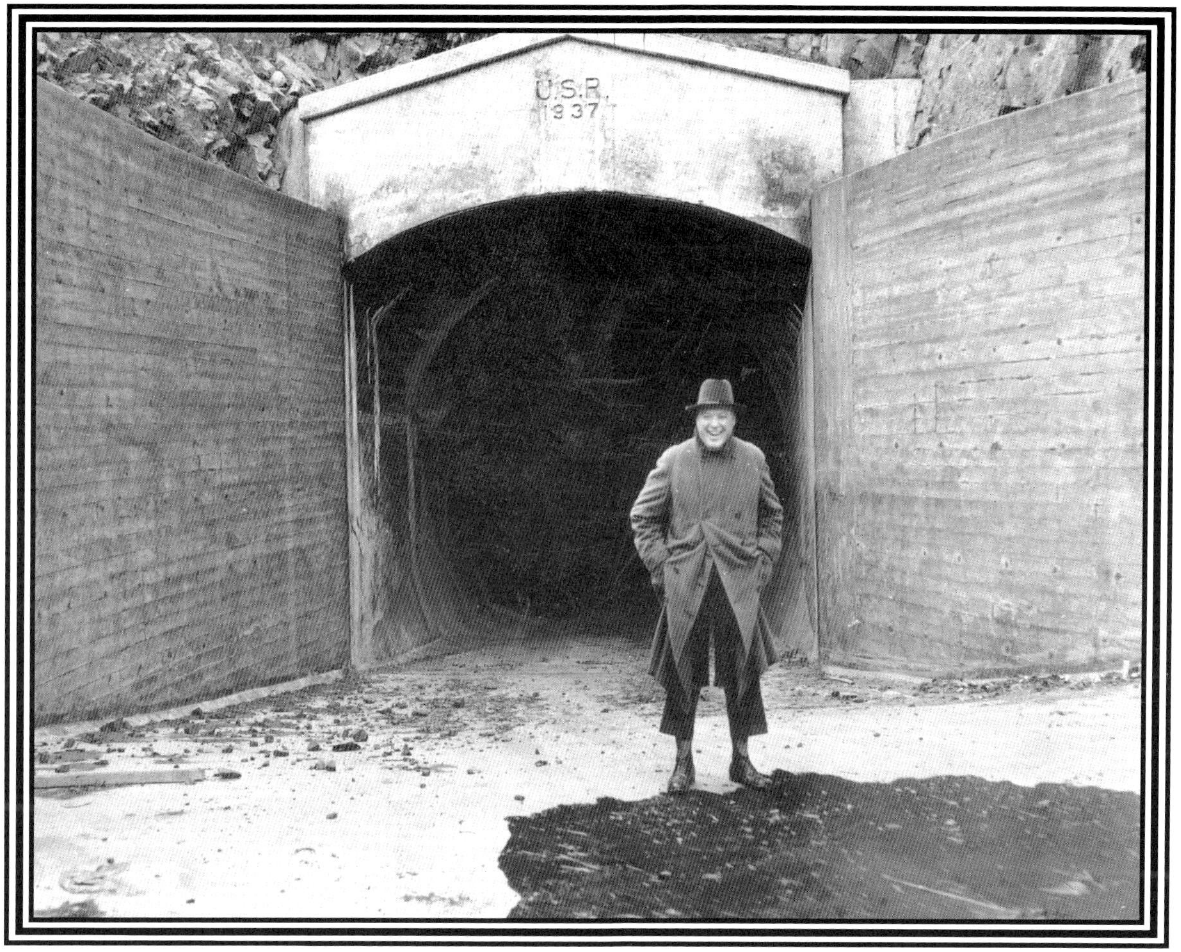

H. Lloyd Miller, president of the Roza Irrigation District standing at the upper portal of tunnel number one as the water reached that point during an operational test in December of 1939. Roza water irrigated its first crops in 1941.

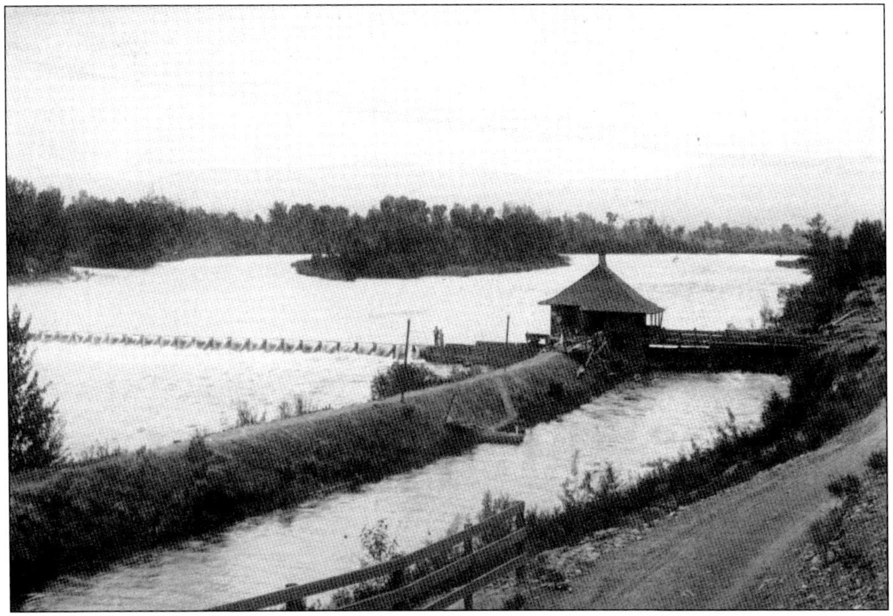

The first Sunnyside Dam and intake was built in 1891.

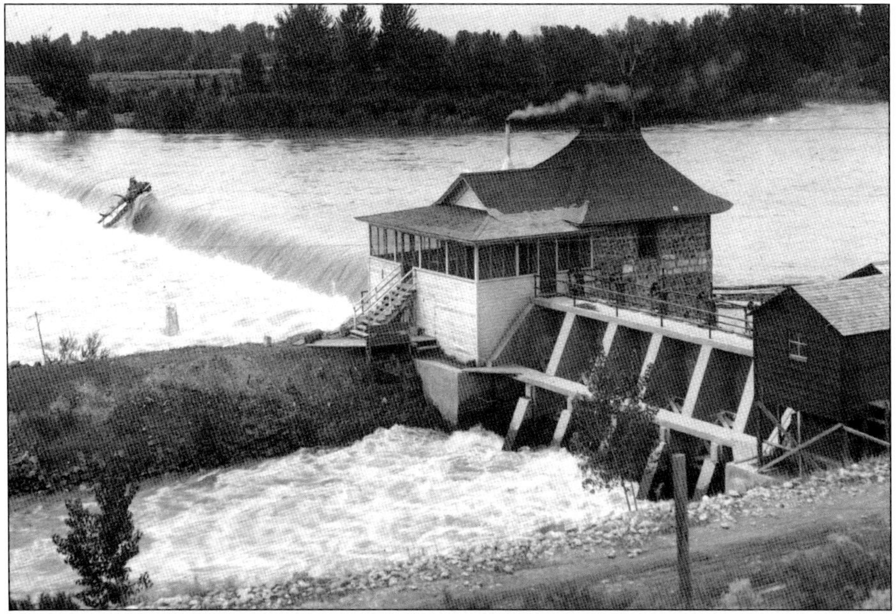

The newly constructed Sunnyside Dam and intake to the Sunnyside Canal in 1906.

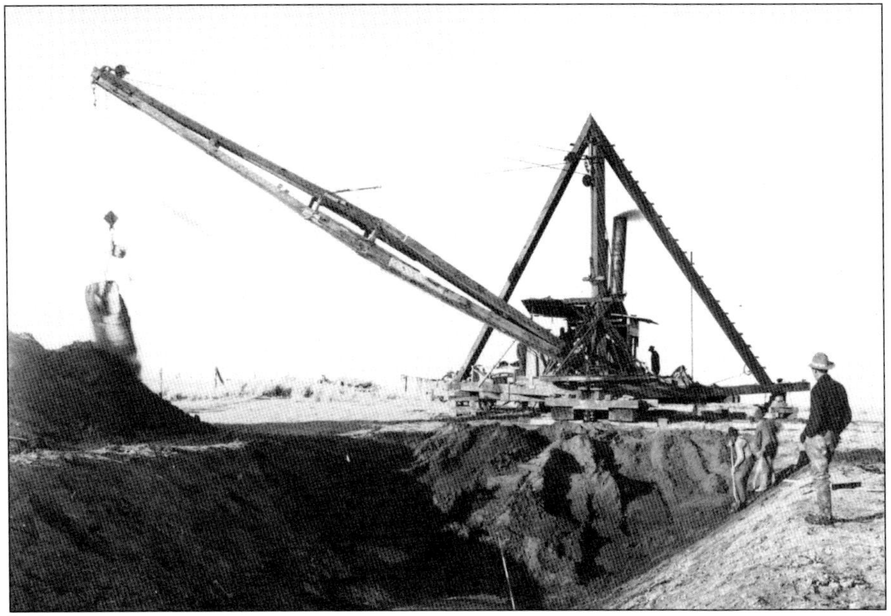

Excavating for Sulphur Creek Wasteway, 1908.

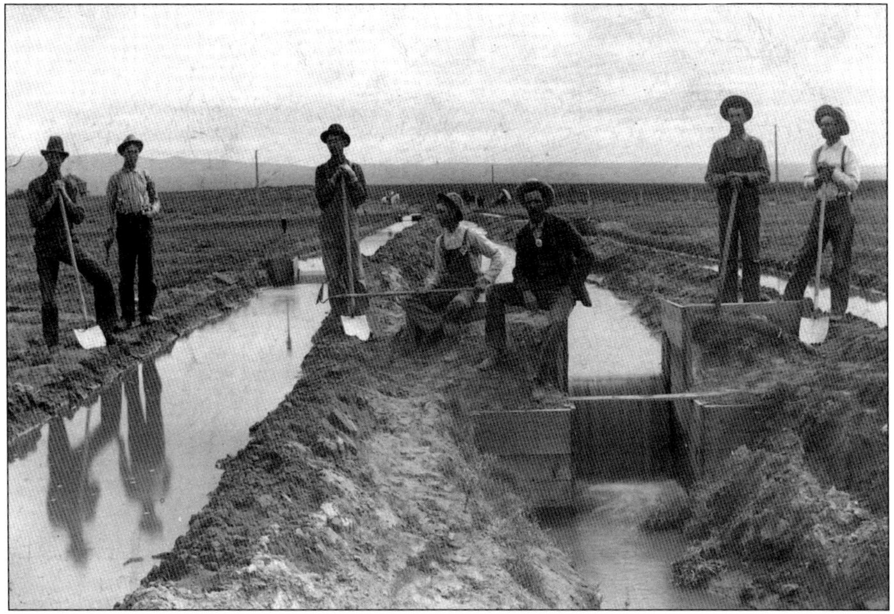

William Stobie and crew at the irrigation head gate, circa 1899.

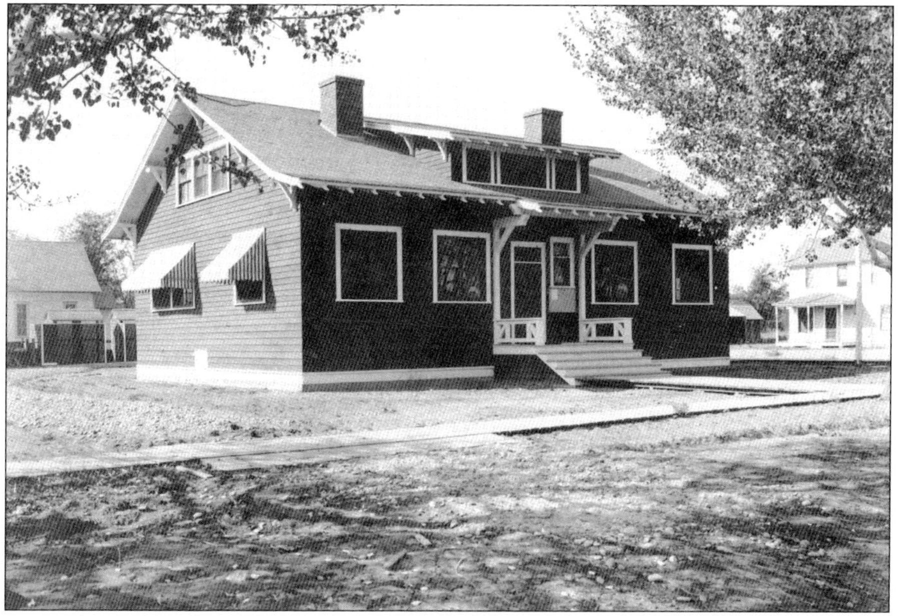

Original Sunnyside Valley Irrigation Building in the early 1900s. Located at the southwest corner of 9th Street and Franklin Avenue.

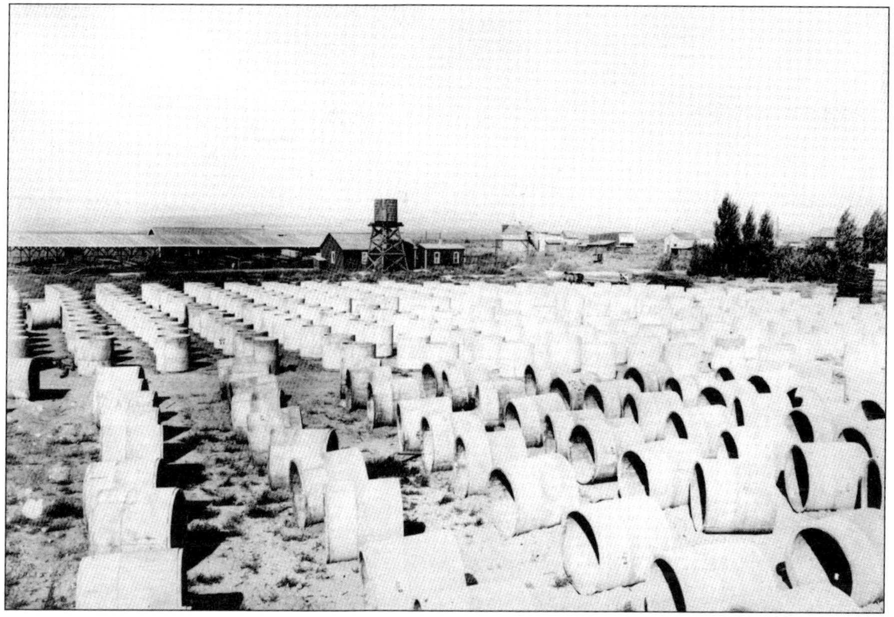

Finished 54" reinforced concrete pipe at pipe plant. The pipe was used on the north side of the Yakima River for Mabton Pipe Crossing, 1908.

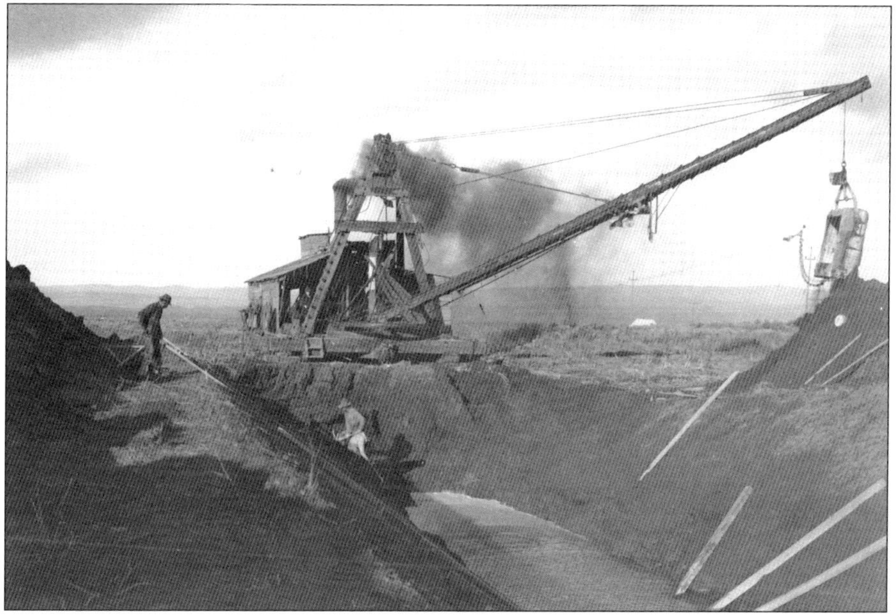

Excavator digging Sulphur Creek Wasteway, 1908.

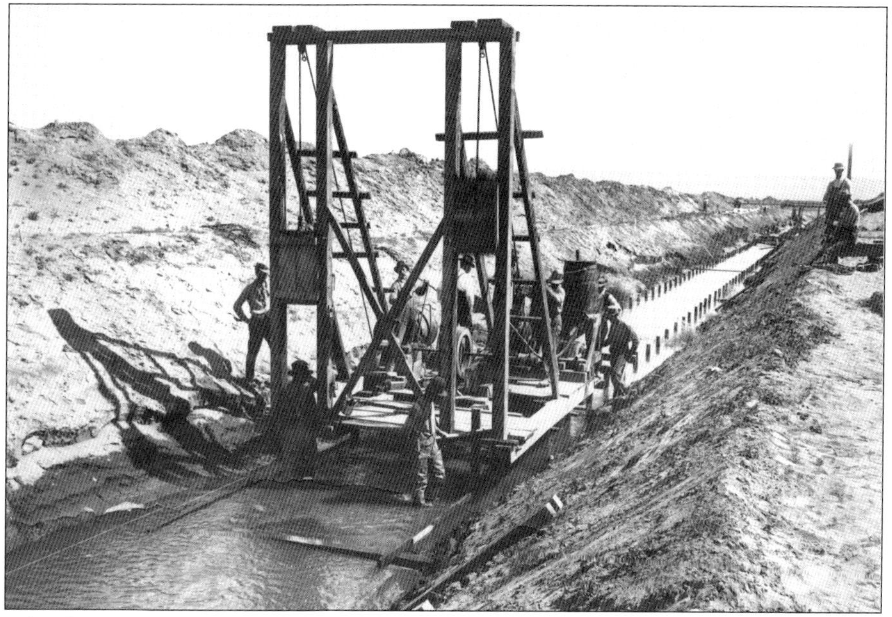

Pile driver at work on Sulphur Creek Wasteway east of Sunnyside, 1909. The Wasteway is still in use today along SR-241.

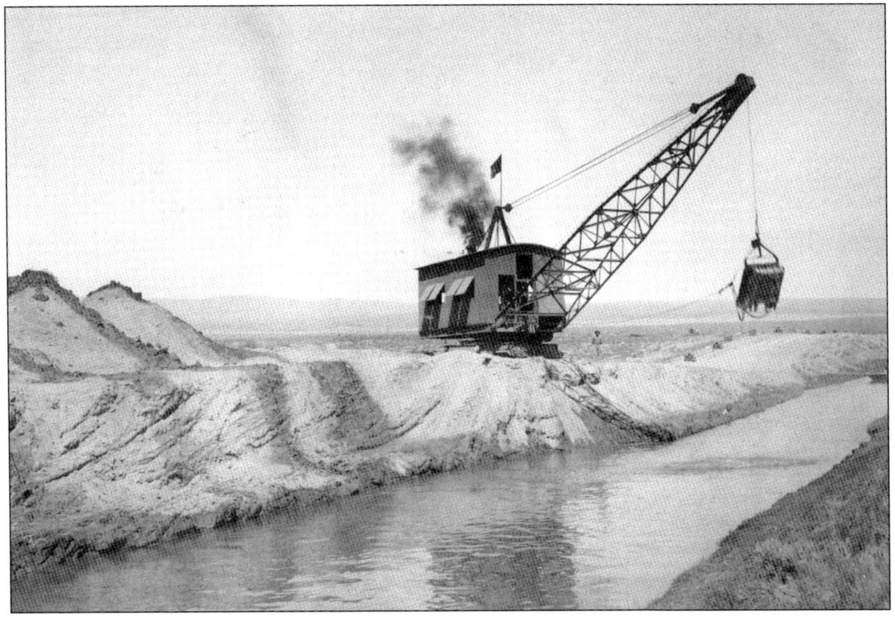

Drag bucket excavator digging the Sunnyside canal. July 29, 1909

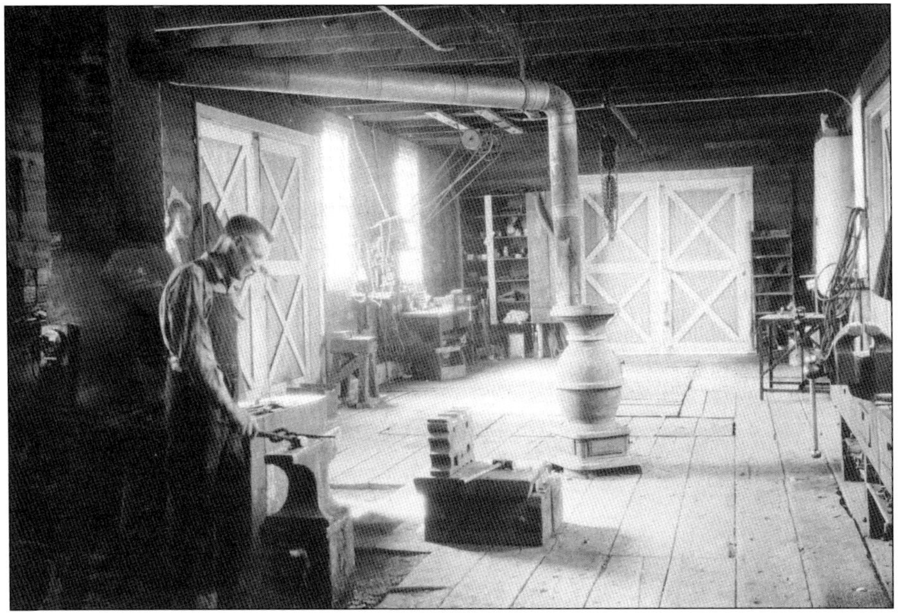

SVID division blacksmith and automobile repair shop in 1928. Nels Mikkleson, blacksmith.

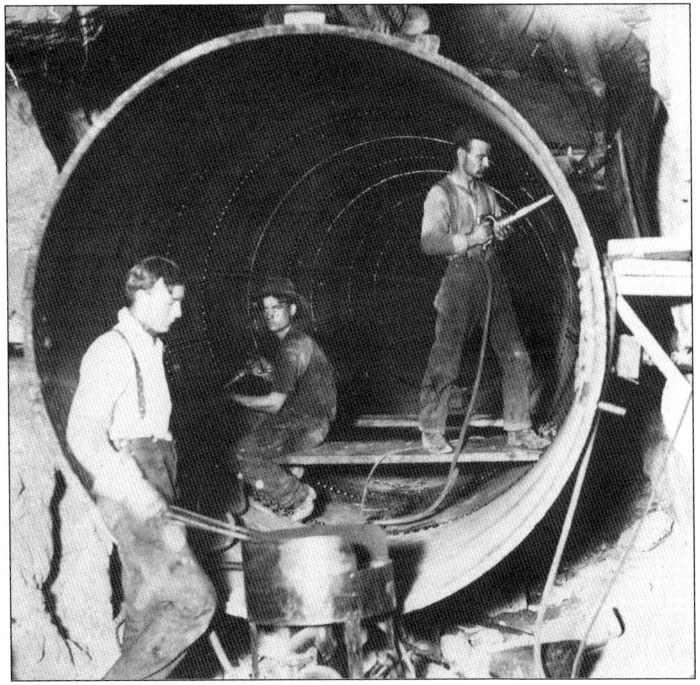

Pipe work, early 1900s.

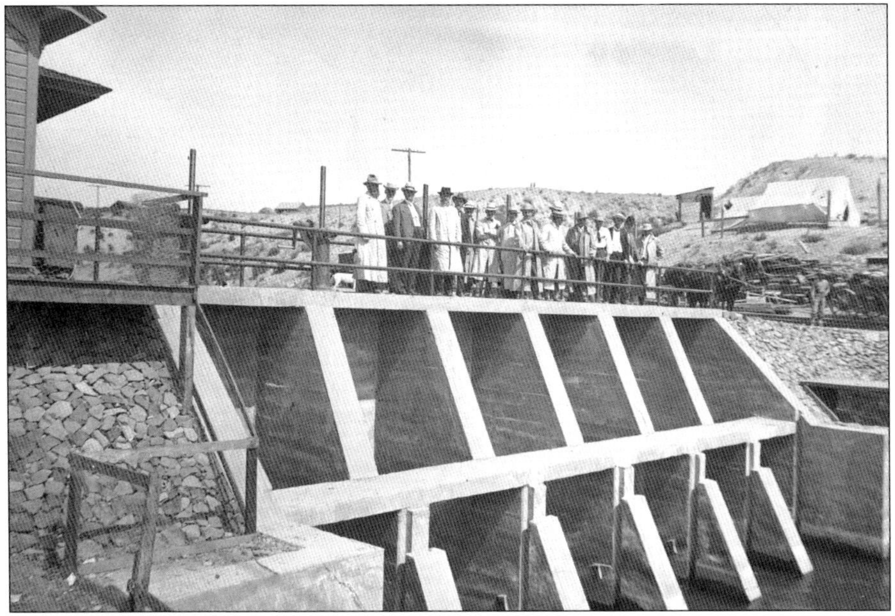

The headgate of the irrigation canal of Sunnyside, circa 1910.

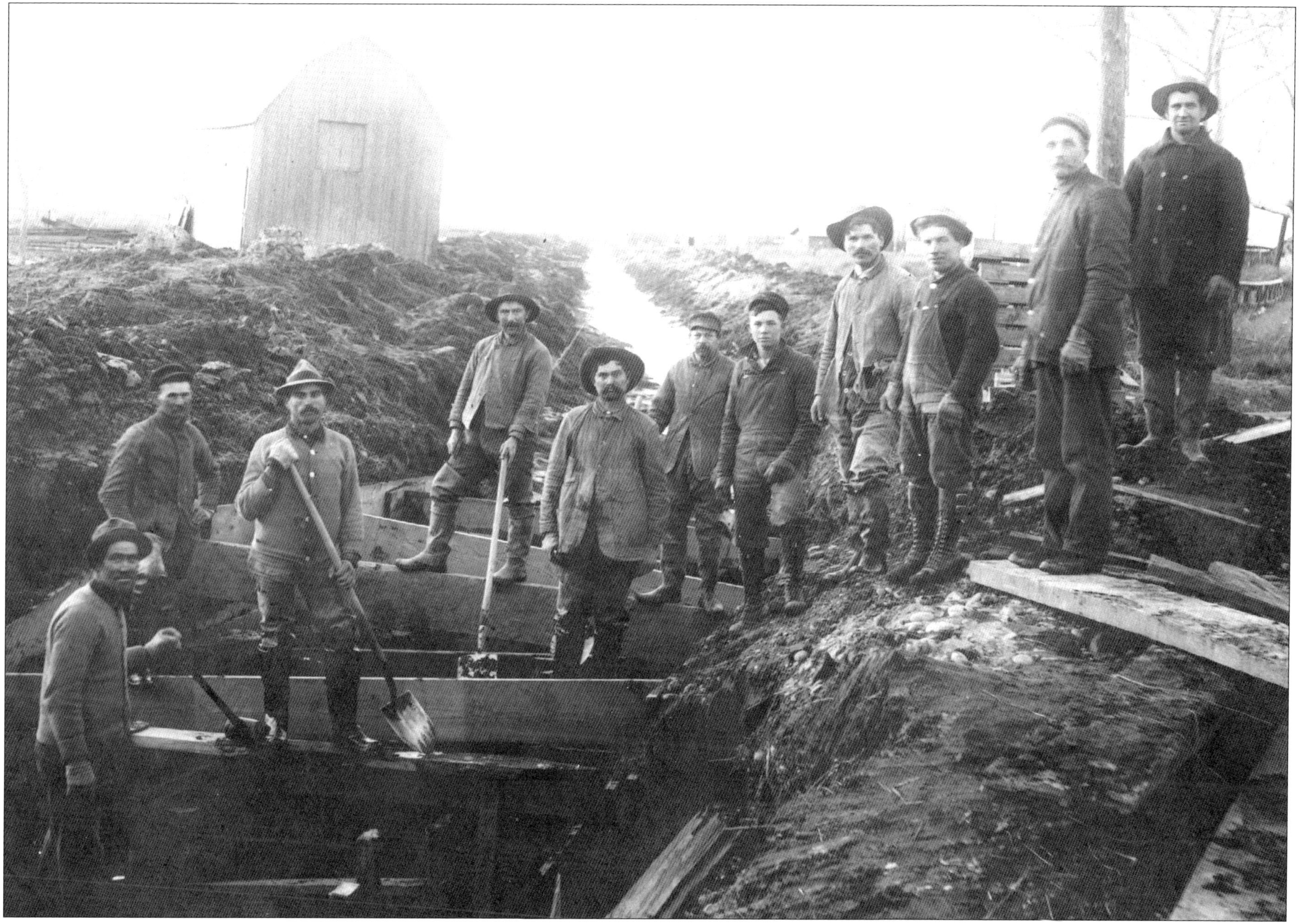

Canal workers, early 1900s. The photo is looking south from Edison Avenue and Park Drive. The barn in the photo occupies the area near the present-day intersection of 4th and Bridge Street. The present-day swimming pool occupies the spot just out of the picture to the left. The depression where the canal was is still visible through Sunnyside's Central Park.

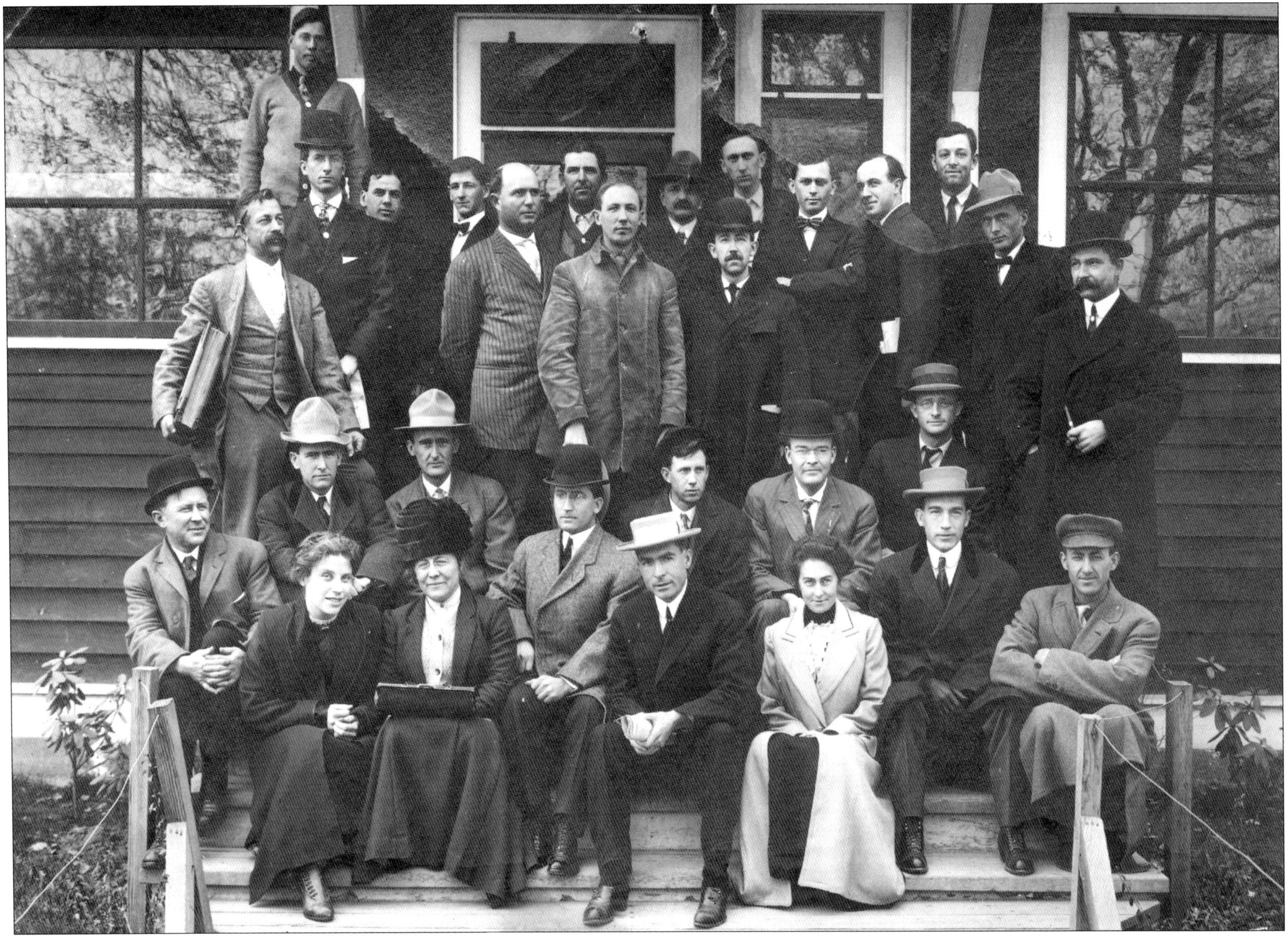

Sunnyside Valley Irrigation District Personnel & Office Building, 1911. Some of the personnel pictured are: Mr. Skeppleman, Mr. Cowin, Mr. Douglas, Mr. Love, Mr. Pheyen, Mr. Burrage, Mr. Schader, Mr. Wooster, Mr. Taschek, Mr. Remington, Mr. Hines, Mr. Horton, Mr. Seivers, Mr. Moore, Mr. Miller and Mrs. Edwards.

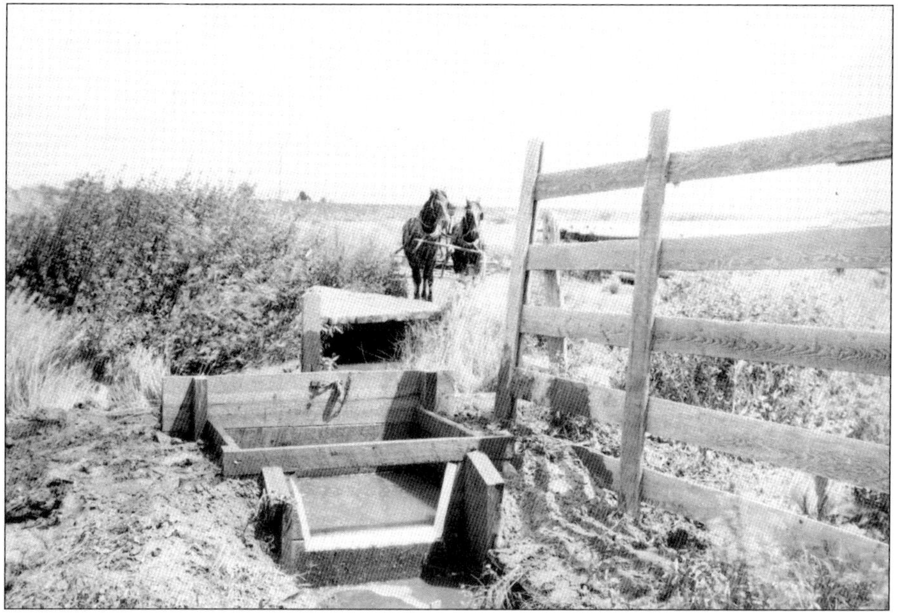

Early-day irrigation water delivery structure constructed from lumber and showing metal weir.

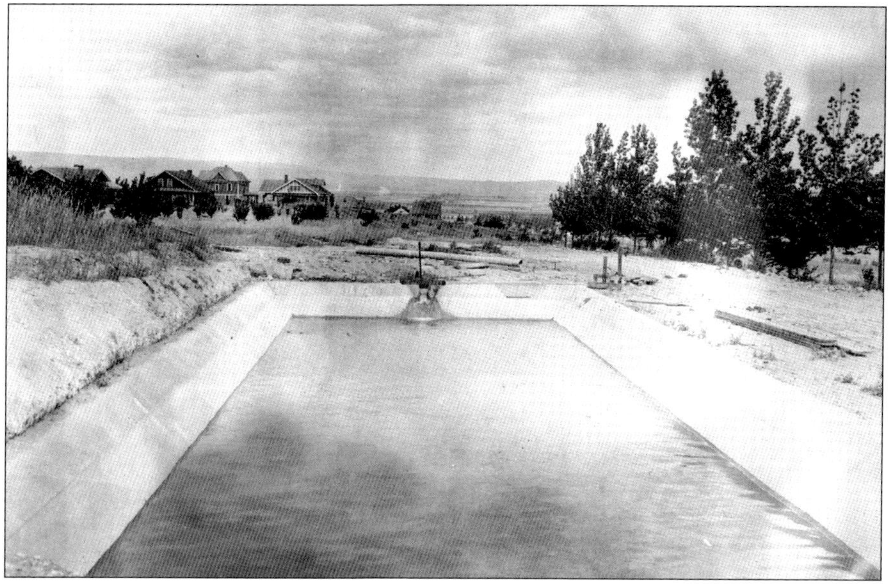

Concrete reservoir for Snipes Irrigation District May 19, 1915. The reservoir is still in use at the intersections of Grandview Avenue, Riverside Drive and Rossier Street, across from Harrison Heights Apartments.

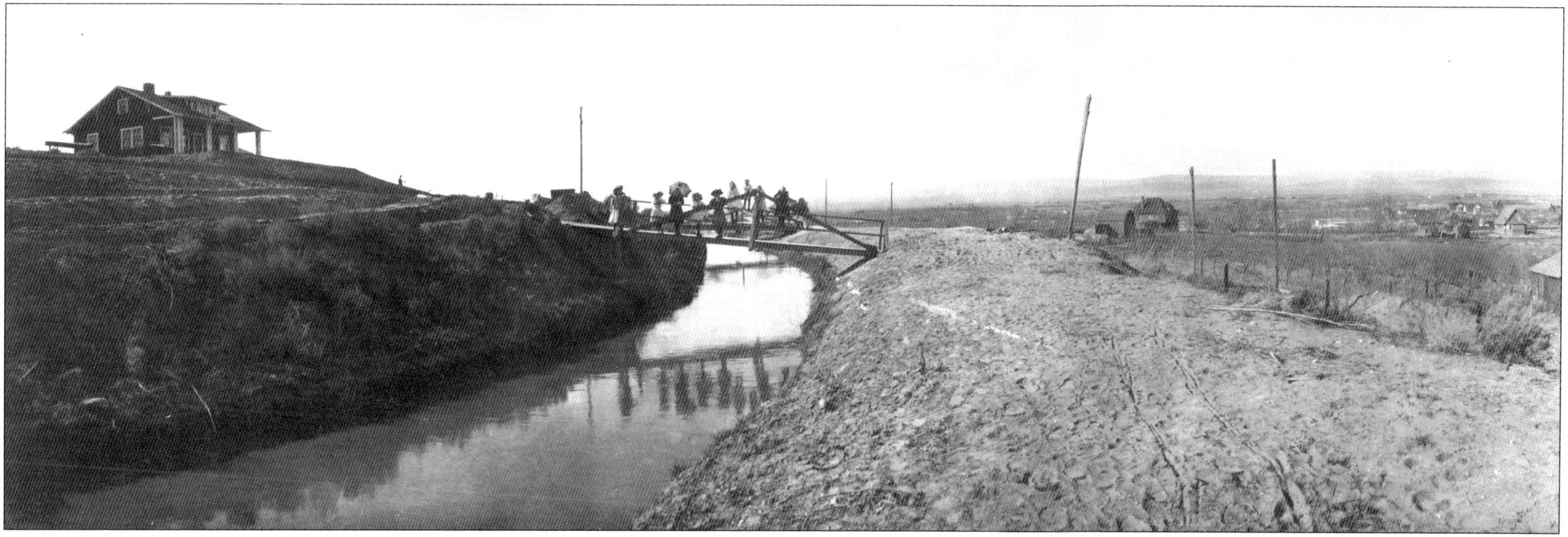

Looking north from the canal bank of S.W. Crescent, circa 1900. The Garin Home, on the left, still stands today on the corner of Crescent Avenue and Bridge Street.

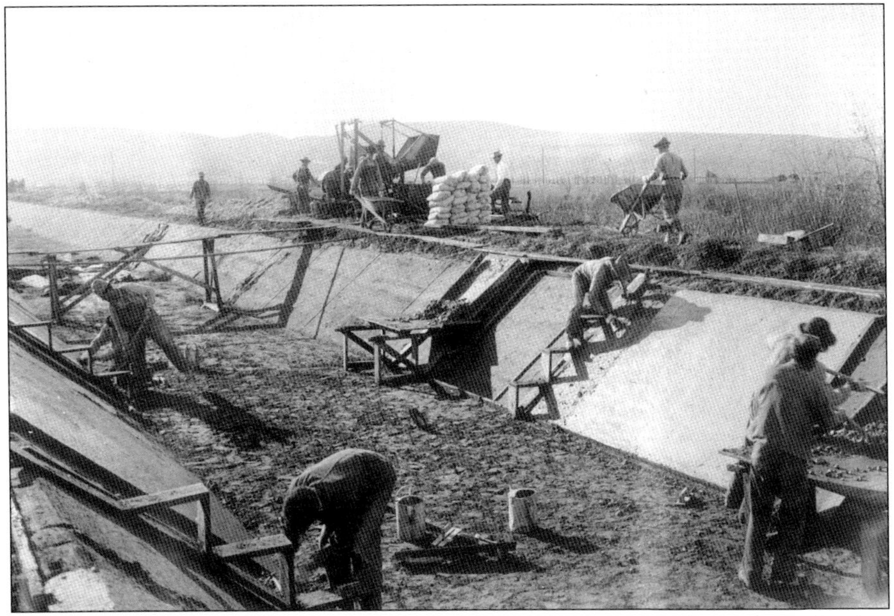

Workers lay the plaster lining on the Snipes Mt. Canal above the highway bridge near Sunnyside. Nov. 25, 1915.

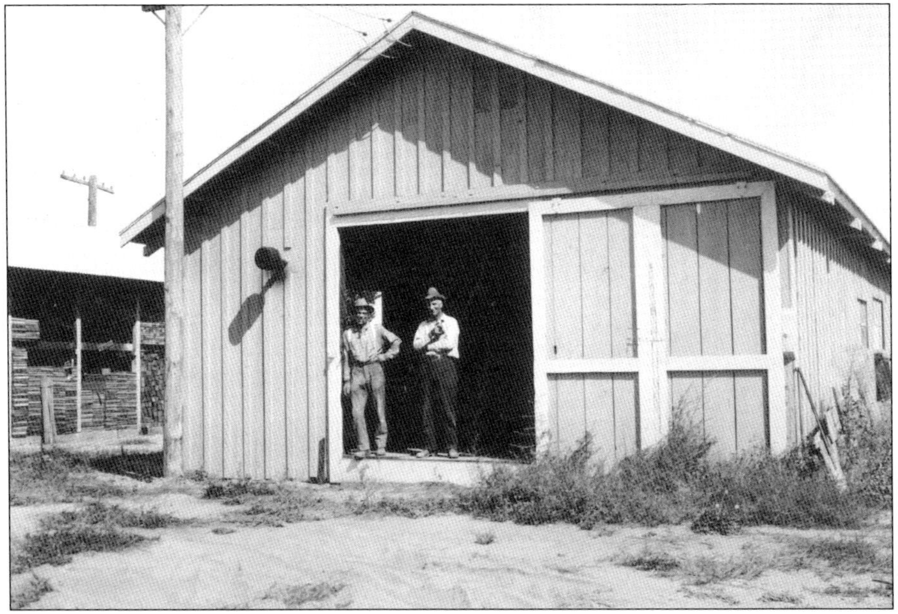

Sunnyside Valley Irrigation Division carpentry shop in 1928. Pictured are Earl W. Myers, Foreman and H.B. Palmer, Power House Foreman.

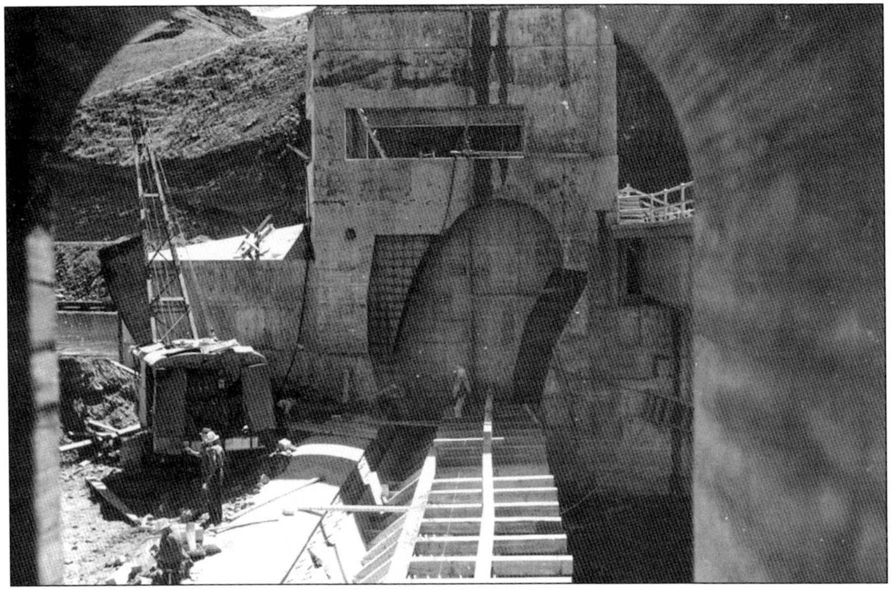

This photo was taken July 19, 1939 during construction of the Roza diversion dam. Here workers are hoisting part of the roller gate plate into place between piers 1 and 2.

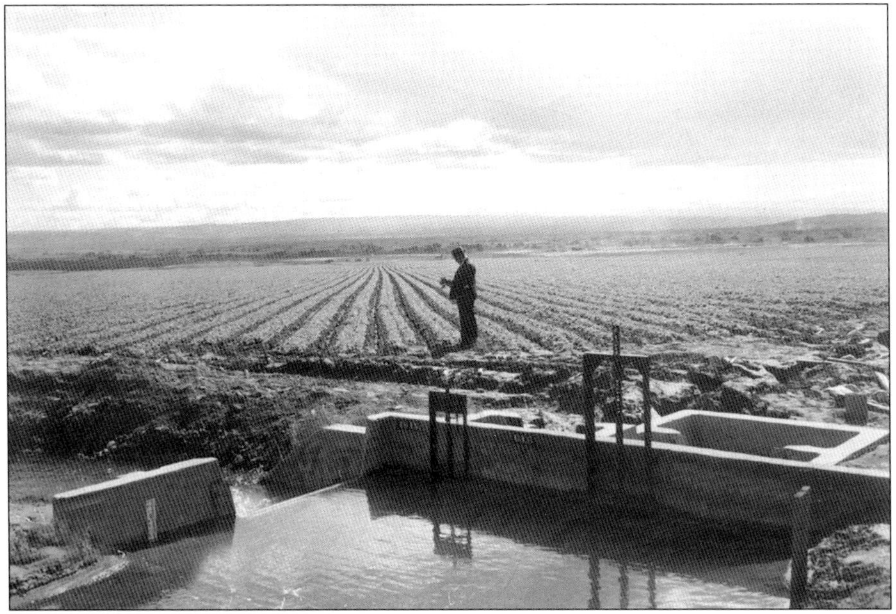

H.L. Miller checks the crop in the early 1940s as water flows through the fields from the newly constructed Roza Irrigation project.

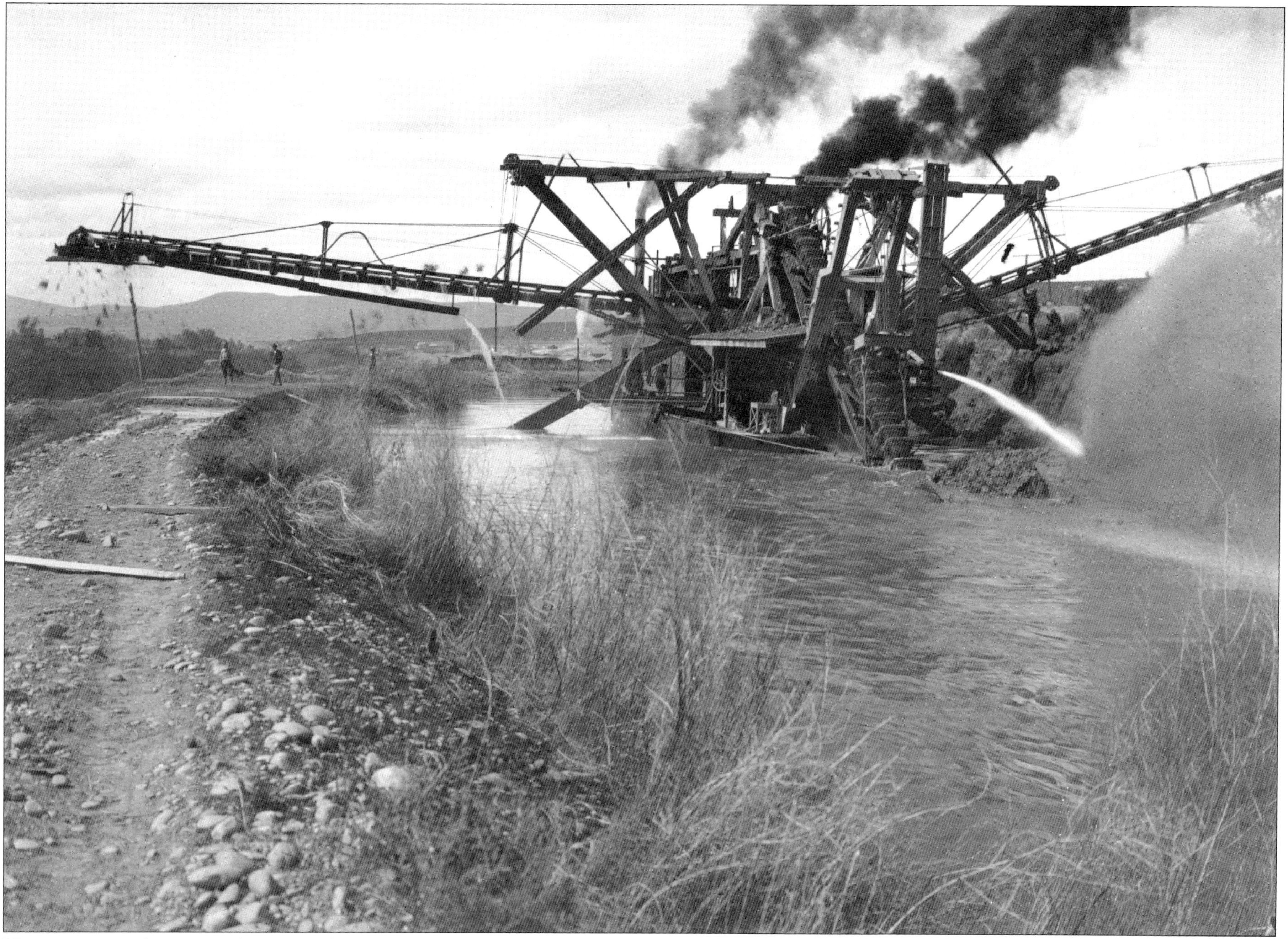

The Bucyrus Dredge was used to widen the canal in 1909 and 1910. The dredge was constructed on-site beginning in July 1909 with the launching taking place on Sept. 27, 1909.

HELPING TO BUILD A BETTER COMMUNITY

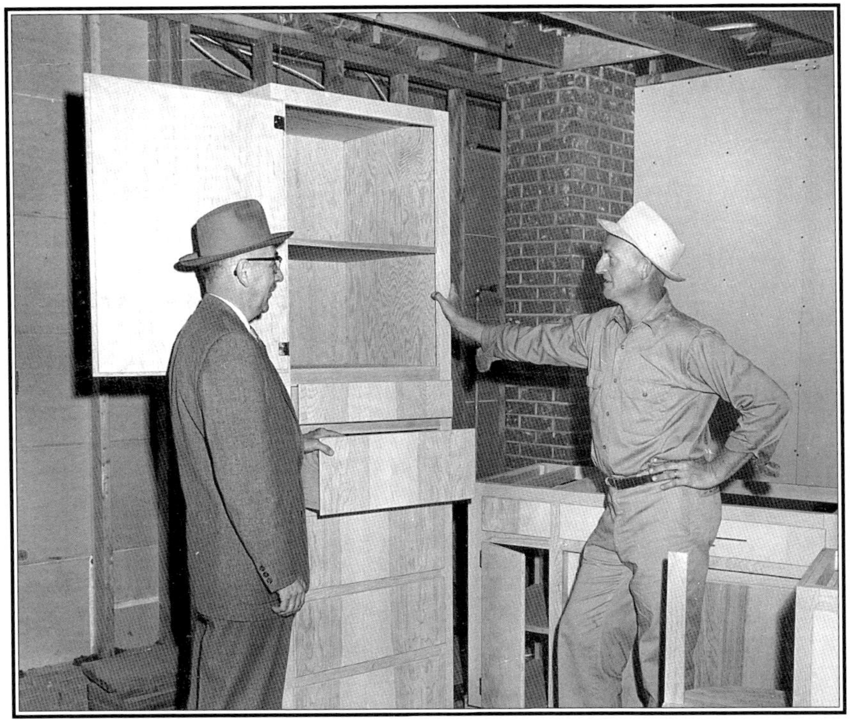

Henry A. Stamschror, right, pictured with M.C. Hansen, a lender from Equitable Savings and Loan in Yakima, began as a residential builder in Sunnyside.

In 1948 Sunnyside became home for Henry A. Stamschror. That same year, Henry began pursuing his dream of becoming a general contractor and began in the area of residential construction. At that time the company built many homes in the Sunnyside area.

After many years as a residential builder Henry felt the need to expand and become more versatile. The decision was made to venture into commercial construction. In 1964, Henry Stamschror Construction, the residential company, became what is known today as Mountain States Const. Co. The company began focusing its interests on concrete and heavy concrete structures. Those roots remain today. The first commercial project completed by the new company, Mountain States Const. Co., was the one million gallon exposed concrete water tank on top of Harrison Hill in Sunnyside.

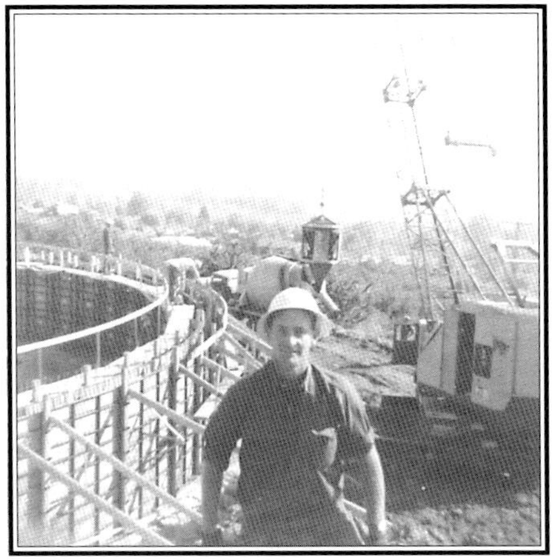

Mountain States Const. Co.'s first commercial project was the one-million gallon exposed water tank on top of Harrison Hill.

Since 1964, Mountain States has continued to pursue projects including commercial and institutional buildings, agricultural and food processing facilities, wineries, underground utilities, water and wastewater treatment plants, and even structures related to the nuclear industry. The company has become a specialist in design build projects such as the Oregon Coast Aquarium, Free Willy/Keiko facility and Passages of the Deep exhibits, and Snipes Mountain Microbrewery and Restaurant here in Sunnyside.

The company has moved forward in both experience and with technological advances. Mountain States continues to expand its knowledge in various industries, taking on many construction projects ranging in size across the Pacific Northwest states while maintaining roots at its Sunnyside location.

For more than thirty-five years, Mountain States has helped "build" the Sunnyside community with projects dating back to the mid 1960s. The residential homes were only the beginning of the company's community involvement. Since becoming a general contractor, Mountain States has been able to participate in helping other local businesses grow and expand their operations and facilities, as well as bring new businesses to the community.

Today Mountain States is under second-generation management, maintaining its goals of being up front in promises, out front in quality and exceptional in versatility, while continuing to be recognized for its dedication, commitment, design build capabilities, and management practices.

MOUNTAIN STATES CONST. CO.

SINCE 1964

803 Scoon Road • Sunnyside, Washington • 509-837-6822

#MO-UN-TS C 352 DC

COMMERCE

William H. Cline arrived in Sunnyside in 1893 becoming the town's first resident and merchant. Cline was given both a residential and a business lot by Paul Schulze, the Northern Pacific Railroad's western land agent, in exchange for setting up a general store. The Railroad, which owned the townsite, wanted to attract settlers and believed that a general store would be a strong selling point to anyone interested in the area.

Cline accepted Schulze's offer on the condition that the proposed name of the town be changed. Schulze wanted to name the town Mayhew, but Cline detested the name so much that he refused to accept the offer unless the name was changed to Sunnyside, the name by which both the canal and the Yakima Valley were known at the time. Schulze agreed and Cline was soon in business.

One of the first buildings to go up after Cline's general store was the Sunnyside Hotel. Built in 1894 the three-story structure would dominate the town's skyline until the early 1920s when it burned down. In 1901 the hotel installed a bathtub, which had to be filled by carrying buckets of water from the town's well. The bathtub was the first such amenity in town, and the hotel proudly advertised this by putting "The Only Bathtub in Sunnyside" on its stationary and business cards. The very next year the hotel had competition after a barber shop installed a tub and started charging customers 25¢ for its use.

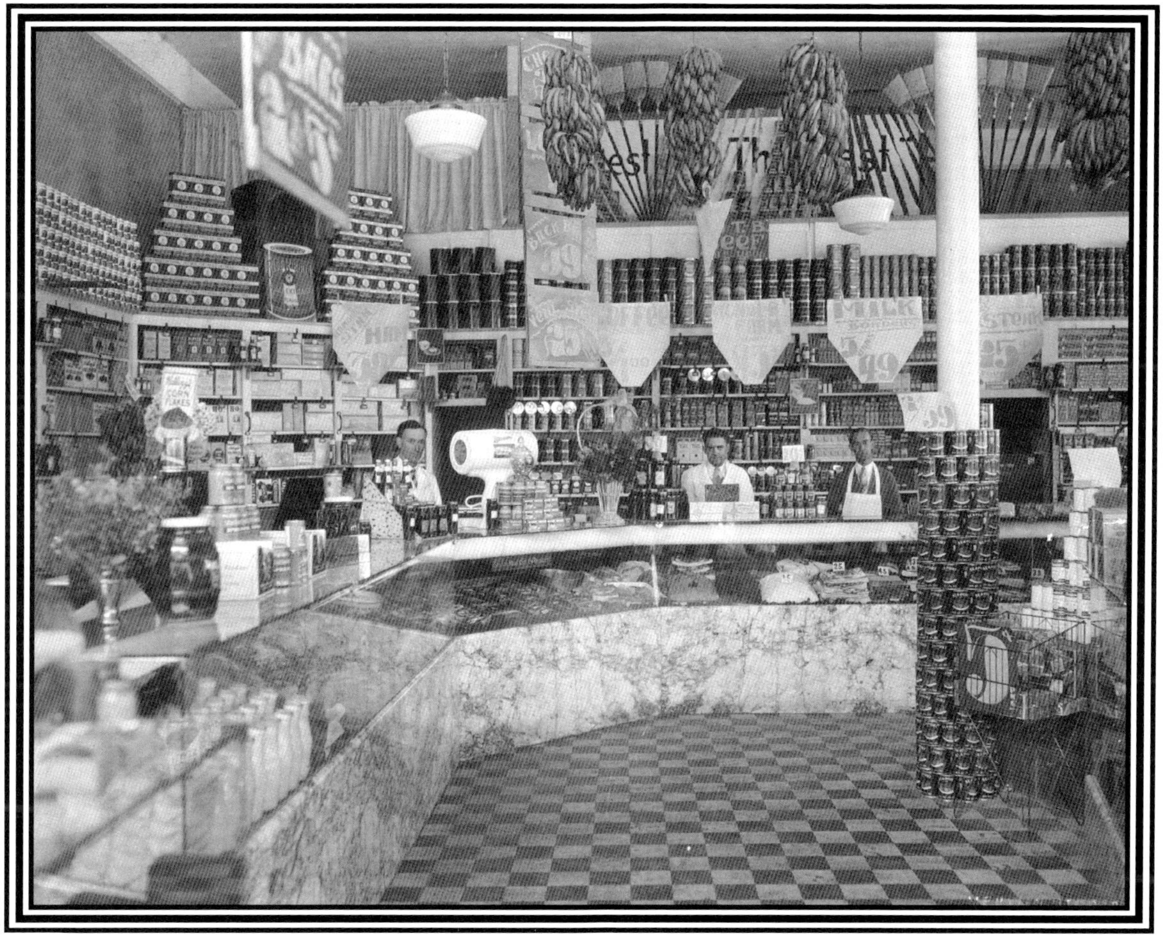

City Market which was located on the southwest corner of 6th Street and Edison Avenue, 1929.

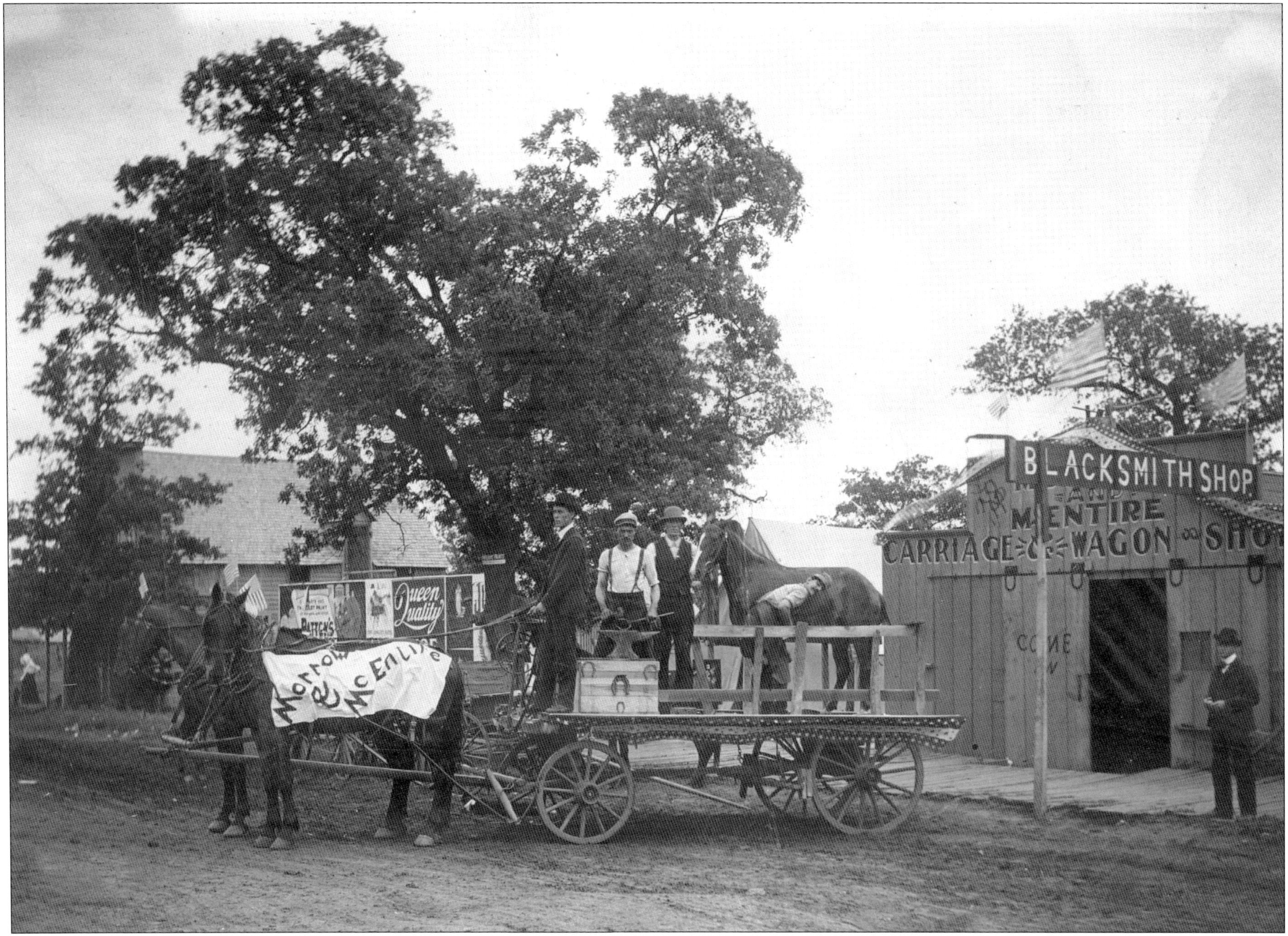

Morrow and McEntire Blacksmith Shop, circa 1900.

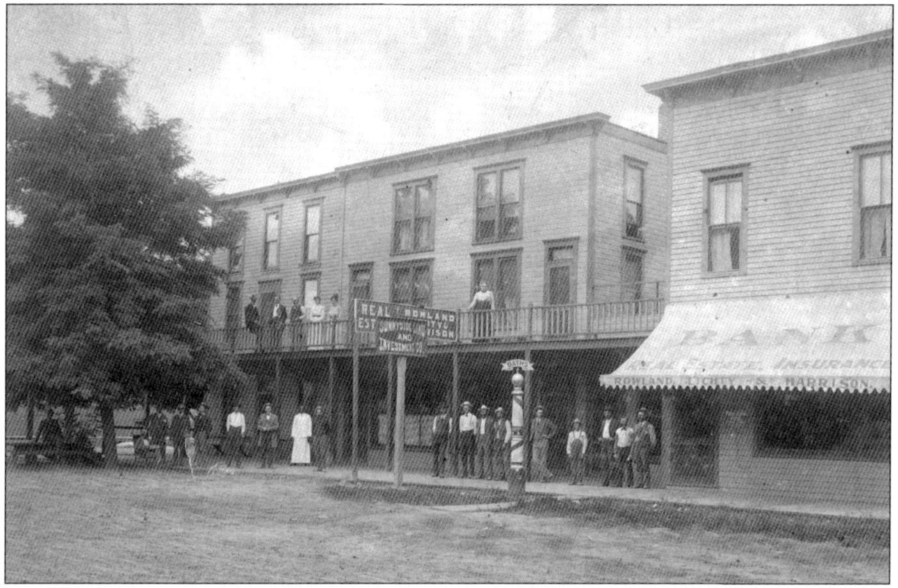

Hotel Sunnyside, Sunnyside Land and Investment Company and the offices of Rowland, Lichty and Harrison located near the corner of 6th Street and Edison Avenue, circa 1900.

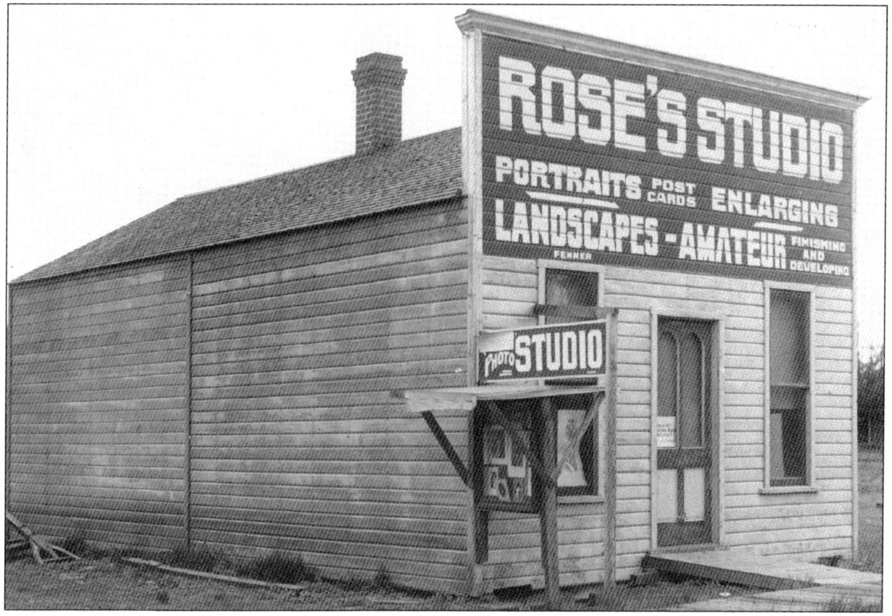

Rose's Studio on Edison. This studio preceded Merwin's Photo Studio and was also the first site of the Sunnyside Sun newspaper.

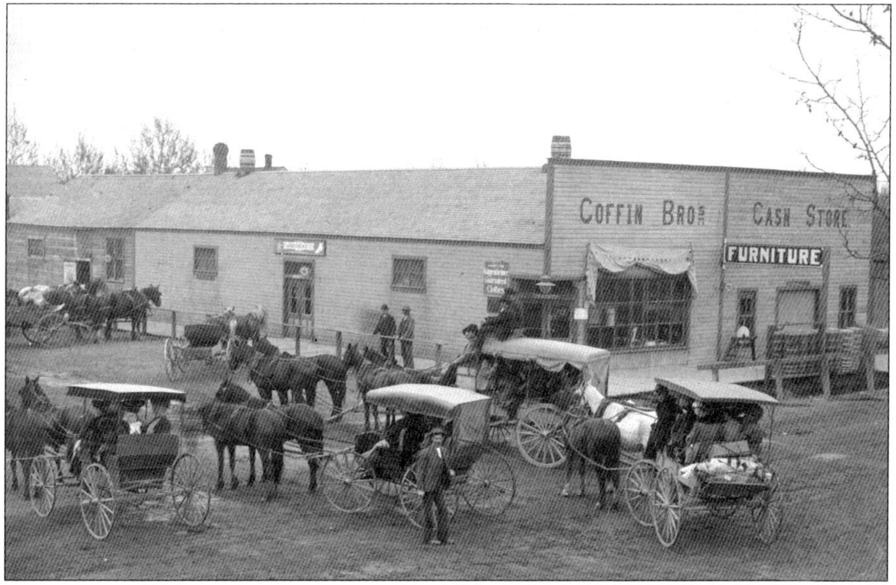

Coffin Brothers store, circa 1905. Located on the southeast corner of 6th Street and Franklin Avenue. Picture taken from the Sunnyside Hotel. Harve Matheson is pictured in the foreground.

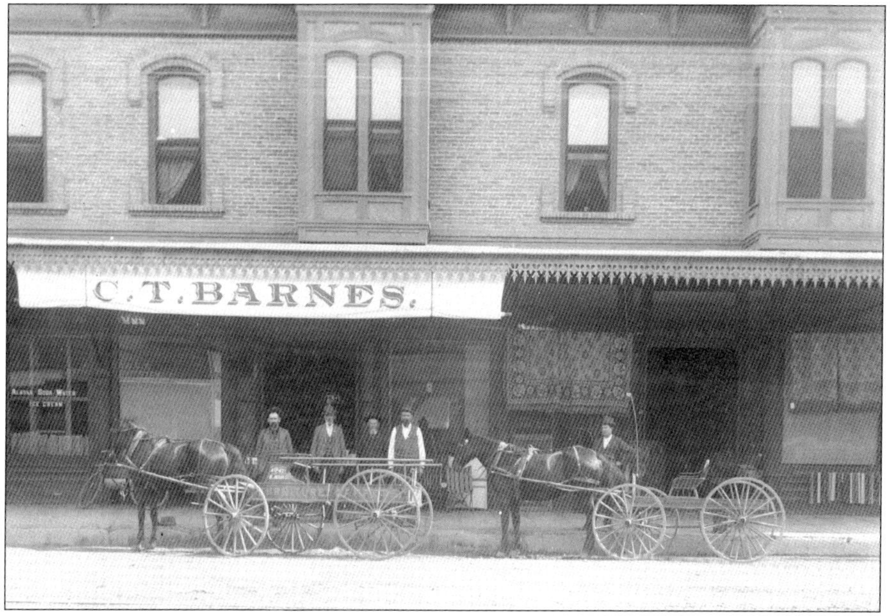

C.T. Barnes, early 1900s.

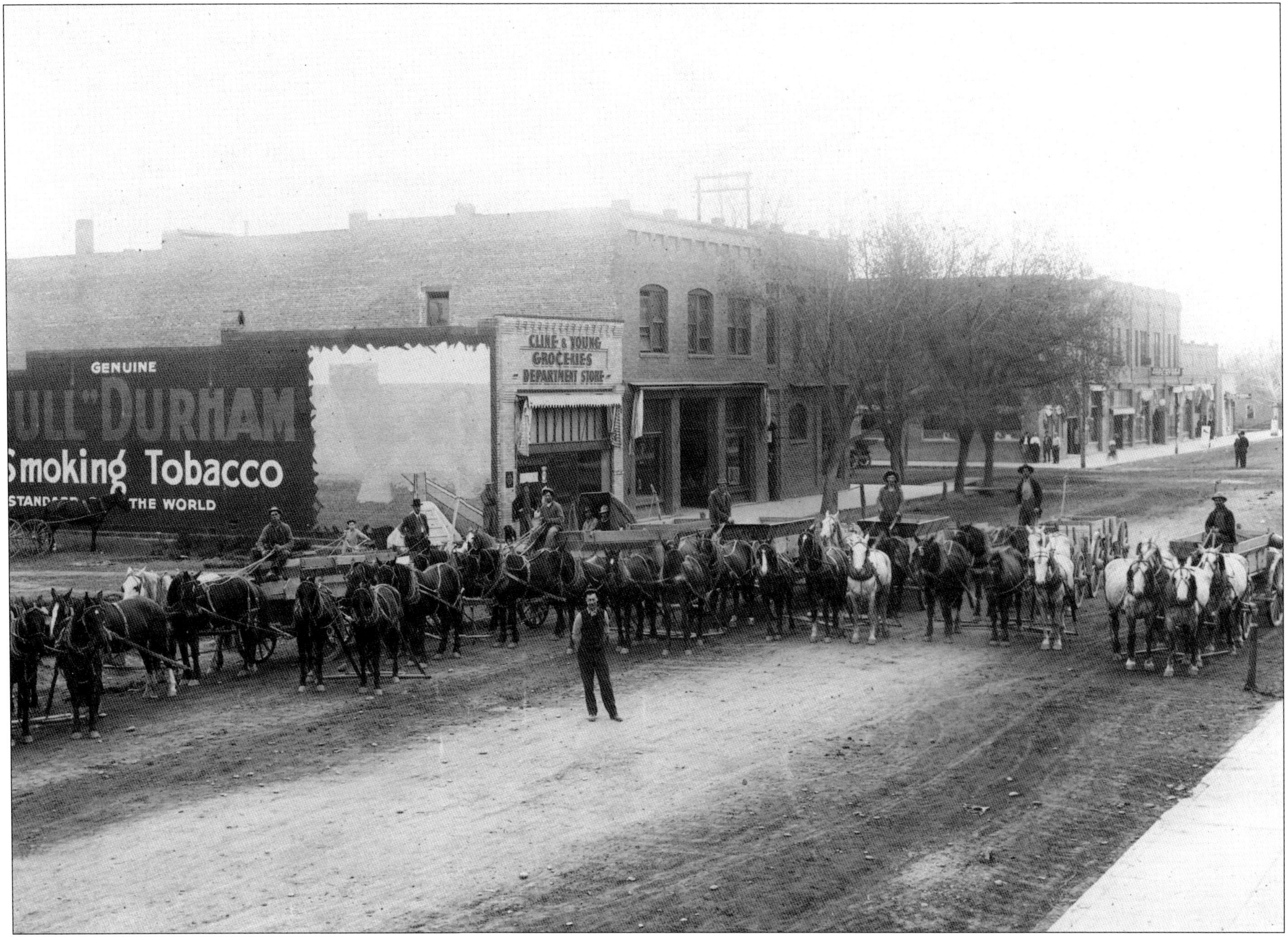

Harve Matheson's grading outfit on Edison west of 6th Street in front of Sunnyside's first store, Cline and Young, circa 1905. The Cline and Young store opened on New Year's Day, 1894.

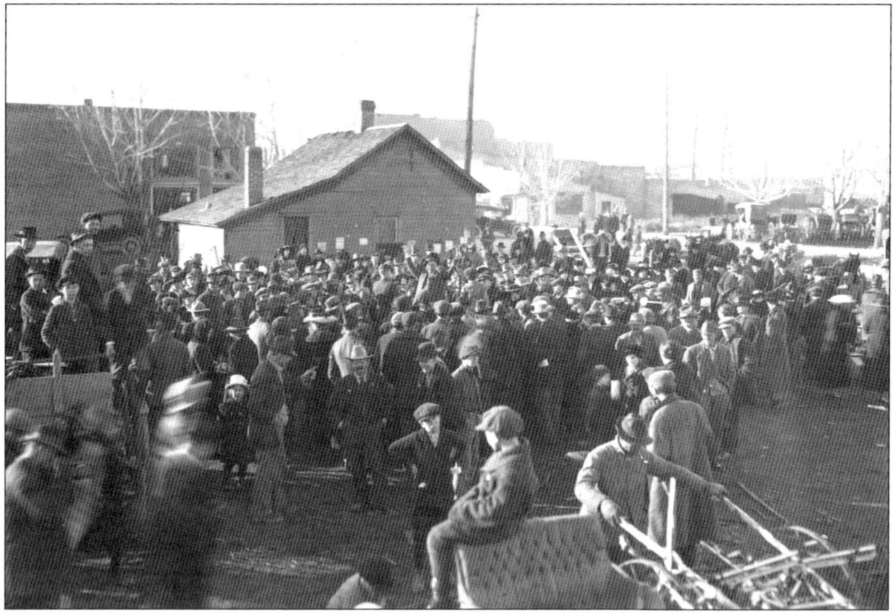

Market Day Sale in Sunnyside. The event was started in 1905 by the Commercial Club and held monthly at the site of the present-day Post Office.

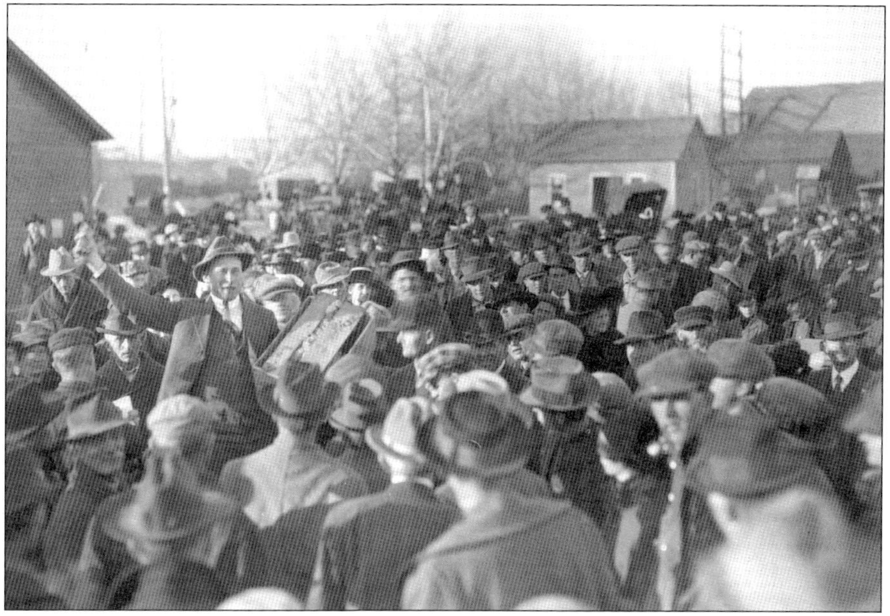

Market Day Sale in Sunnyside, circa 1905.

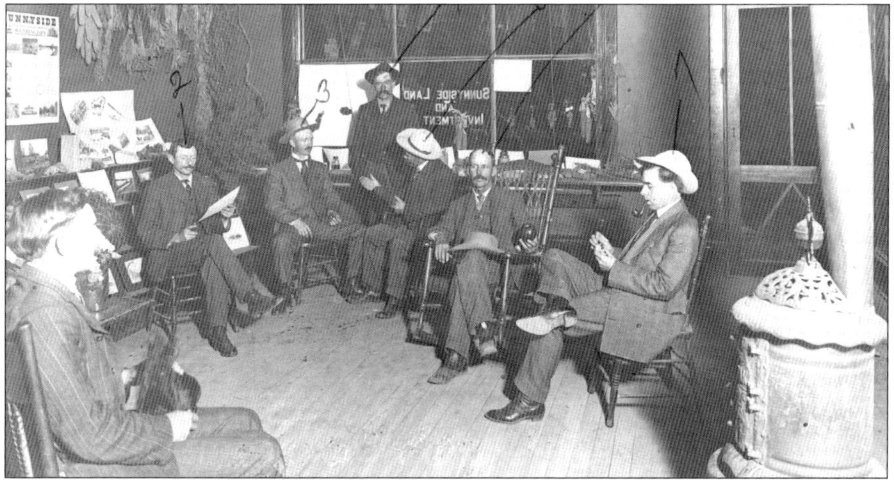

An interior picture of the original Sunnyside Land and Investment Company Office, a small frame building on Sixth Street. Pictured left to right are: A.G. Fleming, barber; James Henderson, Sunnyside's first druggist and mayor; R.G. Page, Banker and first Chamber of Commerce President; W.J. Knight, building contractor; Mel G. Duncan, owner of the S.L. & I. Co.; George Vetter, second Postmaster and Andy Fisk, who purchased Arch Fleming's first barber shop.

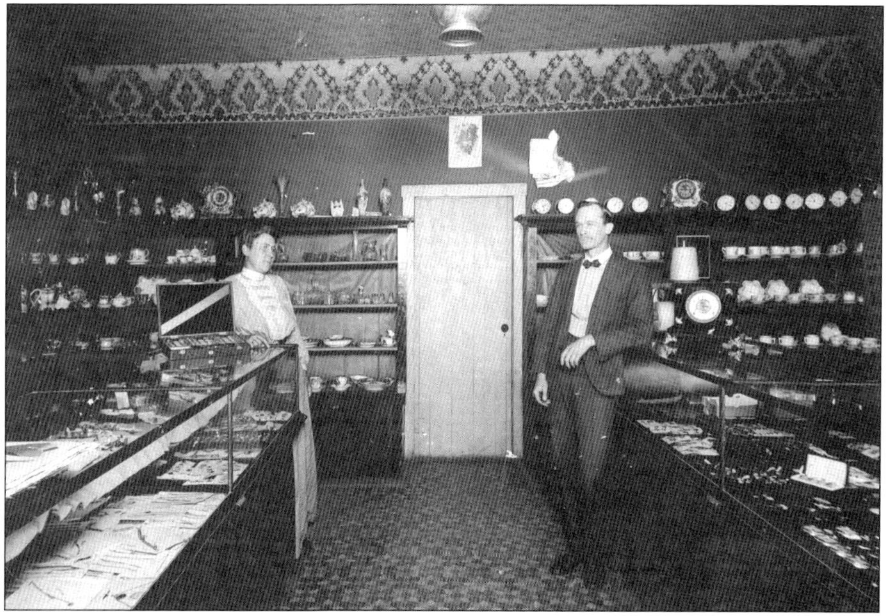

Rachel and Rupert Calkin in their jewelry store, circa 1905.

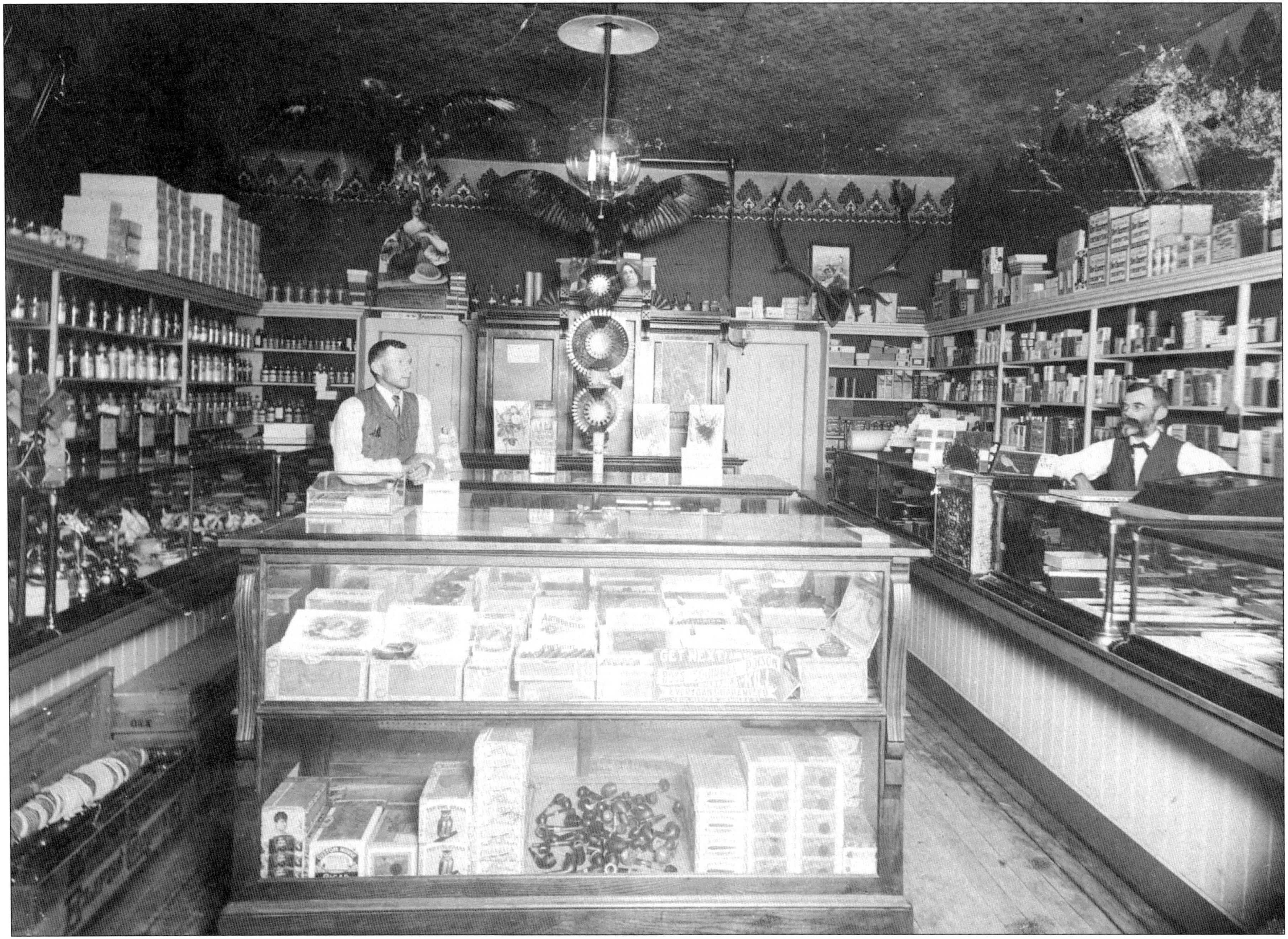

Interior of the first drug store in Sunnyside. The owner, James Henderson is on the left. J. T. Baird, a clerk, is on the right. The store was located next to Cline's on Edison Avenue.

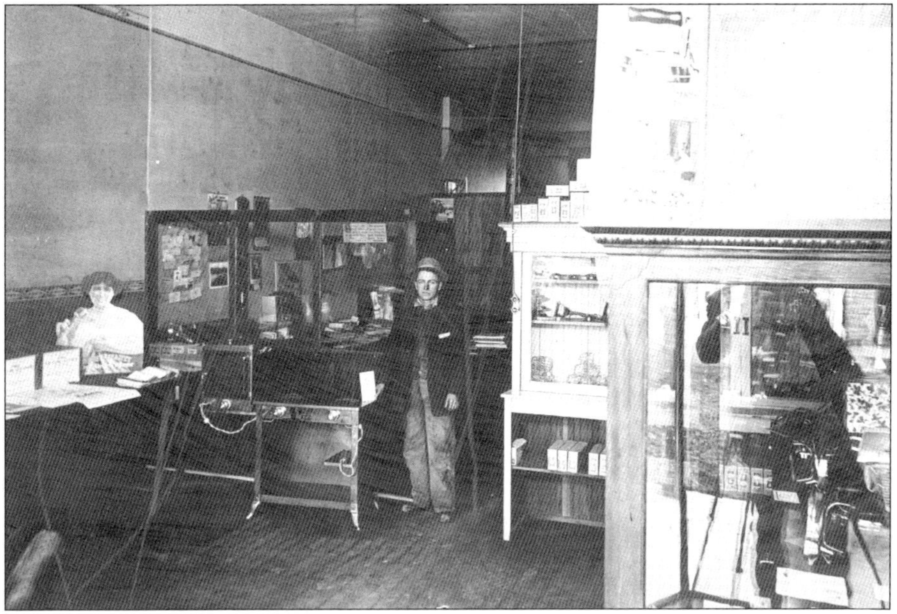

Ted Parke's Electric Shop, circa 1905. The shop was located in the 400 Block of 6th Street.

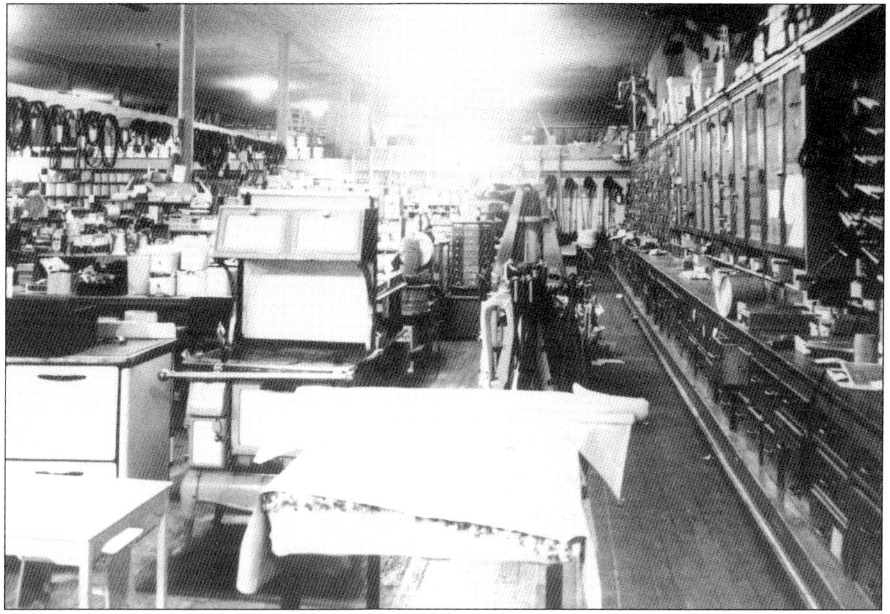

Interior of Amundson's Hardware, which was located where Centennial Park now stands at the corner of 6th Street and Edison Avenue, circa 1920.

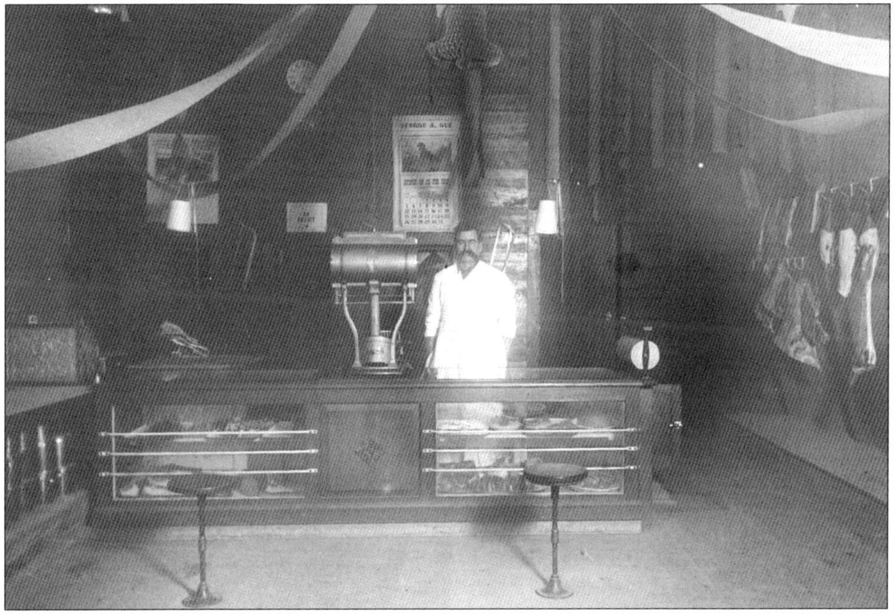

Interior of Sunnyside Meat Market located on the east side of 6th Street between Edison and Franklin avenues, circa 1905.

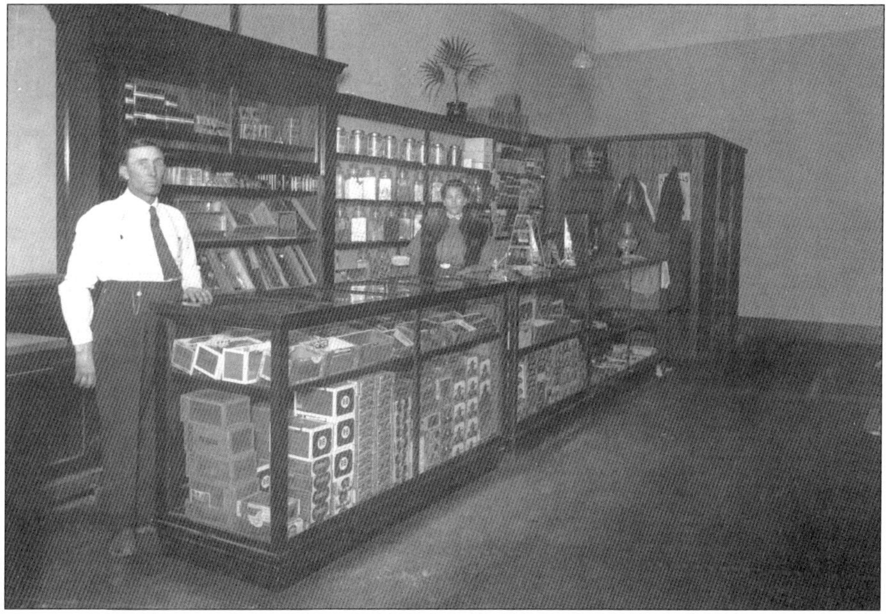

Lou and Libby Eddy in their confectionery store.

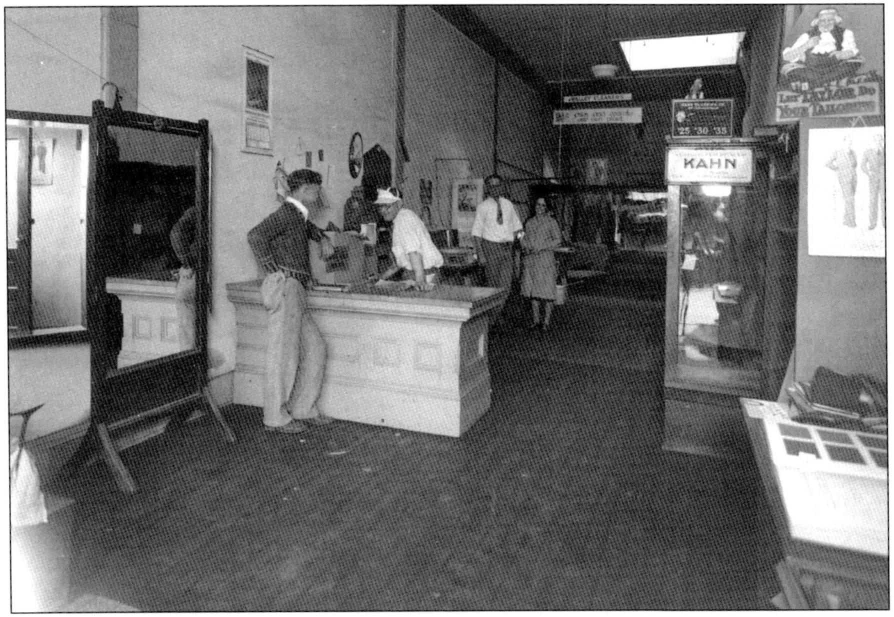

Interior of Valley Cleaners located on South 6th Street. Included in the photo are owners Bill and Nelle Cox. Behind the counter is Art Smith who shined shoes.

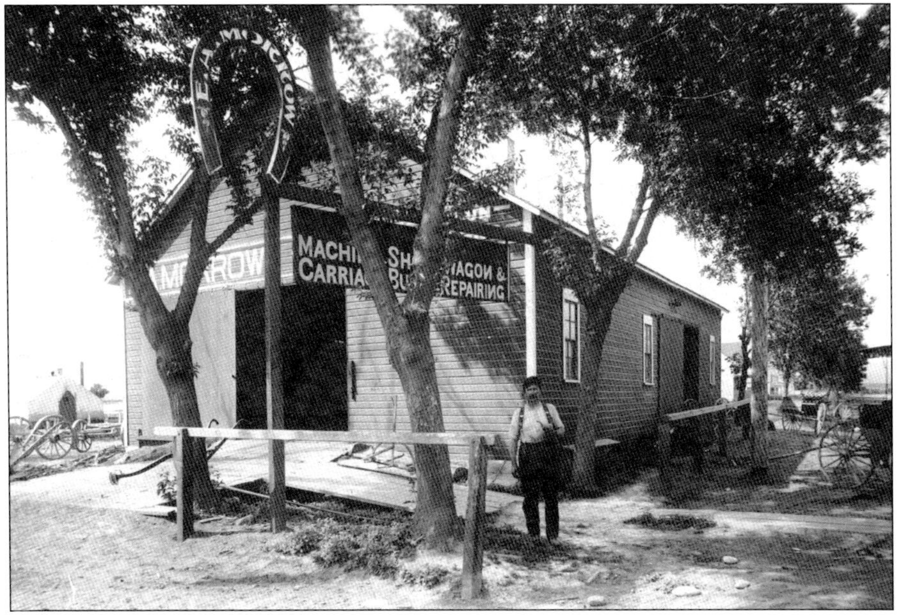

E.A. Morrow outside his blacksmith shop in 1907.

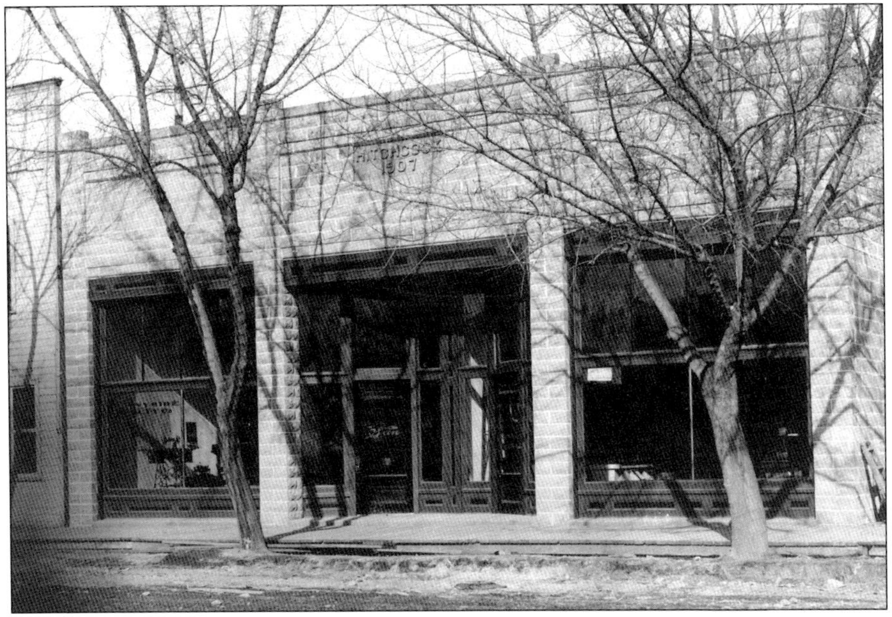

Hitchcock Building, circa 1907. Home of the Sunnyside Sun Newspaper located at 525 East Edison.

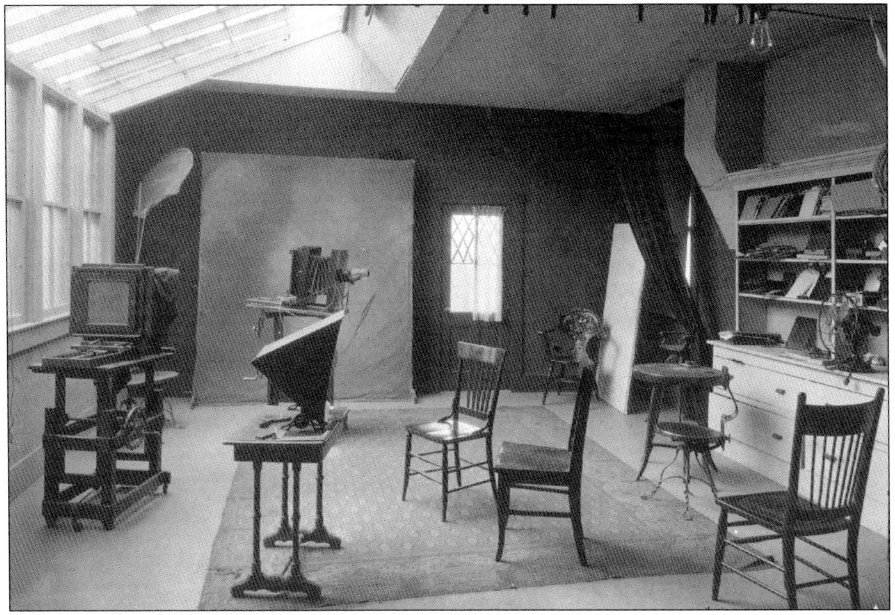

Merwin Photo Studio which later became Morris Floral Shop.

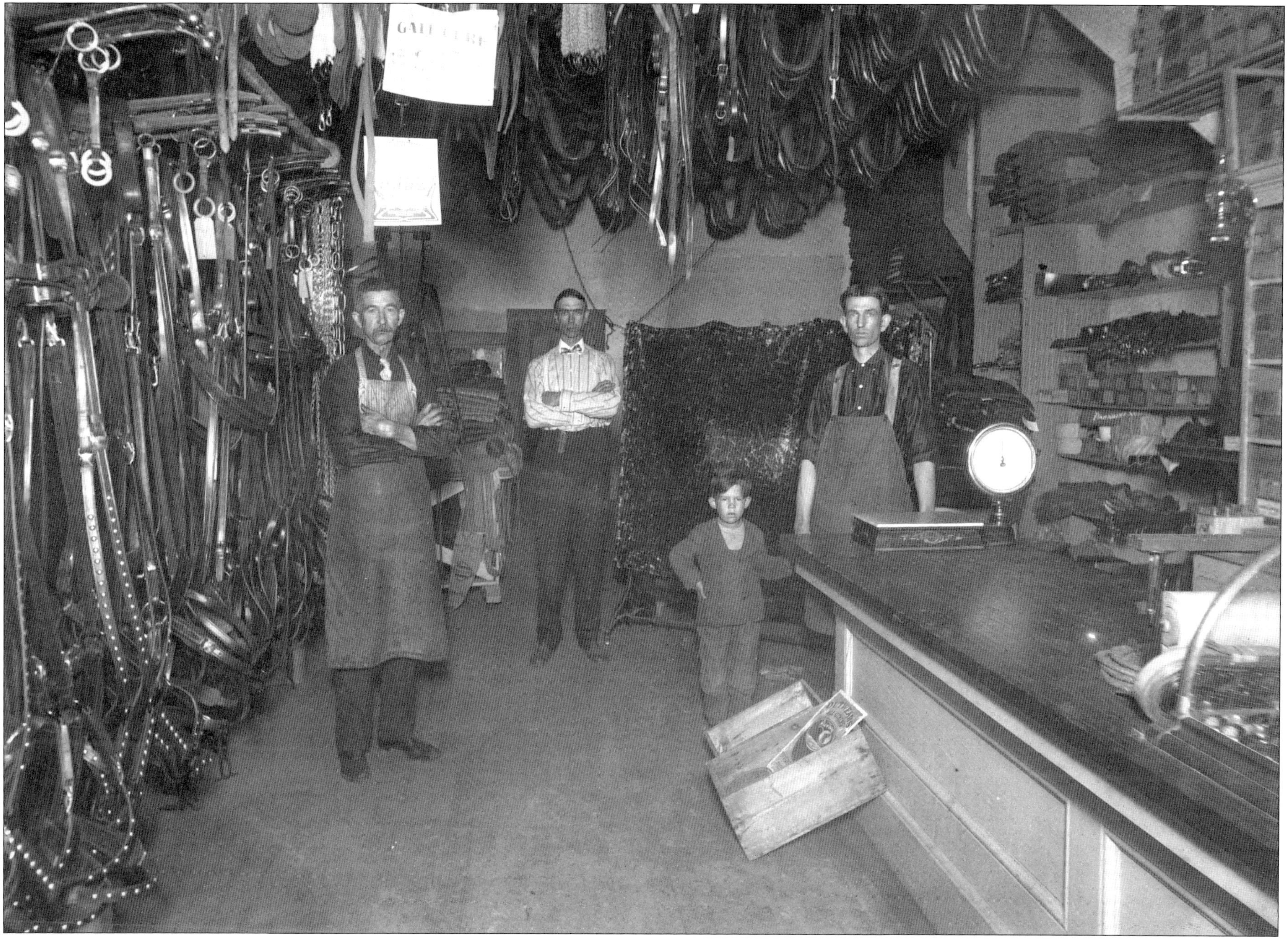

Harness shop in Sunnyside, circa 1906. The man on the left is Mr. Case, the harness maker. The man on the right is the owner Guy E. Root with his son, Clyde. The man in the middle is unidentified.

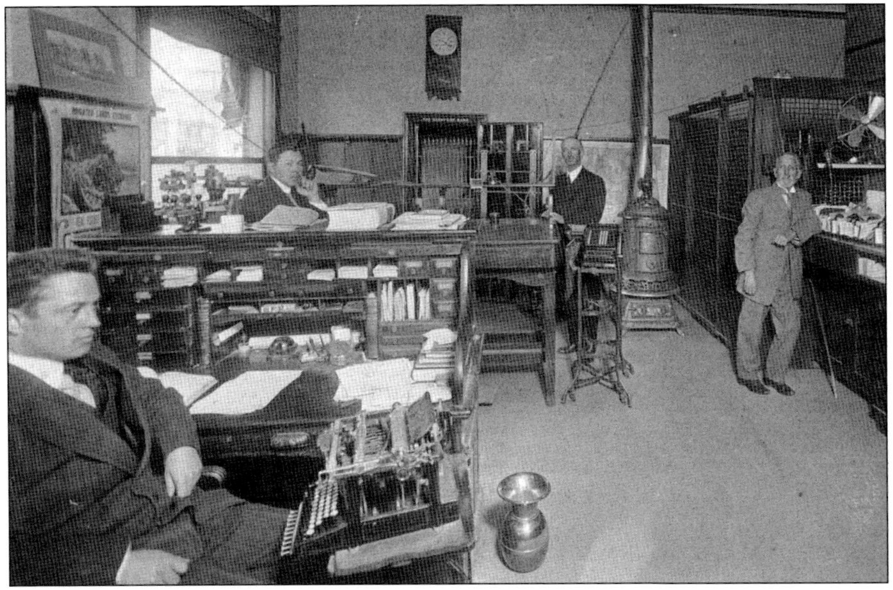

Interior of the Sunnyside Bank in 1908. The bank was located on the northeast corner of Sixth Street and Edison Avenue. Pictured are (L to R) Clarence Zook, Horace Miller, R.G. Page and W.J. Creglow.

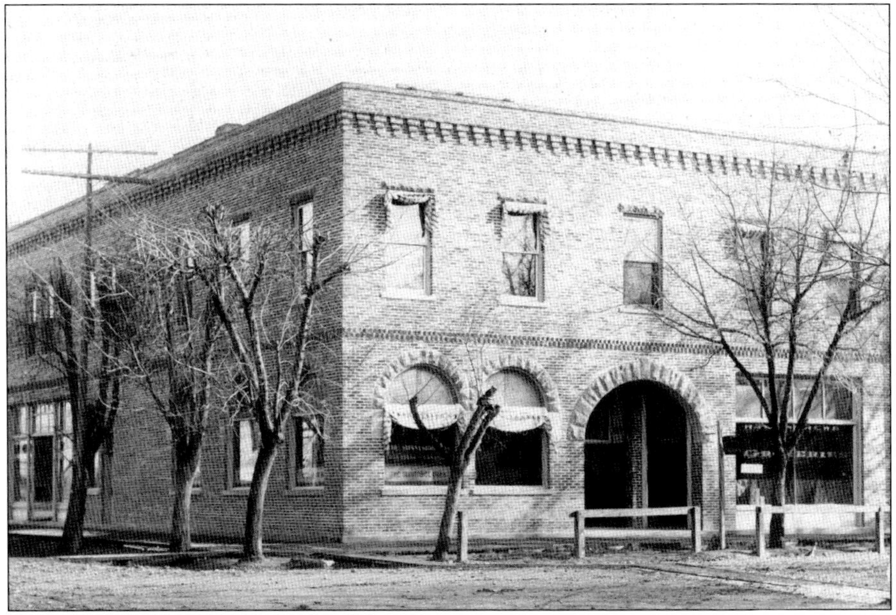

Sunnyside Bank Building was erected in 1906 for $14,000 on the northeast corner of 6th and Edison. The structure would later be called the Central Building.

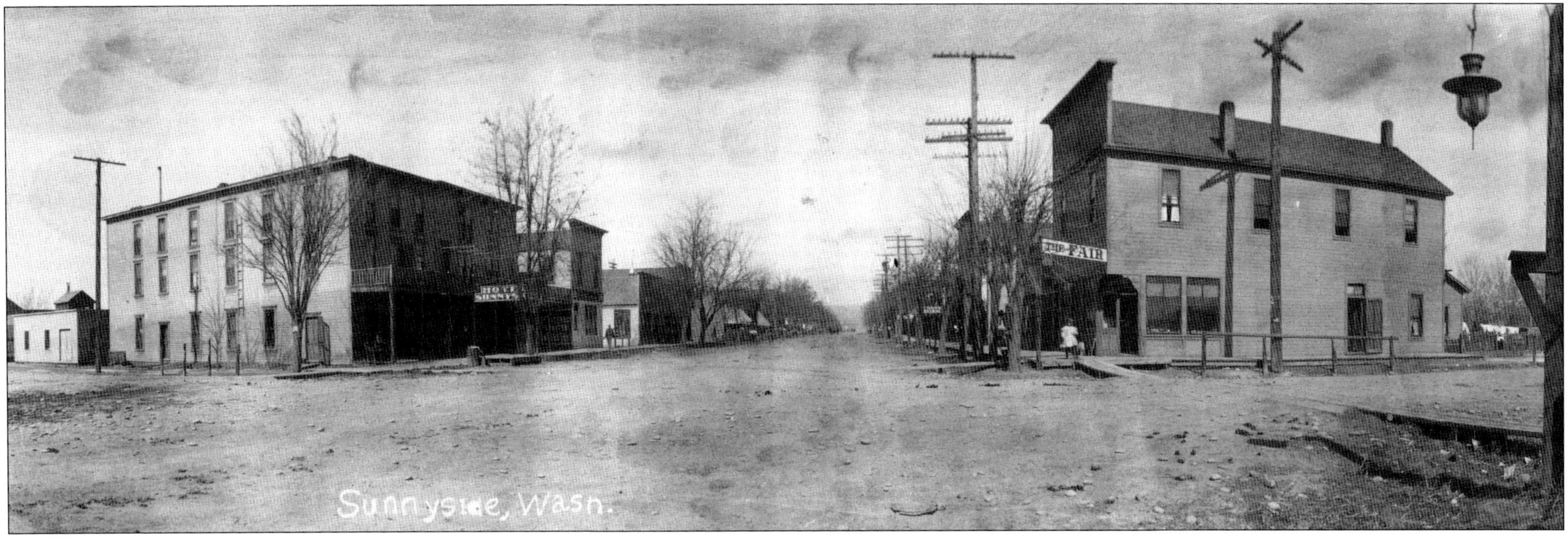

Looking north on 6th Street with Franklin intersection in the foreground. Hotel Sunnyside is the three story building on the left.

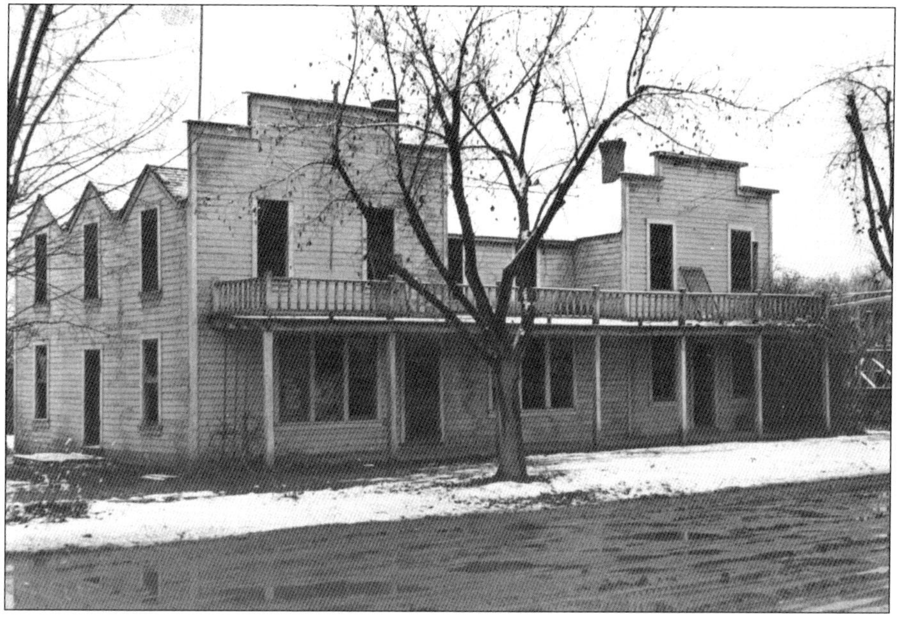

The Globe Hotel at Franklin and 7th streets, circa 1915.

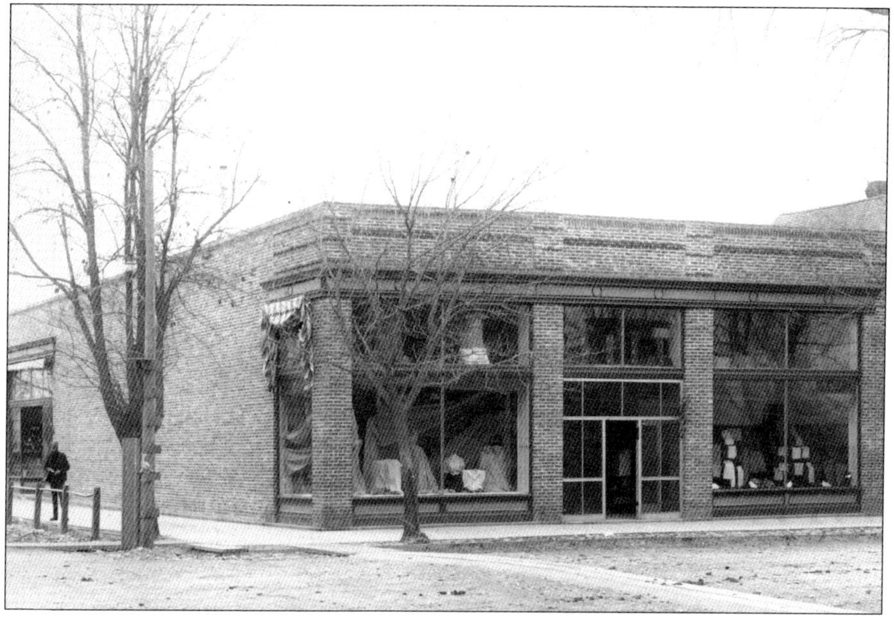

J. B. George Department Store which was built in 1906 on the southwest corner of Sixth and Edison, photo circa 1910.

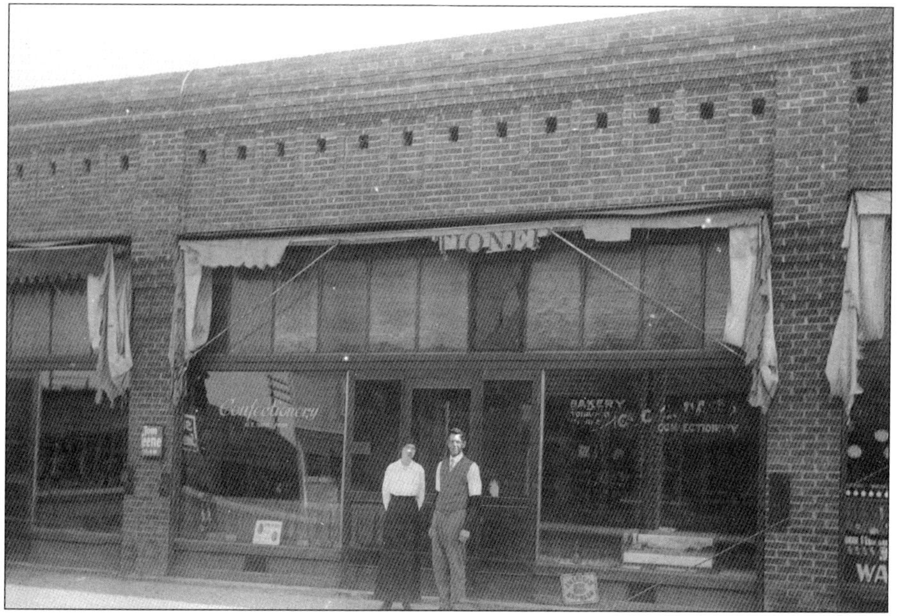

Geo Davis Confectionery, early 1900s.

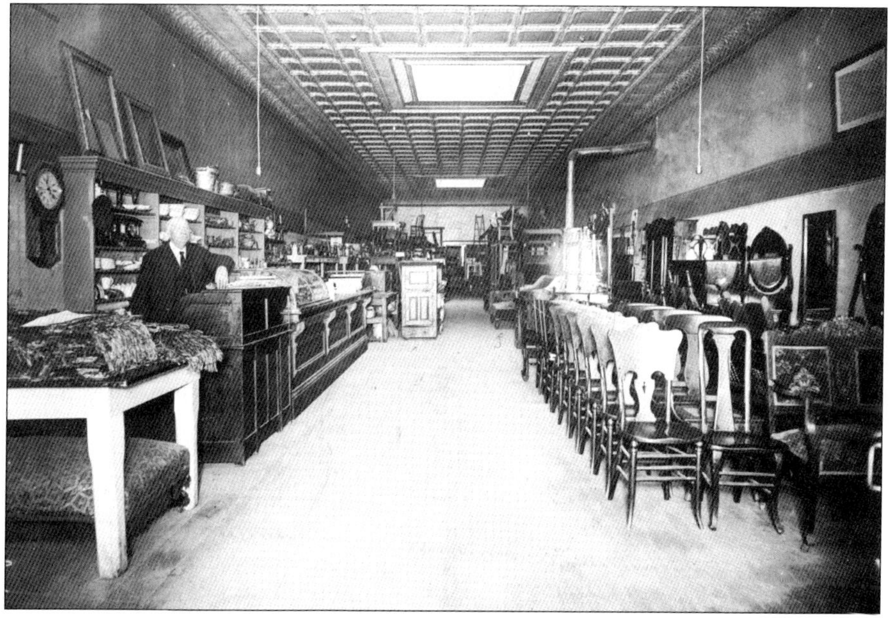

Interior of a Sunnyside furniture store in the early 1900s.

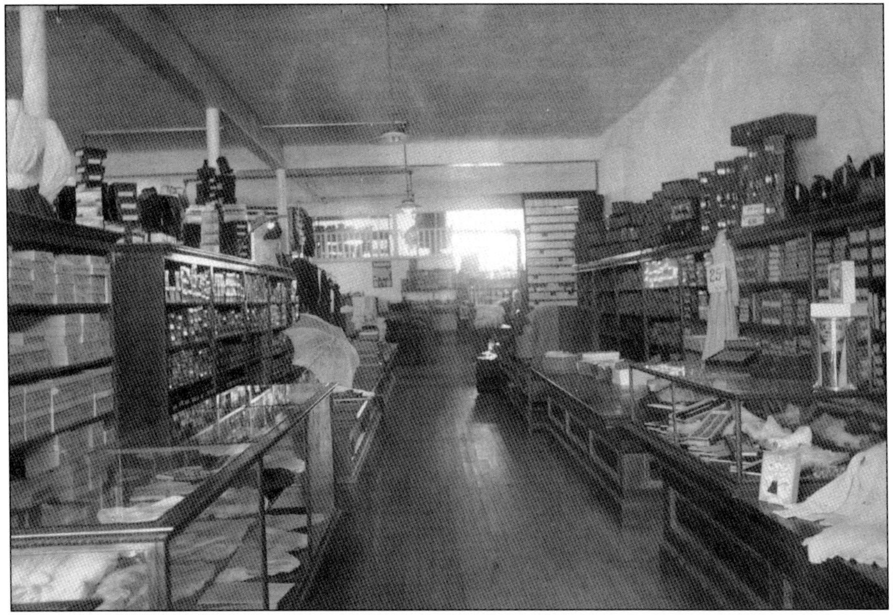

Interior of Cline and Youngs Department Store located on Edison Avenue, early 1900s.

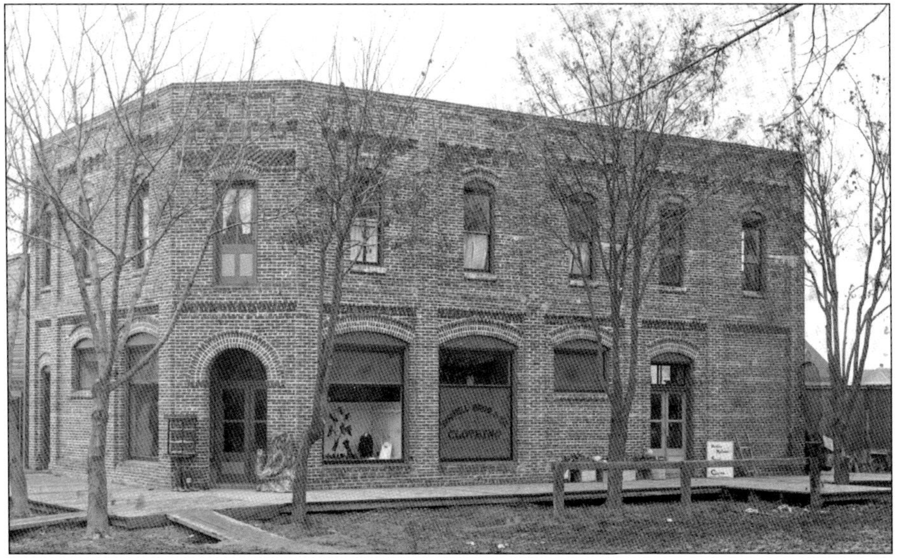

The Boutell Building, built in 1901. The second floor served two years as a high school until September of 1905 when Denny Blaine was opened. The first floor has served as Boutell's Dry Goods, Yakima Valley Bank, Old National Bank, Seattle First National Bank, Dayton Realty and Century 21.

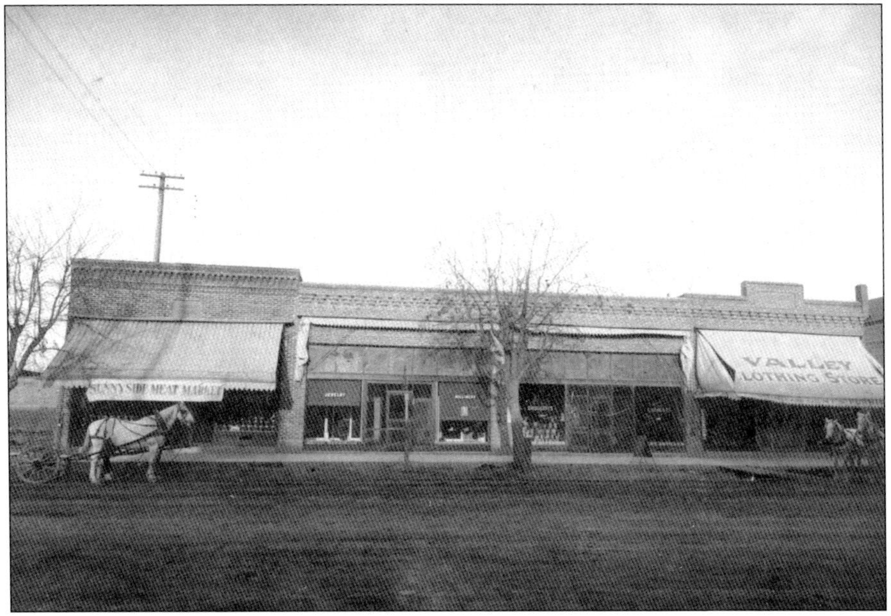

Businesses on the east side of 6th Street between Edison and Franklin including Sunnyside Meat Market, a jewelry store, drug store and Valley Clothing Store.

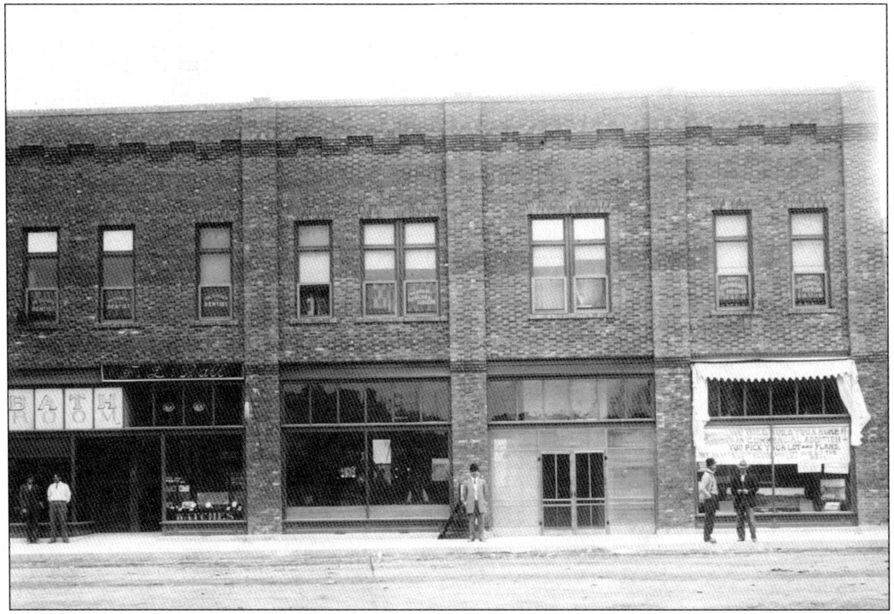

The Allen Building on the north side of Edison between 6th and 7th streets, circa 1911.

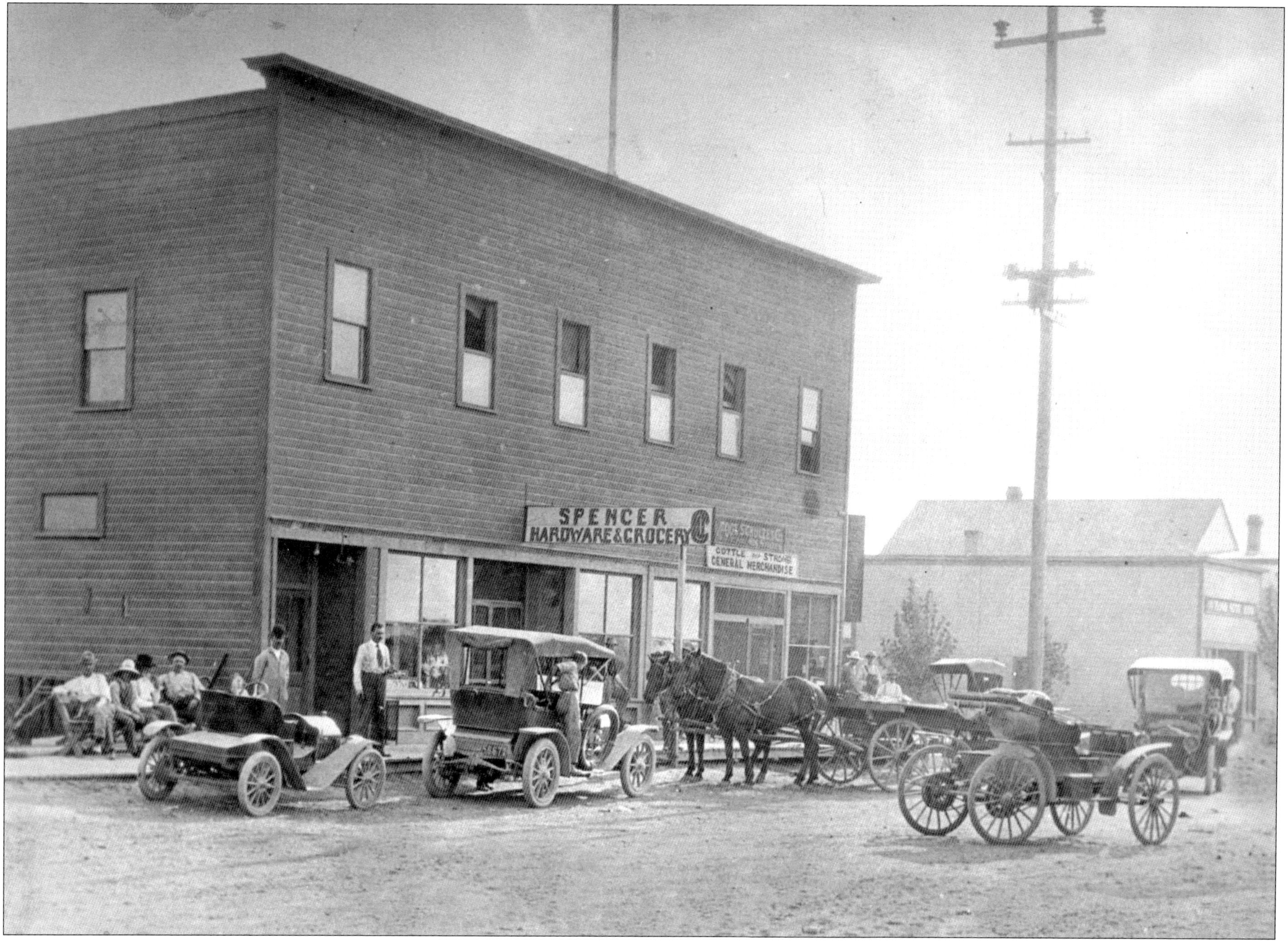

Old Outlook Store and hall, circa 1913.

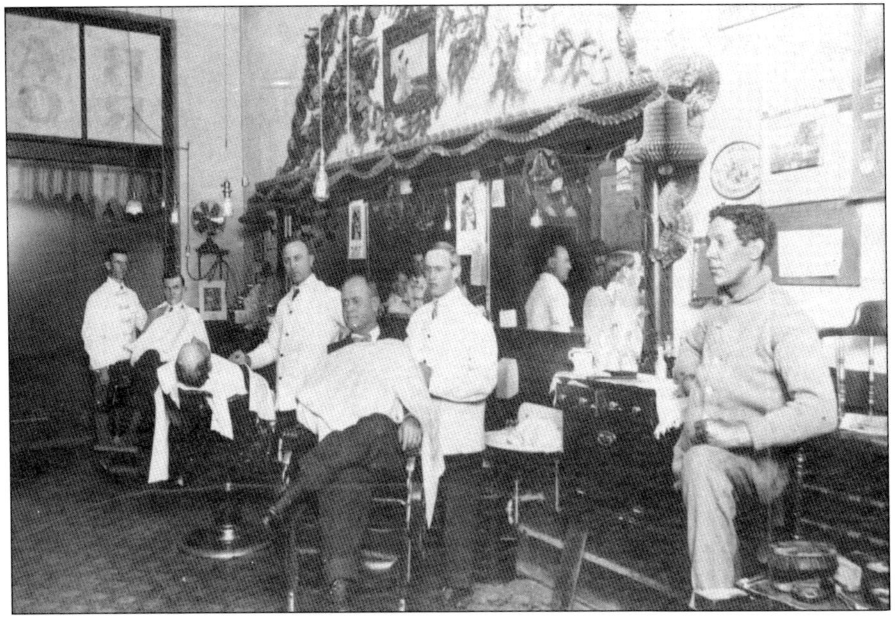

Barber shop located in the Allen Building, circa 1913. This space was later occupied by the Safari Restaurant.

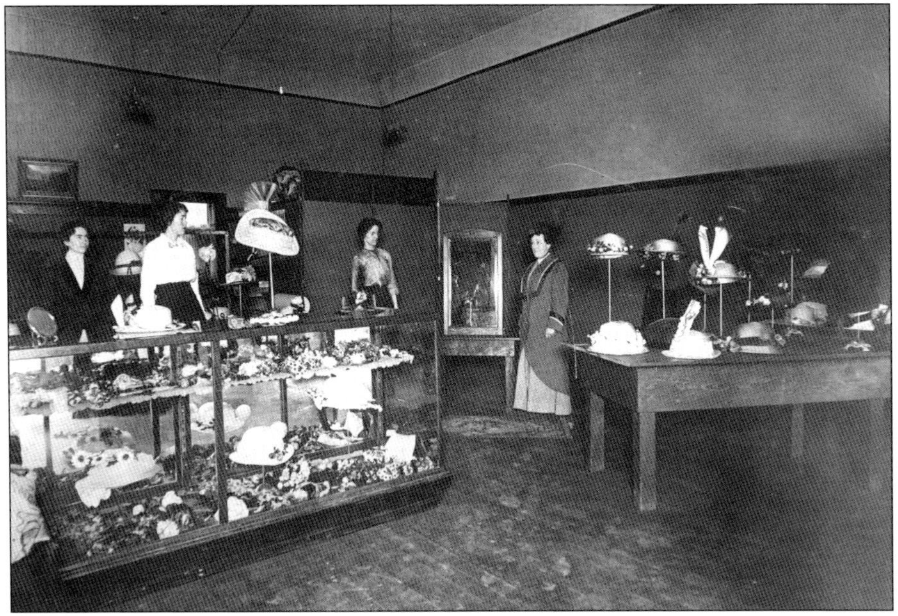

Fanner's Millinery Store, 1914.

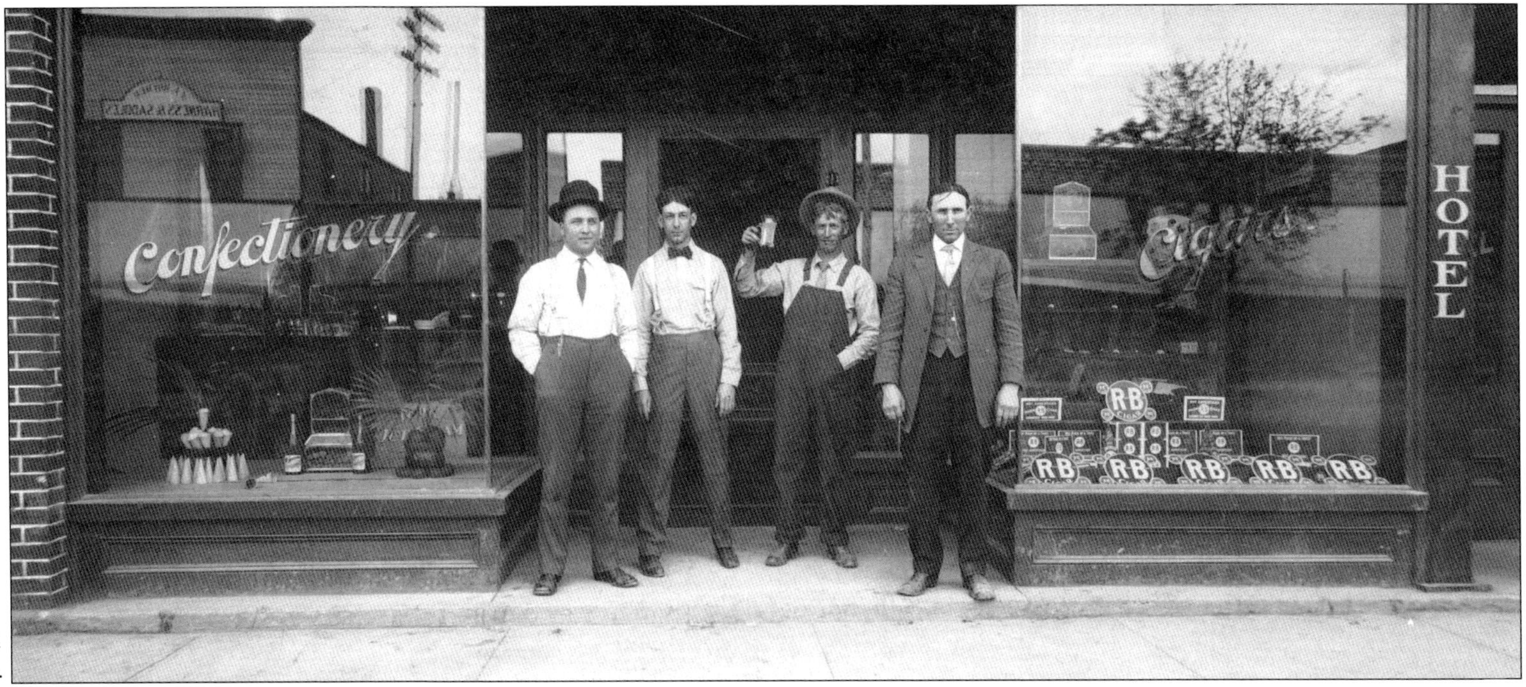

Confectionery, circa 1915.

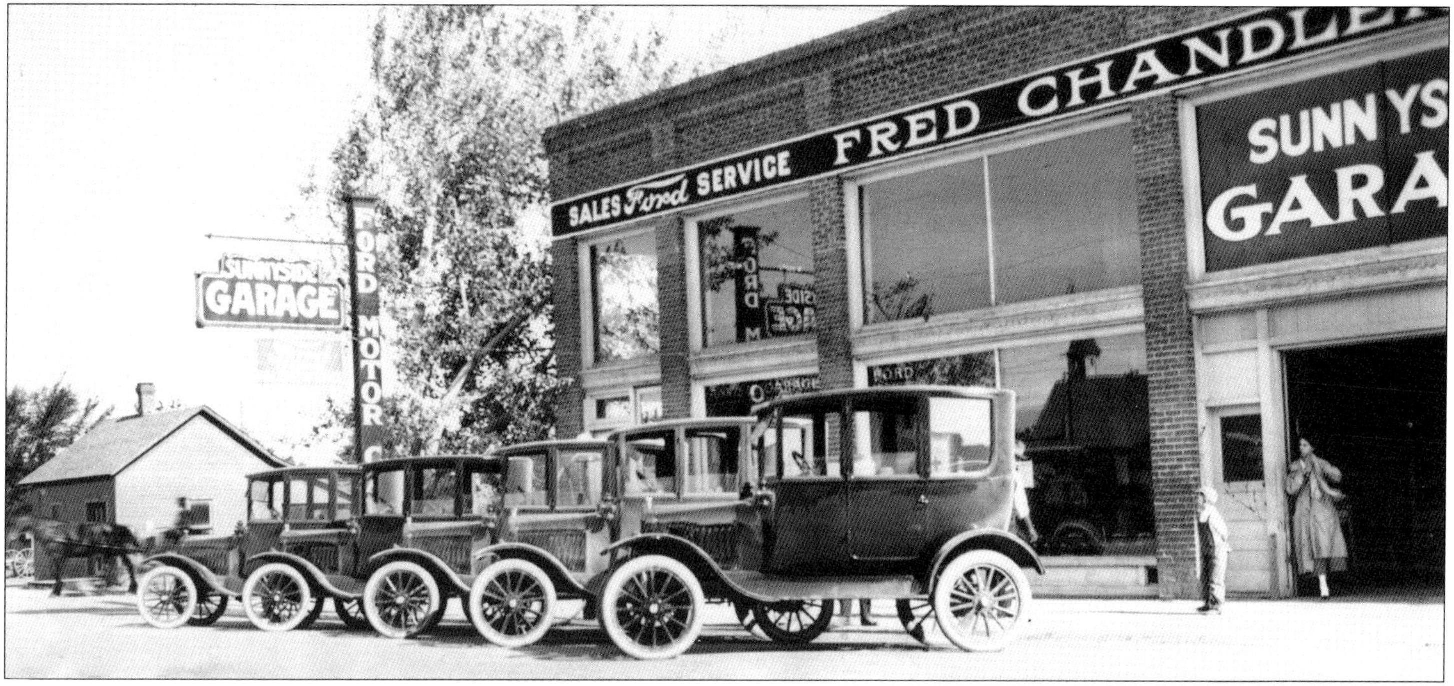

Fred Chandler Ford Dealership and garage at 633 Edison, circa 1918.

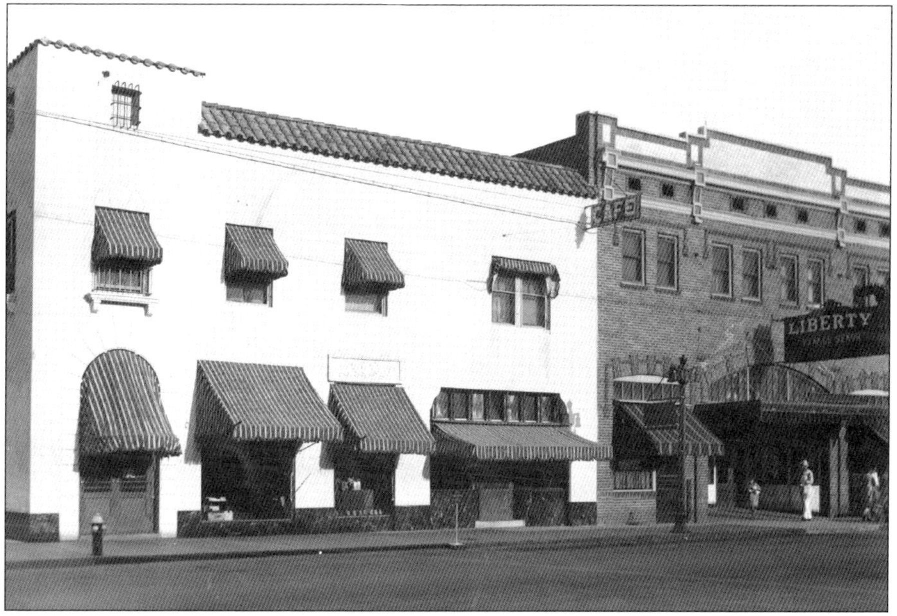

The Planter's Hotel on the left and the Liberty Theater on the right, circa 1915. The Hotel was located on the southeast corner of 6th Street and Decatur Avenue.

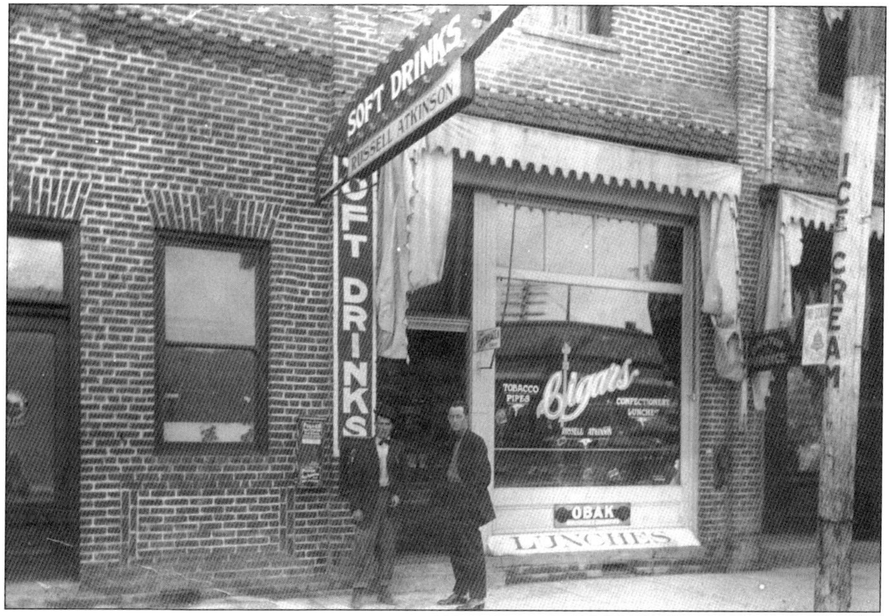

Russell Atkinson's Cigar Store on 6th Street.

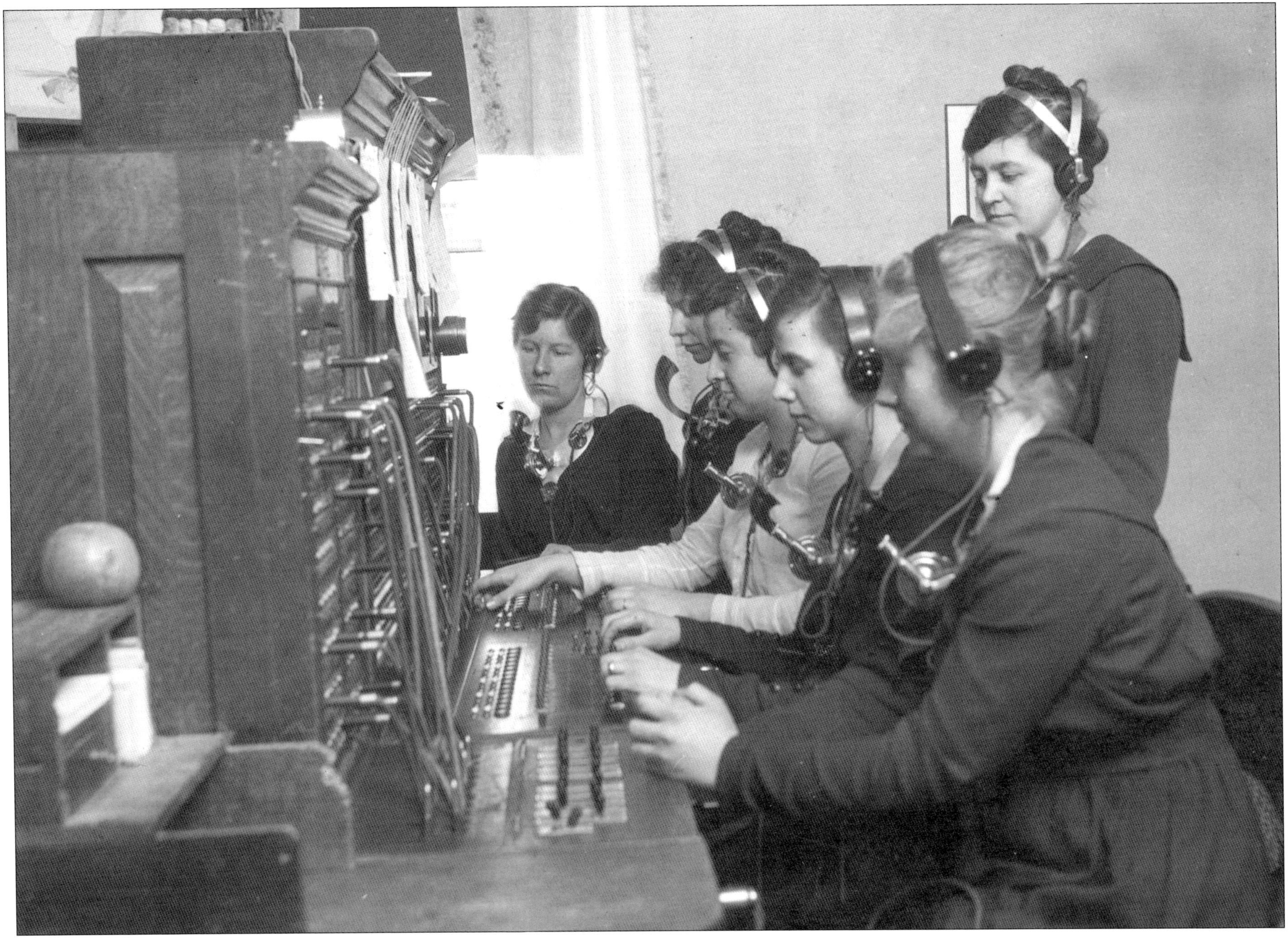

Sunnyside Telephone office, circa 1915. Pictured are Mary Eckstein, Winnie Reynolds King, Daisy Ayers, Leah Davis, and Atha Price Miller.

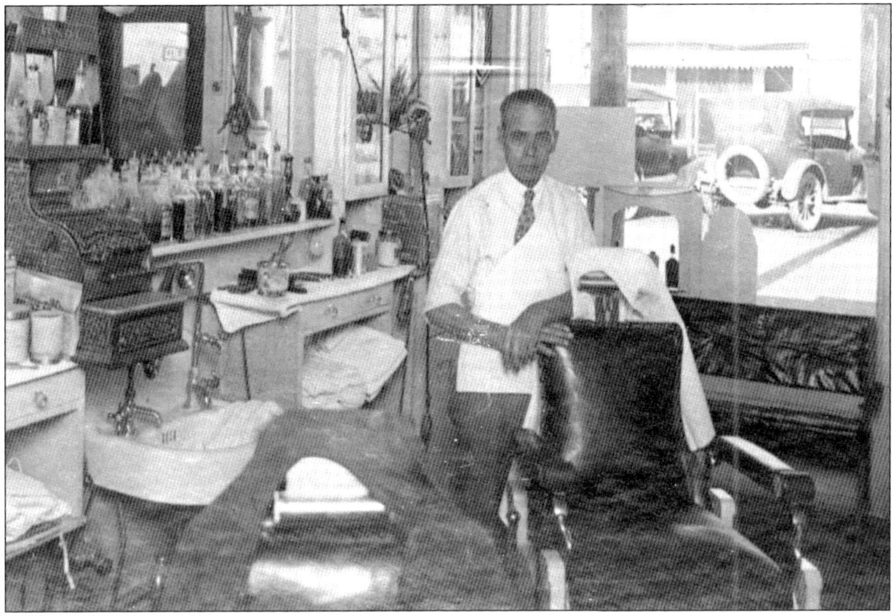

Frank L. Enney in his barber shop located at 422 1/2 South 6th Street, circa 1922.

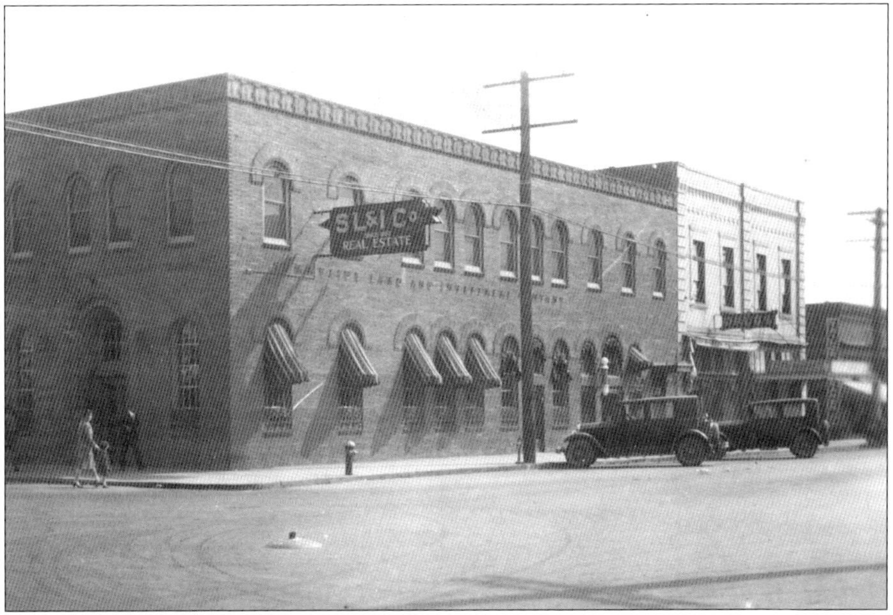

S. L. I. Company at 6th and Edison in the 1920s.

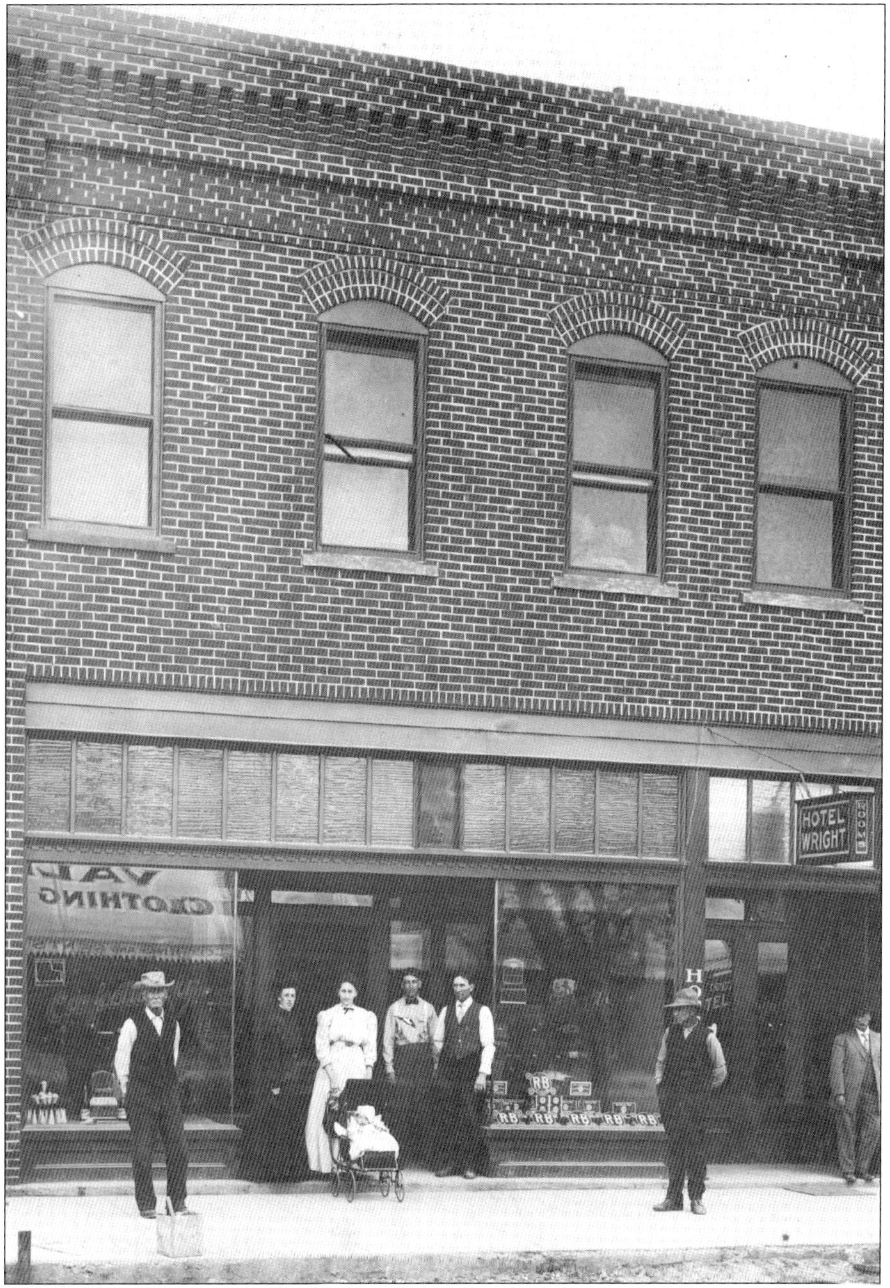

Eddy's Confectionery and Cigar Store. Pictured from left are Hugh McCulloch, Clara Black Libby Eddy with Dorothy Black in the stroller, Ben Howel, Lou Eddy, unidentified, and Billie Wright of the Hotel Wright.

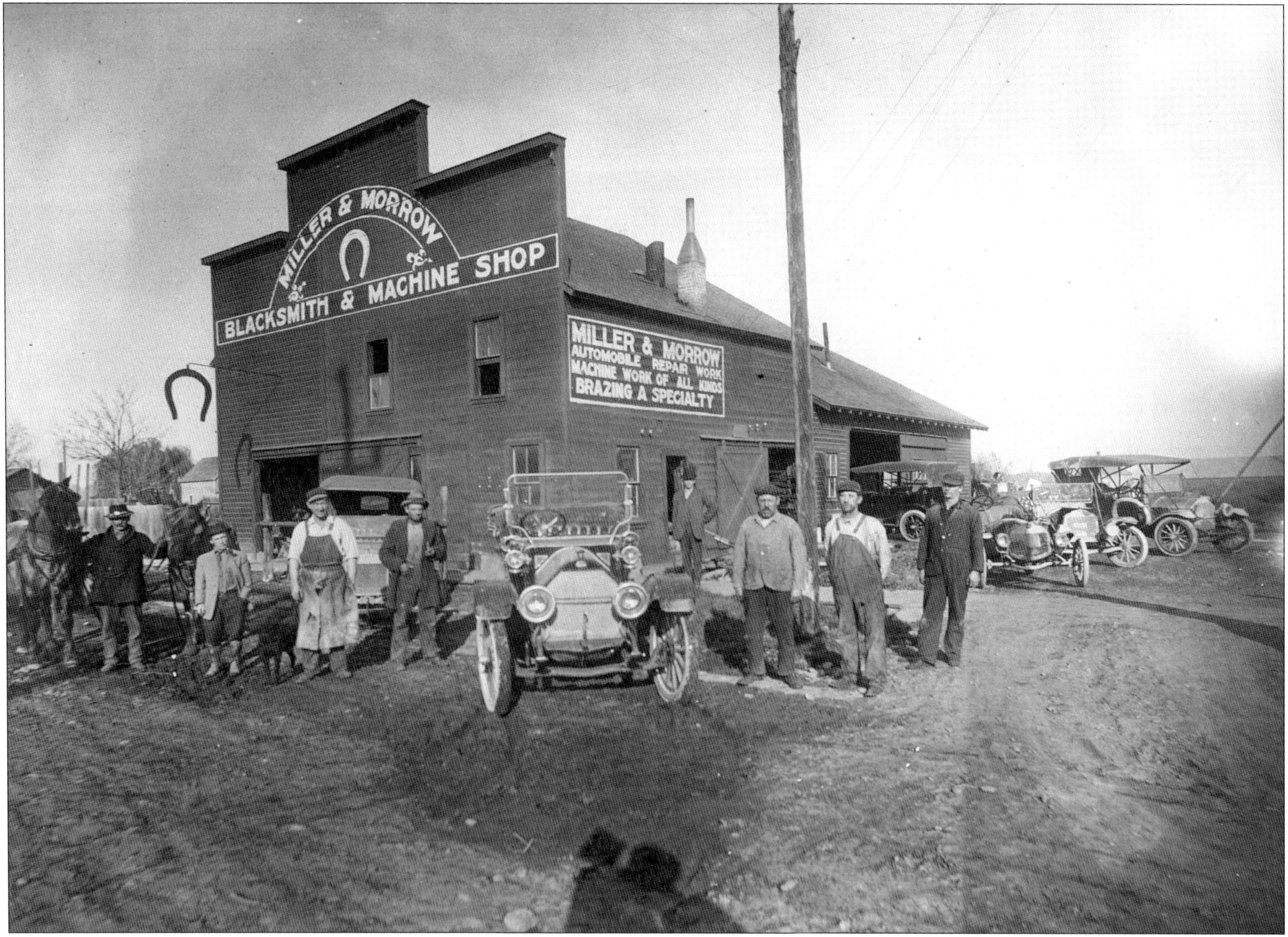

Miller & Morrow Blacksmith & Machine Shop, circa 1922.

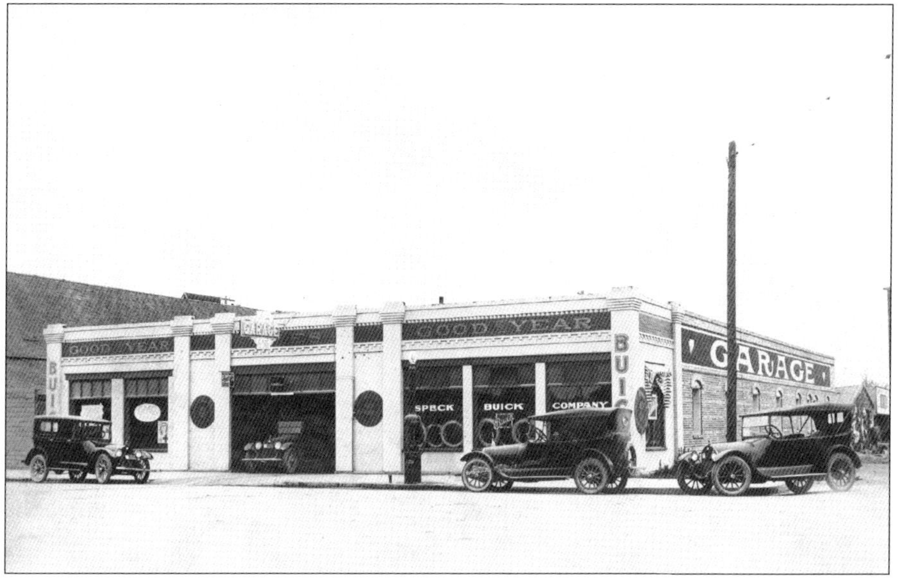

Speck Buick Company first opened in 1912 on the southeast corner of 5th street and Edison Ave. Clayton Speck started the business which was the first Buick dealership in the state.

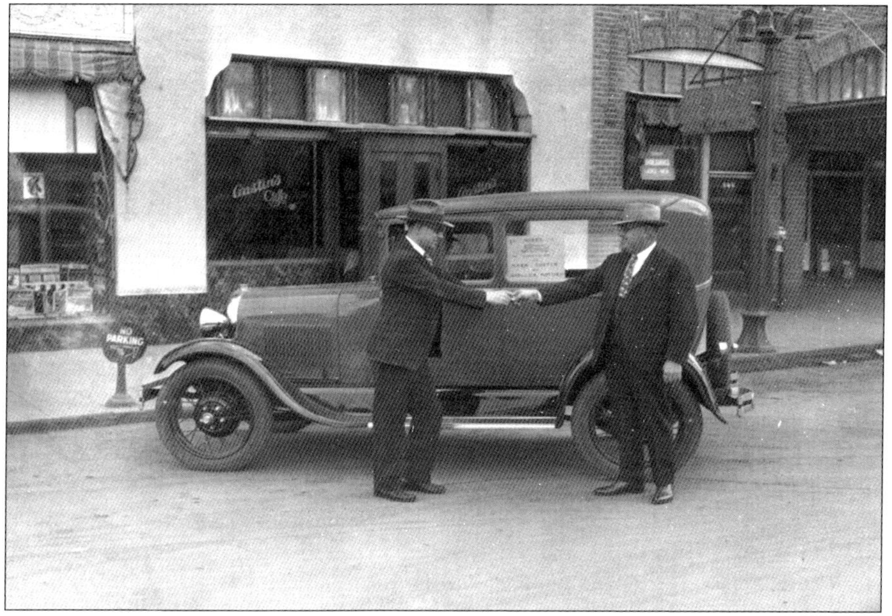

Roscoe Sheller selling a Ford Model A 2-door sedan, circa 1928.

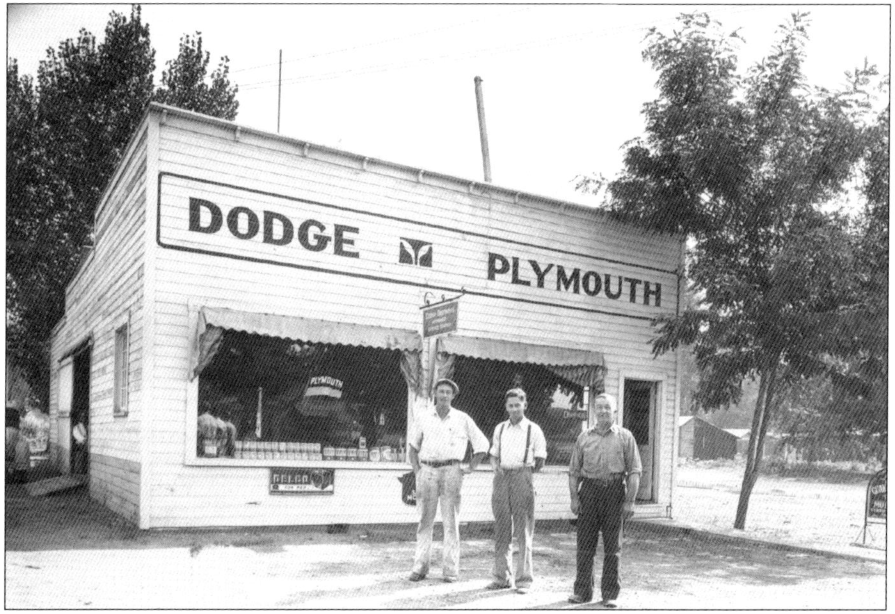

The Dodge-Plymouth Garage located on the southwest corner of 6th Street and Franklin Avenue, circa 1928.

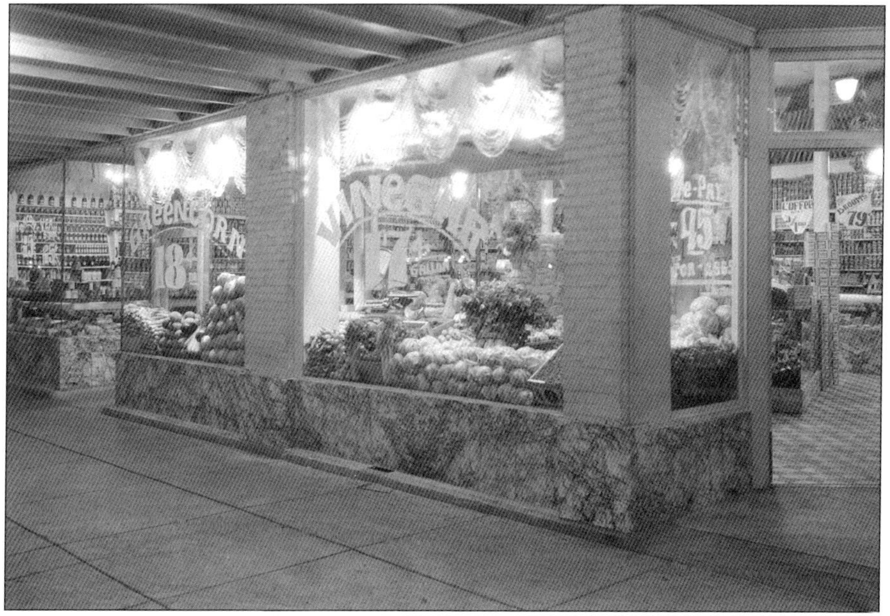

City Market at 6th and Edison, 1929.

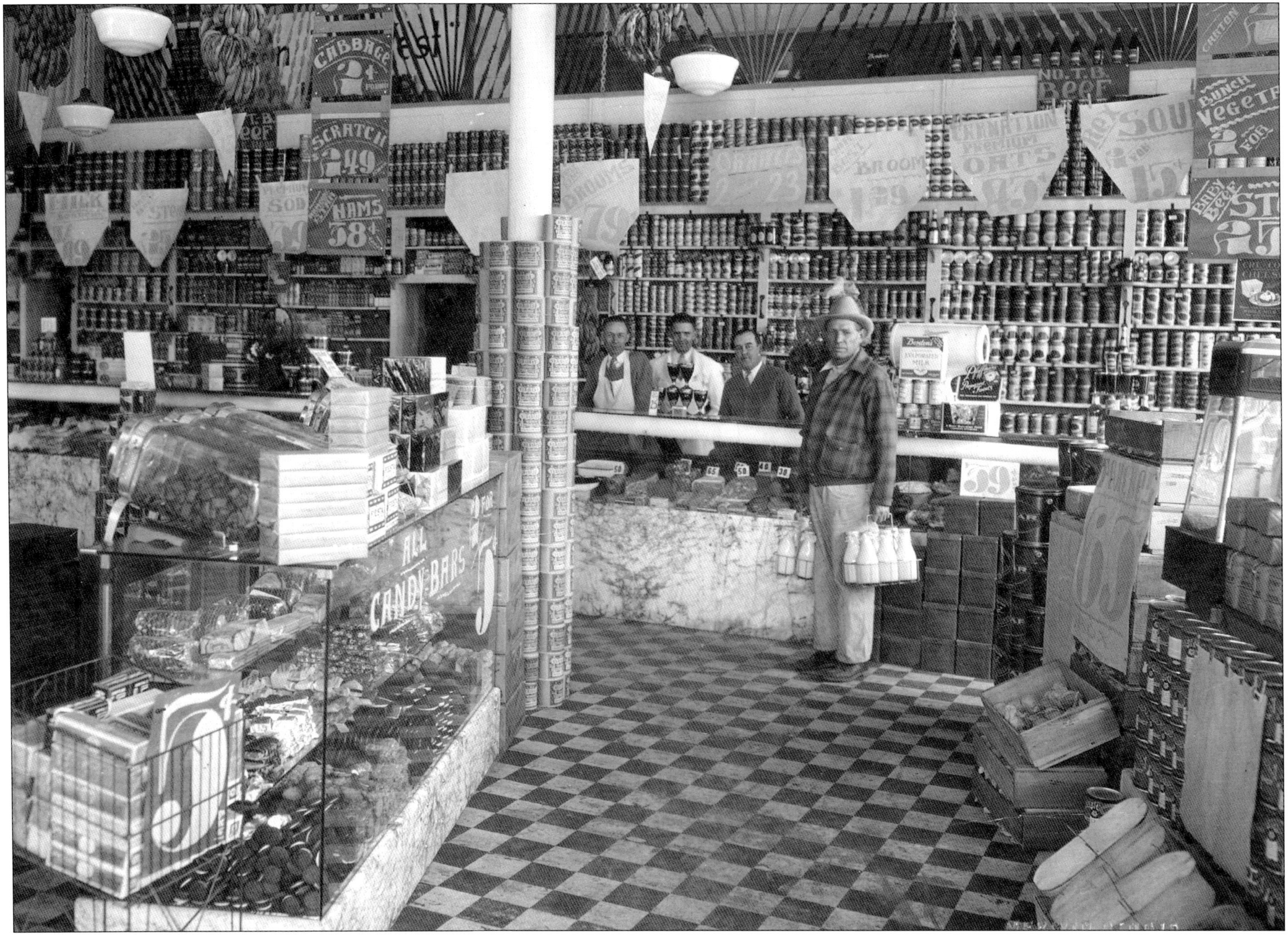

Interior of City Market, 1929. The market was located on the southwest corner of 6th Street and Edison Avenue at the site of the present-day Centennial Park.

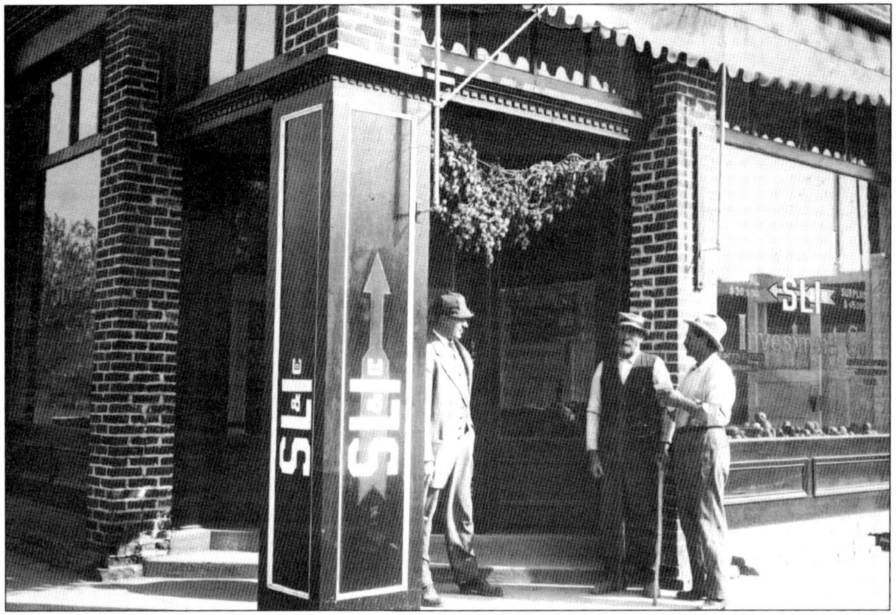

Sunnyside Land & Investment Company, circa 1930.

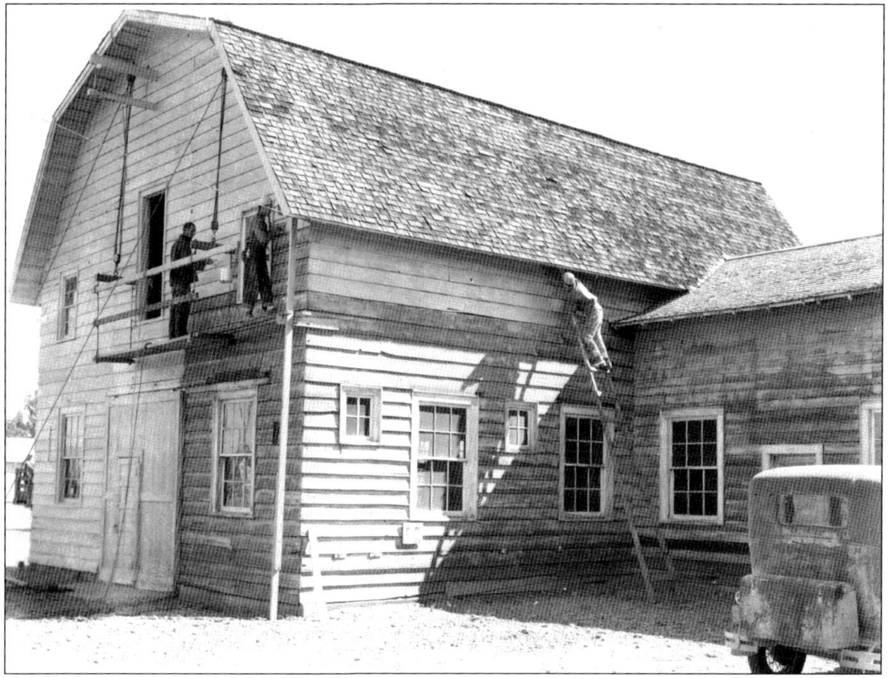

Civilian Conservation Corp (CCC) enrollees painting the Bureau of Reclamation Machine Shop in Sunnyside May 19, 1939. The shop sat at the corner of 11th Street and Blaine Avenue where the present-day Sunnyside Valley Irrigation headquarters now stands.

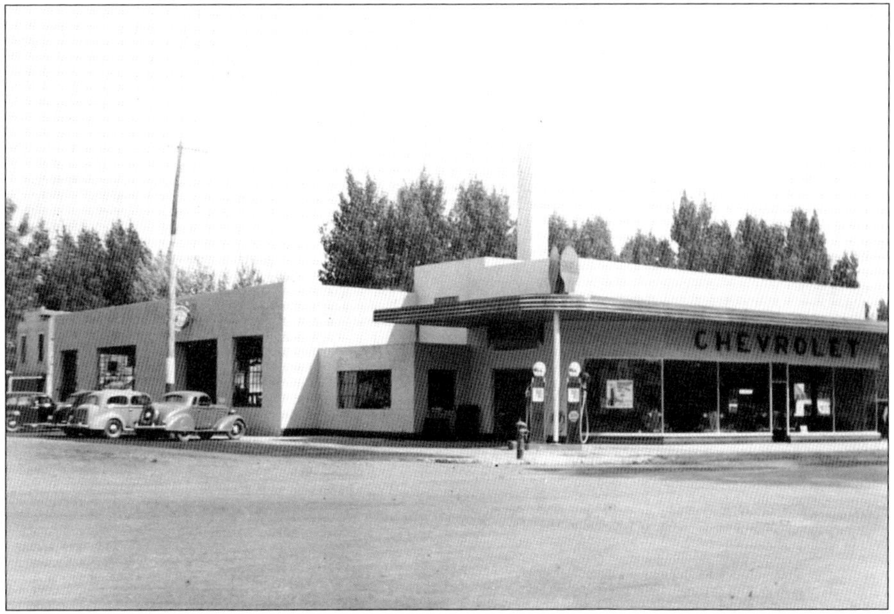

Speck Motor Company, circa 1940. This is the present-day location of the Sunnyside Daily Sun News on 6th Street and Franklin Avenue.

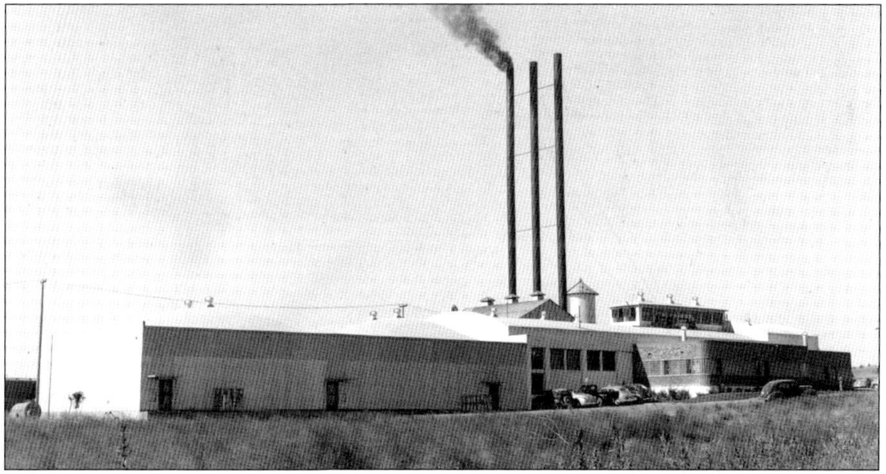

Morning Milk Company's evaporated milk plant in Sunnyside. Building still stands at the corner of Lincoln Avenue and 1st Street.

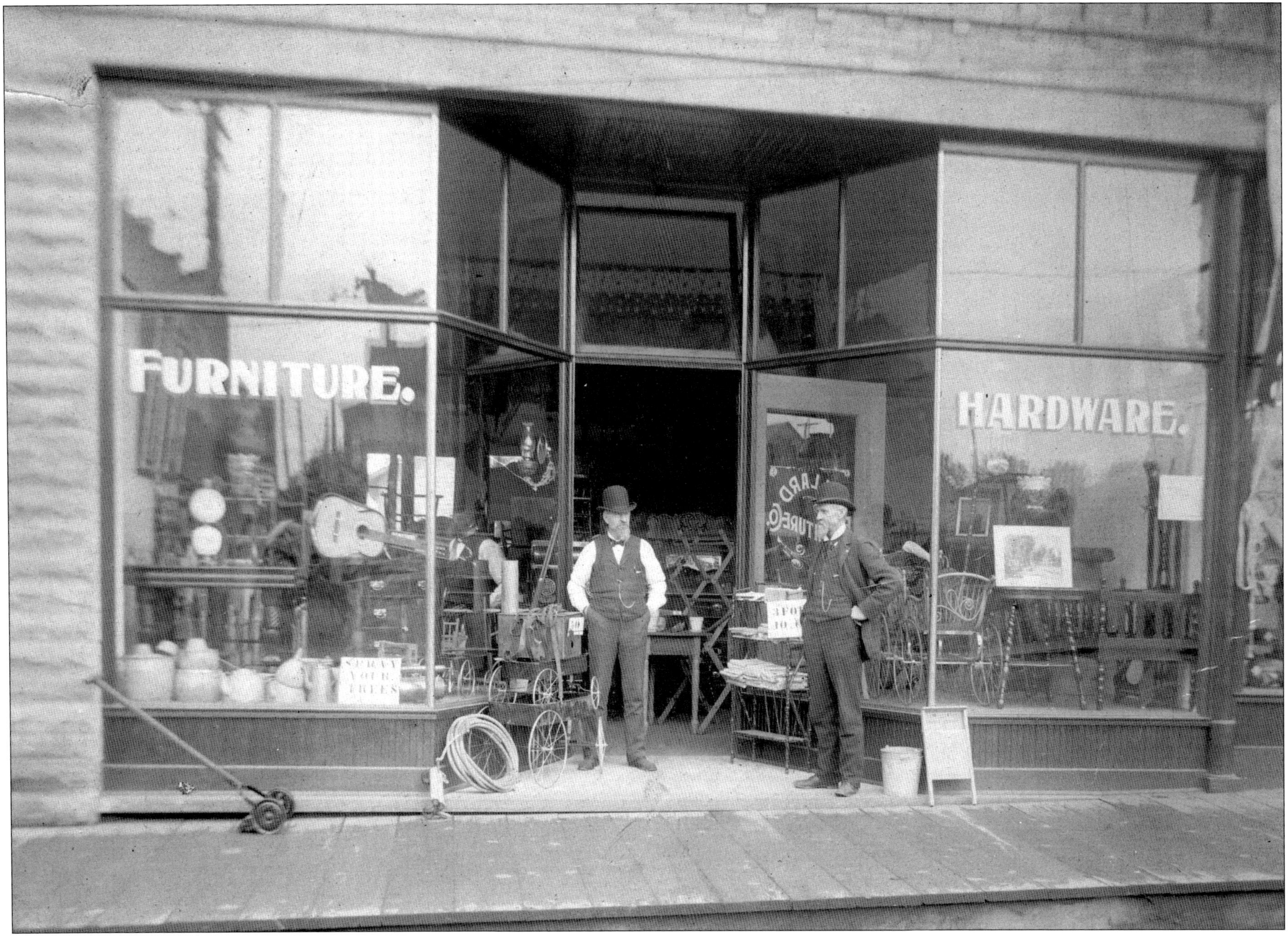

Furniture and hardware store.

PUBLIC SERVICE

As early as 1901 Sunnyside's citizens began clamoring for incorporation. Incorporation would allow the town to elect officials, pass taxes, sell municipal bonds, and engage in projects to better the community. To qualify for incorporation, Sunnyside needed a minimum of 300 residents. A census was taken, and the town was found to be 20-25 people short of the required number. Unwilling to accept defeat, the town persuaded a few tent dwellers in the country to pitch their tents inside the city limits. At the same time Christian Rowland, the Christian Cooperative Colony's recruiter and one of it founders, arrived from the Midwest with a number of new immigrants. A new census put the town's population at 314.

With the population hurtle cleared, an election was set for September 2, 1902. On the ballot were candidates for mayor, town council, and the measure to incorporate. All of the town's 45 qualified voters cast a ballot. When the votes for incorporation were tallied, it was found that two had left their ballots blank, one had voted against the measure, and 42 had voted for it. Sunnyside was officially incorporated.

James Henderson, a druggist and one of Sunnyside's first residents, became the town's first mayor. One of the first ordinances set the town marshal's salary at $5 a month, and another raised money for street improvement by accessing a $2 annual poll tax from every male citizen 21 years of age or older.

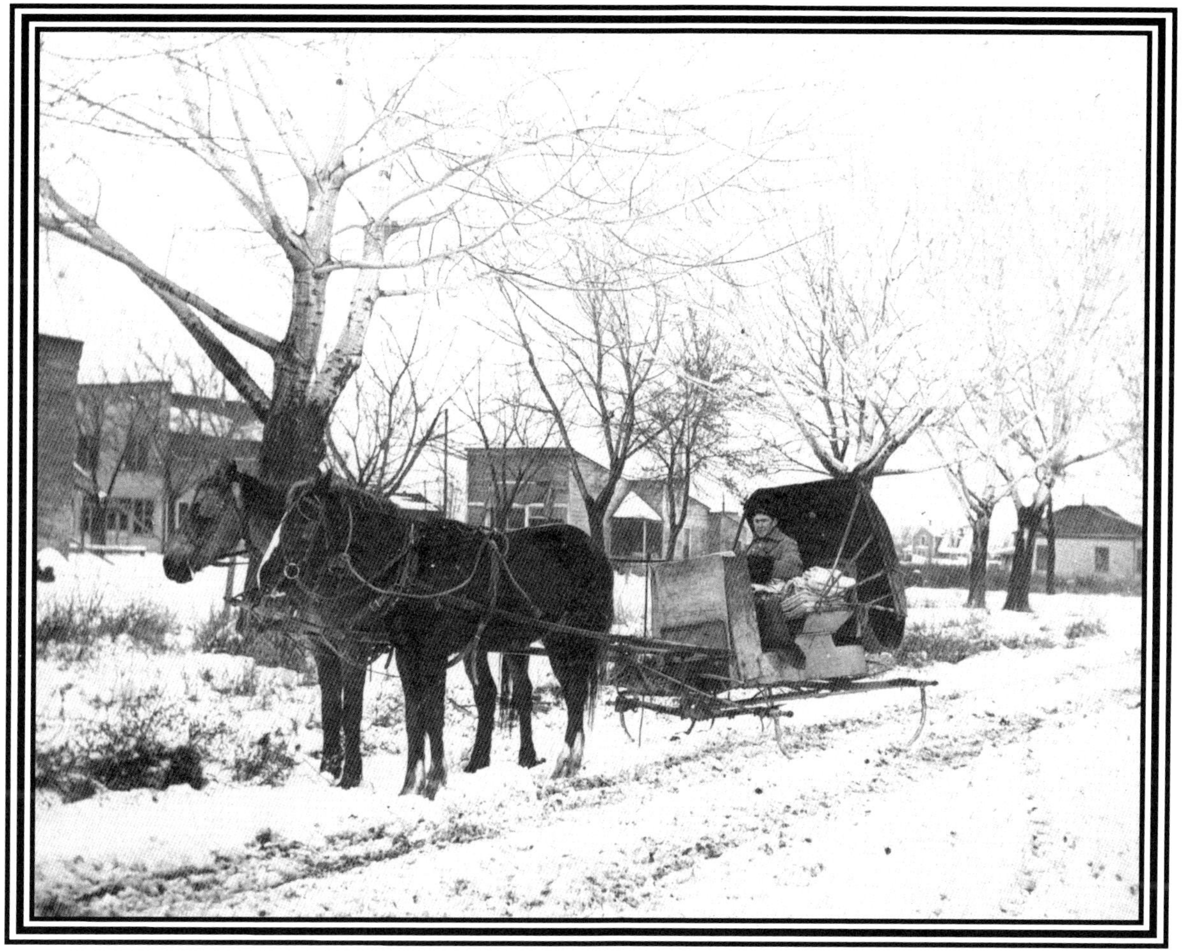

Orin B. Gregory on his mail route, November 17, 1907.

CITY OF SUNNYSIDE, WASHINGTON

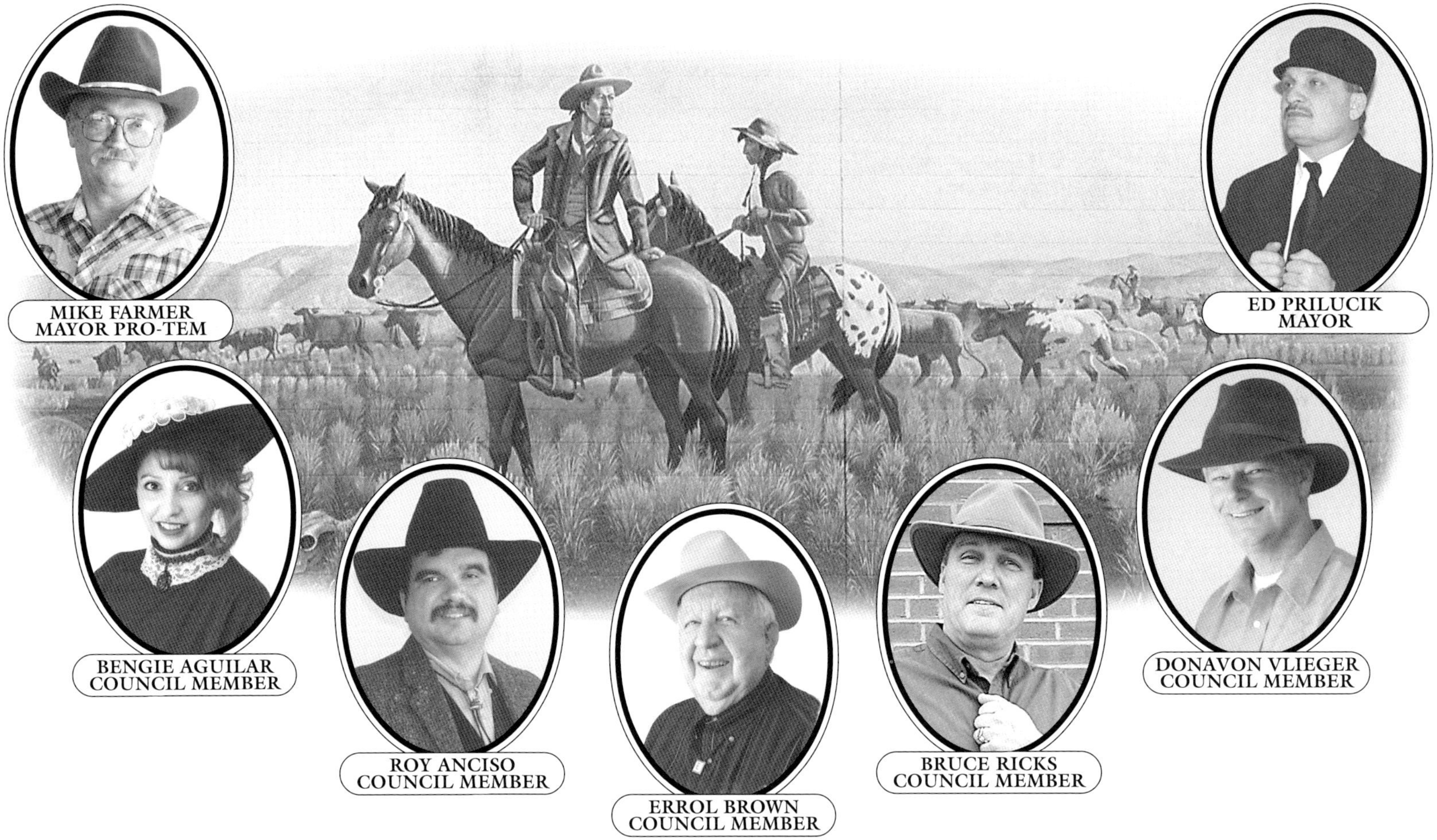

1902 ~ 2002

Join The Sunnyside City Council In Recognition Of The Grand History Of Sunnyside And Its Transition From A Sagebrush-Desert Environment To An Outstanding Northwest Community.

~ SUNNYSIDE CENTENNIAL CELEBRATION ~

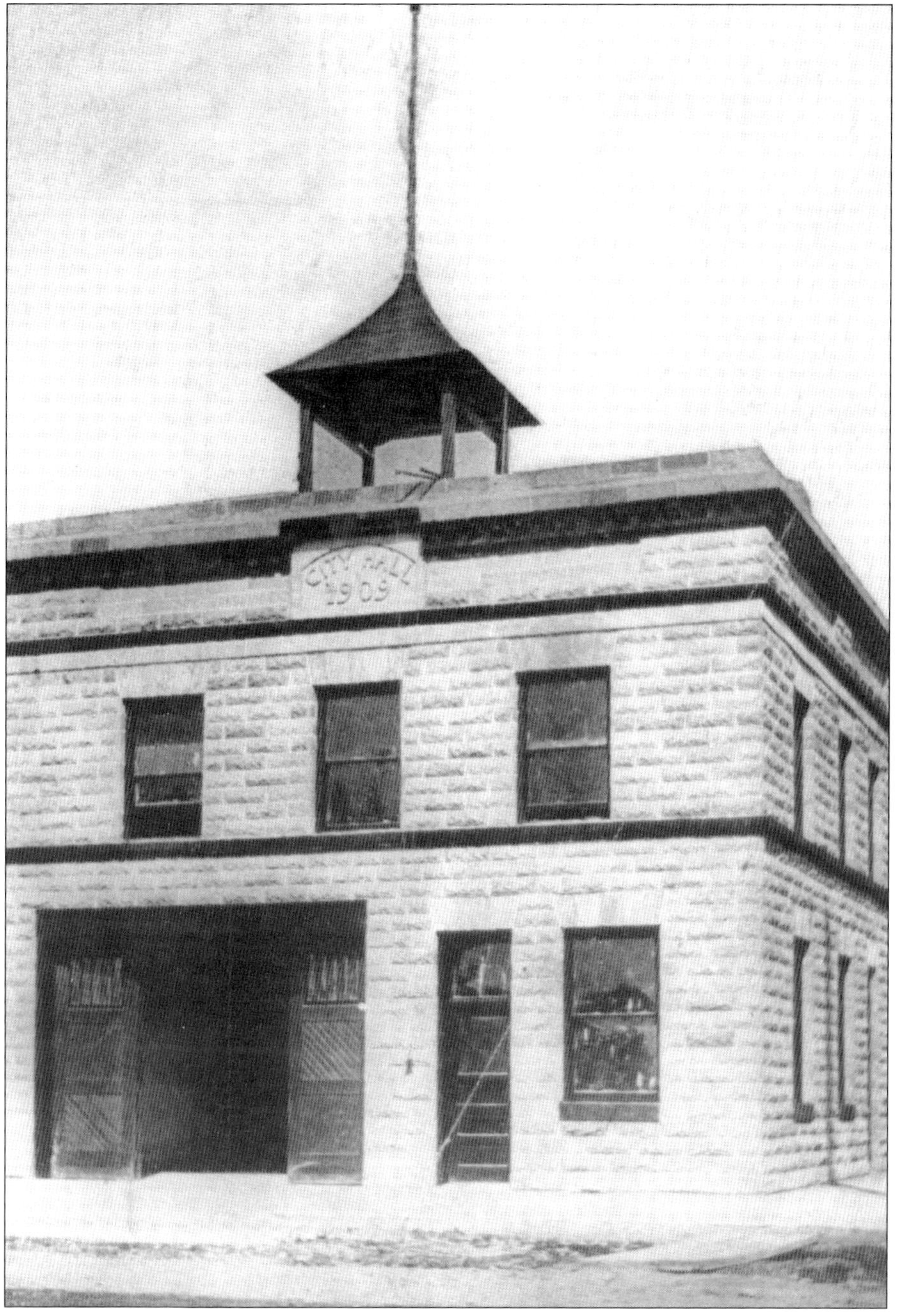

Sunnyside City Hall, circa 1915. The building still stands on the northeast corner of 6th Street and Decatur Avenue.

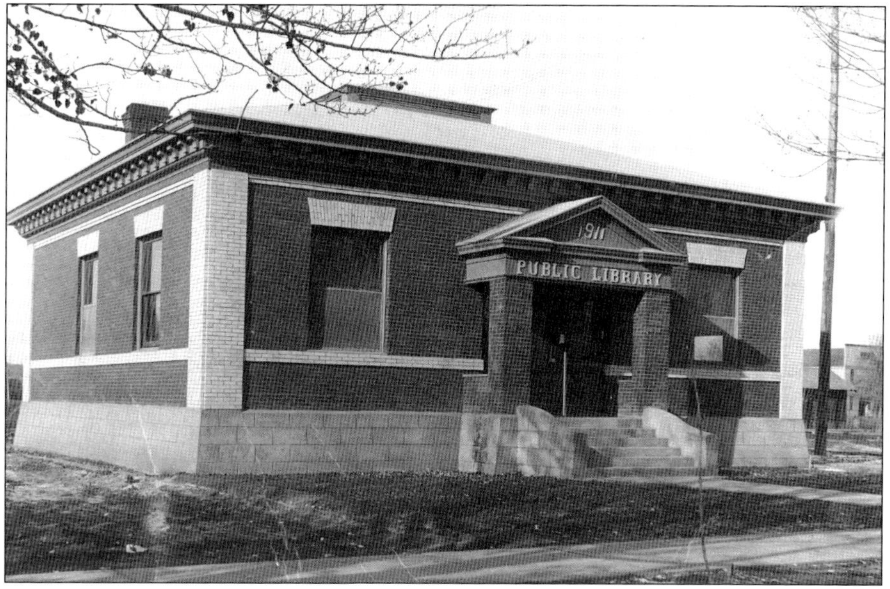

Sunnyside Public Library shortly after its completion in 1911. It was one of the many Carnegie Libraries. Located at the present-day Library location of 7th Street and Grant Avenue.

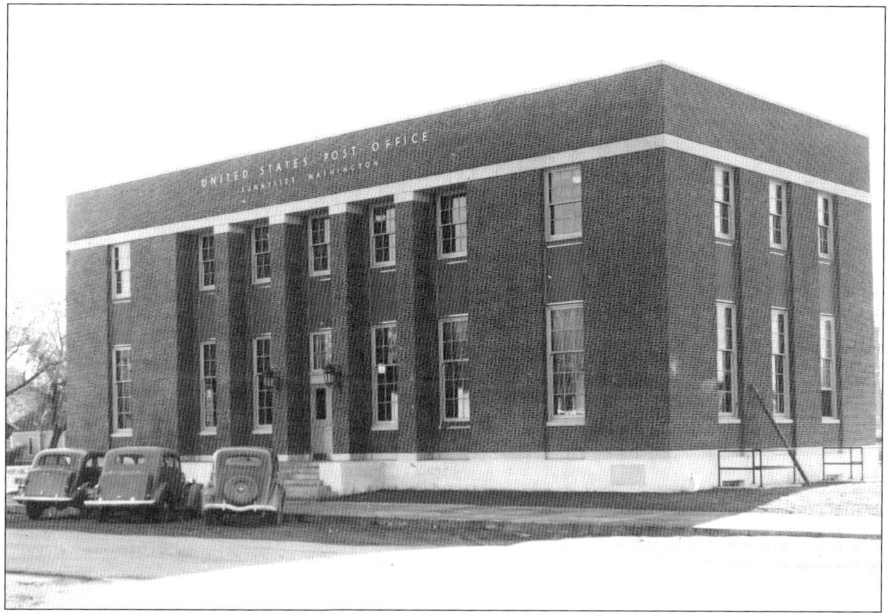

The Sunnyside Post Office opened in November of 1937 at 7th and Edison.

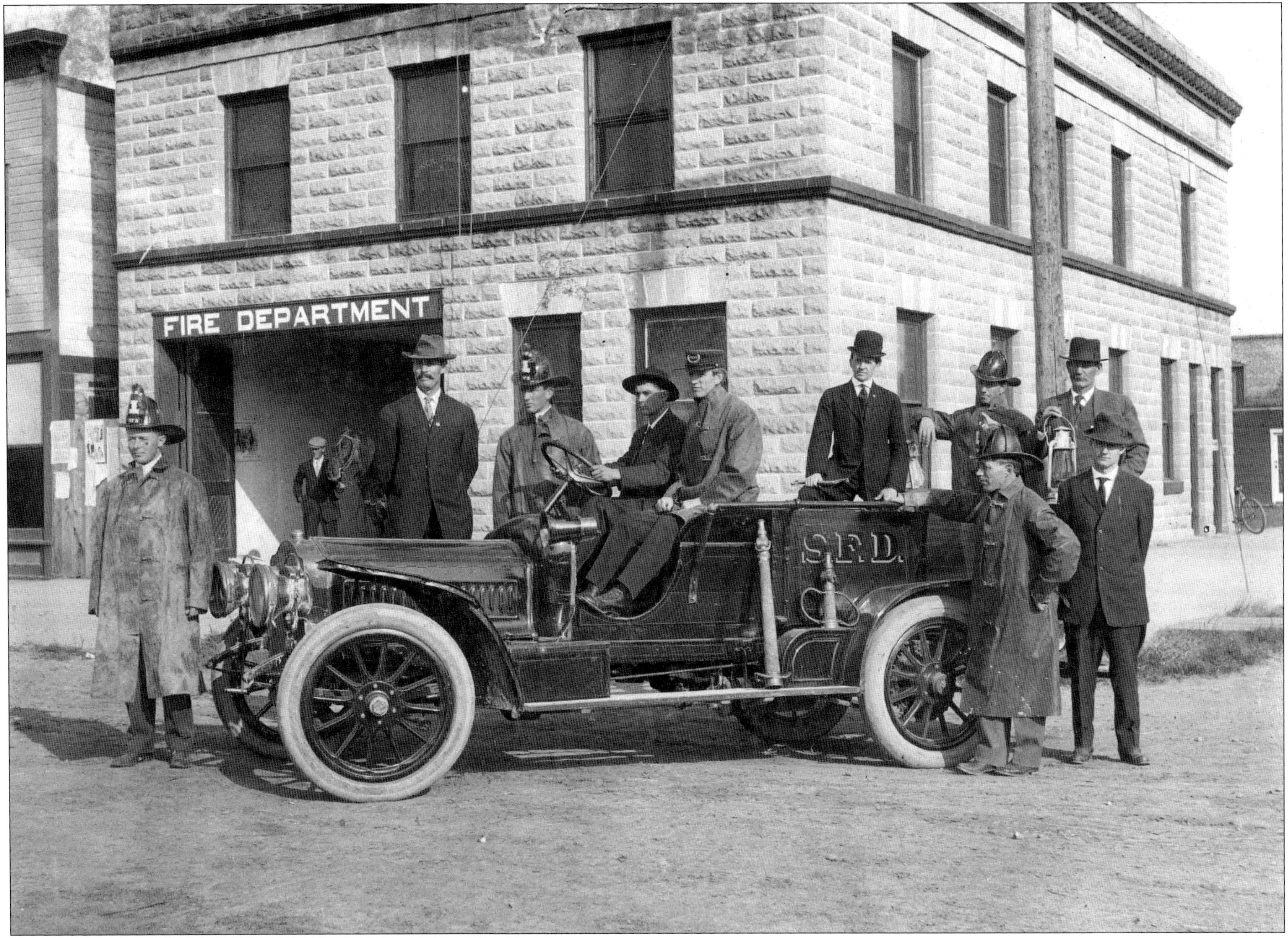

The Sunnyside Fire Department gathered around their new motorized truck which they purchased from Mark Sharp of Outlook. Located in front of the original City Hall at the corner of 6th Street and Decatur Avenue. Photo circa 1913.

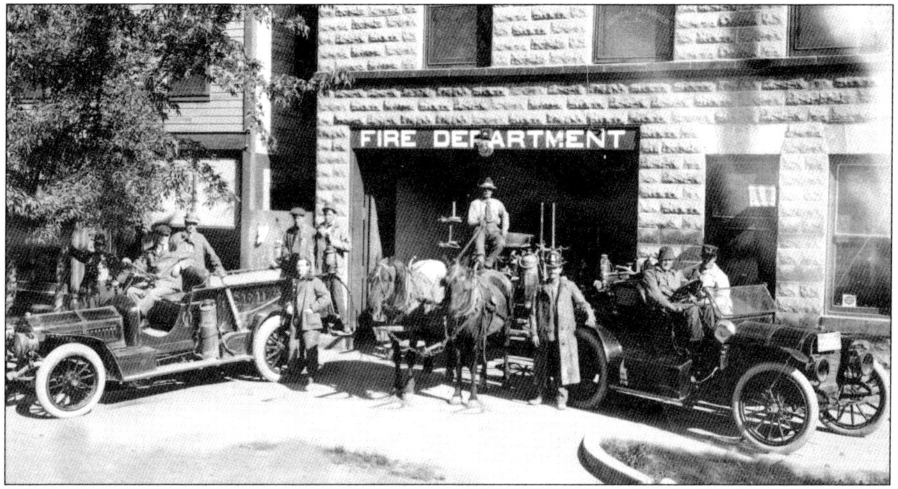

Sunnyside Fire Department, circa 1920.

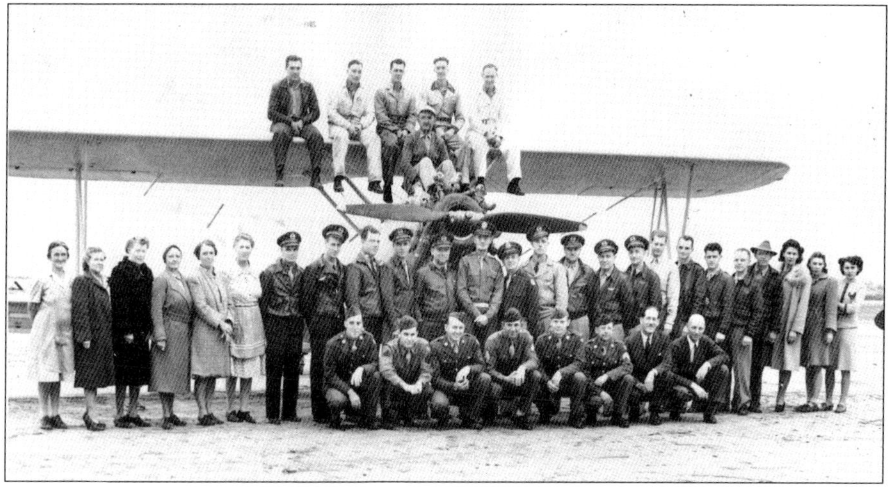

This is a photo of Army and Air force pilots and support crew who trained at the present-day Airport Ranch site on Bethany Road, Northwest of Sunnyside. Photo was taken approximately 1944. Pictured are front (left to right) Cpl. Davies, Art Whitaker, Cpl Higgins, Mr. Brown, Sgt. Lake, Sgt. Ripley, Sgt. Stanley, and Cpl. Cob. Second Row (L to R) Mrs. Alice Van Eaton, Eloise Asselstine, Mrs. Fannie Forrestt, Martha Aiken, Mrs. Nell Zilliox, Emily Tester, Mrs. Hazel Cline, Ernest Schokley, Maxine Mitzlaff, Jimmie Doaks, Mrs. Goldie Hoon, George Fane, Lyle Bonney, Dave ?, Ralph Stevens, Wayne Dugan, Joe Halsey, Bob Owens, Andy Silani, Doyle Dayton, Chet Stinson, Frank Barker, Lt. Robinson, Milton Donner and Lt. Thom. Top of the engine Mac McCarty. Top of wing (L to R) Antone (Tony) Steinback, Van Ott and Wallace St. Mars.

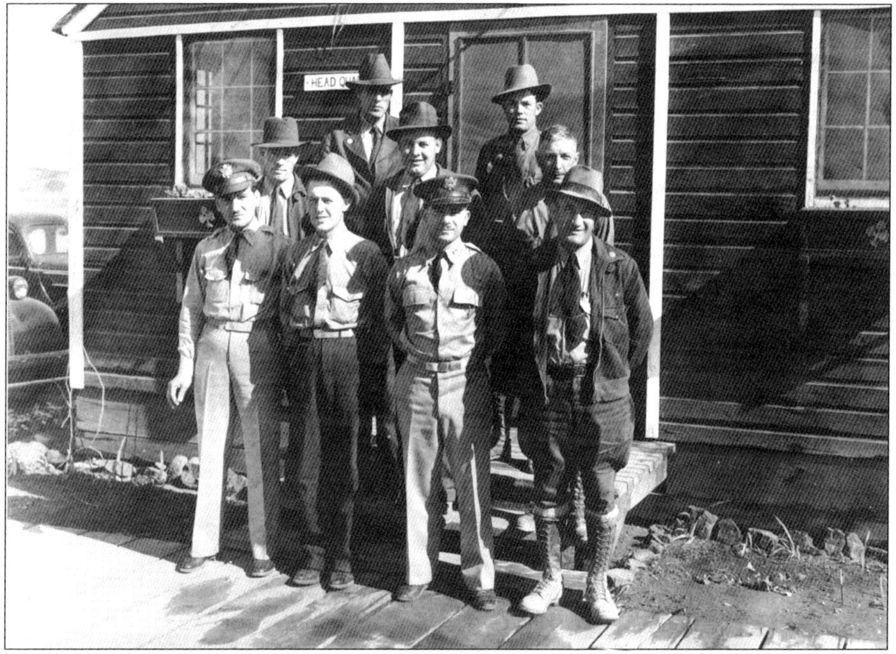

Camp BR-58 Army and Bureau of Reclamation personnel in 1939. Front row, left to right: Lt. Gaspard Massie; John Simpson, Jr. Foreman; Lt. Benedict Giacalone and Mike Waszack, Jr. Foreman. Second Row - W.L. Granger, Machine Operator; Robert Hansen, Jr. Foreman, and Robert Dick, General Foreman. Third Row - Paul Turner, Camp Superintendent and F.E. McCoy, Jr. Foreman.

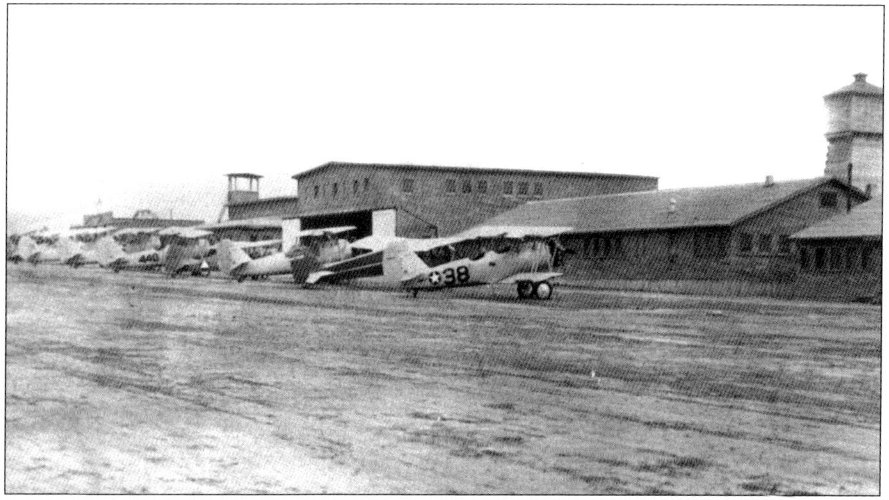

This line up of planes at the Airport Ranch was taken by Frank Barker, Chief Pilot in 1944. It shows the line of airplanes used to train pilots.

PEOPLE

The Panic of 1893, one of the worst economic depressions in U.S. history, hit Sunnyside hard in the mid 1890's. By the end of 1894 Sunnyside was a bustling little town with a growing business district and a population of about 100. By 1898 every business except William H. Cline's general store had closed, and the population dipped to just seven families. The Northern Pacific Railroad went bankrupt, and the Sunnyside townsite company, a subsidiary of the railroad, also failed.

The town was brought back from near death by Stephen J. Harrison, a minister from Iowa; Harvey M. Lichty, a banker and former college professor from Nebraska; and Christian Rowland, a bank president and farmer from Illinois. All three men had dreamed of building a Christian community. After meeting at a church conference, they agreed to pool their resources and form the Christian Cooperative Colony. The group purchased the Sunnyside townsite in 1898 and began recruiting. Ads were put in church newspapers across the Midwest. One such ad read, "We are building a community of church people who have no fear to express their conviction against saloons, Sunday desecration, dancing, horse racing, gambling, and other such vices."

The town's population began quickly to grow again. To insure that the community kept its Christian values the founders of the colony put a forfeiture clause into every real estate deed. The clause prohibited alcohol, gambling, and prostitution. Anyone found guilty of engaging in such vices forfeited their property back to the colony.

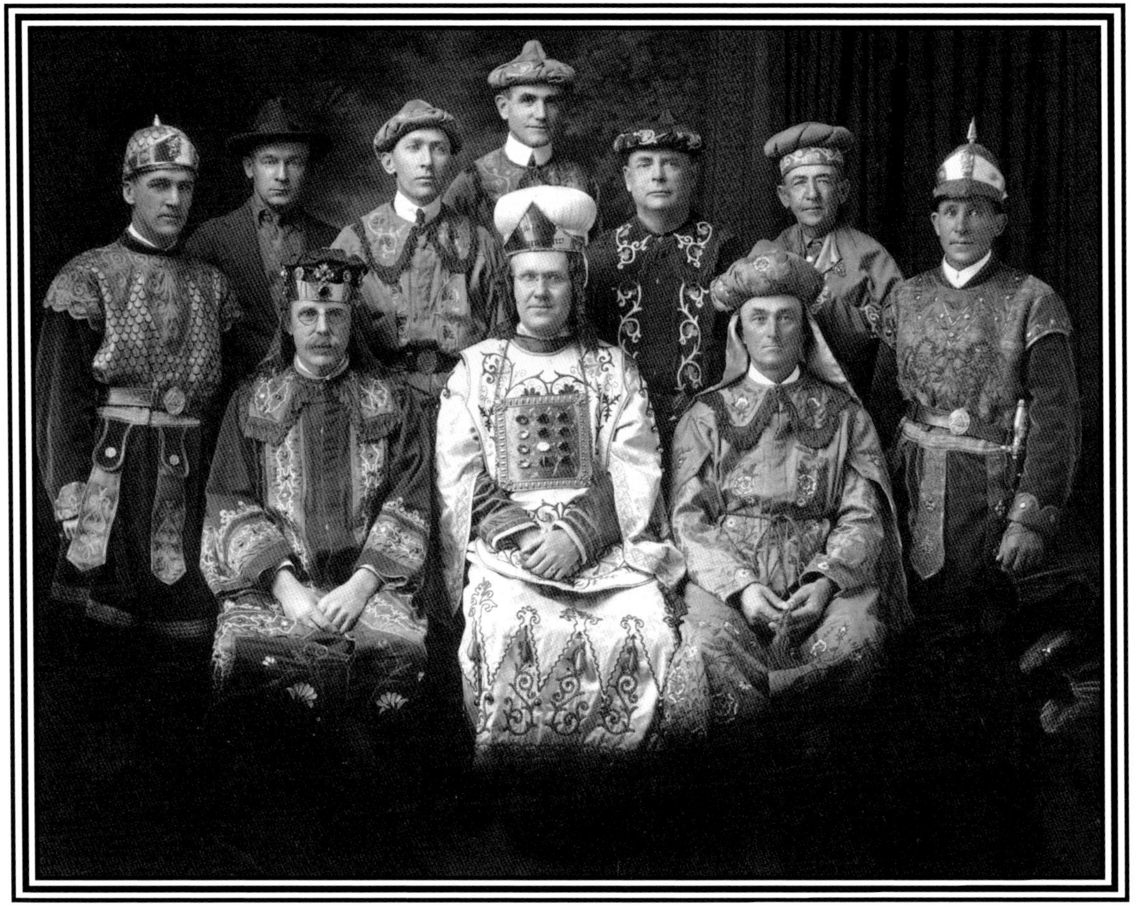

From left, top row, Thad Hall, Fred Langford, Oscar Boose, Arthur Murfin, H. Webber, C. Langford and Harry Gochnour. Front row, Robert McCredie, John Heinze and unidentified.

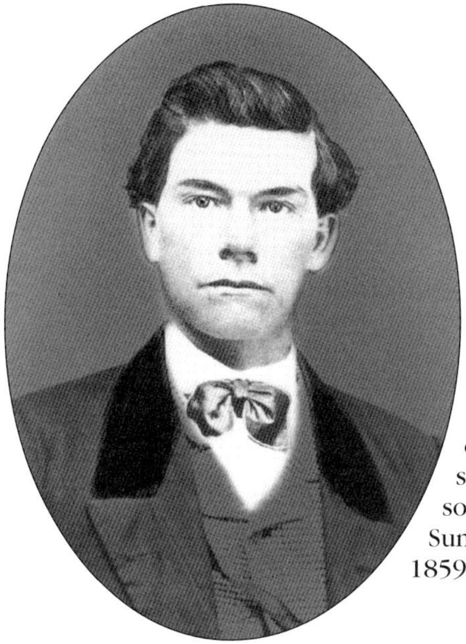

Ben Snipes, Northwest cattle king; settled in southwest Sunnyside in 1859.

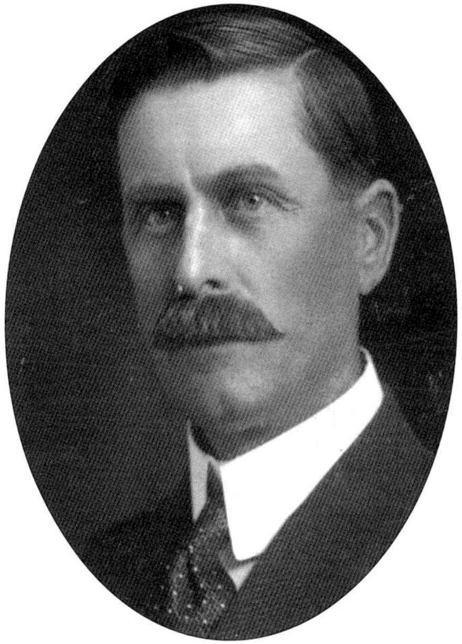

Oliver Renwick Ferrell (Ren) was Ben Snipes' foreman. He was born in California in 1864, came to the valley in 1878 and settled here in 1880.

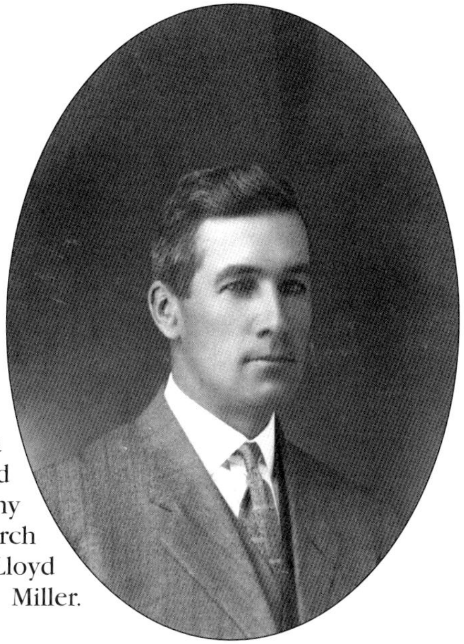

W. H. Harrison, pioneer, businessman and farmer, circa 1901. He formed the S. L. I. Company along with Arch Fleming and Lloyd Miller.

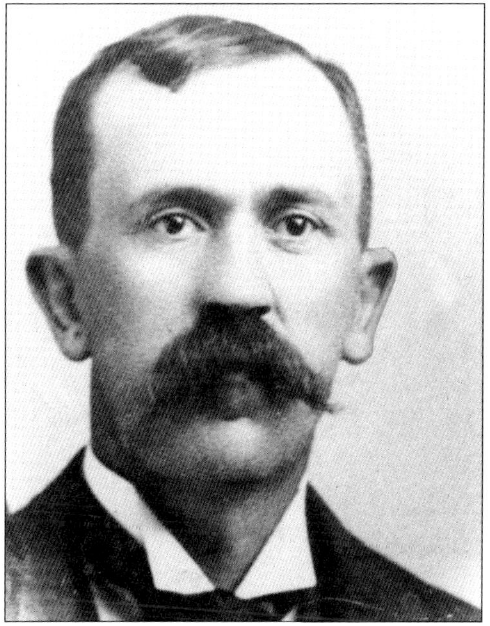

H. M. Lichty moved his family to Sunnyside and co-founded the Christian Cooperative Colony in 1898. He later opened Lichty Market.

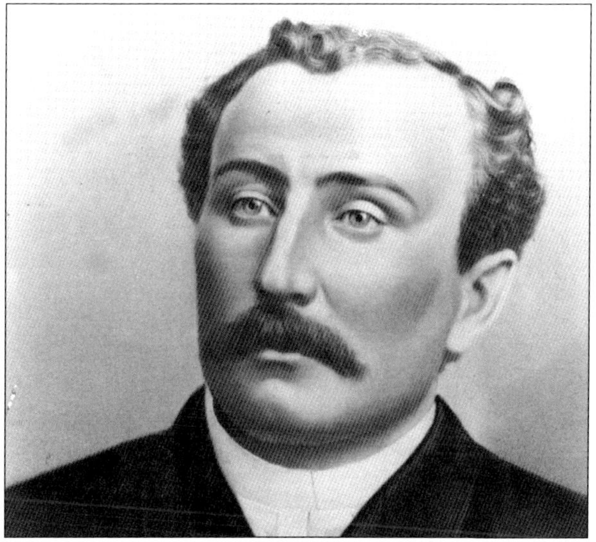

Christian Rowland, Co-founder of Christian Cooperative Colony in 1898.

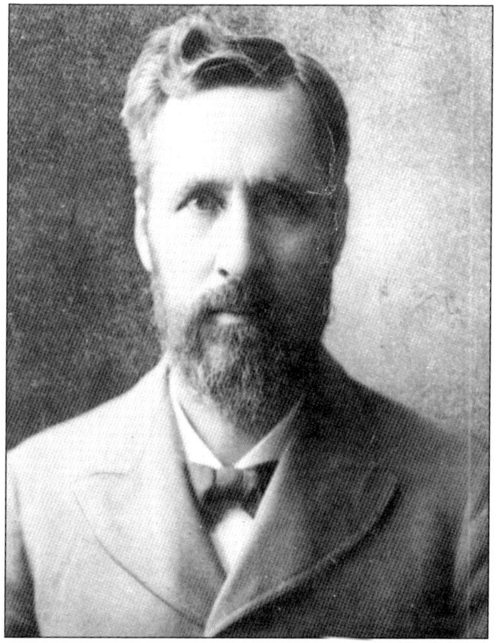

S. J. Harrison came to Sunnyside in 1899. He was a co-founder of the Christian Cooperative Colony.

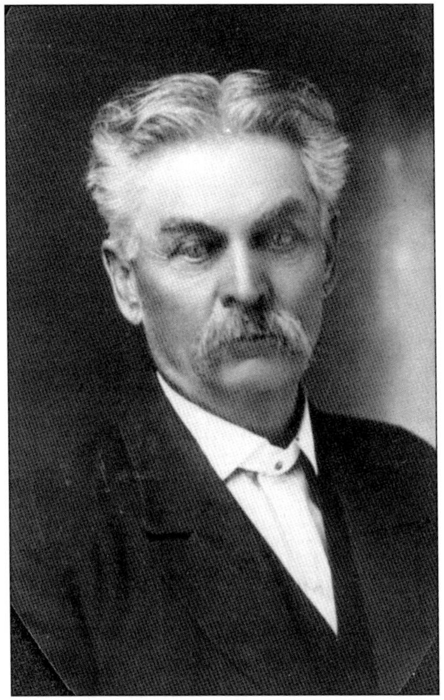

Caleb W. Taylor landed in Mabton in 1893 with his children Emmette and Clarence. He built the community's first school, Cline's store, the Gillis Building, almost all the early buildings in Sunnyside.

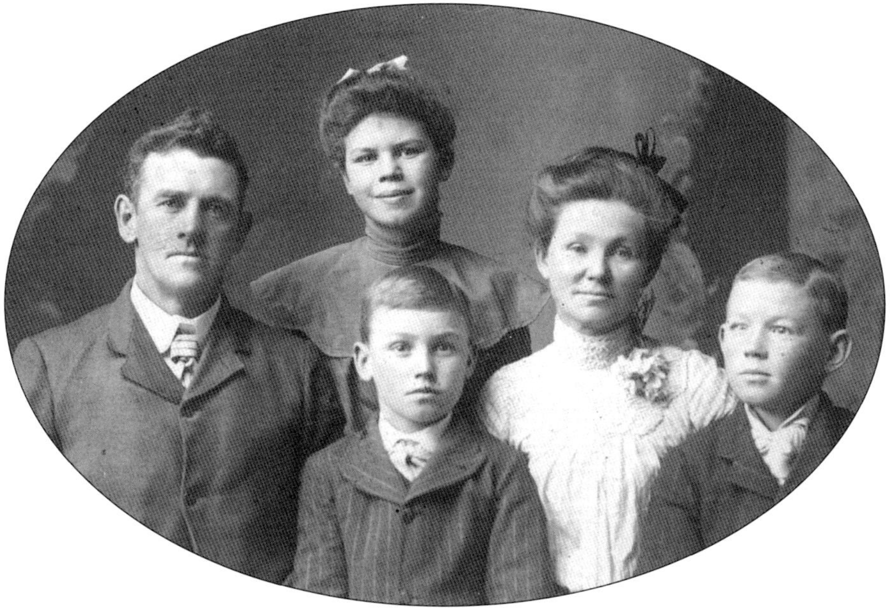

The Emory Thompson family came to the valley in 1893.

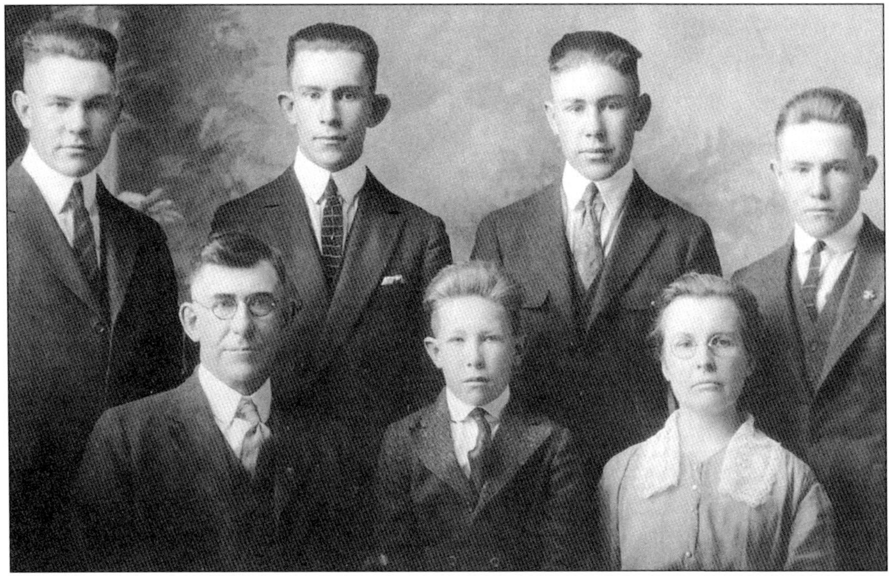

E.A. Morrow Family. Front row from left: Eluster A. Morrow, Paul Morrow and Flossie May Morrow. Back row from left Arvelo Morrow, Ray Morrow, Leonard Morrow and Clint Morrow. Photo circa 1920.

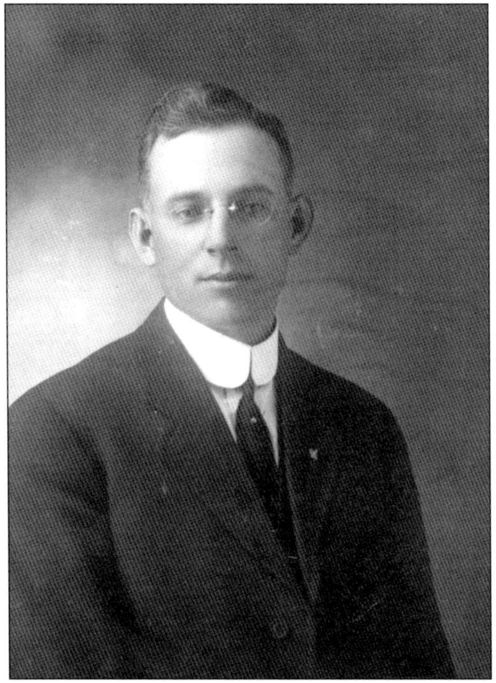

Archie G. Fleming came to Sunnyside in 1899 and held clerical positions in local stores. He later got into the drug business until 1908 when he and W. H. Harrison acquired the Sunnyside Land & Investment Company.

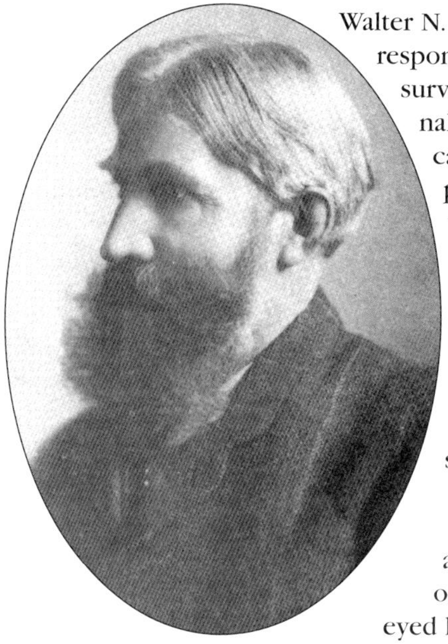

Walter N. Granger, was responsible for surveying original Sunnyside canal and platting the town of Sunnyside.

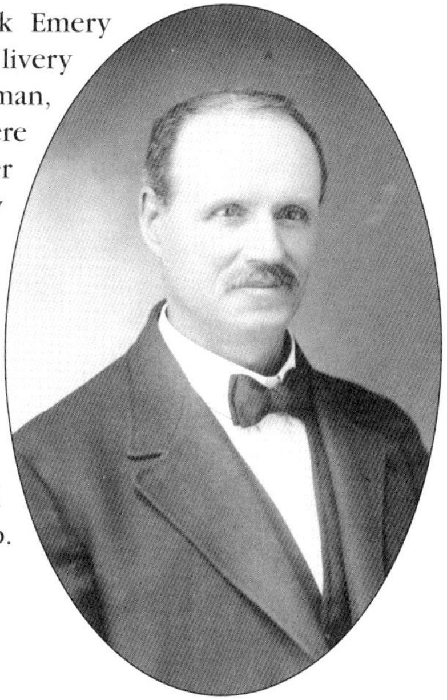

Mark Emery a livery stableman, where never a balky or one-eyed horse was ever hired out for service. Mark's buggies and hacks were always well greased and ready to go.

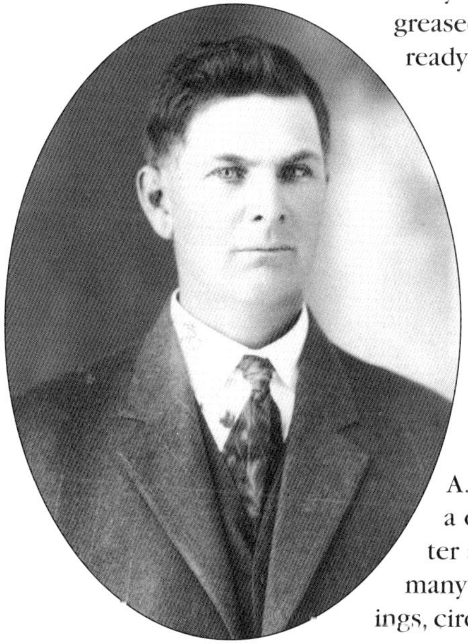

A.P. Eckles was a early carpenter and built many early buildings, circa 1904.

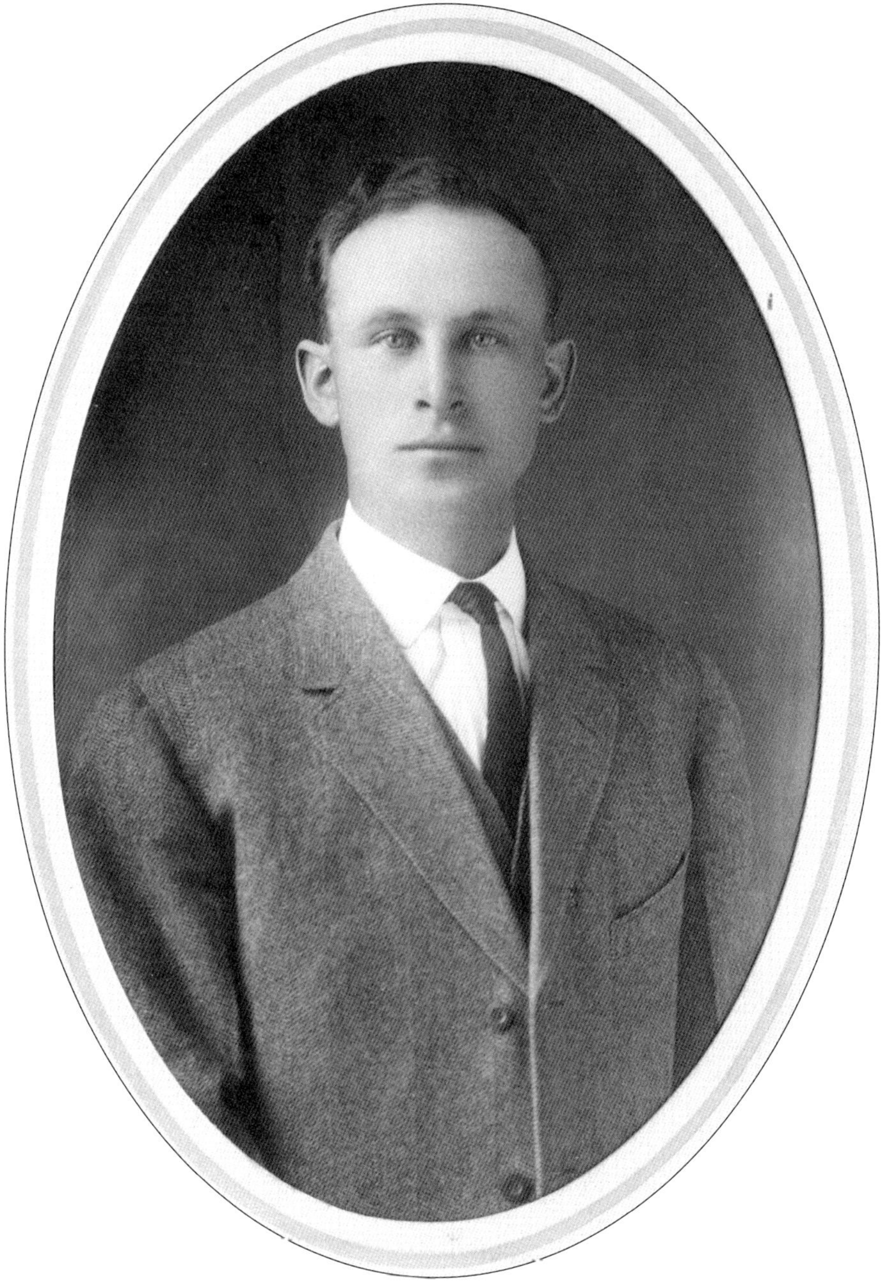

George Gochnour a prominent Auctioneer in Sunnyside's early days.

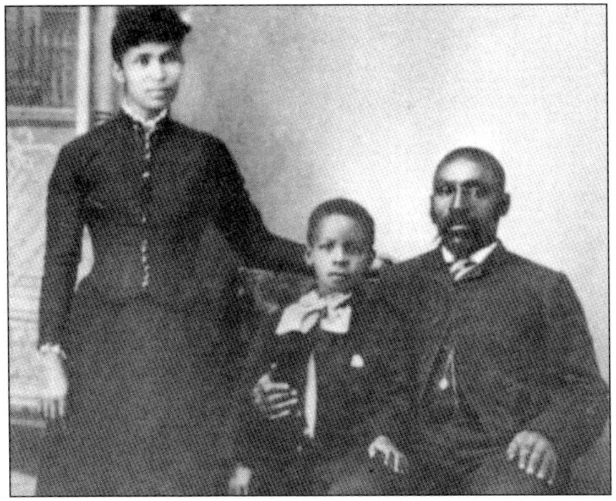

The Ole Washington Family moved to the Sunnyside area in 1891. Always concerned about schools in the area, they donated the land for the Waneta School in 1901.

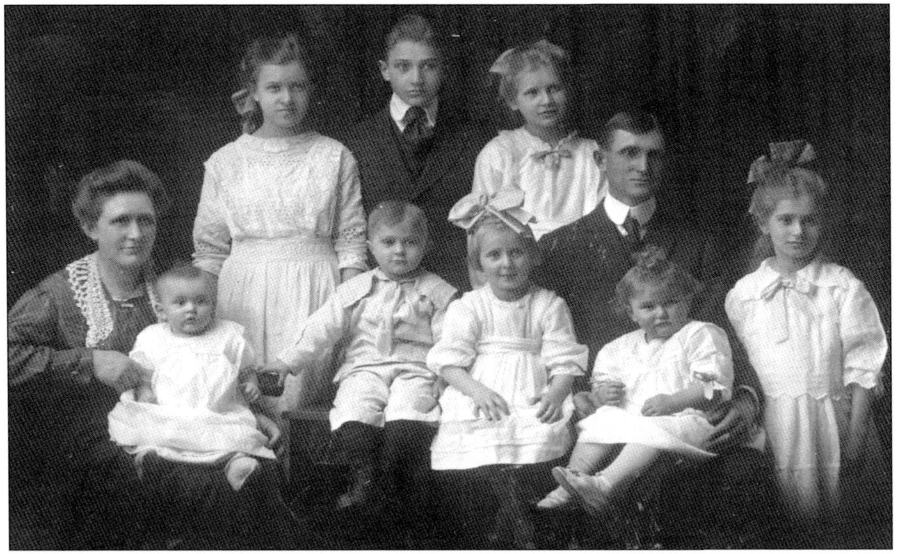

The Herbert Padgham Family. Herbert Padgham came from Farmington, New York and Gertrude Cochram came from Mt. Sterling, Iowa. They met in Naches and married in 1903. They moved to Sunnyside in 1907 and bought acreage on Allen Road. They raised nine children; Kester, Zada, Roberta, Roena, Paul, Pauline, Roxine, Birdena and David.

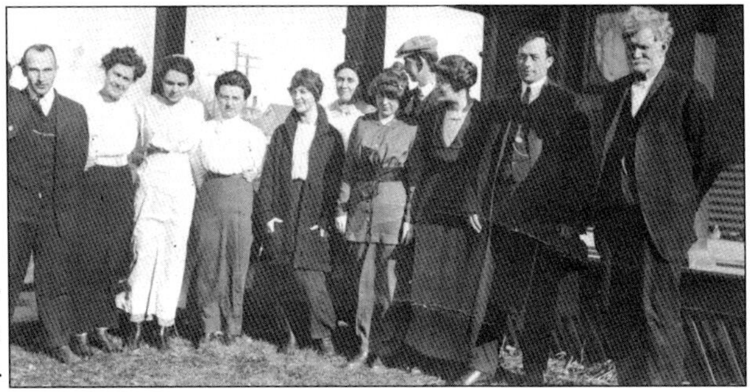

The Peter Shockley Family settled in Outlook in 1910.

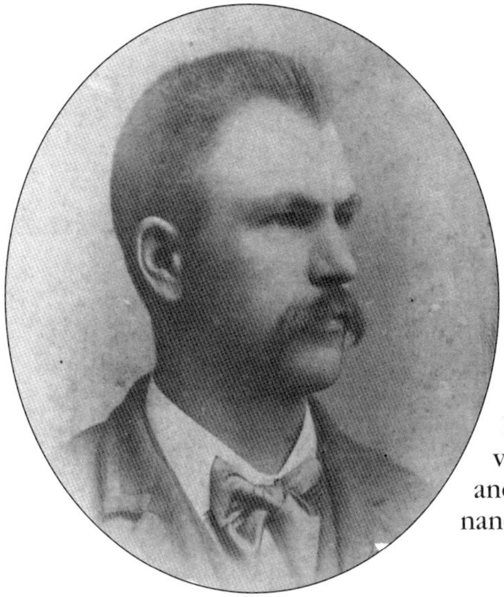

John L. Stackhouse served as engineer on the Sunnyside Project. He built the dam at Parker and he surveyed and laid out the Sunnyside Canal and supervised its digging and maintenance until his death in 1903.

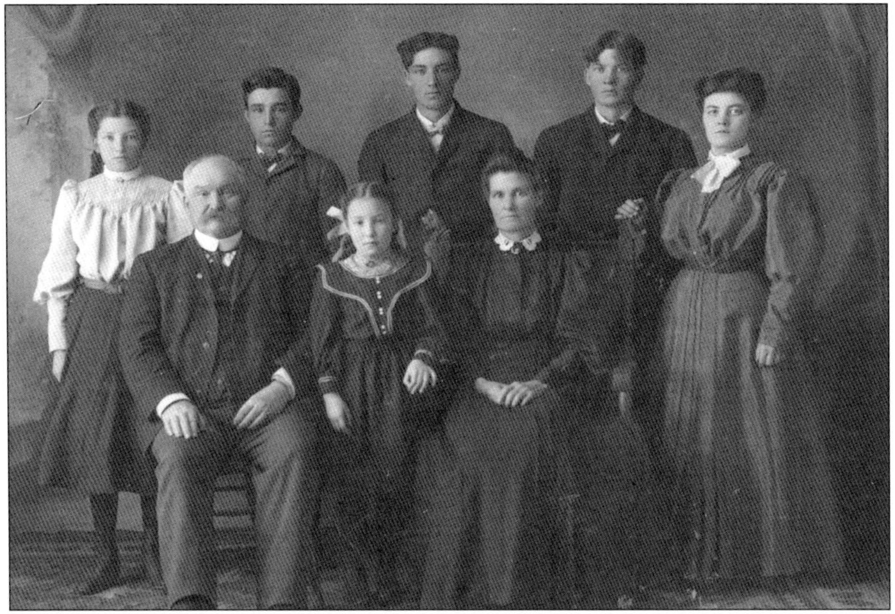

The Peter Shockley Family settled in Outlook in 1910.

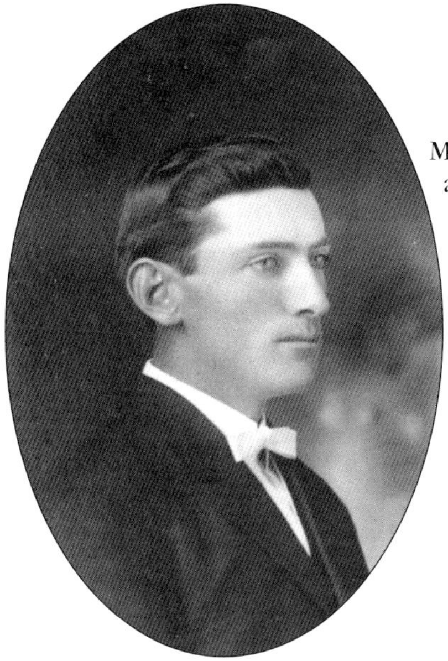

Mr. And Mrs. Eber Vincent arrived in the valley in 1905 and handled cattle on the site of the present golf course. Mrs. Vincent taught school at the Wheatland School near the present Airport Ranch.

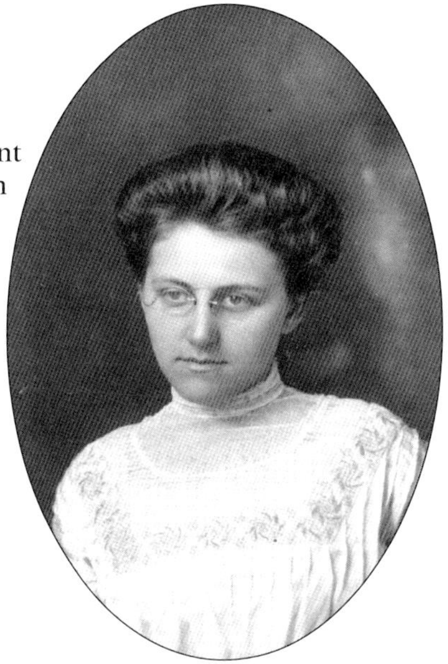

Ed Young was an early day bunch grass merchant who would take your eggs and butter in exchange for flour, red flannels or a corset. While Ed was a bachelor, he owned the only driving horse which knew the way home without Ed touching a single line.

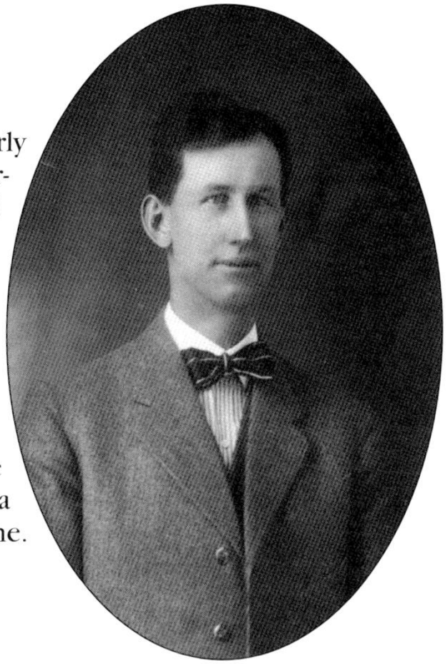

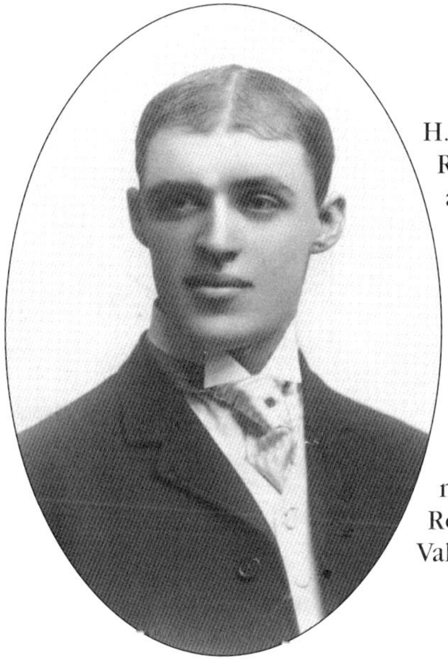

H. Lloyd Miller and his wife Ruth, circa 1907. The Millers arrived in Sunnyside in 1907. H. Lloyd Miller first sold real estate and buggies, but later was made a full partner in the Sunnyside Land and Investment Company. He will always be known for Airport Ranch and his major role in bringing the Roza Irrigation Project to the Valley.

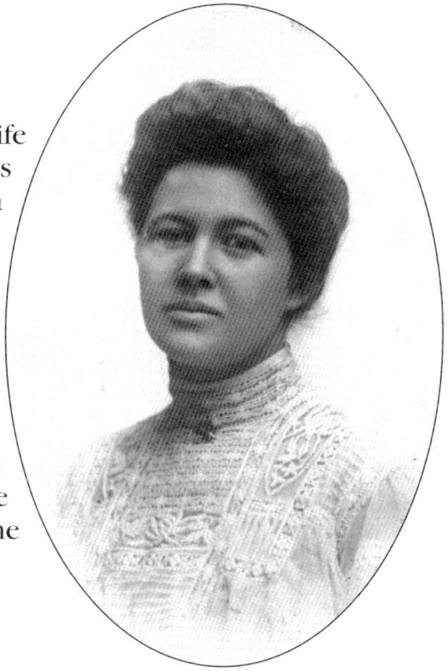

J. B. George, pioneer merchant who "grubstaked" hundreds of pioneer settlers with credit for food and clothing, hardware and implements as they dug homes out of the desert. He was a community builder, school board member, and beloved pioneer citizen who always gave good measure.

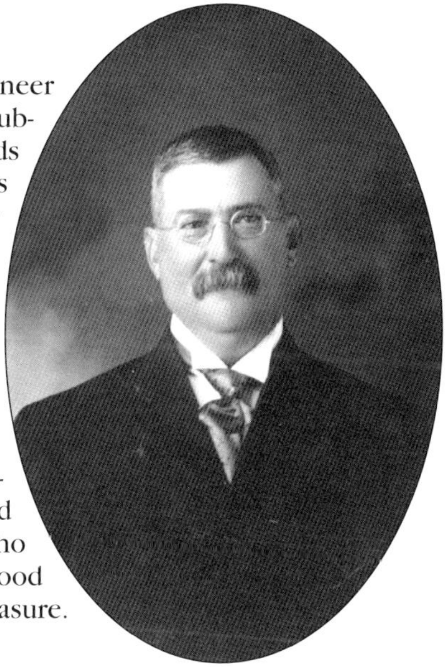

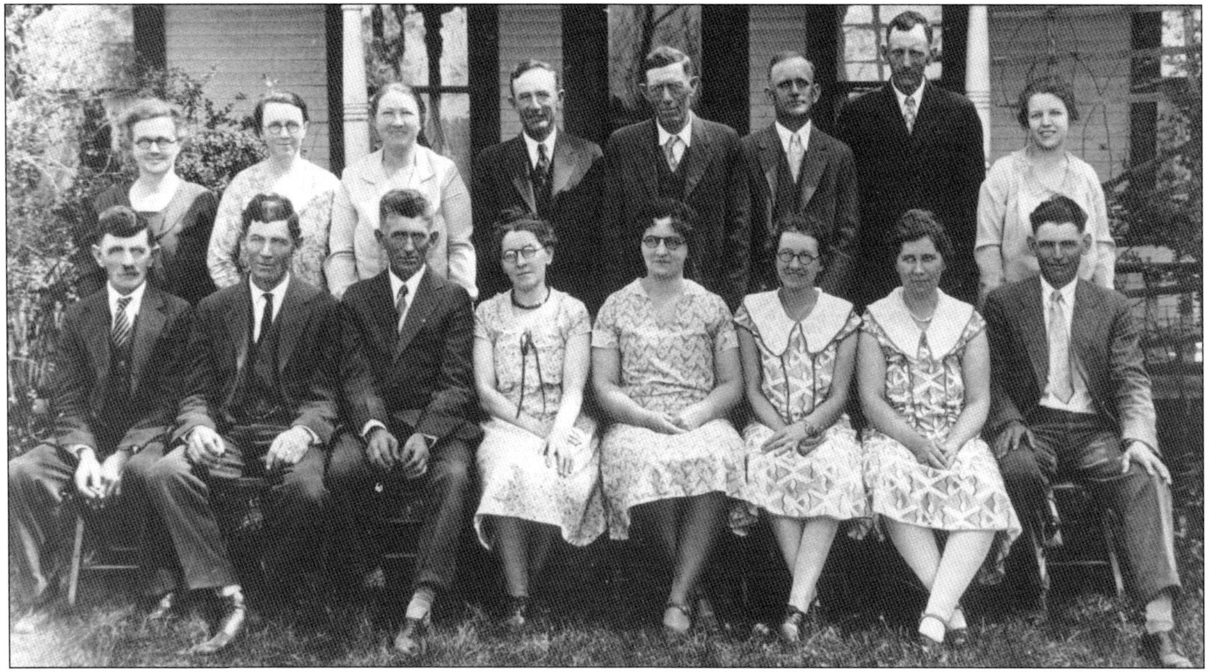

The Bos family, circa 1930.

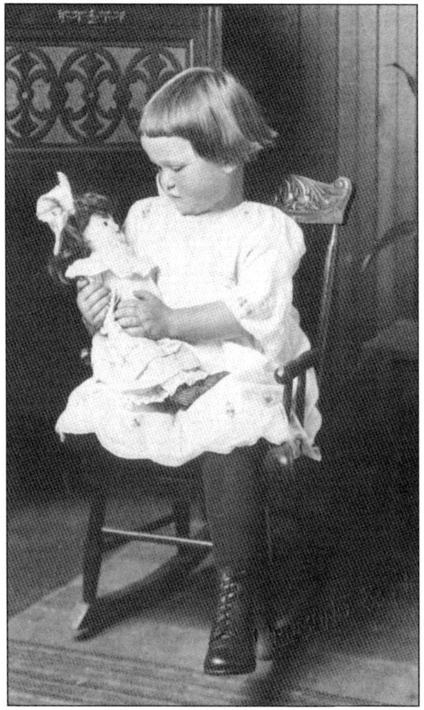

Dorothy Sheller at home with doll, 1920.

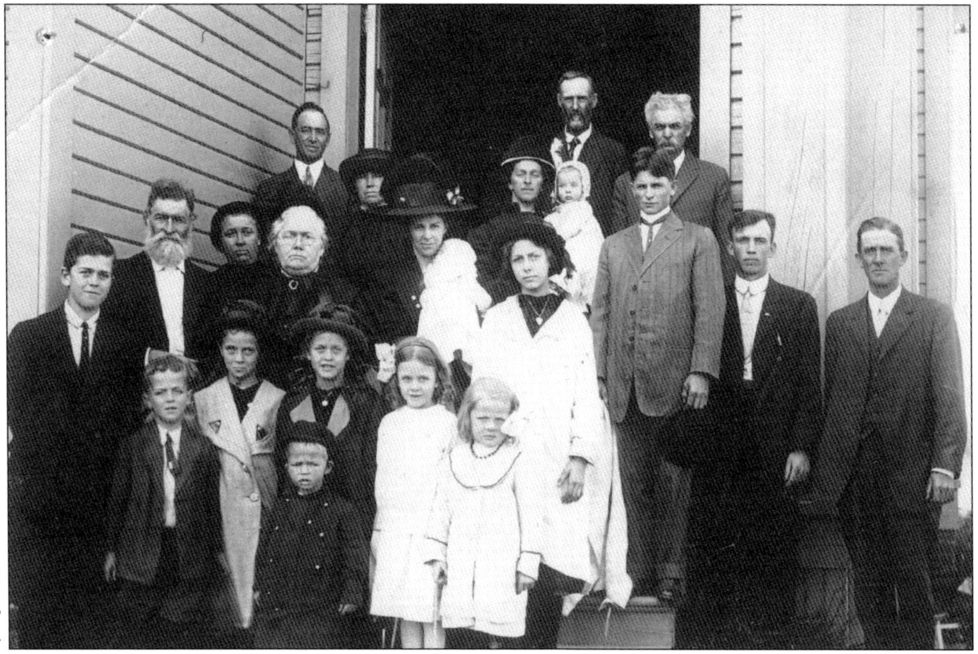

The Taylor and Peck families, circa 1907.

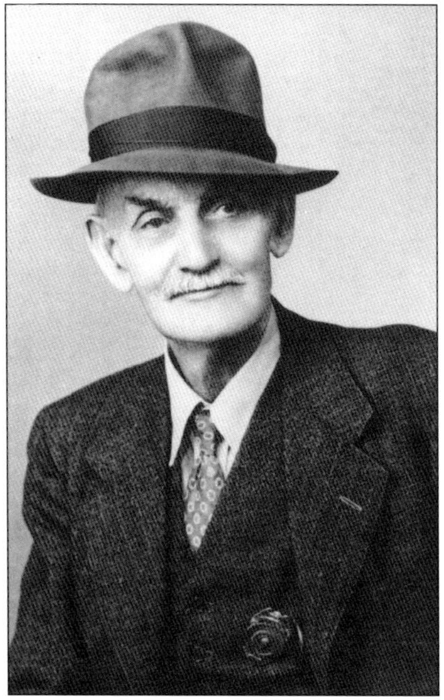

I.W. Colby, circa 1947. Colby was named the first chief of police in 1908. For many years he was the only officer. The City of Sunnyside bought him a silver star police badge, which Colby always wore. He retired in March of 1948 after serving 40 years.

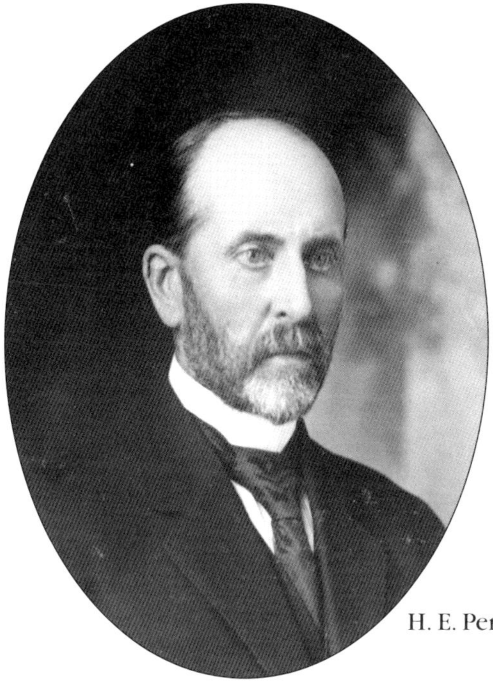

H. E. Perrin, teacher and city clerk.

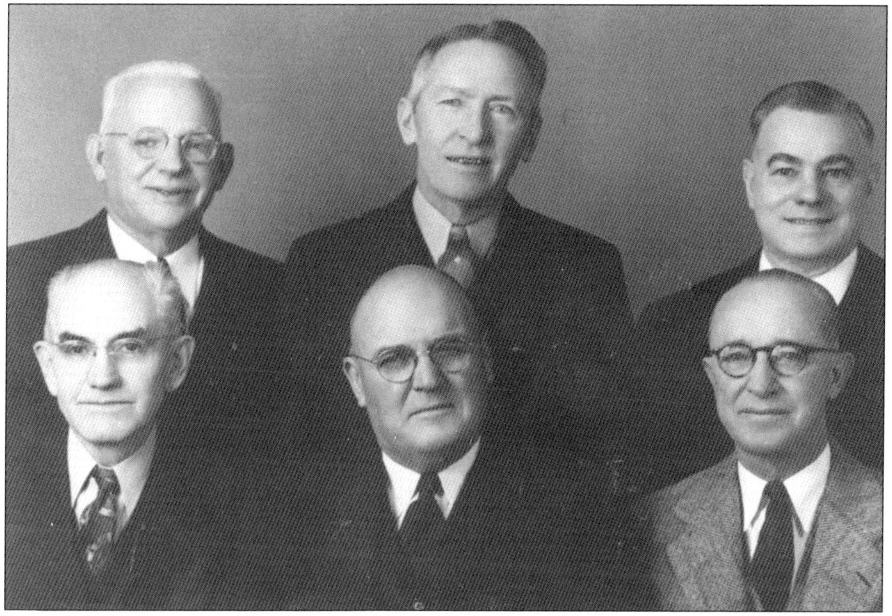

Sunnyside businessmen. From left, back row, A. G. Fleming, Oscar Boose and Al Hillyer. Front row, A. M. Murfin, Roscoe Sheller and Clayton Speck.

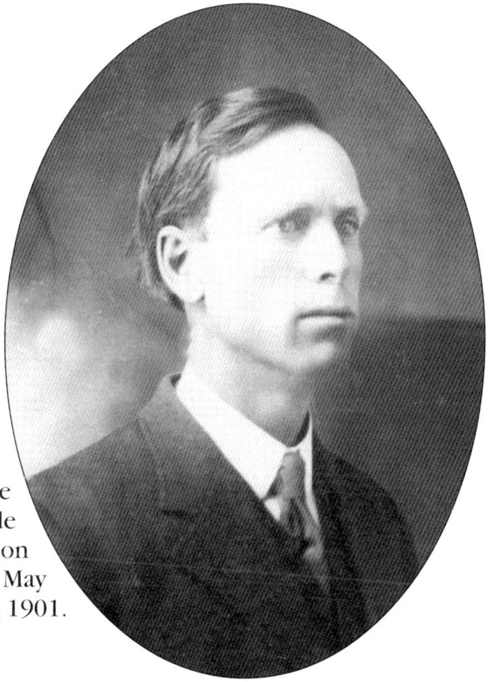

Bill Hitchcock who was the first publisher of the Sunnyside Sun newspaper. The first edition of the paper was published May 24, 1901.

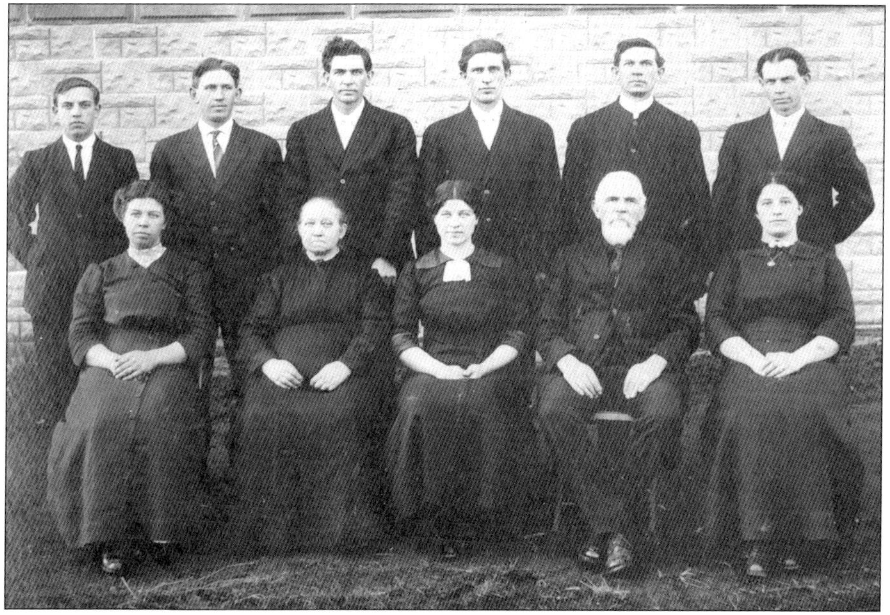

The Taylor Family. From left, front row, Alice, Mary (mother), Nanny, Peter, Zechariah, and Ada. Back row, Ernest, John, Henry, Wesley, Samuel, and George.

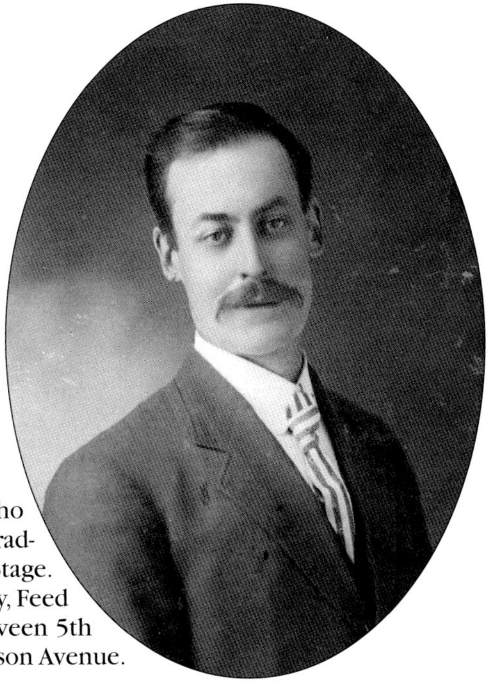

Harvey Matheson who had horses for road grading and the Mabton Stage. He operated a Livery, Feed and Stage business between 5th and 6th Street on Edison Avenue.

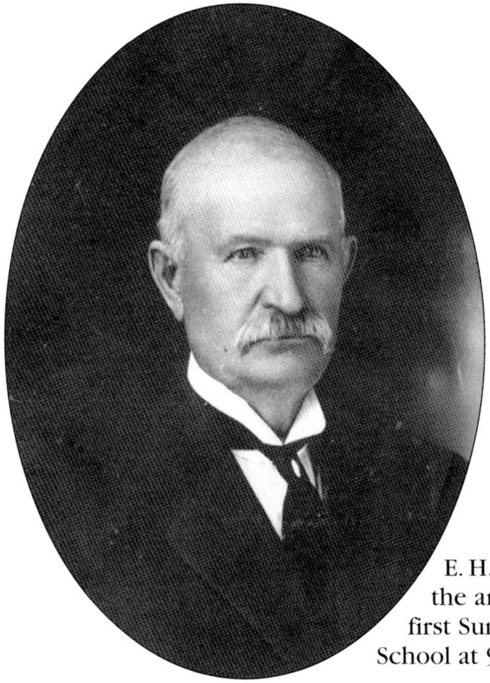

E. H. Ragland was the architect for the first Sunnyside High School at 9th and Edison.

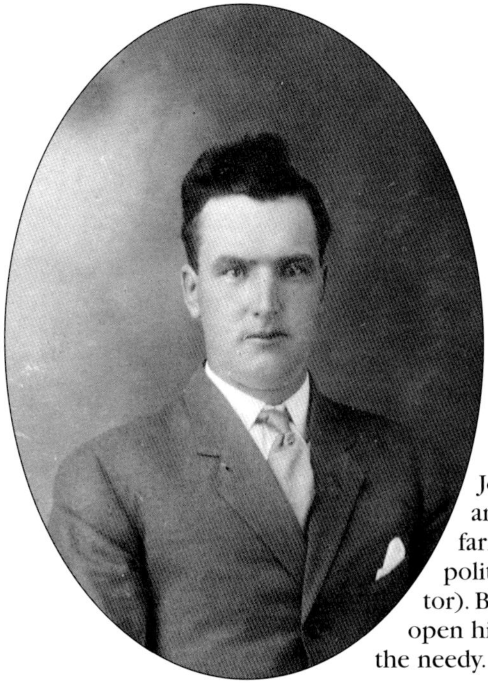

John Heffron was an early promoter, farmer, cattleman, and politician (state senator). Bad years saw him open his pear orchard to the needy.

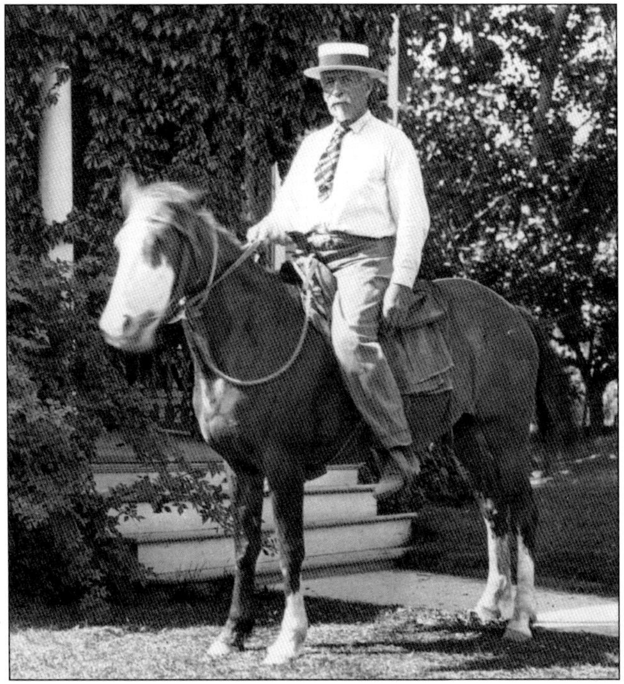

Henry E. Nicolai came to Sunnyside in 1905 where he raised tomatoes, vegetables, melons and cherries. In 1906 he built one of the first homes on Harrison Hill at 301 Grandview Avenue. He was the president of the Good Citizen's League and an advocate of a "dry" community.

TRANSPORTATION

The arrival of the first train to Sunnyside on February 2, 1906, was an event to remember. Despite the time of year, a crowd of some 3,000 had gathered at the depot. People had come from all across the state to join in the celebration.

An inaugural train carrying Governor Albert E. Mead and other dignitaries was making its way towards Sunnyside. The train was to be greeted by a brass band and a welcoming committee headed by Mayor William B. Bridgman. After the necessary exchange of pleasantries, the whole party was to be taken to the top of Harrison Hill for a huge barbecue.

Everything was going well until the train came into view. The train visibly slowed down, stopped, and then rolled over on its side half mile from the depot. The Train had been the victim of Sunnyside's drainage problems. Irrigation had made the desert bloom but no one had thought of the need to drain off the excess water. As a result the town's water table had risen to the point that most of Sunnyside was mired in mud. The tracks had been laid but not tested with a heavy locomotive. The train's weight had pushed the railroad ties and rails into the mud. Without the support of the rails, the train tipped over.

Fortunately, no one was hurt, and the celebration continued as planned. The train was righted, more stable tracks were laid, and despite the accident, train service to Sunnyside started on schedule.

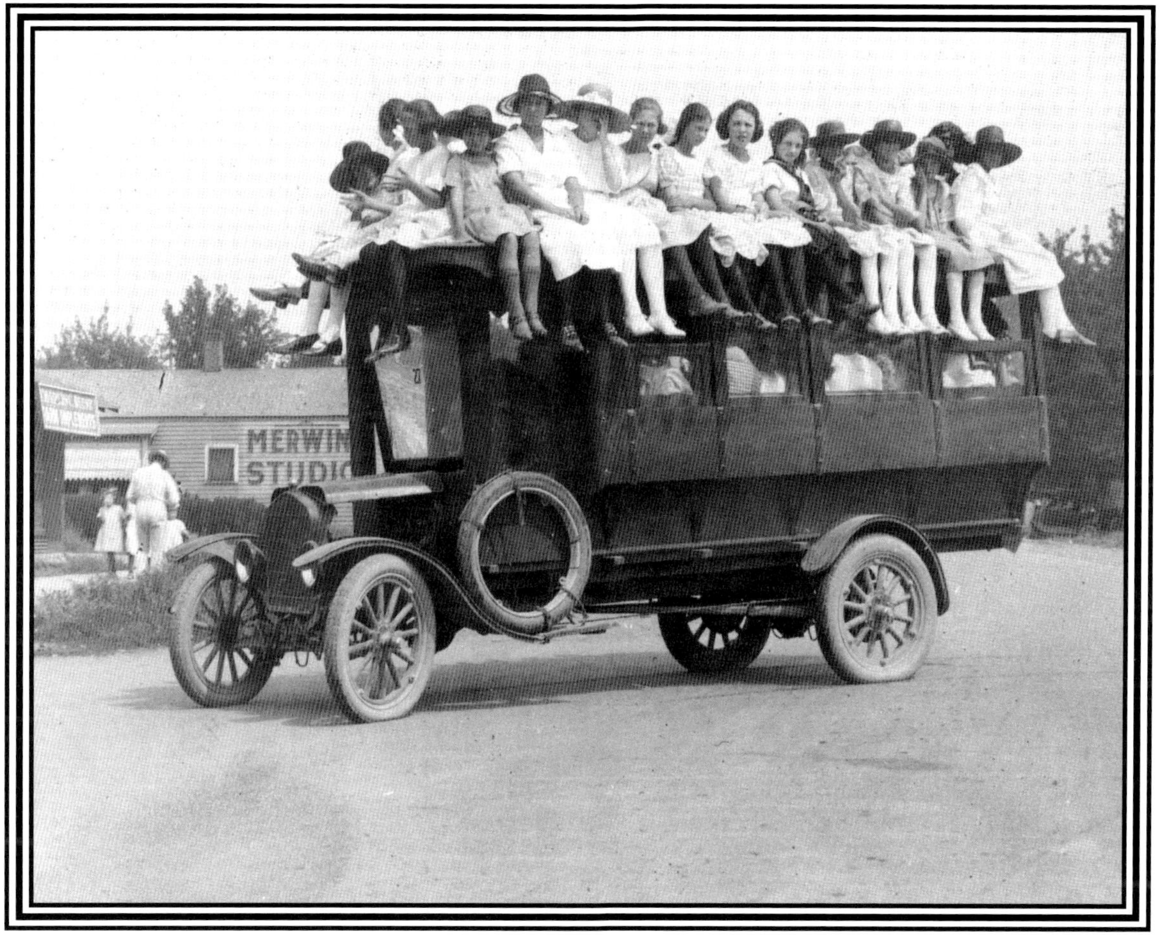

An early day bus in Sunnyside. Passengers normally would ride on the inside.

Proudly Serving Sunnyside's Transportation Needs Since 1912

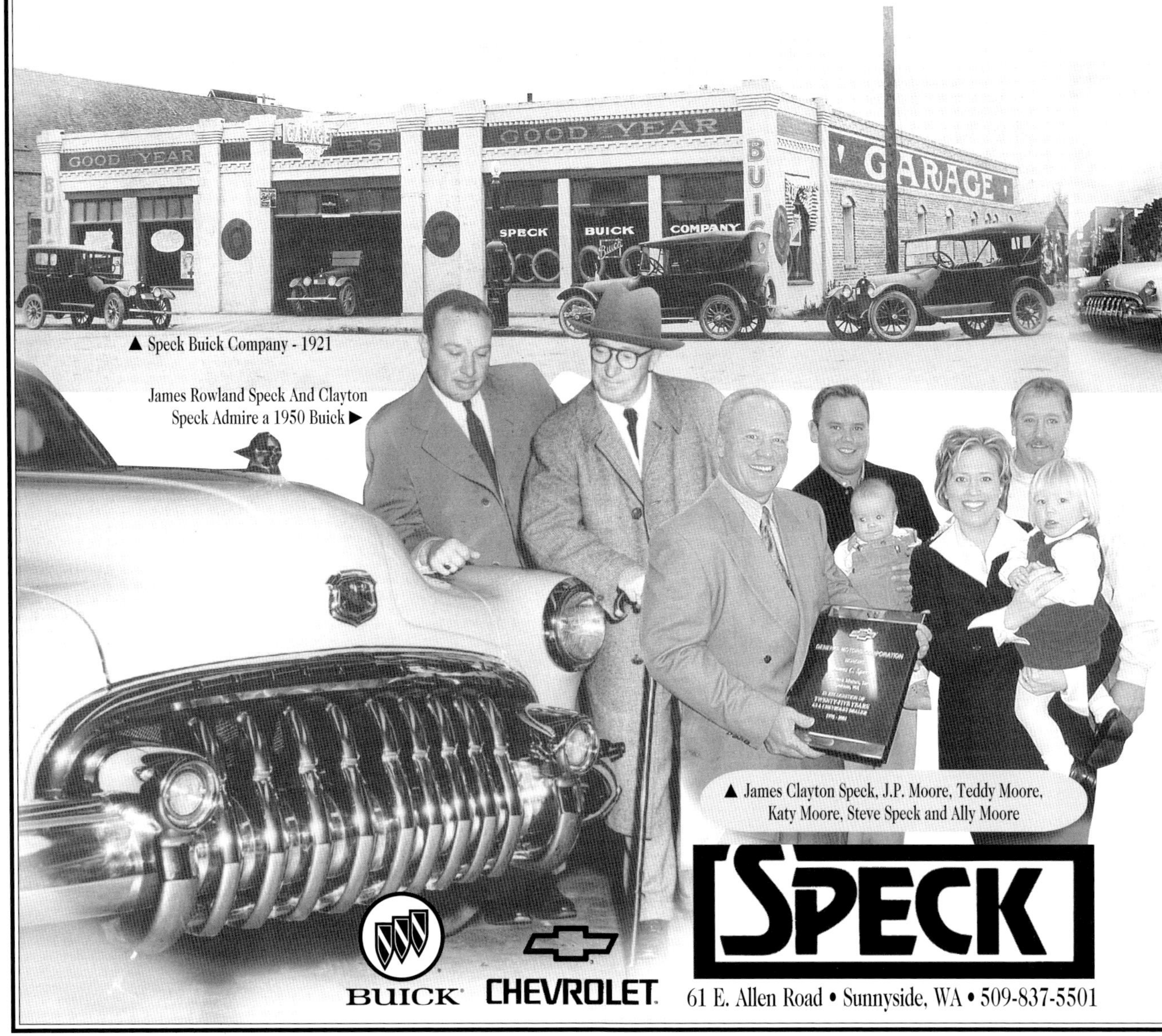

▲ Speck Buick Company - 1921

James Rowland Speck And Clayton Speck Admire a 1950 Buick ▶

▲ James Clayton Speck, J.P. Moore, Teddy Moore, Katy Moore, Steve Speck and Ally Moore

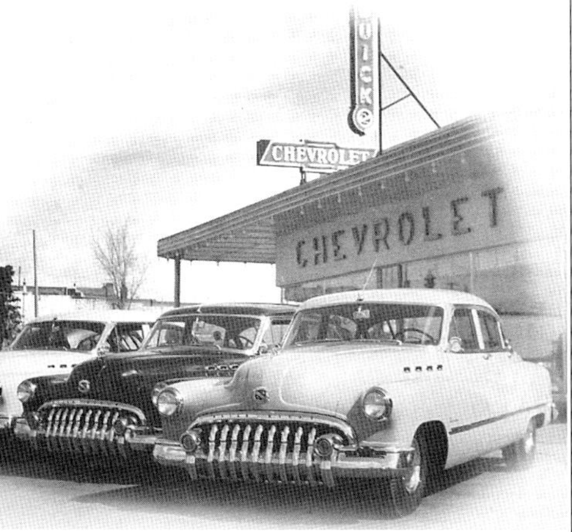

When Clayton Speck founded Speck Buick Company in 1912, little did he know that the Speck family would continue on with his tradition of quality automobiles, service and customer satisfaction for years to follow.

Today the tradition continues into its fourth generation proudly serving the Yakima Valley with quality General Motors automobiles.

Speck Motors is proud to be the oldest Buick dealership in the state of Washington and one of Chevrolet's premiere dealerships.

BUICK CHEVROLET

SPECK

61 E. Allen Road • Sunnyside, WA • 509-837-5501

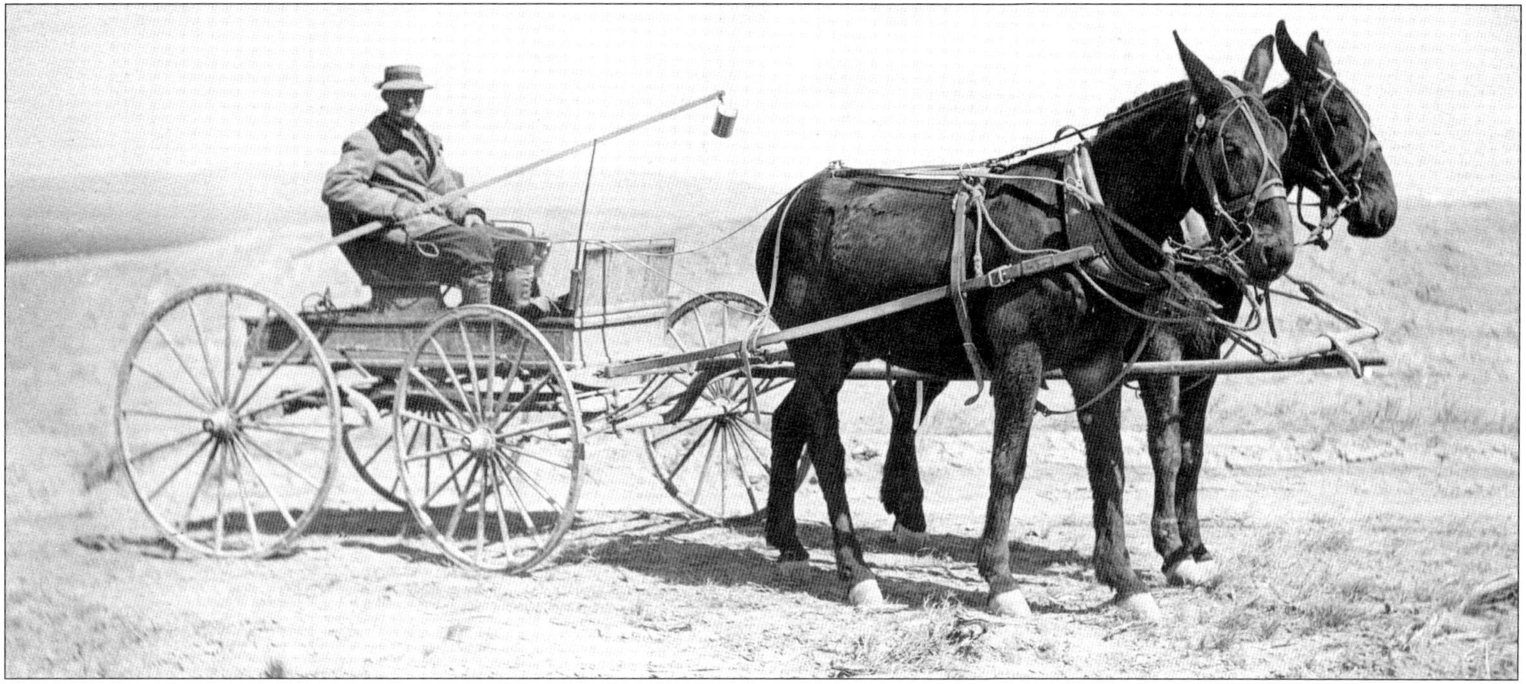

Hydrographer's team of mules showing a patent whip, circa 1900.

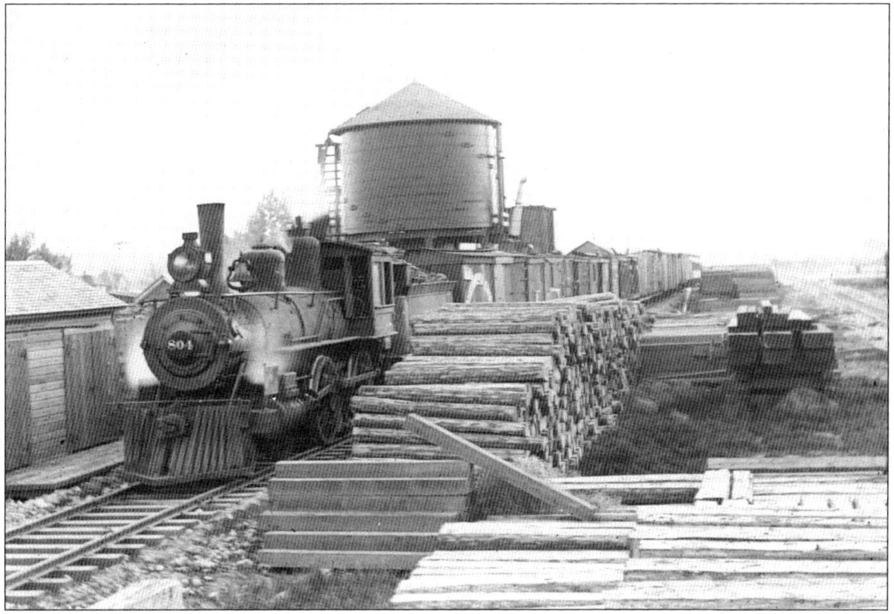

A Northern Pacific train, circa 1906. Photo take when siding tracks were still under construction.

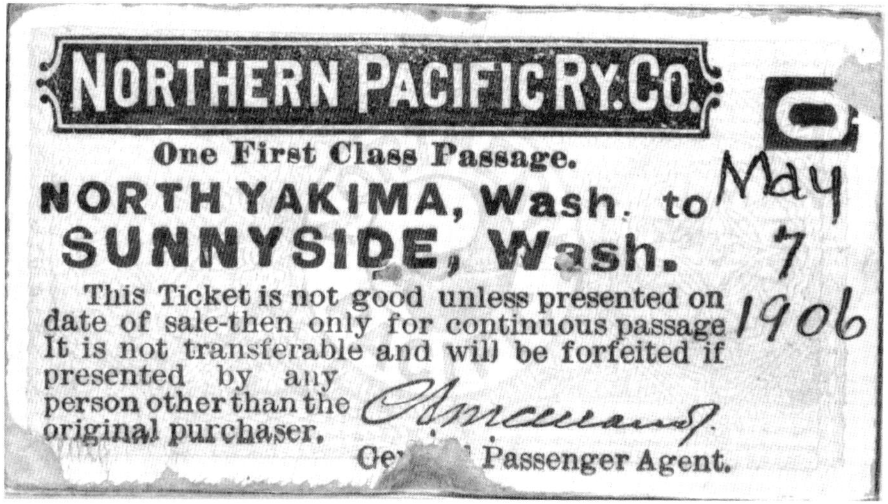

NORTHERN PACIFIC RY. CO.

One First Class Passage.

NORTH YAKIMA, Wash. to SUNNYSIDE, Wash.

May 7 1906

This Ticket is not good unless presented on date of sale-then only for continuous passage It is not transferable and will be forfeited if presented by any person other than the original purchaser.

Ge[illegible] Passenger Agent.

First passenger ticket sold in Sunnyside. The ticket was sold to S. J. Harrison on May 7, 1906 by Northern Pacific's Agent, R. P. Haney.

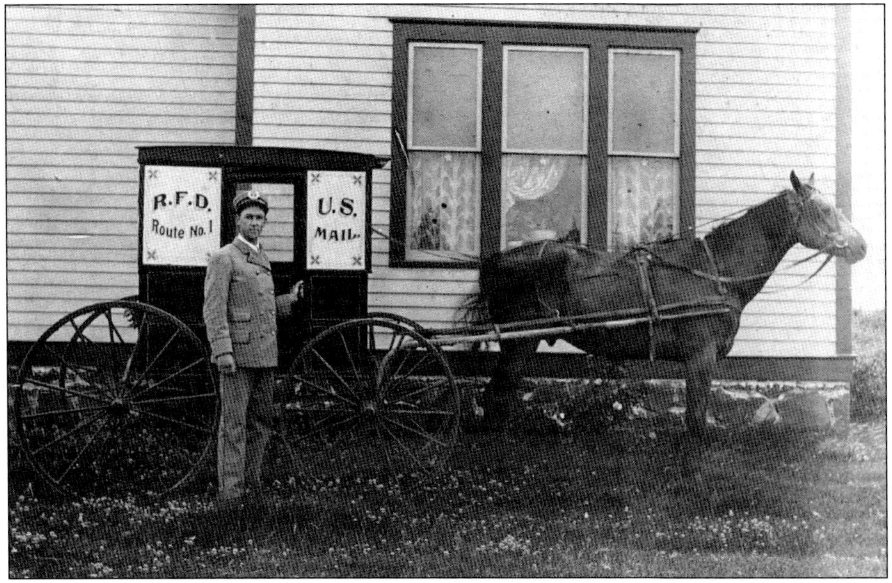

A mail delivery wagon in 1908. Orin Gregory, mailman and owner who earned his wagon by selling 150 subscriptions to "Popular Mechanics" magazine.

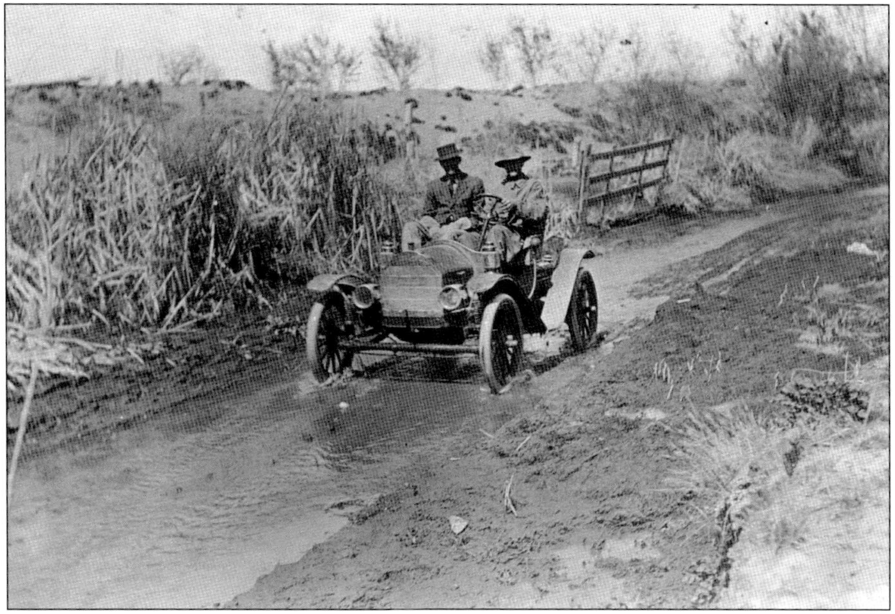

A car in a washed-out road, circa 1910.

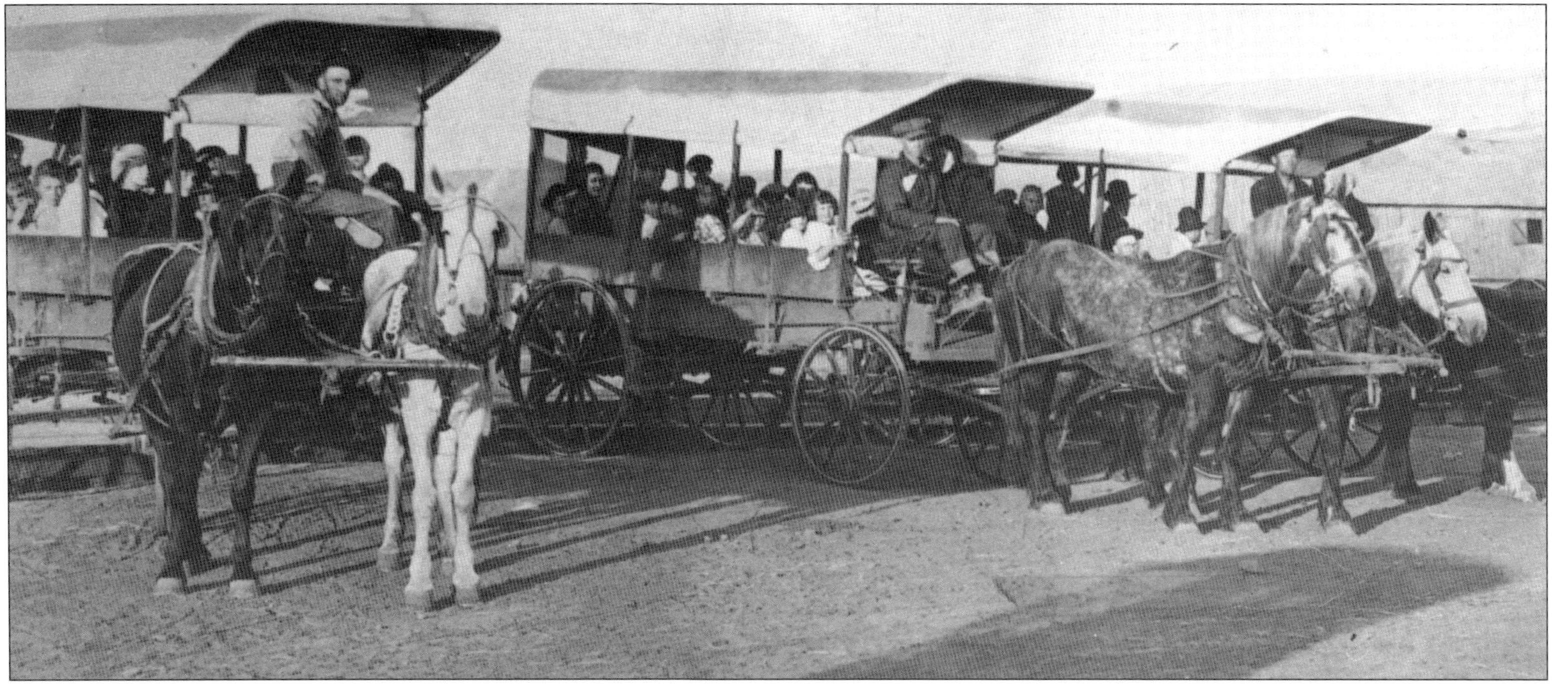

Horse drawn school buses, circa 1910.

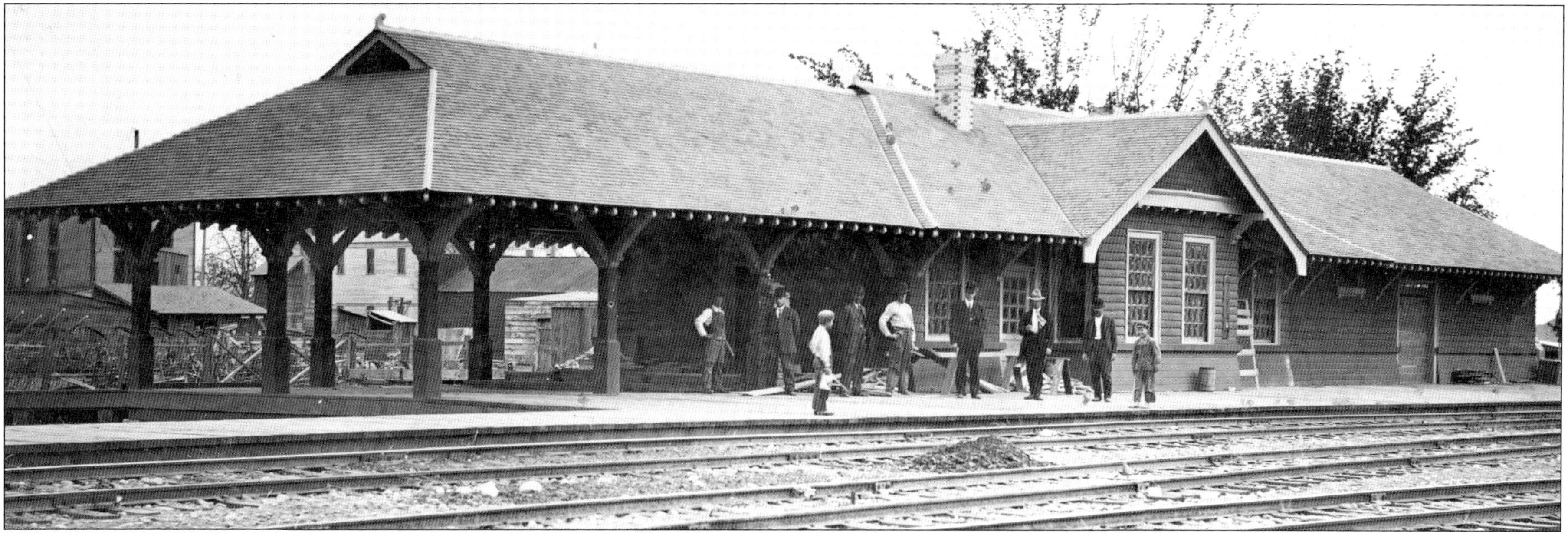

The construction of the North Coast Railroad Depot.The structure was demolished in the late 1970s.The train schedule commenced on March 3, 1911, photo circa 1911.The depot stood at the southwest corner of 5th Street and Edison Avenue, and later became in Union Pacific Railroad Station.

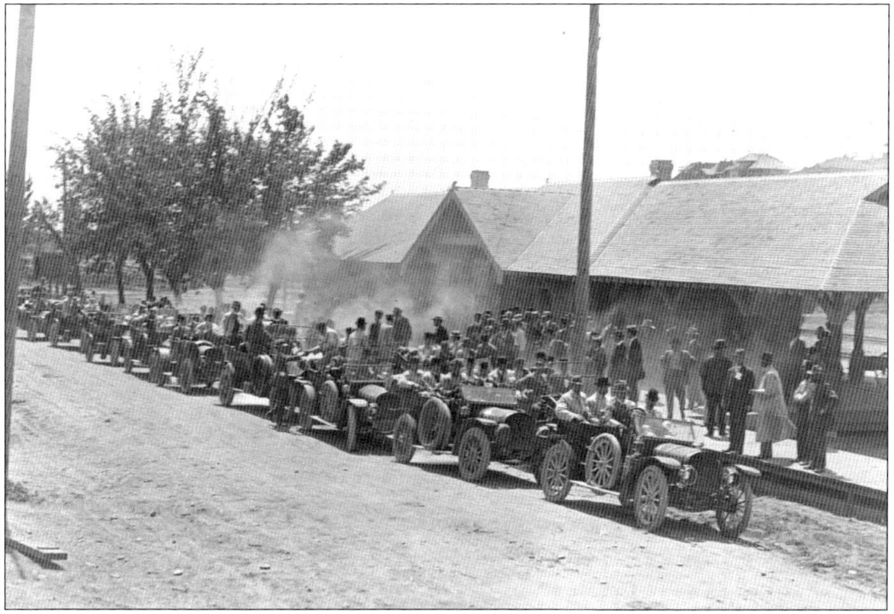

The Union Pacific Railroad Station, circa 1912.

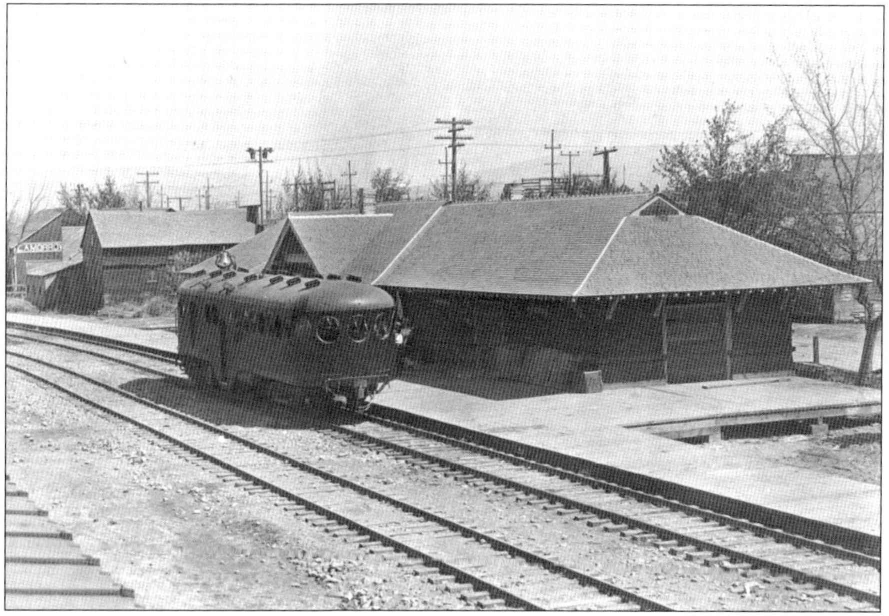

North Coast Railroad Depot and "Galloping Gertie or Ghost," circa 1911. Photo taken looking North towards Edison Avenue from atop a railroad car.

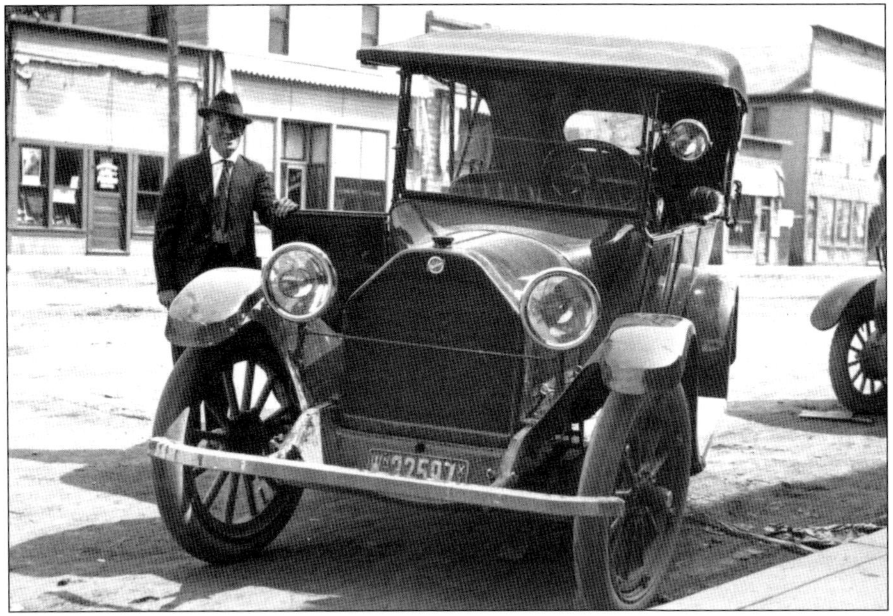

Gentleman with his car on 6th Street in Sunnyside, circa 1918.

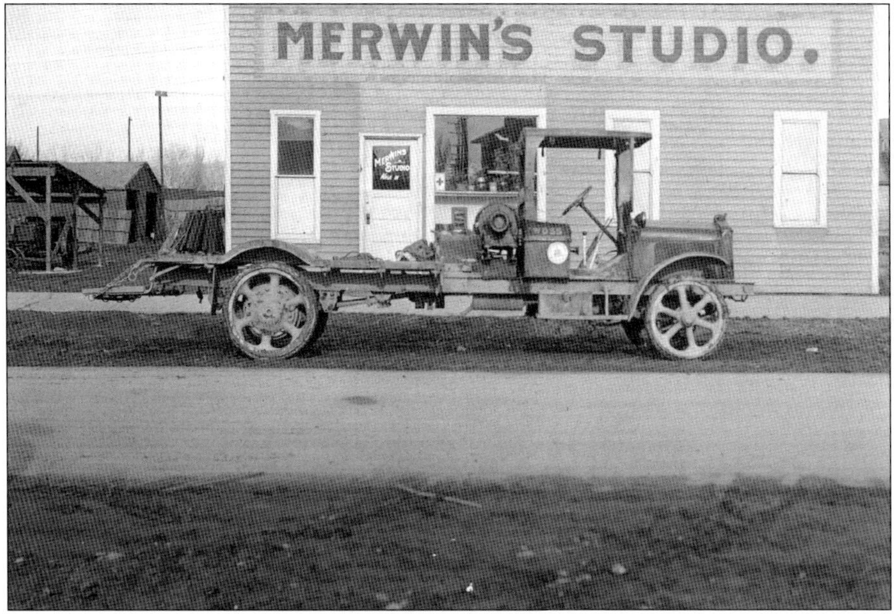

Truck outside Merwin's Studio, 1920s.

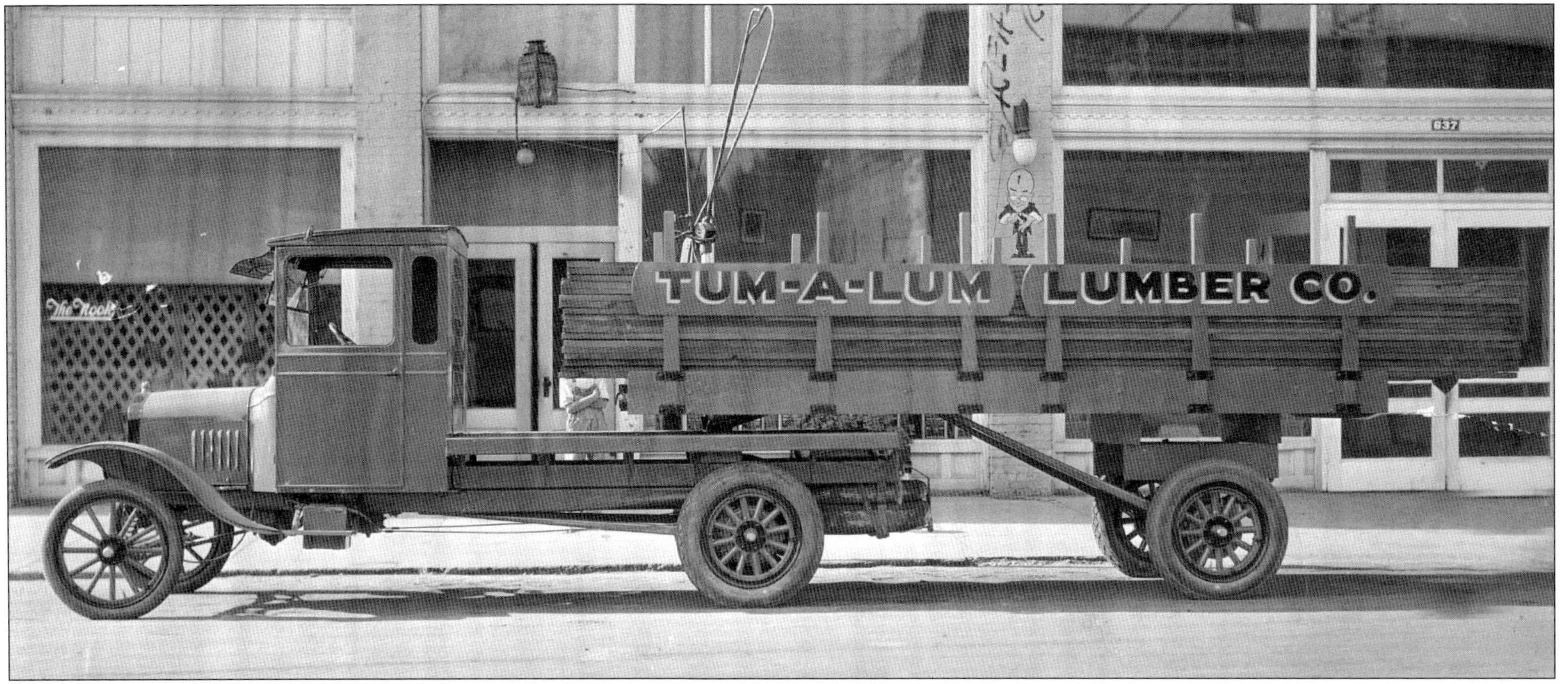

Tum-A-Lum Lumber Company's semi-truck which hauled large loads of lumber, circa 1925.

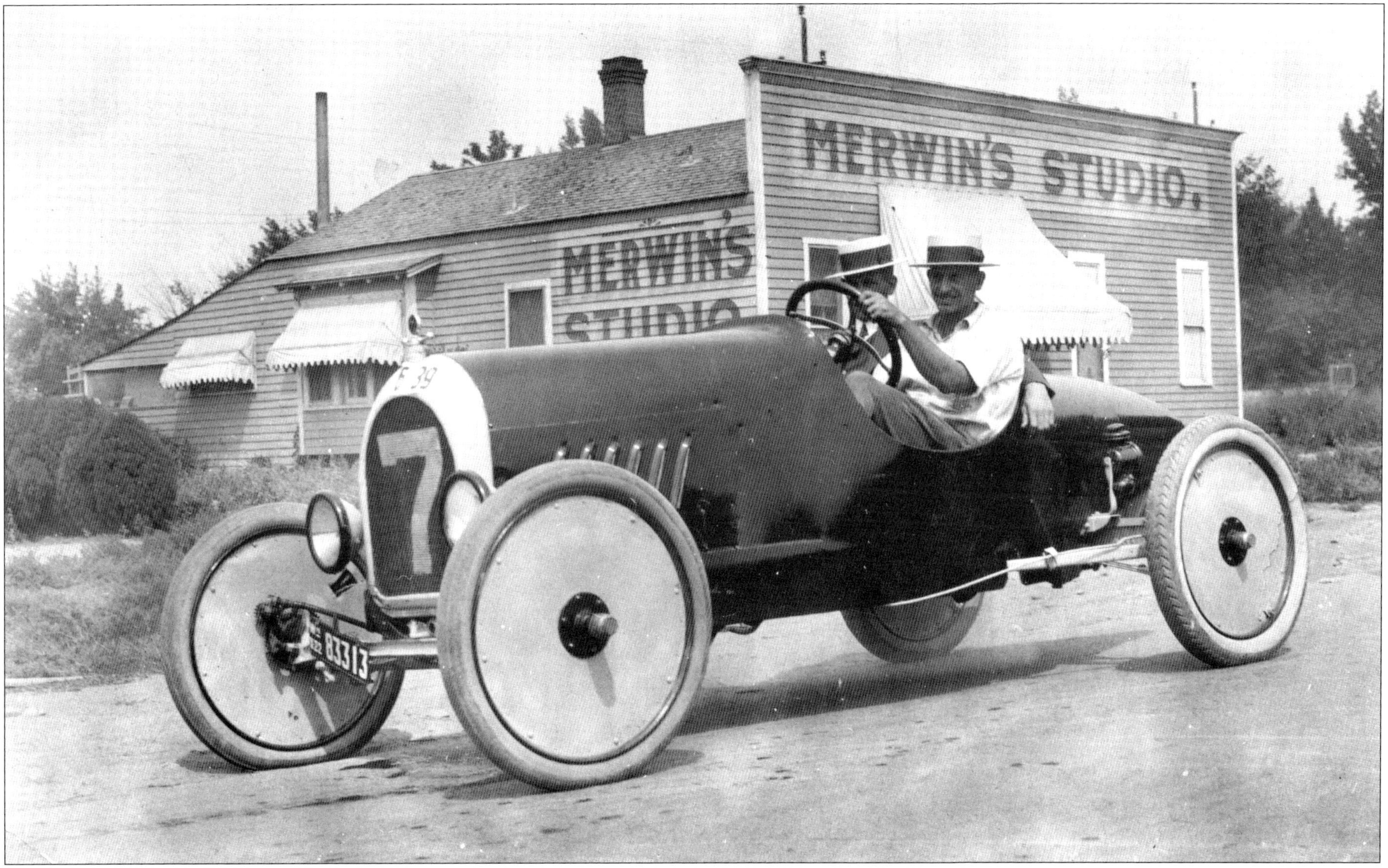

"Bug" body mounted on a used Model T chassis, popular with young swains in the 1920s.

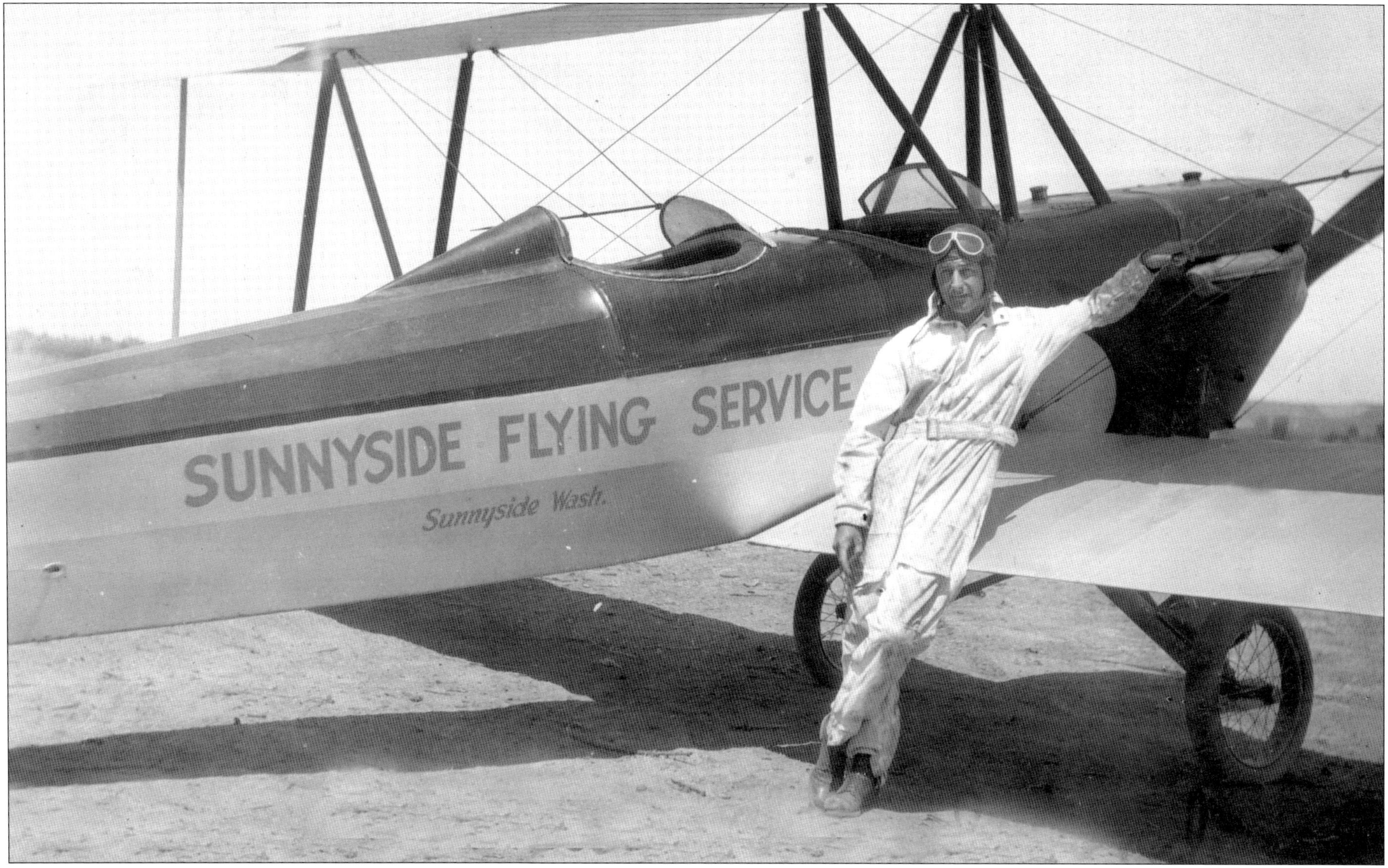

Oscar Bolin and his aircraft, circa 1925.

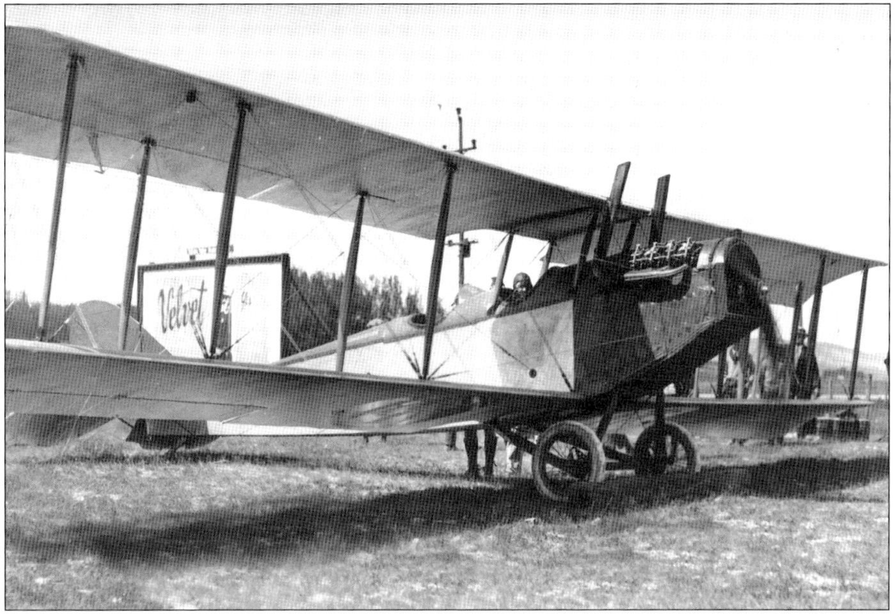

An aircraft on June 4, 1925, Ford Day.

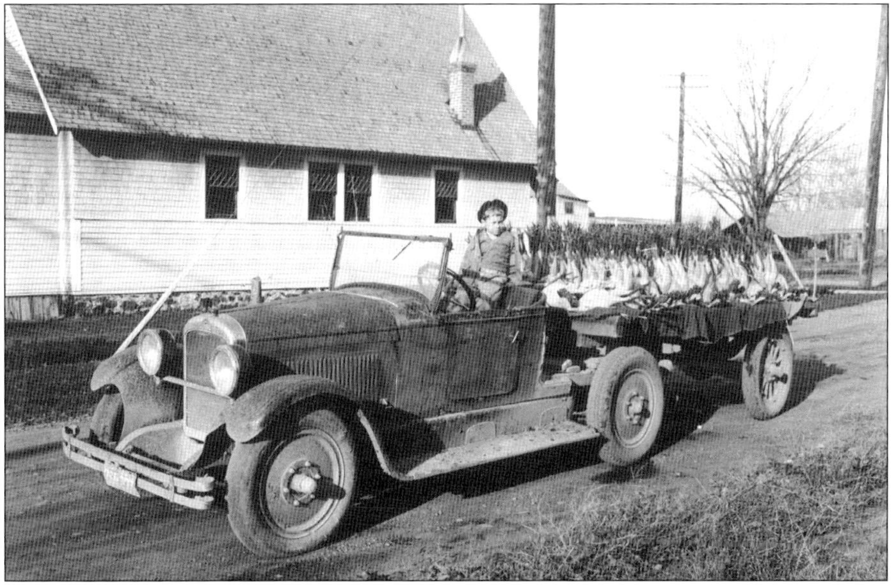

December 16, 1933 found this young man helping with the delivery of Christmas turkeys destined for the Washington Co-operative Egg & Poultry Association plant in Sunnyside.

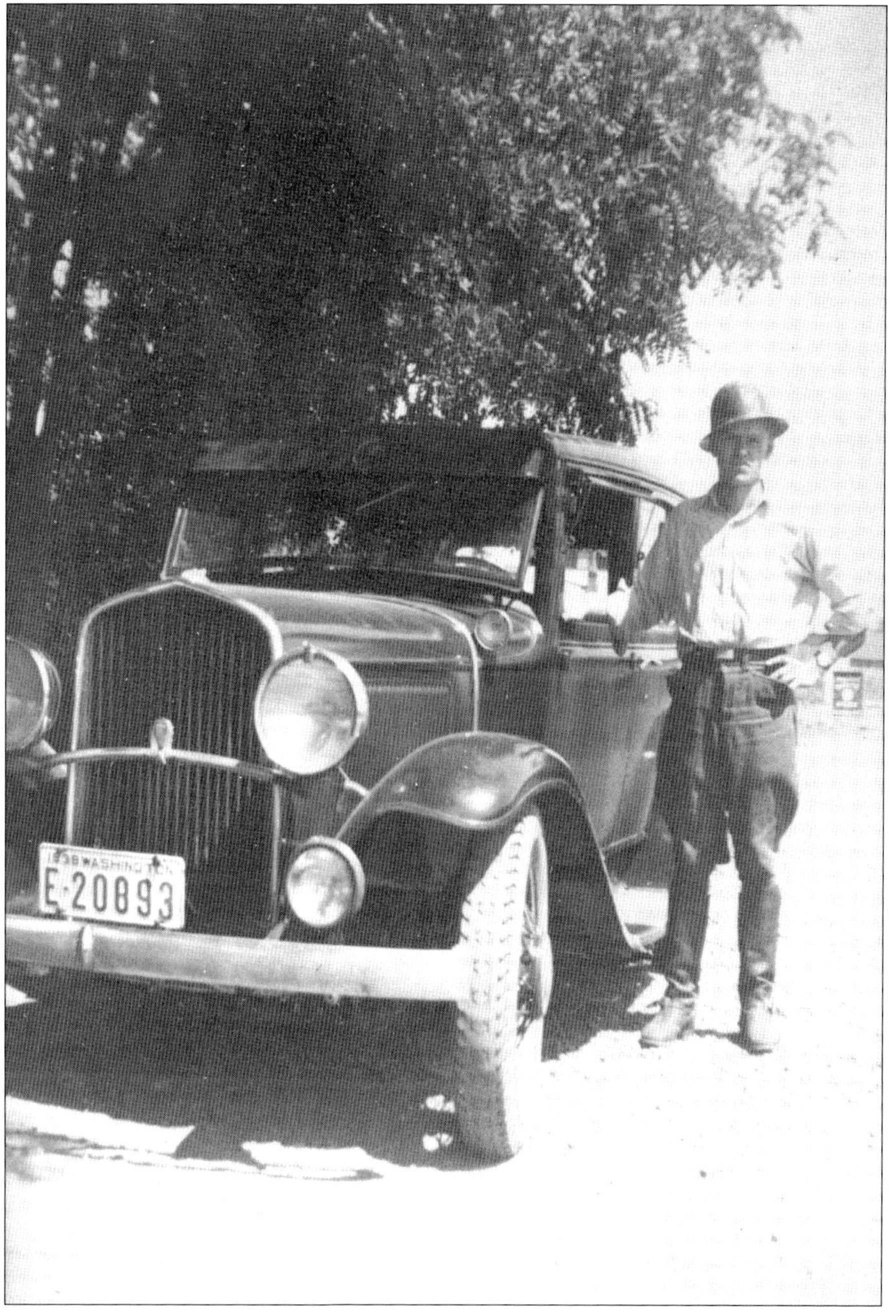

Wilbur Jenkins next to his 1930 Chrysler.

Partners in time.

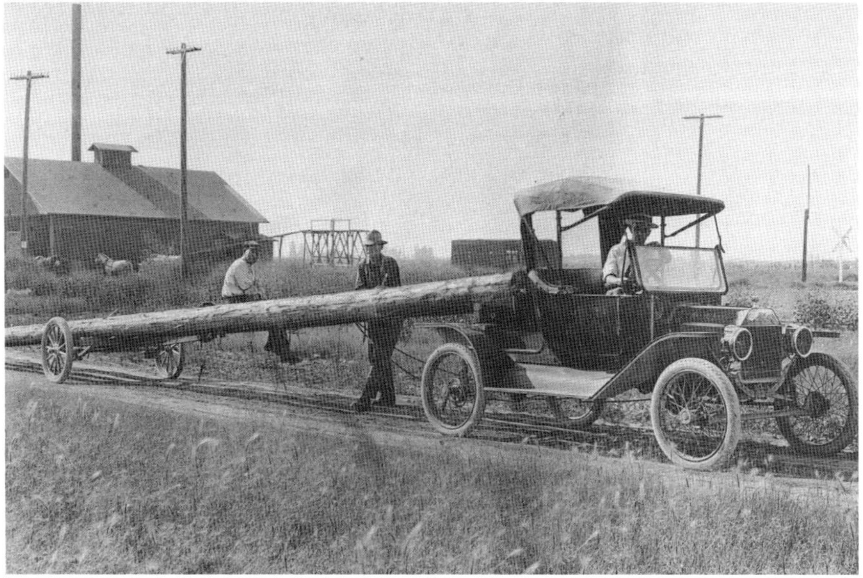

Citizens of Sunnyside, a 100-year anniversary is a measure of your strength and an extraordinary occasion to celebrate.

Pacific Power is proud to have been a working part of your community for almost as many years – since 1910, we've provided power to your families, schools, churches and businesses. For the privilege of being your energy partner for the better part of a century, we thank you.

You can reach us 24 hours a day, 7 days a week. Just call 1-888-221-7070. Or visit our Web site at www.pacificpower.net.

PACIFIC POWER

Making it happen.

RECREATION

Hunting, sports and dramatic presentations are listed as popular recreational pursuits of early Sunnysiders. While school sports dominated most of the community's organized activities, large hunting parties were often seen bringing in large numbers of the Lower Valley's most plentiful wildlife - jack rabbits.

Many early accounts given by Sunnyside hunters recall a time when the skies were black with migrating geese, ducks and assorted feathered fowl looking for a resting spot at the ponds and marshes surrounding the nearby Yakima River.

One of the community's first pubic improvements was the establishment of Central Park in 1908. As soon at the newly planted trees were of any height, families began spending Sunday afternoons picnicking in the city park. Along with picnics came organized baseball games attracting huge crowds. At a time when girls were just beginning to attend school on a regular basis sports activities for the female gender also provided a well deserved diverse from pioneer life in the Lower Valley.

Besides sports, public recreation activities in early Sunnyside included barn dances, outdoor band concerts and the occasional visit by chautauquas, an event eagerly looked forward to by early Sunnysiders. Families would pack up their overnight gear for a week-long stay in town to listen to the visiting lecturers and musical presentations.

The area grange organizations, of which the Outlook Grange is the oldest in the area, also offered an entertainment break from the day-to-day monotony of pre-radio and television days. Dances and dinners were regularly hosted by the local grange halls for as little as 50 cents admission.

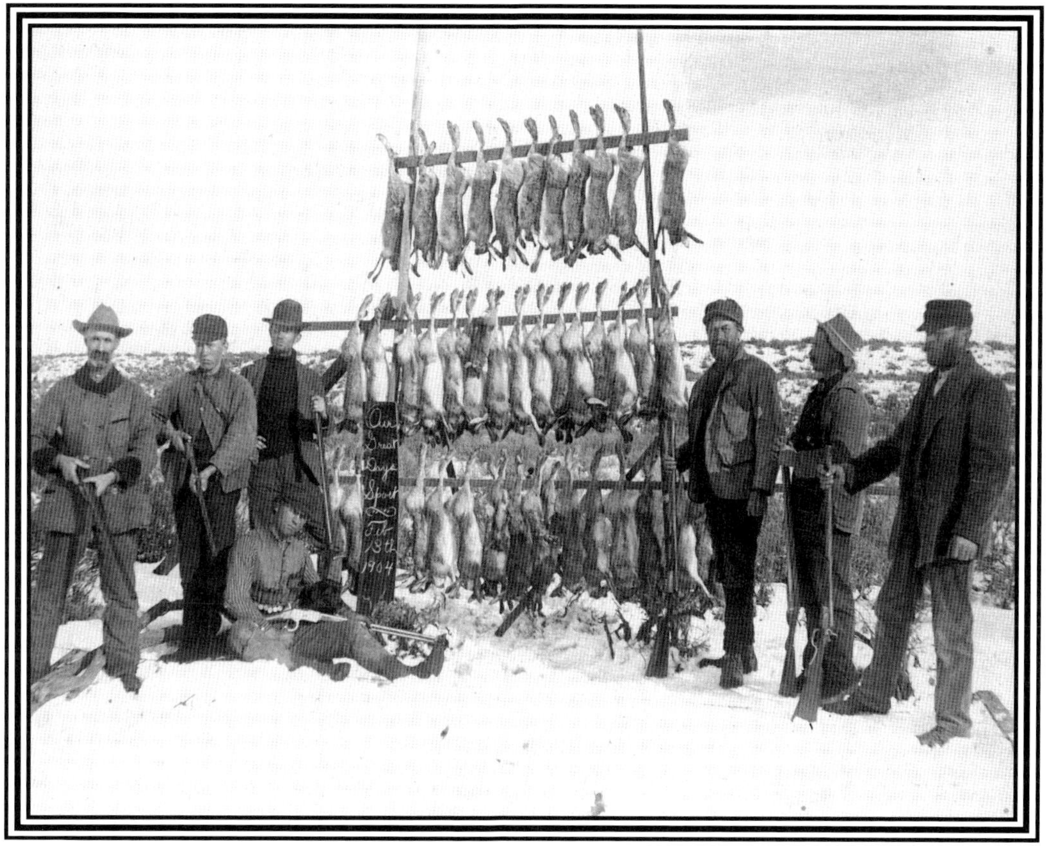

Hunters with a large catch of rabbits, February 13, 1904.

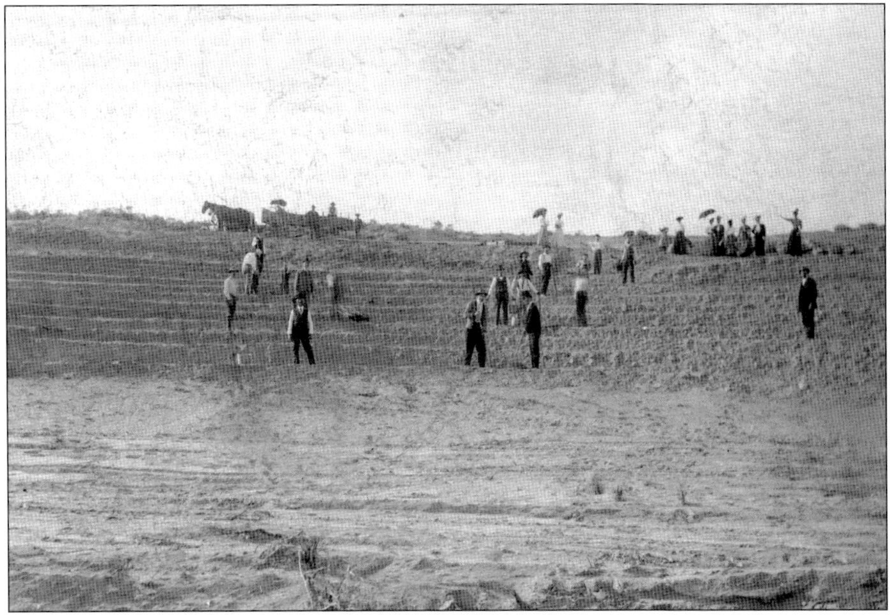

Sunnyside businessmen plant trees at the dedication of the City Park, 1908.

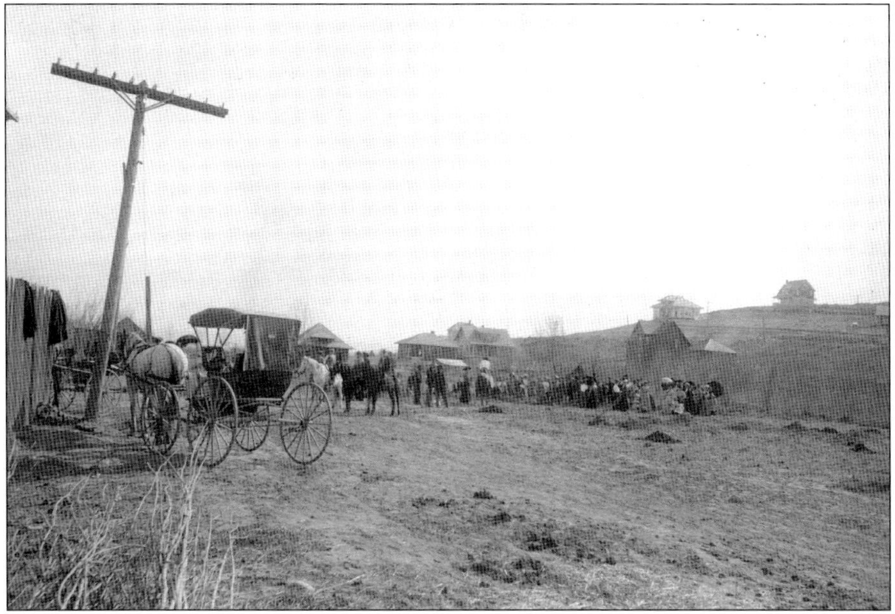

The City Park, 1908.

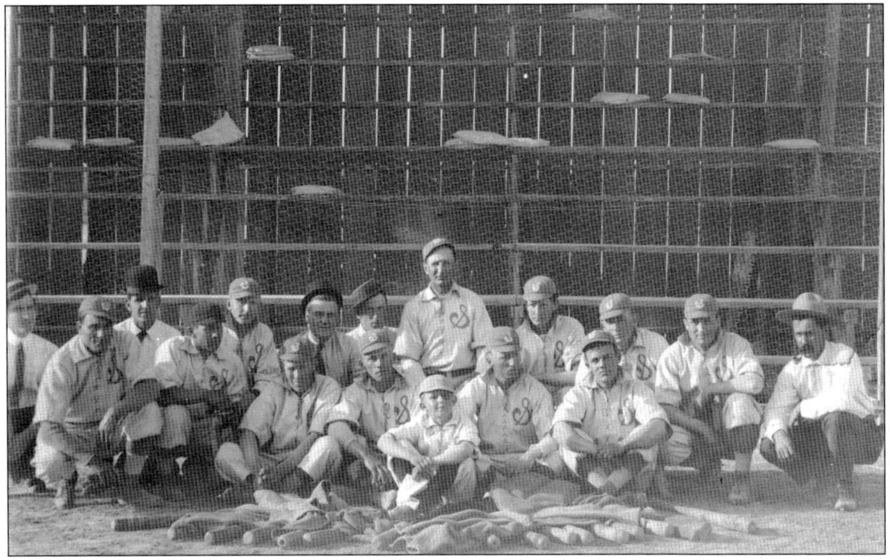

Sunnyside baseball team, valley champions, 1908. L to R: Walker, Jim Scoon, Chester Ferson, Chappy Chapman, Alva Hilderbrand, Roscoe Sheller, Guy Lichty, Alva McClain, George Smith, Joe Myers, Wilbur Searle, Perry (Slim) Johnson, Merle Yeager, Wilfred Searle, Earl Rowland and Lee (Stony) Stonebreaker.

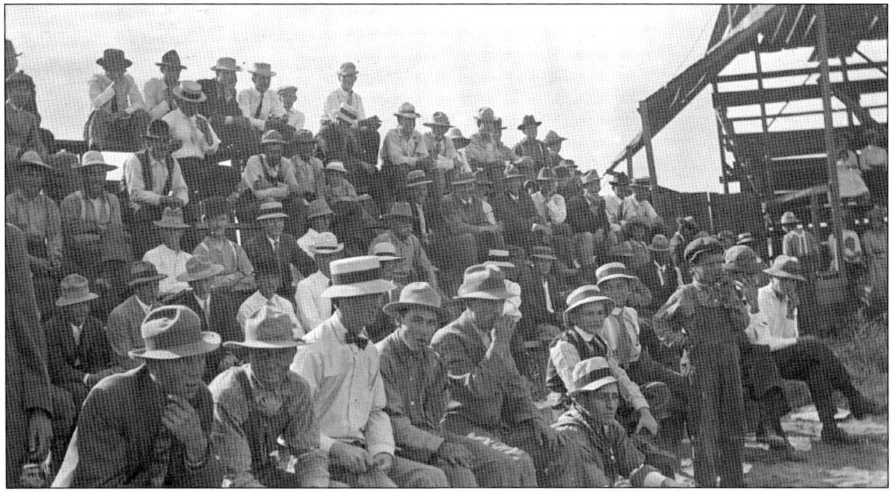

Baseball spectators, circa 1910.

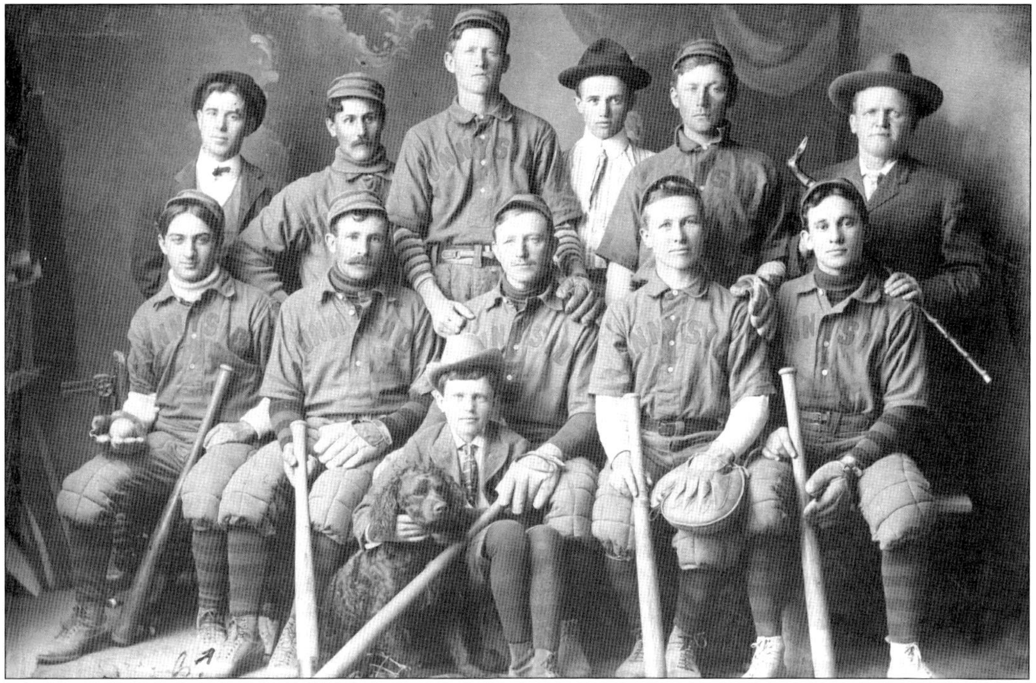

Sunnyside's first baseball team. Each player was allowed only one shower each season.Seated from left: Nels "Lefty" Franklin, Harry Gochnour, Ira Miller, Lawrence "Shorty"Whorton and Elmer Gochnour. Standing from left:Andy Fisk, Lee "Stony" Stonebreaker, Capt. George "Bo" Reed, Frank Vetter Howard Miller and Manager Doc Belyea. Mascot and boy in front unidentified.

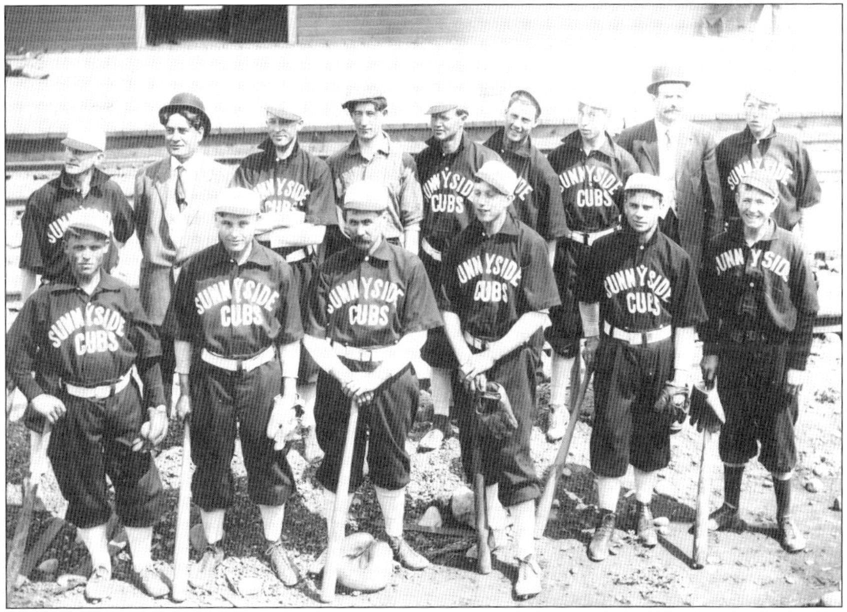

Sunnyside baseball team, early 1900s.

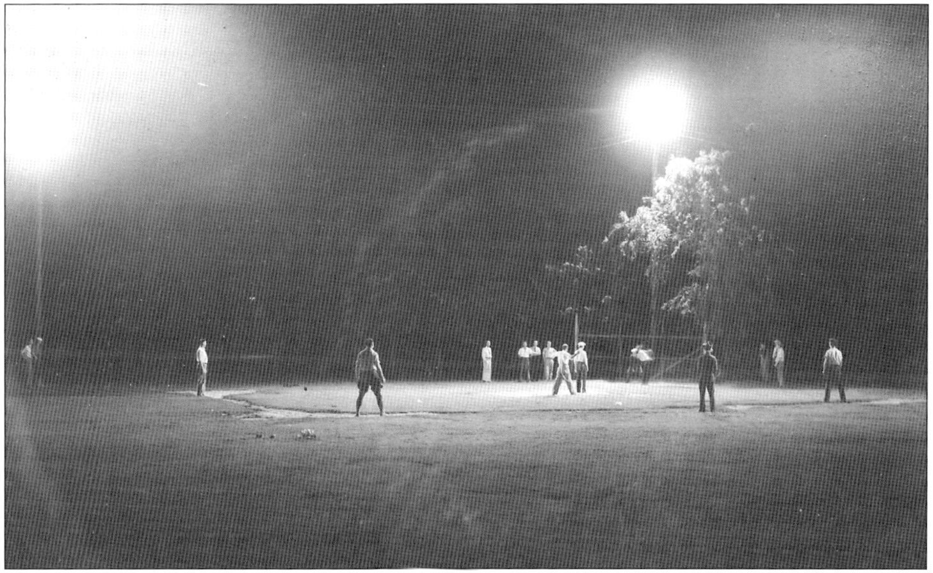

Night baseball game on Lincoln's Lighted Field. Sunnyside was also the first city in the Lower Valley to have street lights.

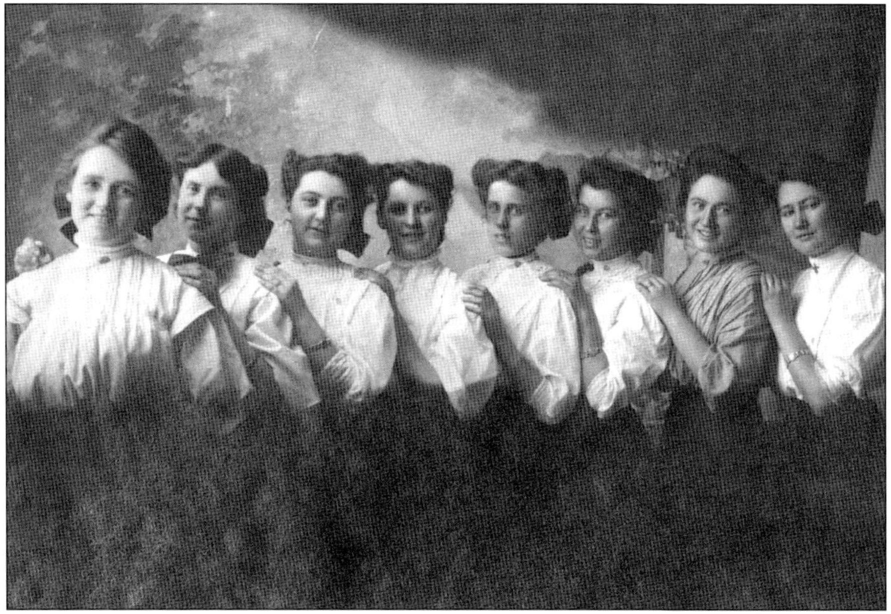

Outlook girls basketball team, 1910. Left to right are: Susie Core, Nell Williams, Miss Dopps, Sadie Jones, Blow Williams, Hazel Dickenson, Ruby Core and Ethel Scheyer.

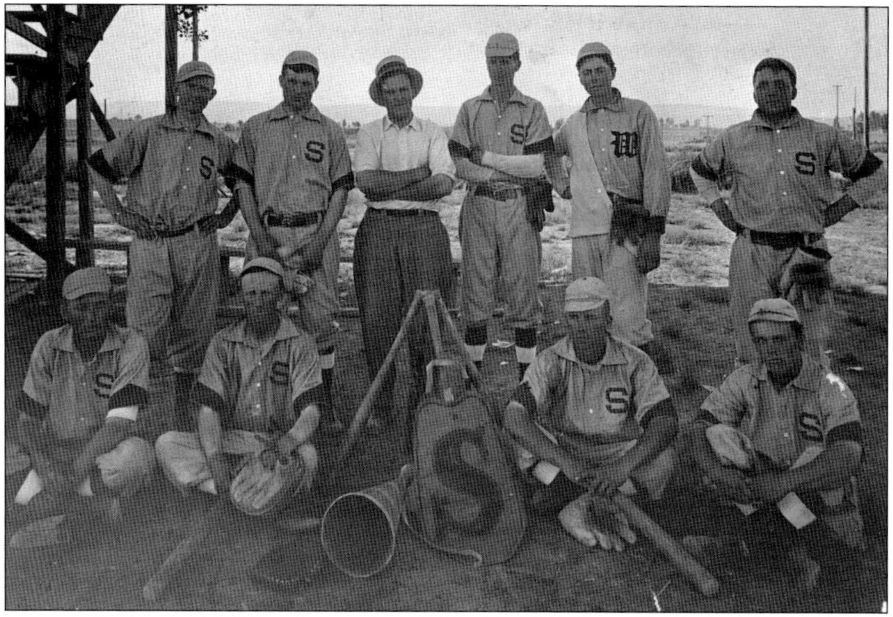

Sunnyside basesball team, circa 1910.

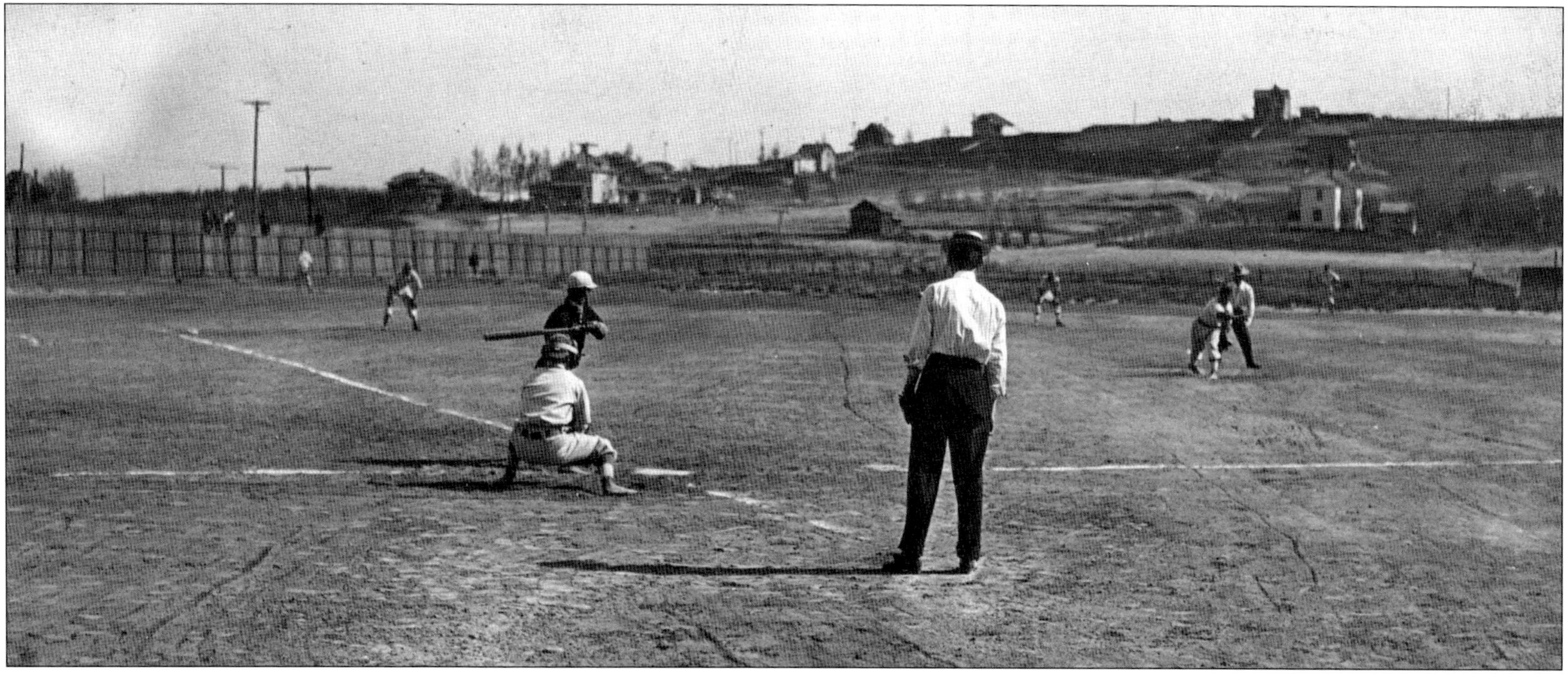

Early baseball game, 1910.

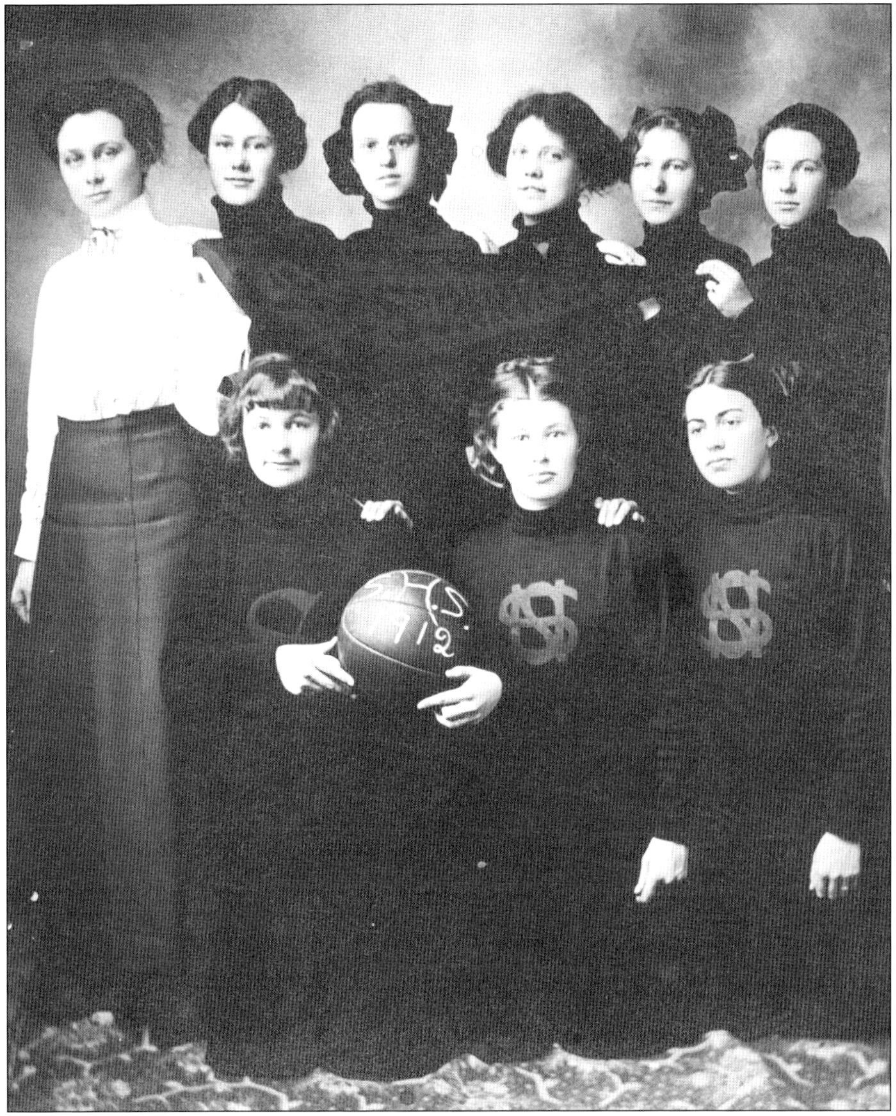

Sunnyside High School Girl's Basketball Team of 1912.

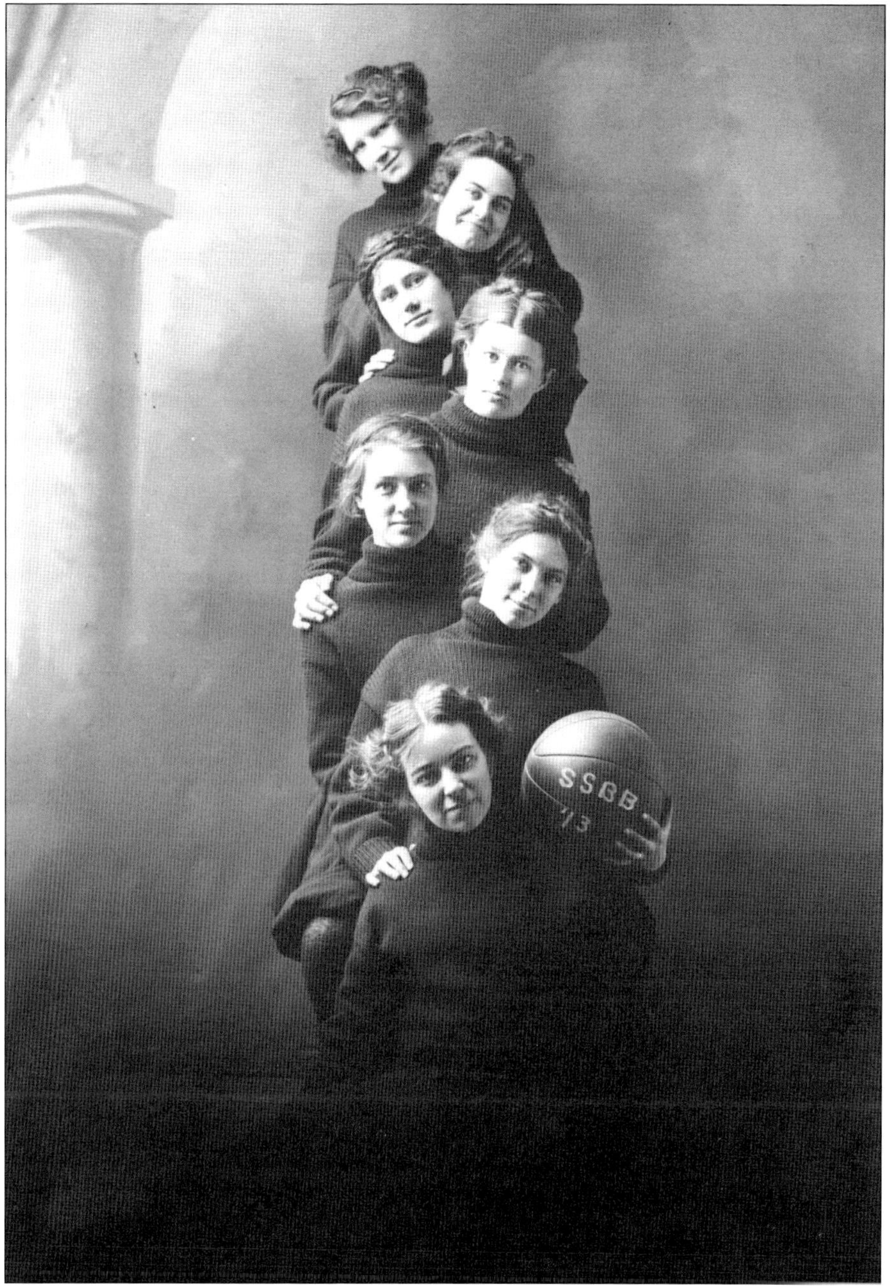

Sunnyside High School Girl's Basketball Team of 1913. From top to bottom, Austa Stackhouse, Lora Cafferty, Lois Hutchinson, Florice Nicolai, Jessie Thomas and Florence Mahaffy.

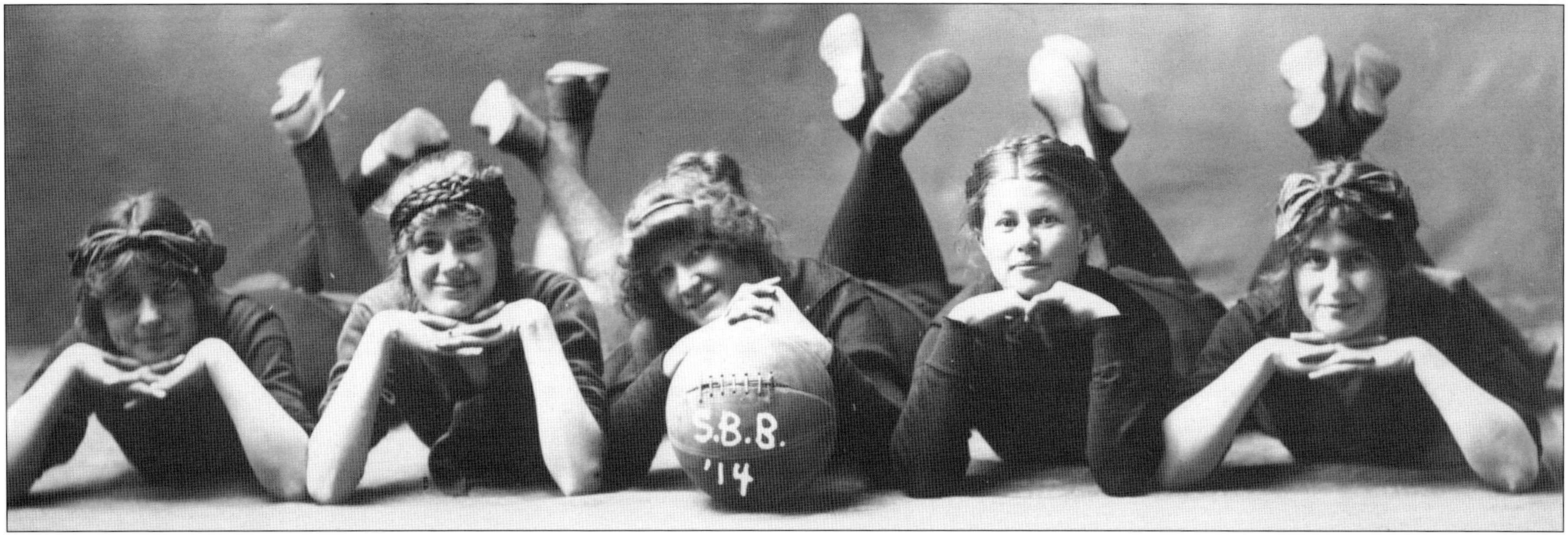

Sunnyside High School Girl's Basketball Team of 1914.

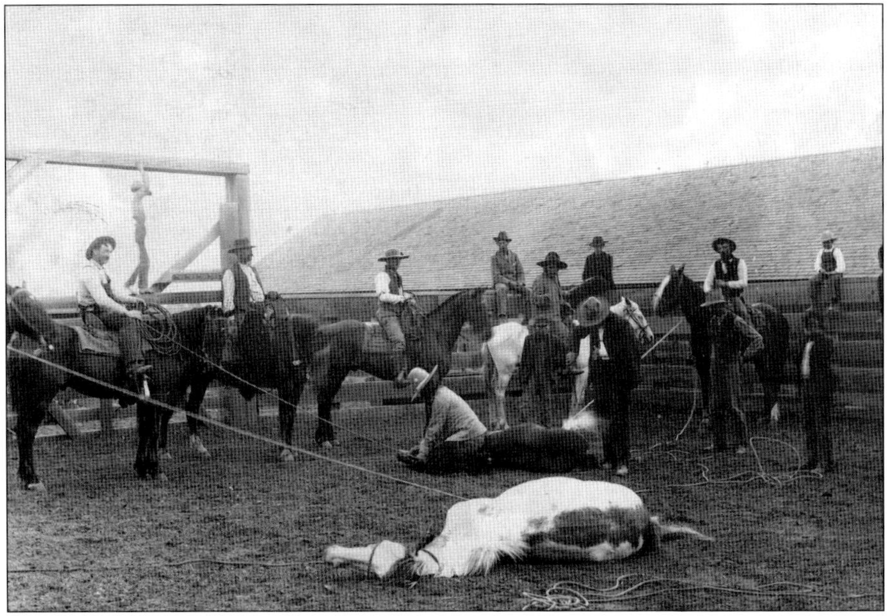

Cowboys branding their horses, early 1900s.

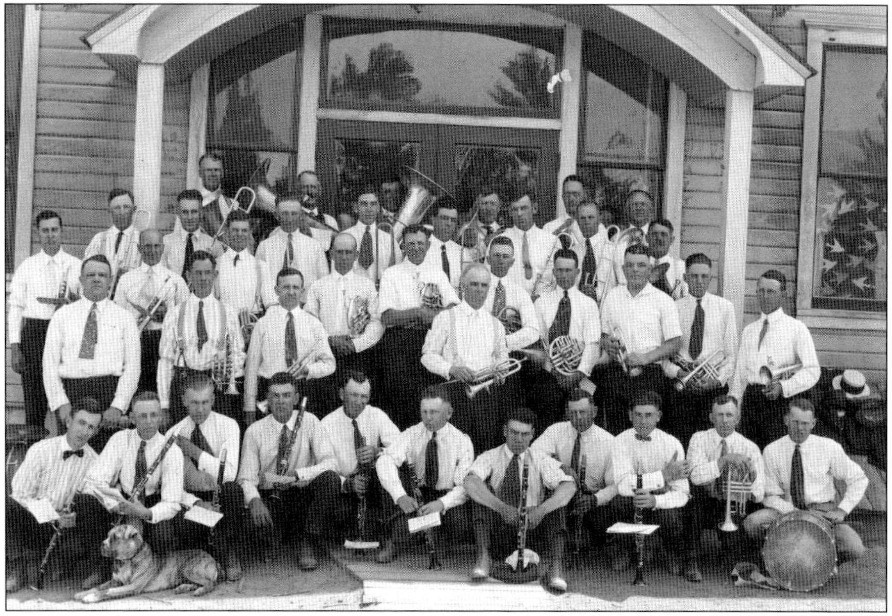

Band members from both the Grandview and Sunnyside bands before a parade in Grandview, 1920s.

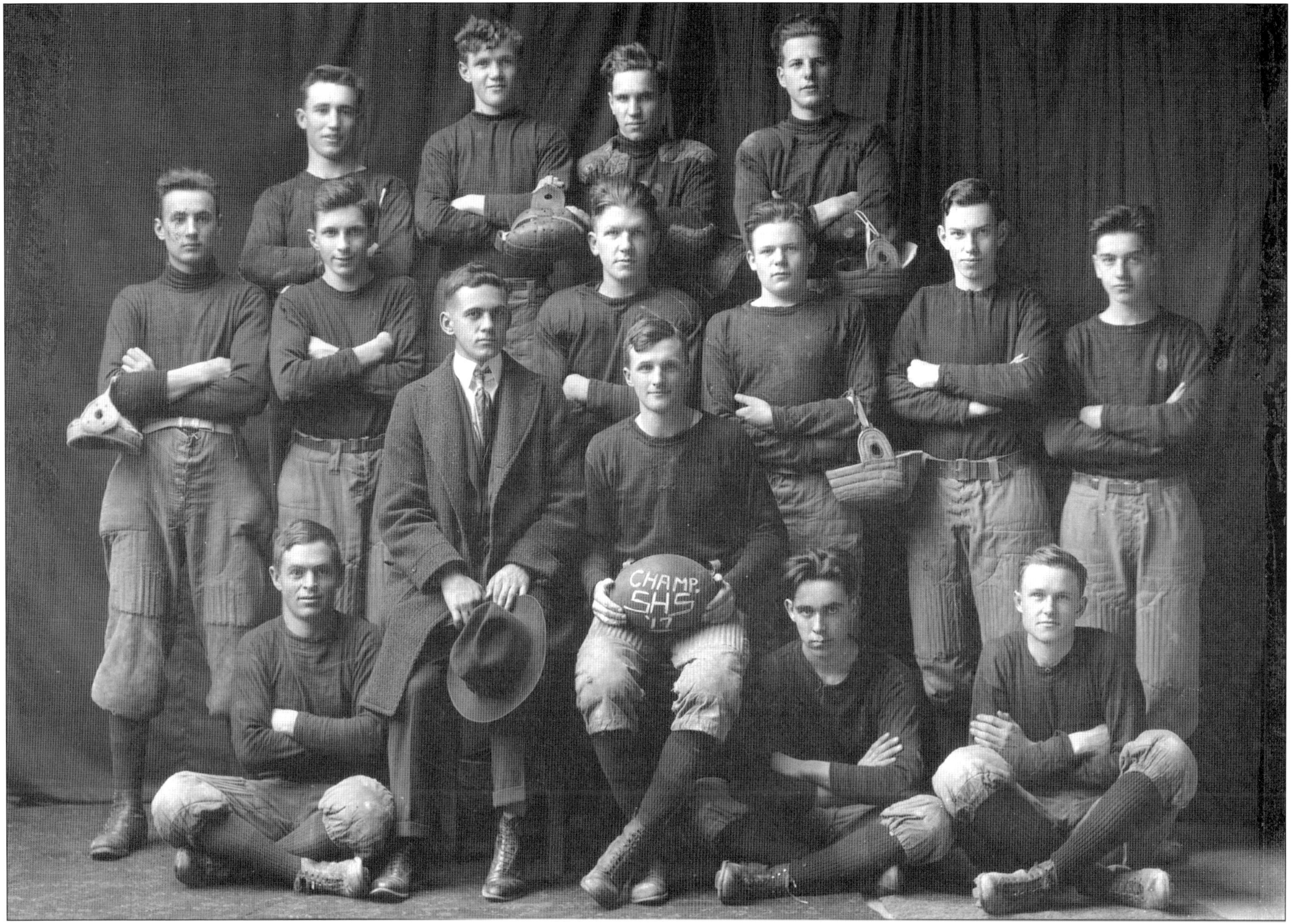

Sunnyside High School football team, league champions, 1917. Front row, left to right: Howard Martin, coach Schwenk, George Toner and Eldon Foreman. Middle row, left to right: _____ Terry, Ed Funk, John Stackhouse, Norman Rutenik, Ralph Rhebock and Frank McKibben. Back row, from left to right: Hobart Bond, Homer Wisner, Jenry Balcom and Harry Searle.

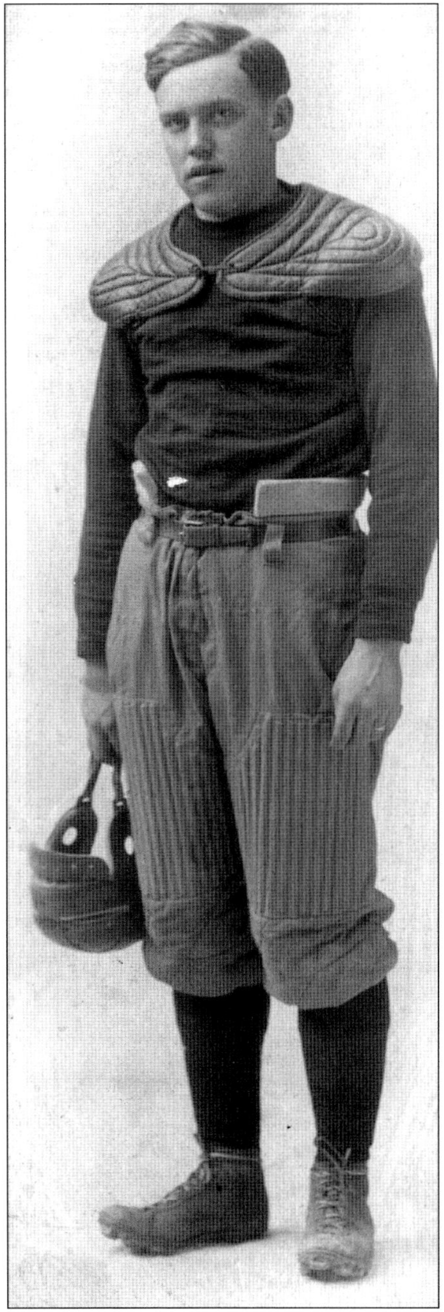

Perry Duncan, a member of the 1916 Sunnyside football team.

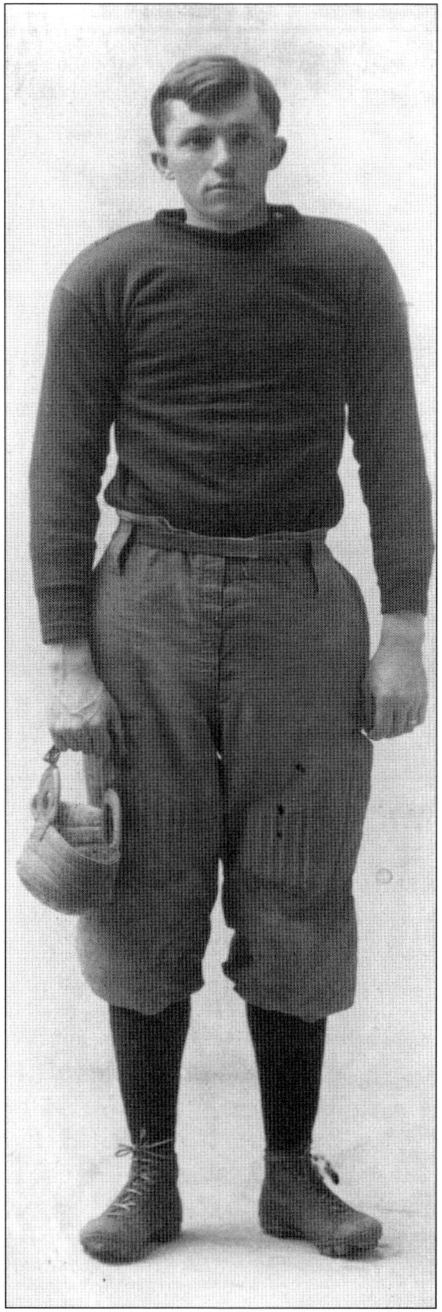

Earl Meyers, a member of the 1916 Sunnyside football team.

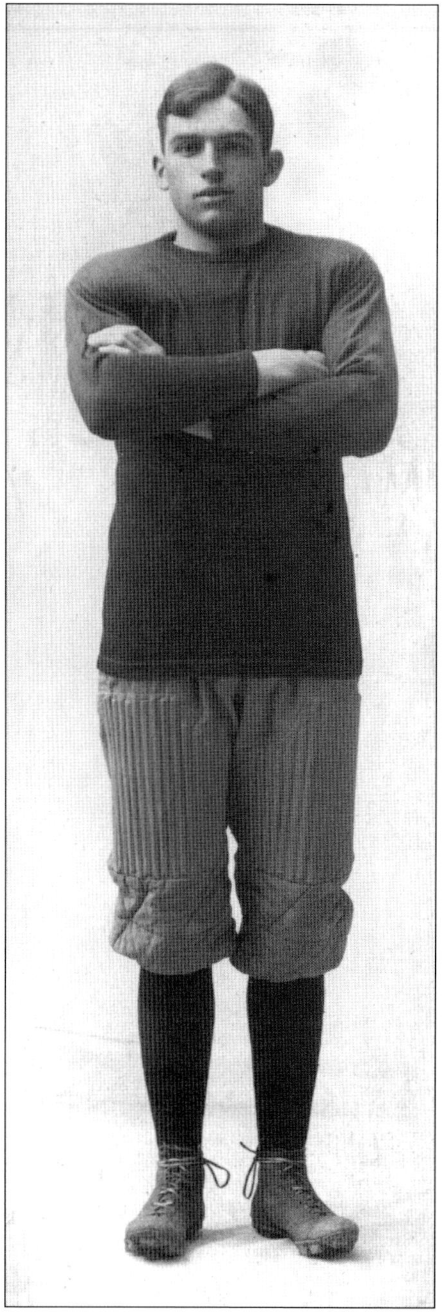

Bert Colby, a member of the 1916 Sunnyside football team.

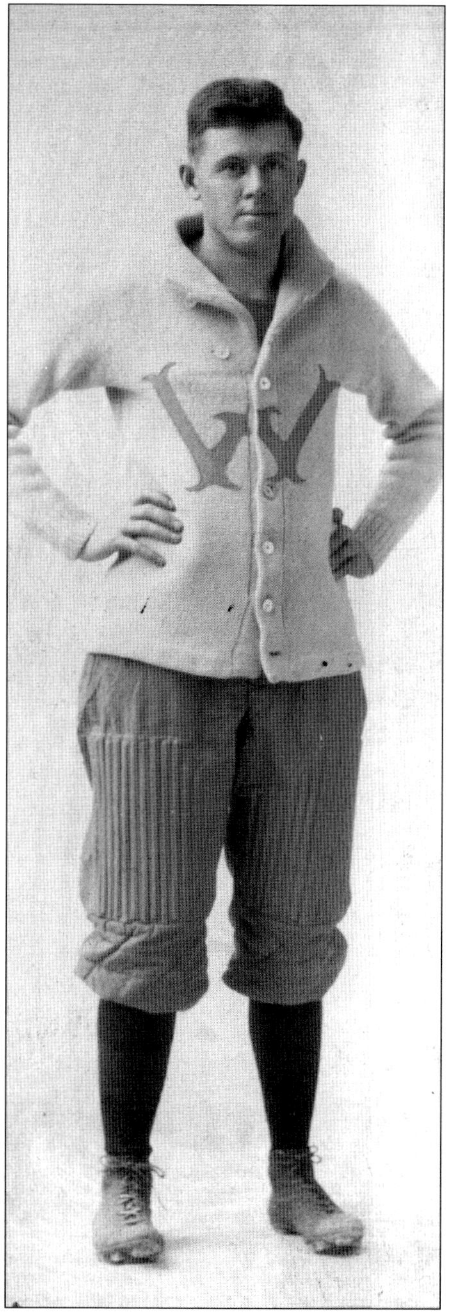

Don Thompson, the coach of the 1916 Sunnyside football team.

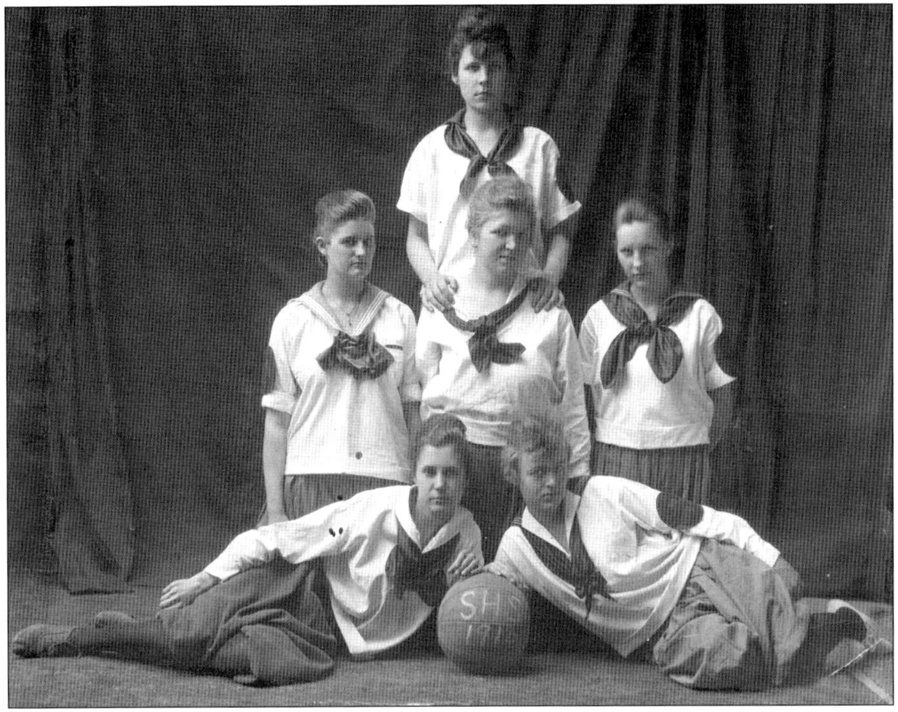

The 1918 Sunnyside High School girl's basketball team. Front row, Olive Warner and Laura Martin. Kneeling, Alice Morrison, Helen Stackhouse and Opal Boynton. Top, Clara Davis.

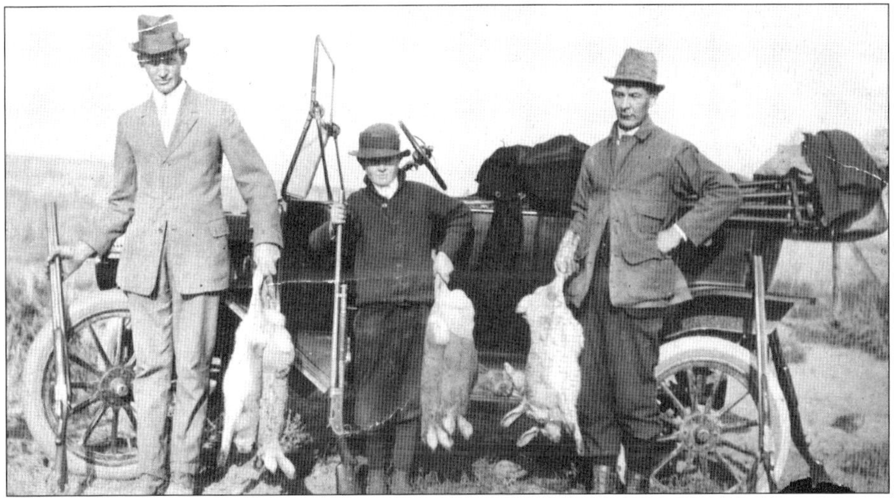

Hunters with their catch of rabbits, circa 1919. Left to right: P. Thornberry, Roy Brackett and Mr. Brackett.

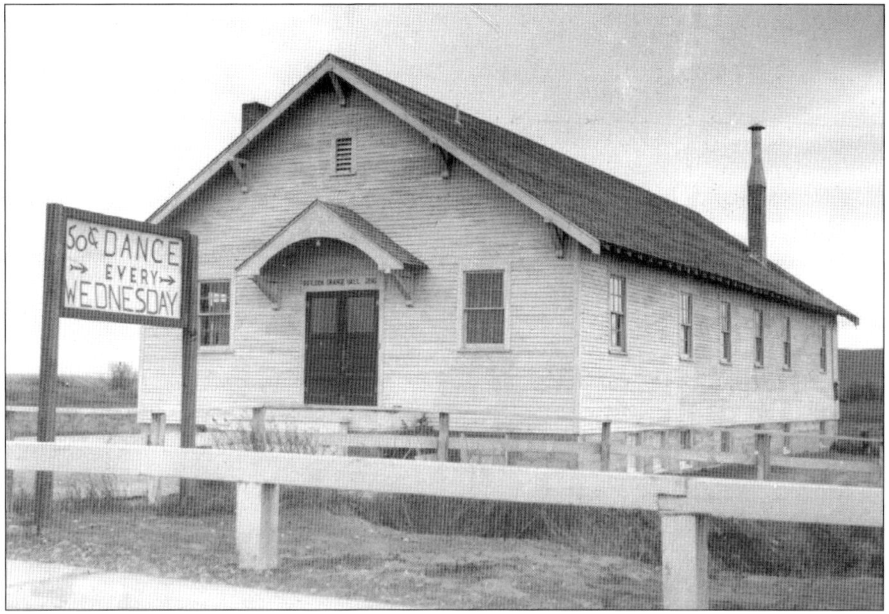

Outlook Grange Hall at the same site of present day Grange on Outlook Road, 1931. Note the 50¢ dance every Wednesday night

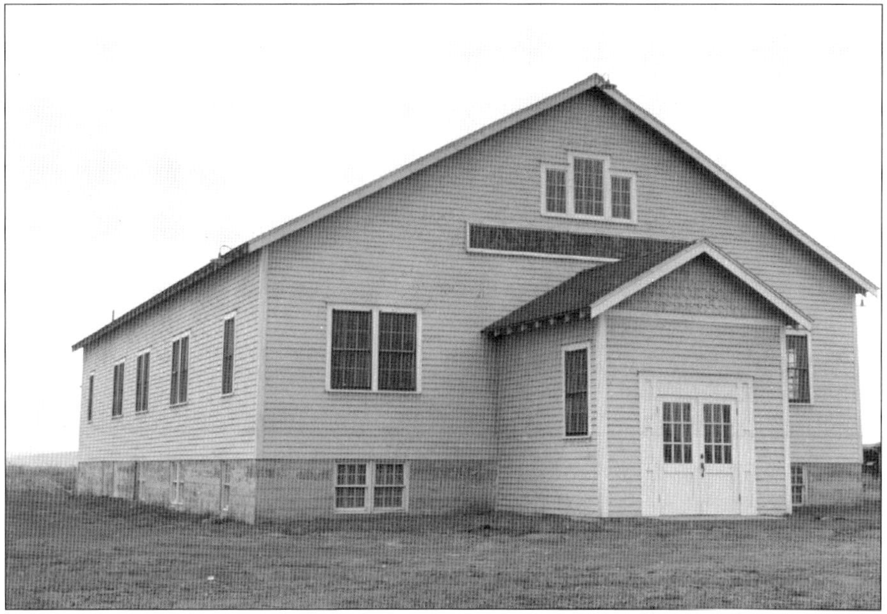

1931 Wanita Grange Hall on Sunnyside/Mabton Road.

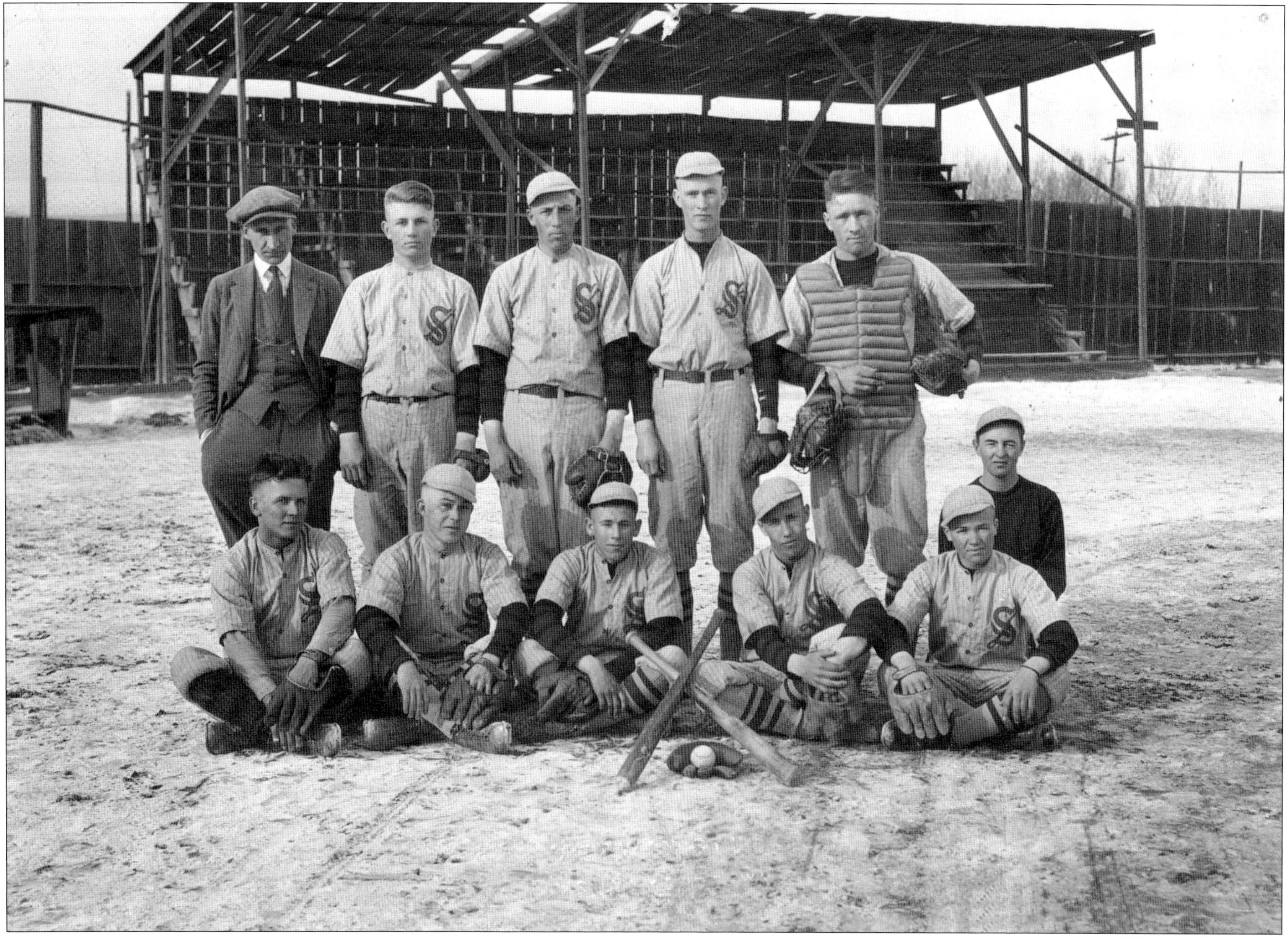

Sunnyside baseball team, 1922.

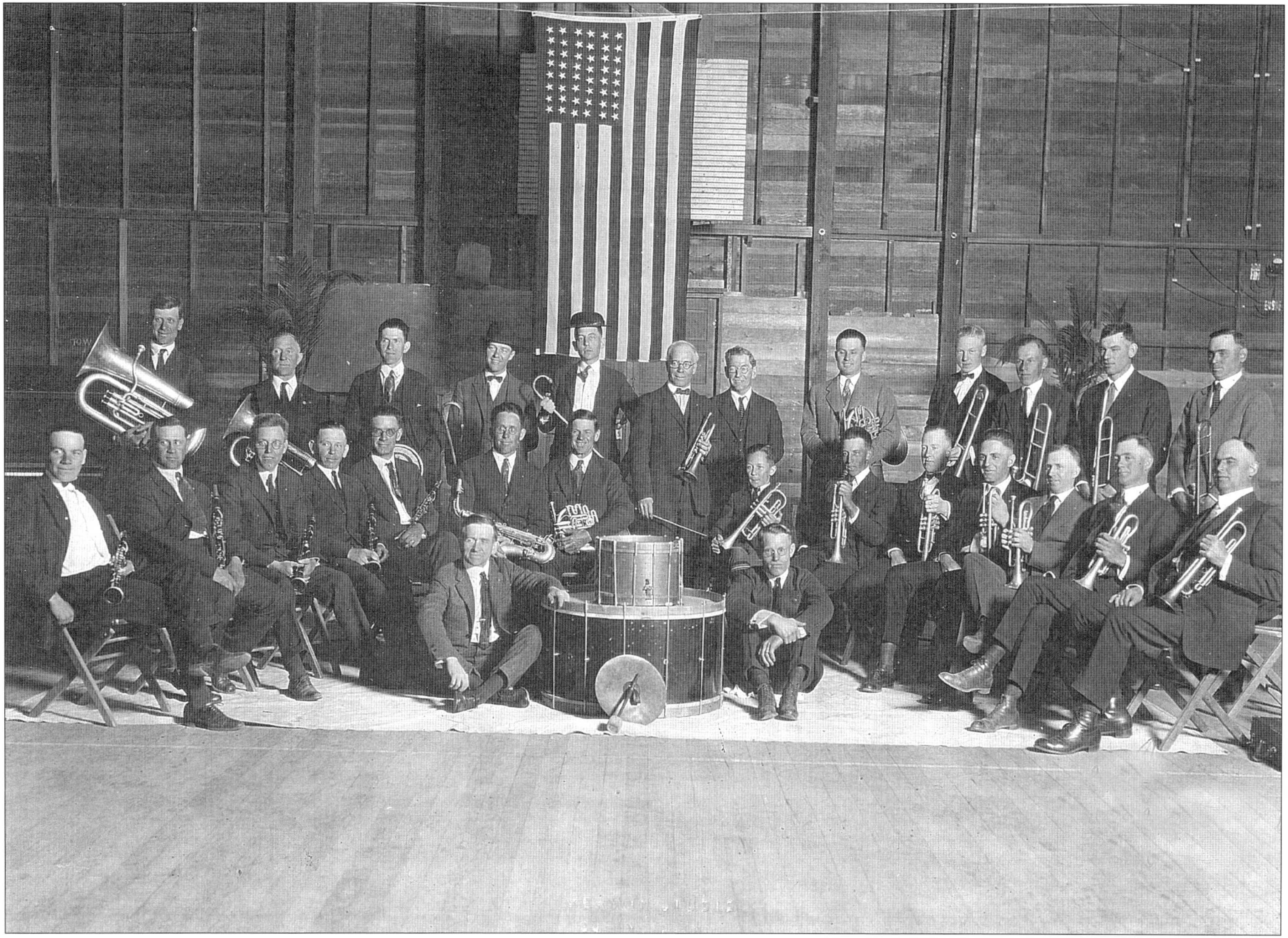

The last concert under Professor Hare. Professor Frienmuth took over, 1923.

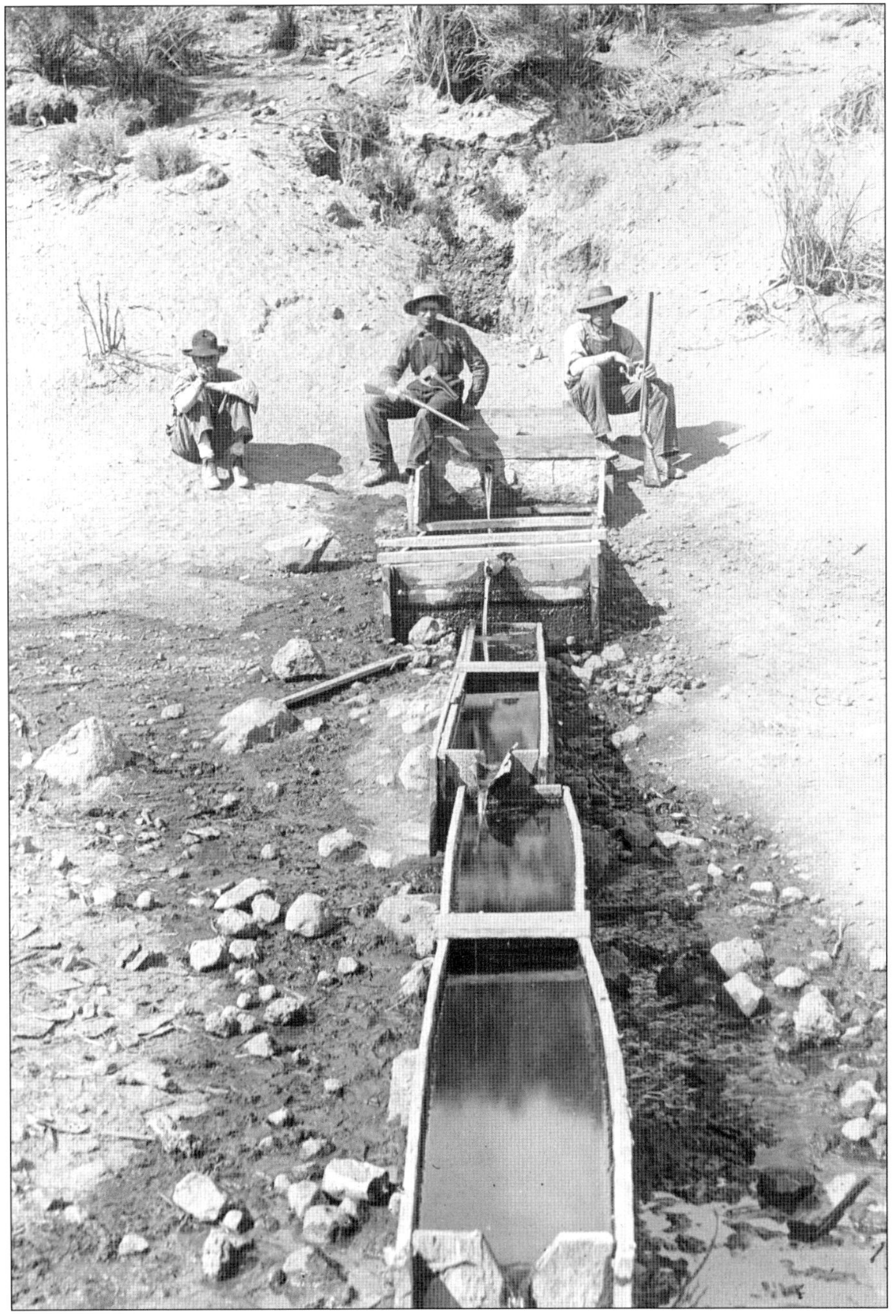

Men on a hunting trip northeast of Sunnyside at Barrel Springs near the Stuart Ranch. Mark Hetterick is known to be one of the three men.

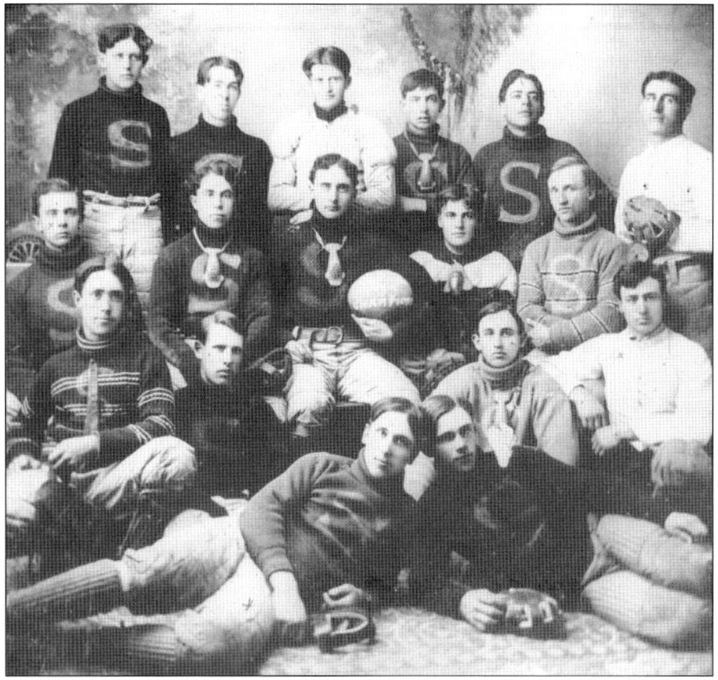

1905 Champion Football team. Some of those pictured are: Lee Ehmer, Albert Resliff, Hugh Crawford, Archie Campbell, John Dyke, Spruce Cox, Horace Miller, Harry Ehmer, Roscoe Sheller, Wilbur Searle, Real Lichty, Guy Lichty, Herb Shanefelt and Alva McClain.

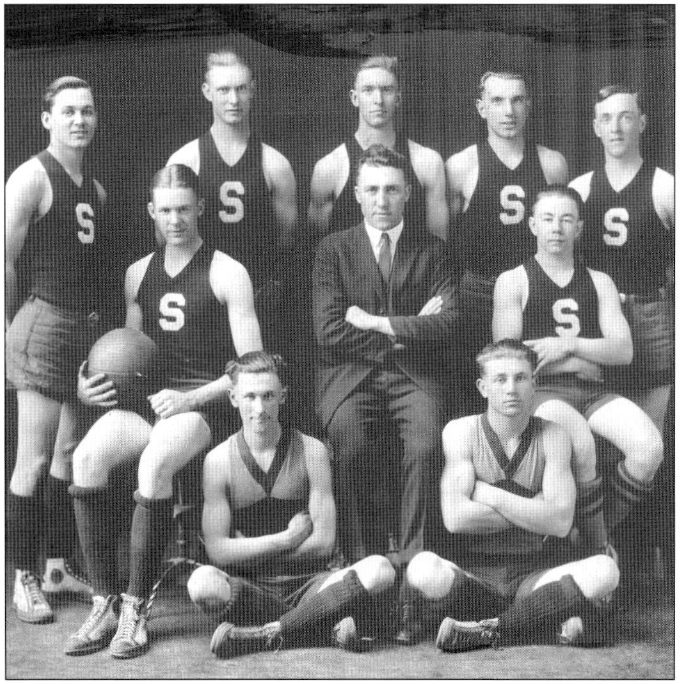

1923-1924 Sunnyside High School Basketball Team. Pictured in front from left: Joe Morgan and Riley Antler. Second row from left: Wendell Hitchcock, Coach Bush Lewis and Floyd Ingraham. Back row from left: Claude Maurey, Reese Cochran, Clayton McMinimee, Desmond Shearer and Howard Bagley.

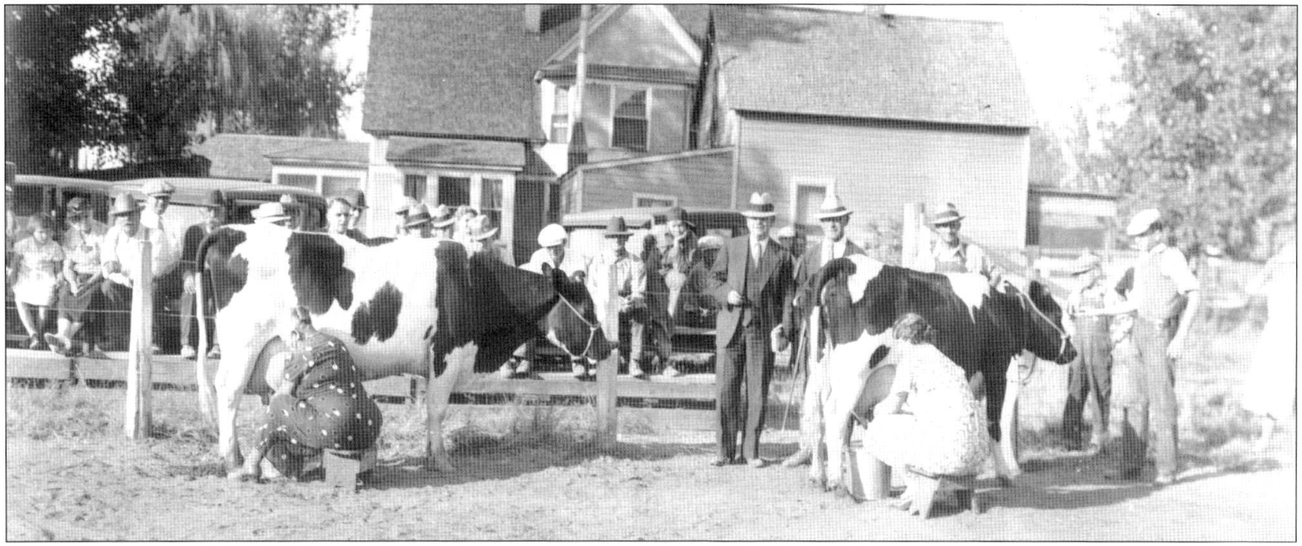

September 28, 1934 - Two women contestants compete in a milking contest during the Sunnyside Dairy Show. September 28, 1934.

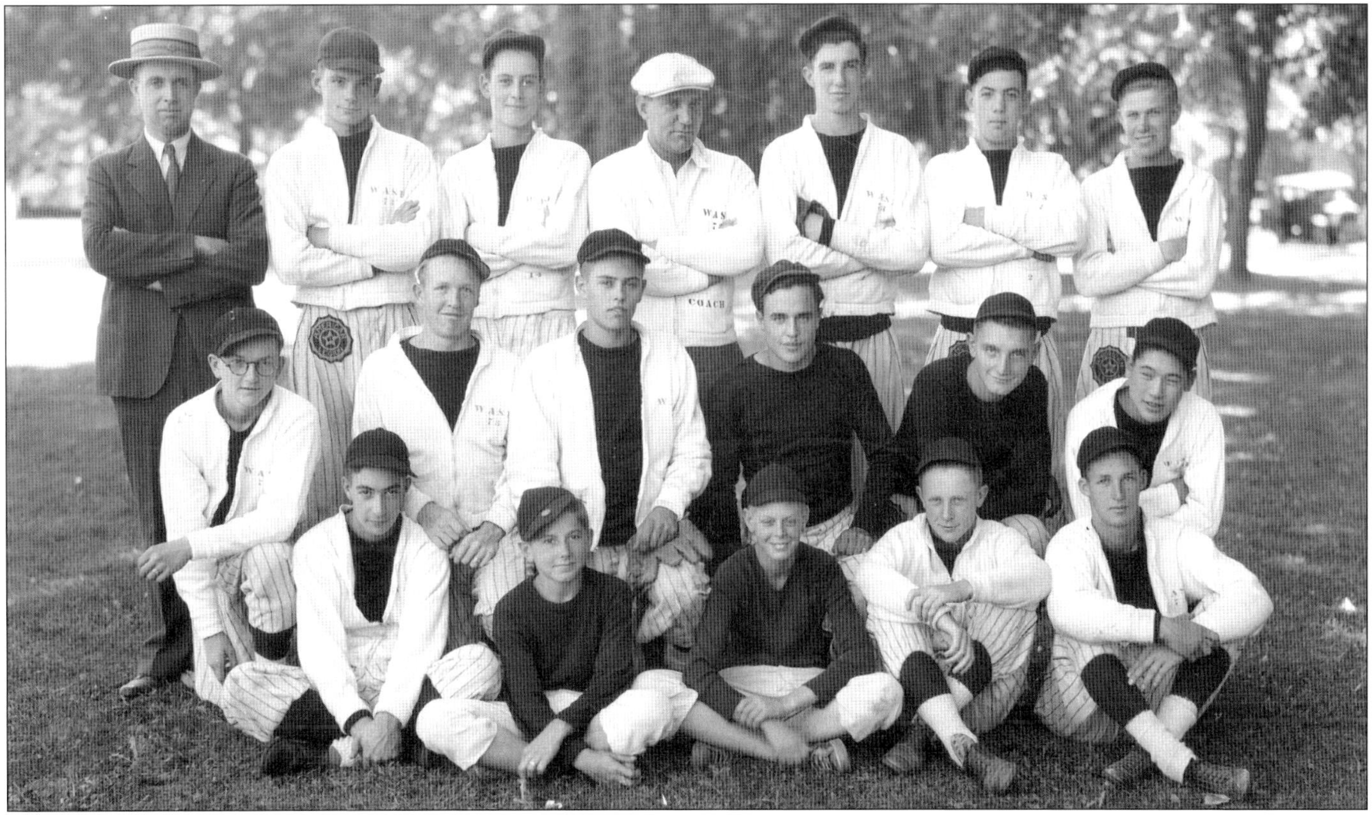

Sunnyside American Legion baseball team, 1930s. Some of the players pictured are: Phil Langford, Chuck Langford, Floyd Yamiro, Chuck Greer, Elden Greer, Flenn O'Neal, Gene Emery, Coach Jackson, Ellis Taylor, Bud Van Horn, Telford Anderson, Walter Hagerman and ____ Hickenbottom.

CELEBRATION

Today one of Sunnyside's most popular celebrations is the Sunshine Days. The event has been held since 1983, but its roots go back much further than that. Some of its previous incarnations include Ben Snipes' Day, the Sunnyside Grande Stampede, Neighbor Day, Roza Day, Fete day, and Ford Day.

Each celebration was unique, but Ford day was perhaps the most unusual. The event was held from 1922-1932 and was a celebration of the Model T. Festivities included a parade, street fair, prize drawings, Model T races and contests, the crowning of a Ford Day Queen, a street dance, and fireworks.

The parade was exclusively for Ford owners, which at the time included just about everybody who owned a car. Various awards were given out for such things as the noisiest Ford, the greatest number of people in a Ford, the five prettiest girls in a Ford, and in the days before political correctness, the fattest man and largest woman in a Ford.

The most unusual event of the day though was the auto-polo contest. The contest was a cross between a polo match and a demolition derby. It involved two stripped down Model T's with primitive roll bars welded on to the frame near the driver's section and at the rear of the car. Besides a driver each car had a mallet-man who stood on the passenger side running board gripping the front roll bar with one hand and a croquet mallet with the other. The object of the game was to score by hitting a basketball through a goal. There were numerous collisions, a few rollovers and amazingly no serious injuries.

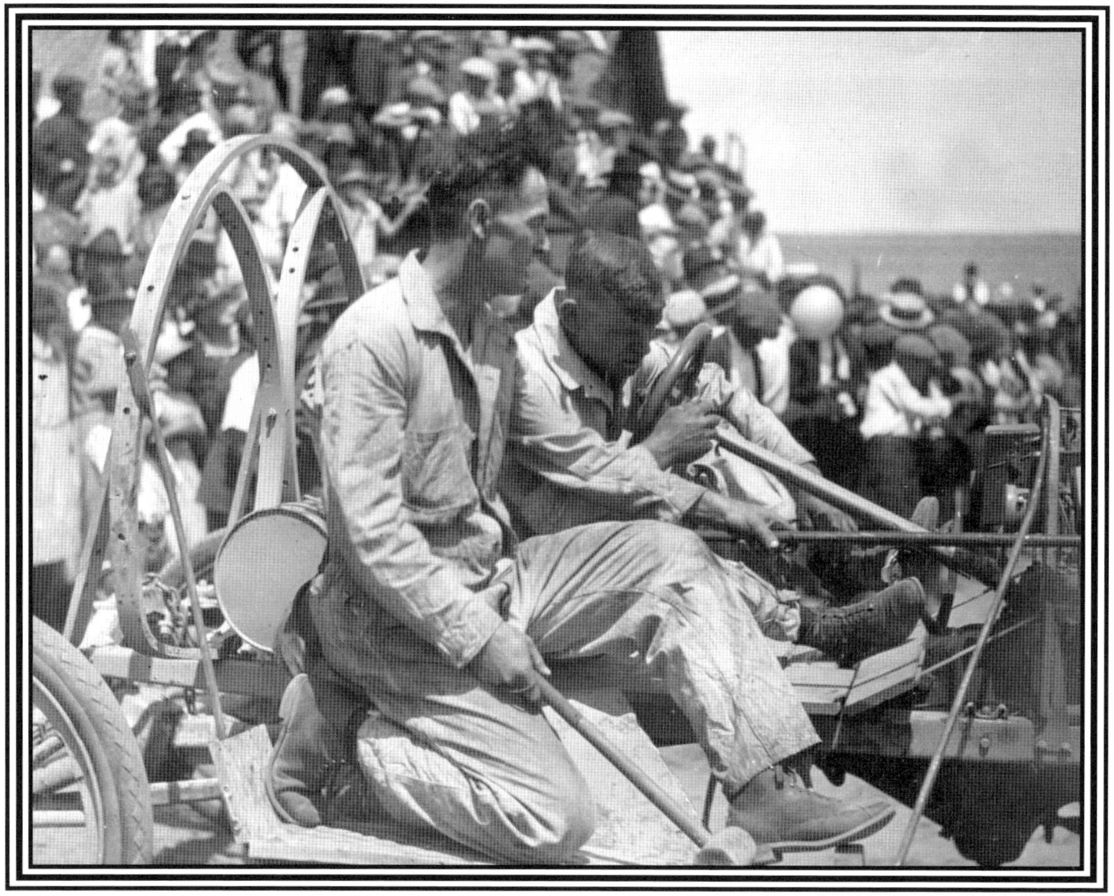

Ford Day, 1925. The passenger has a mallet that was used to play "Model T Ford Polo." Note the roll bar.

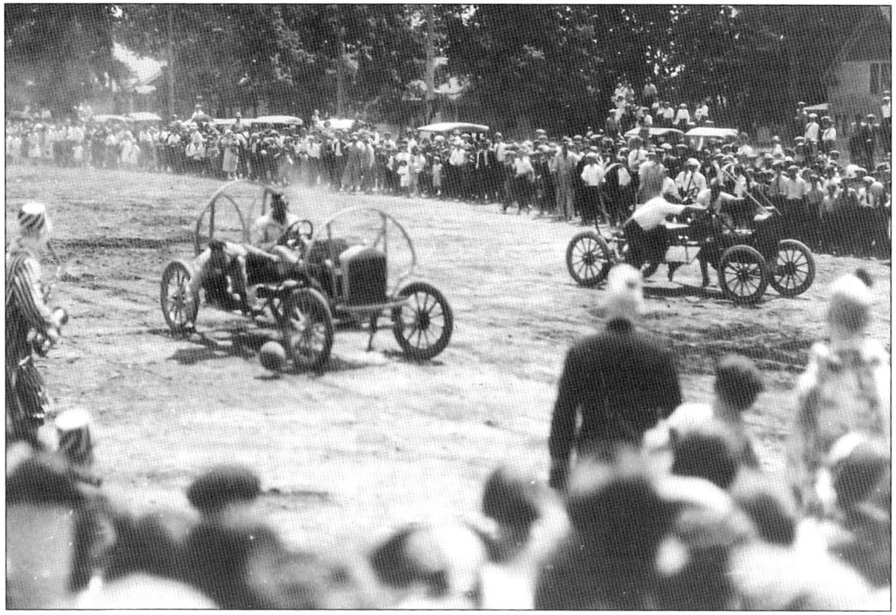

Model T Ford Polo event. Very popular attraction during Ford Day. Two cars, one ball, things happened!

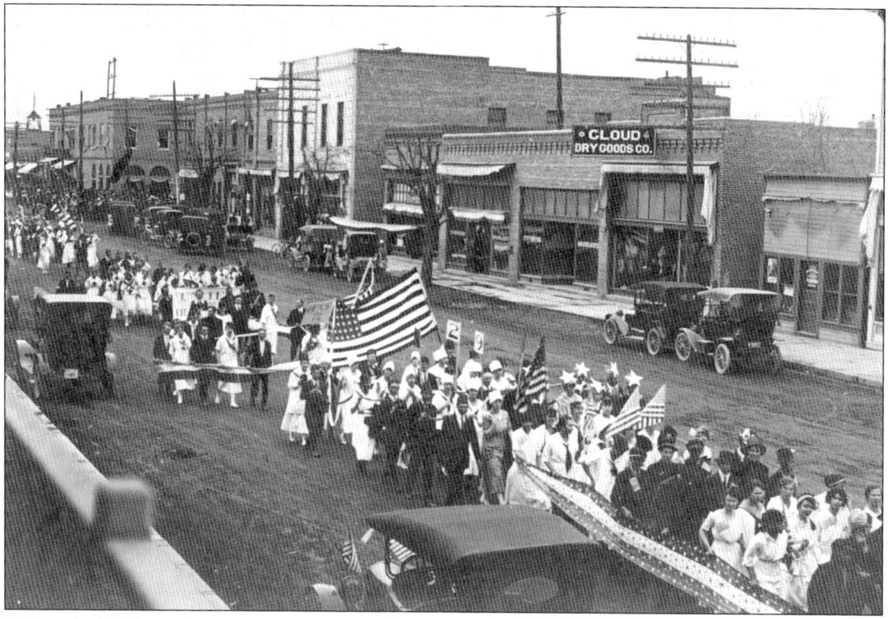

School children in a patriotic parade, April 20, 1917.

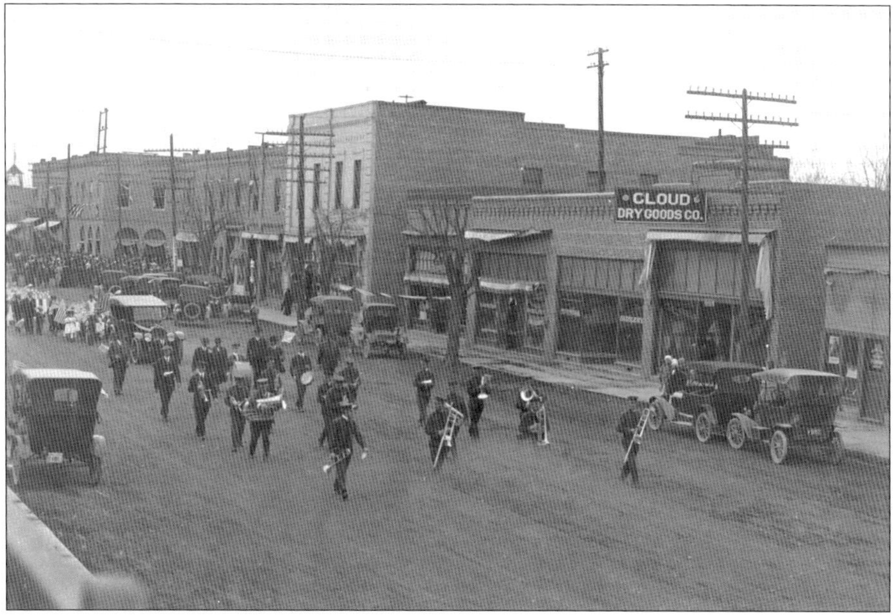

Sunnyside Band in a patriotic parade, April 20, 1917.

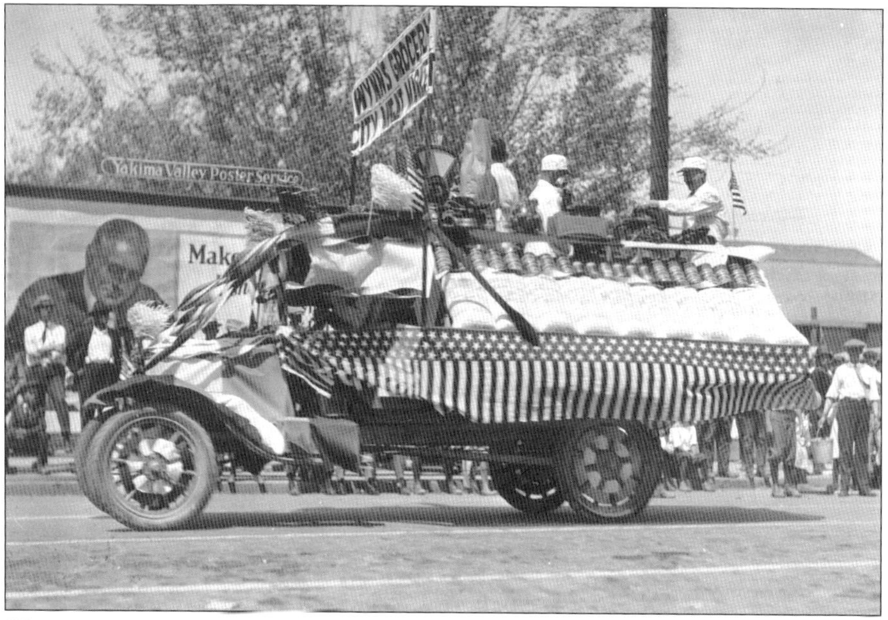

Wynn's Grocery City Meat Market float which took first prize in a parade, circa 1920.

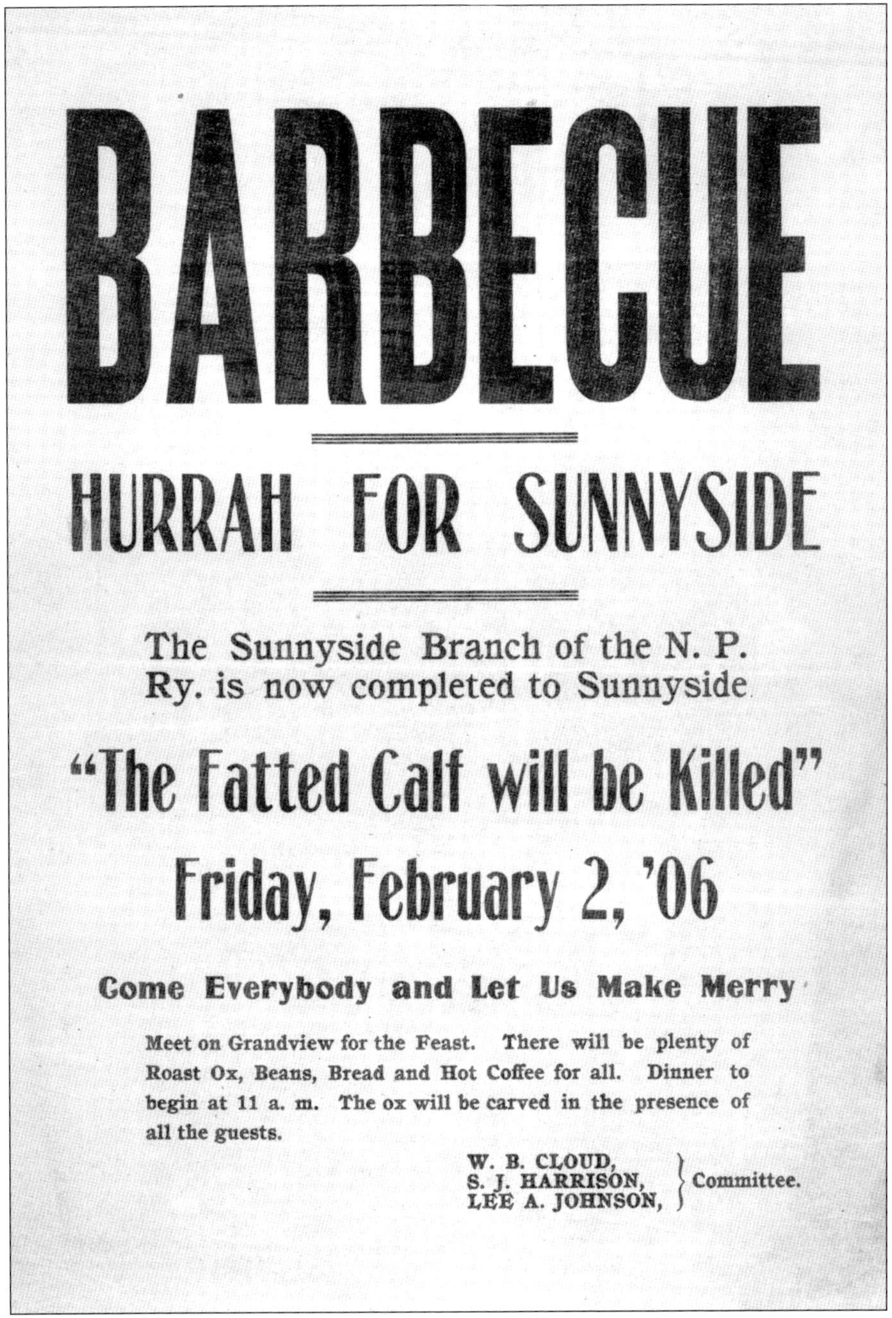

Advertisement for a Sunnyside barbecue in 1906.

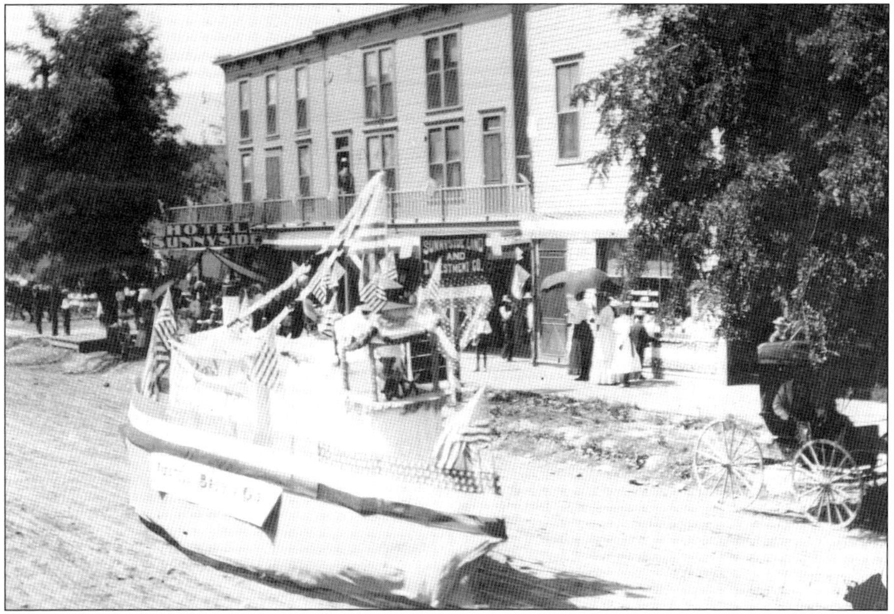

A float outside the Sunnyside Hotel on July Fourth, 1905.

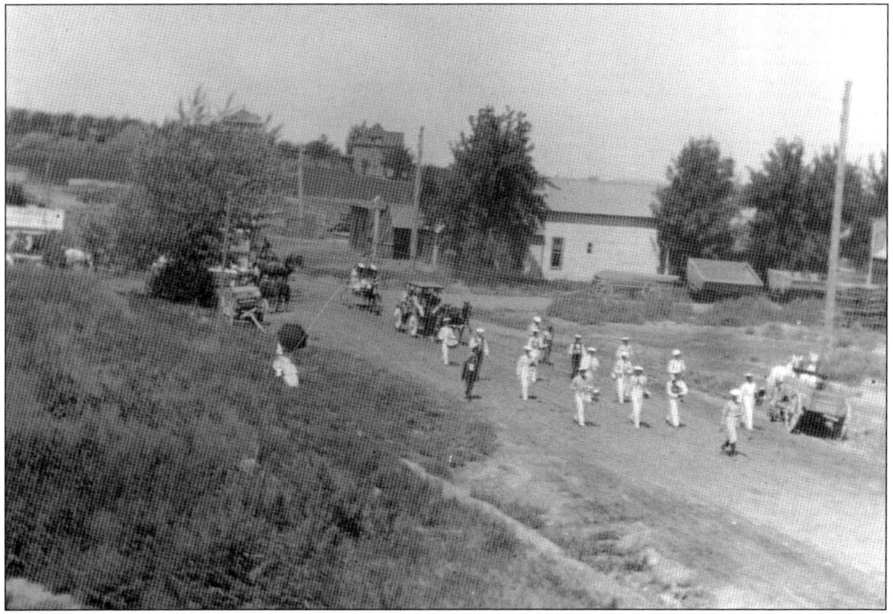

Fourth of July parade down Fifth Street, 1905.

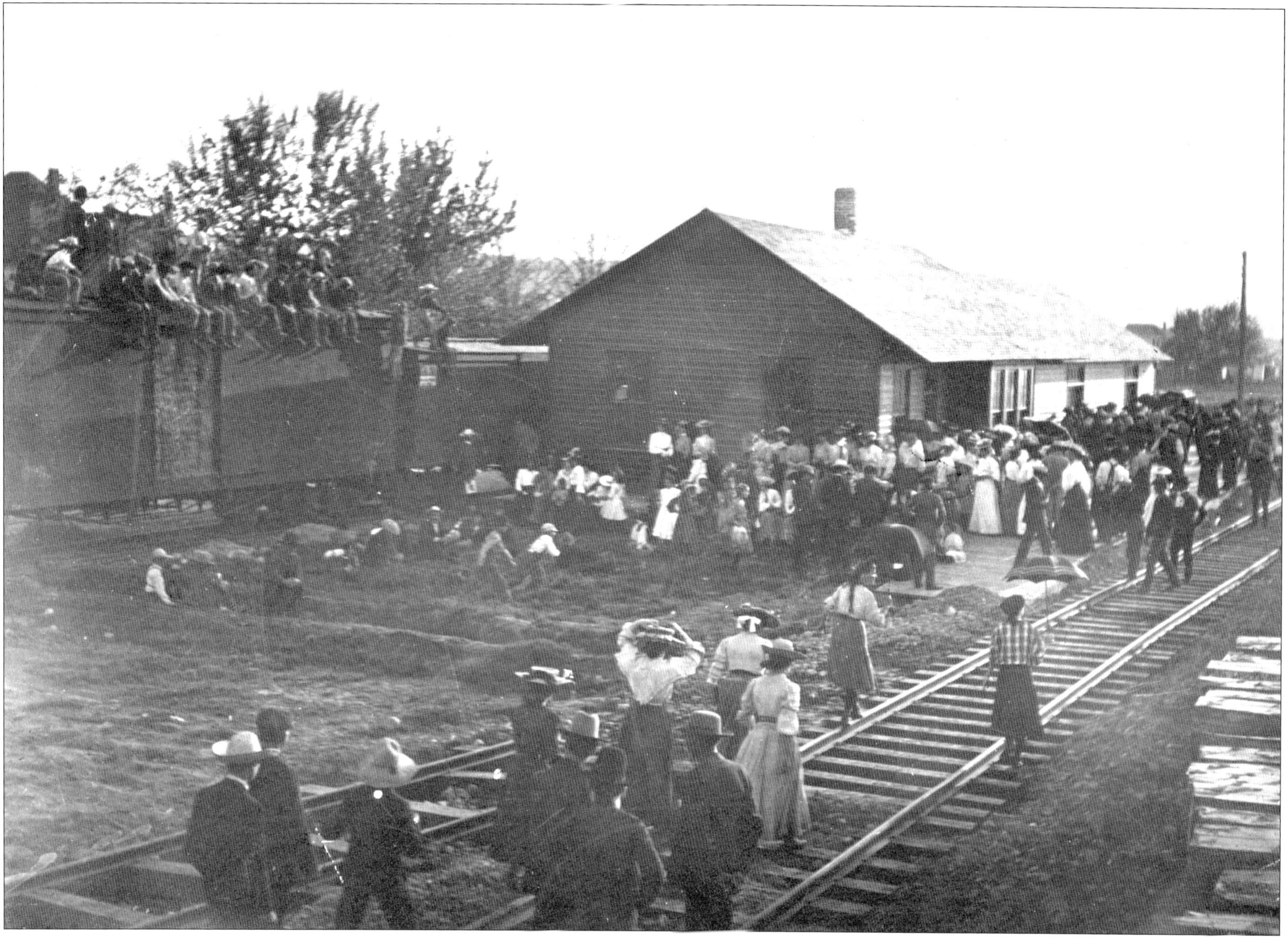

Arrival of Governor Mead for Commercial Club's first community celebration, May 23, 1907.

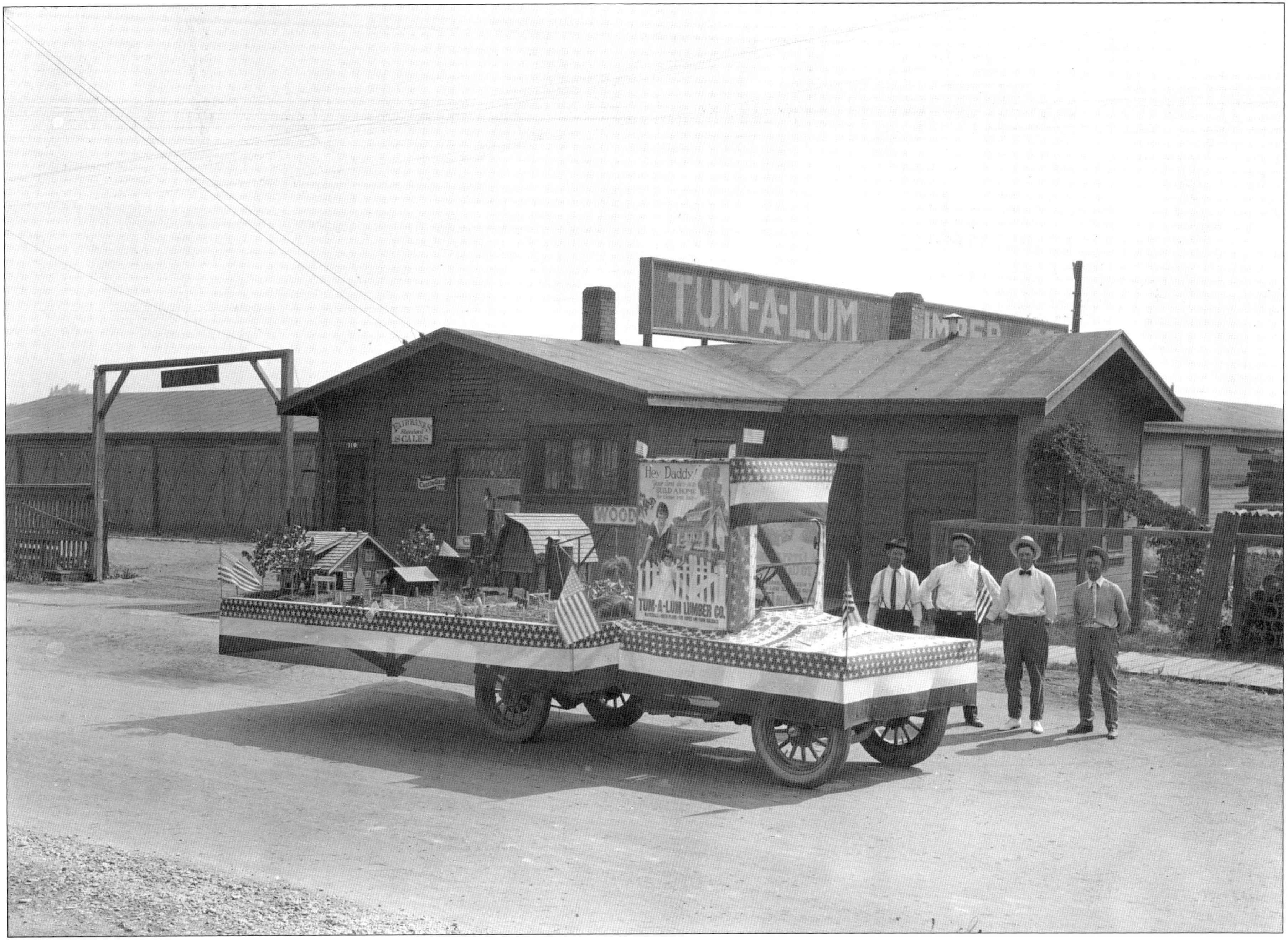

Tum-a-Lum Lumber Company was the first place float in the 1922 Fourth of July Parade. The lumber company was located on the east side of 6th Street between the railroad tracks and Custer Avenue.

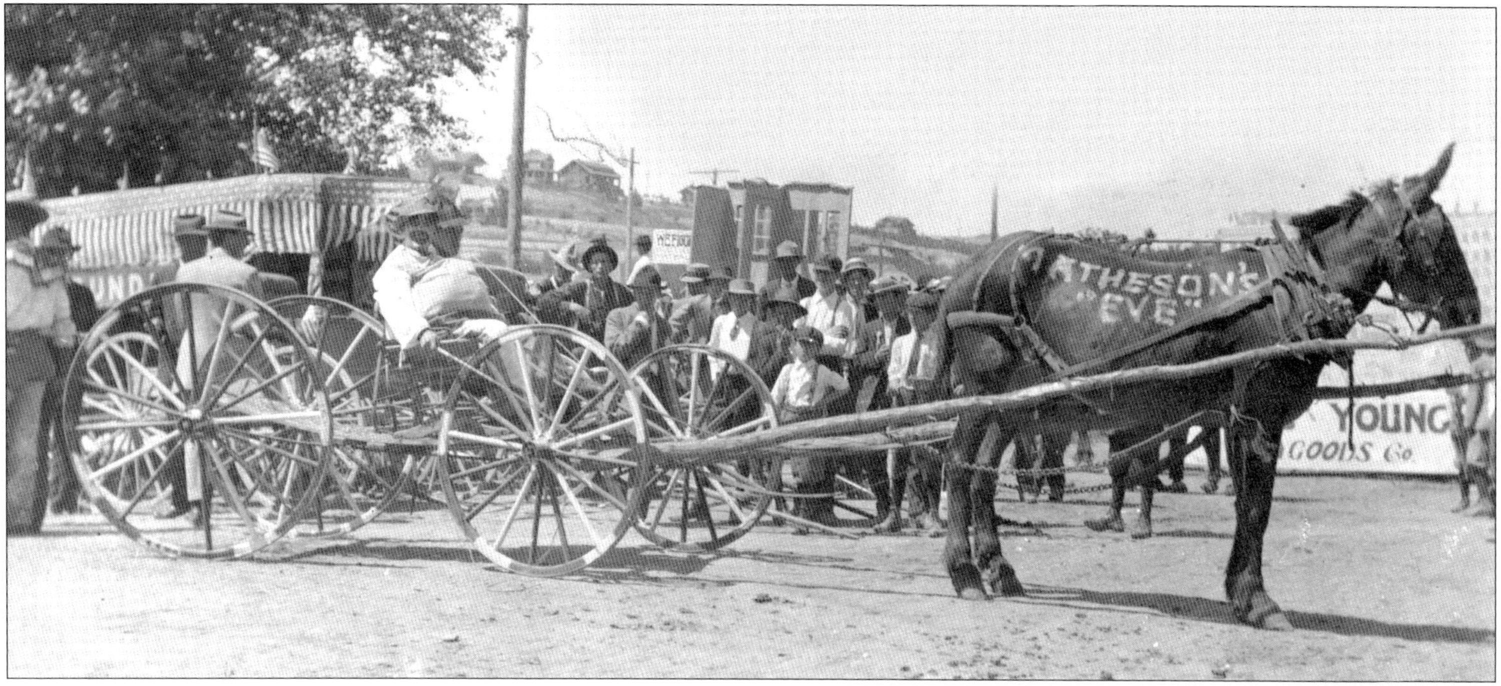

Harvey Matheson's float in the Sunnyside Picnic, circa 1896.

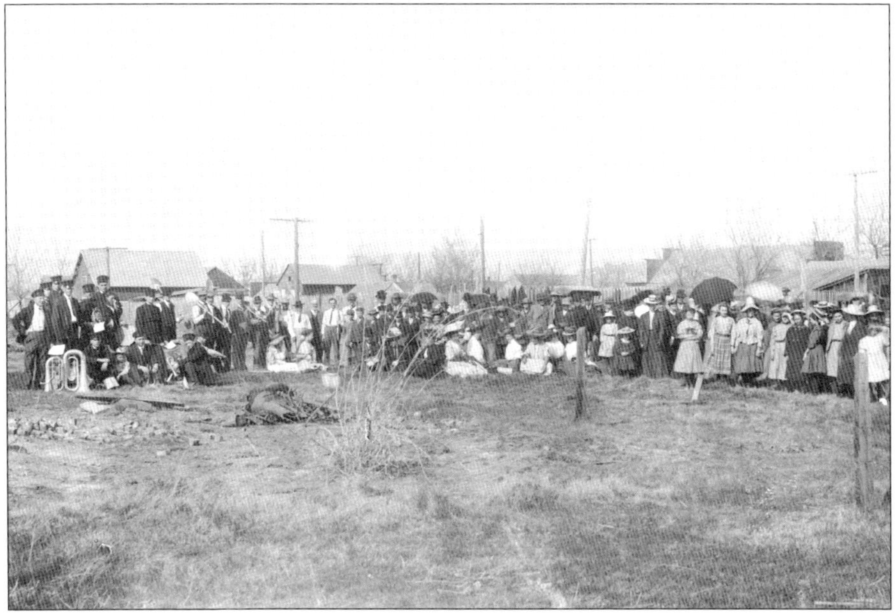

Arbor Day at Sunnyside Park, 1897.

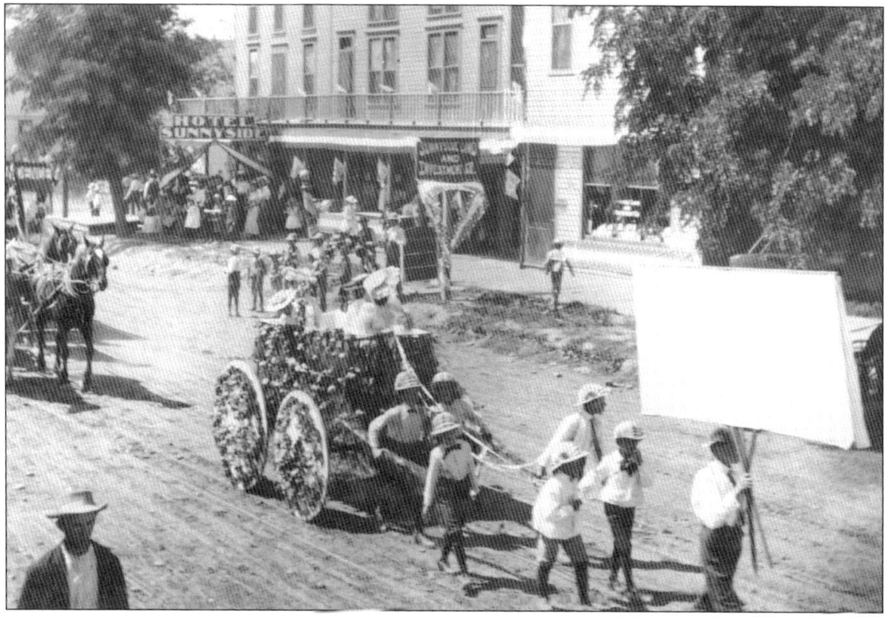

The July 4th Parade, 1905.

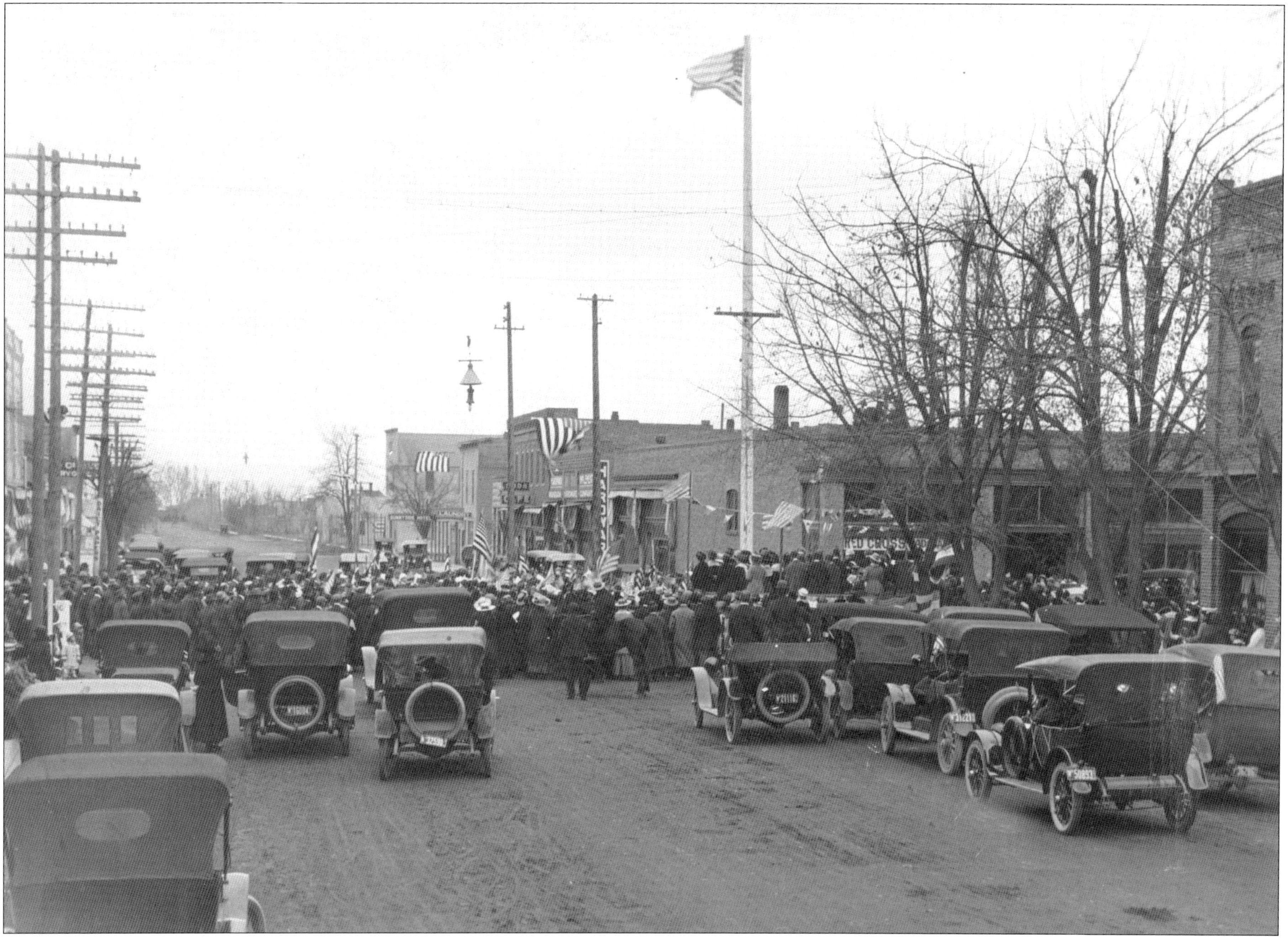

Crowd gathers for flag raising in the early 1920s. Two high school boys who wouldn't salute the flag were tied up and given a good soaking with a fire hose, and they got no sympathy.

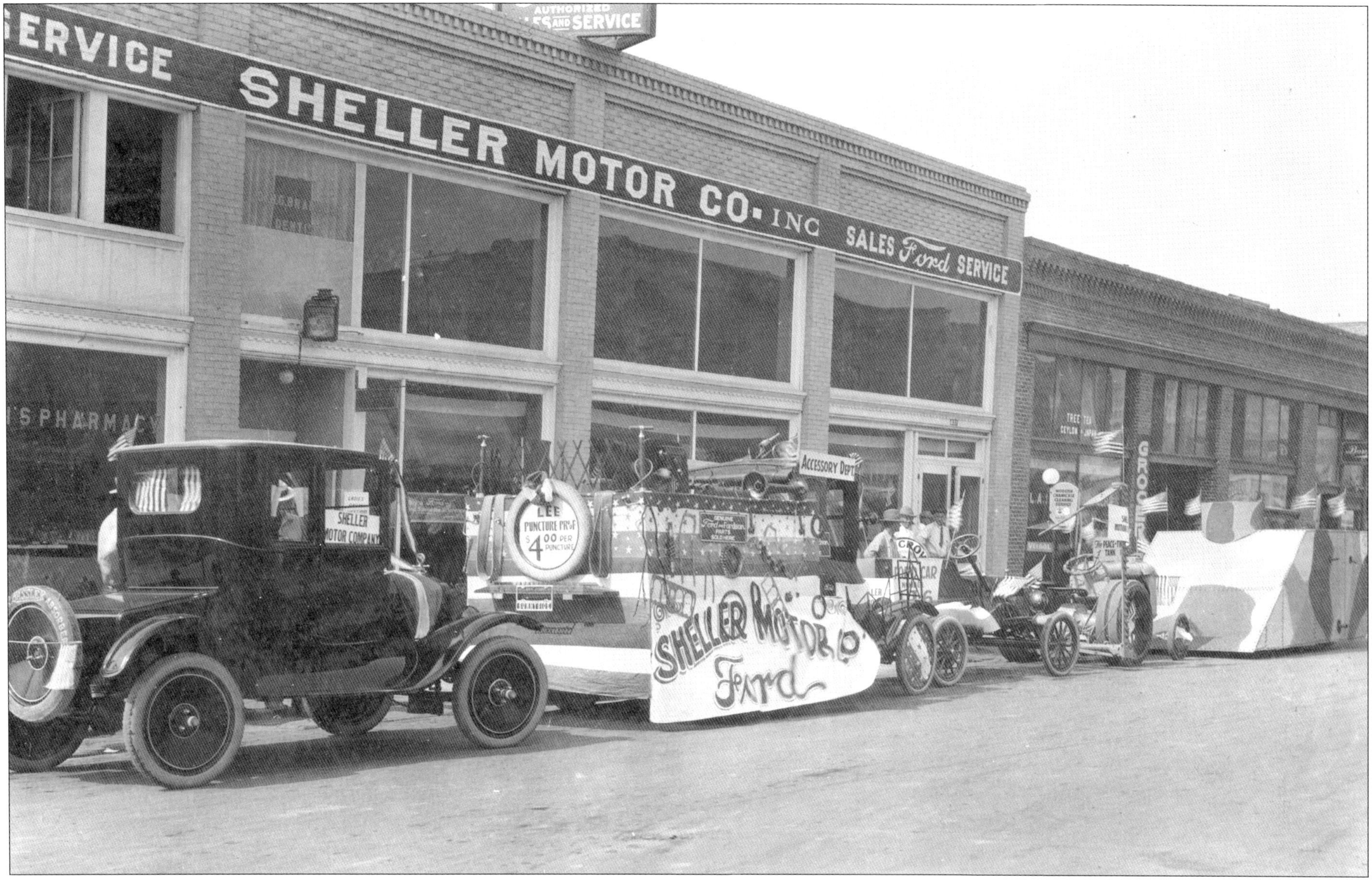

Ford Day in Sunnyside.

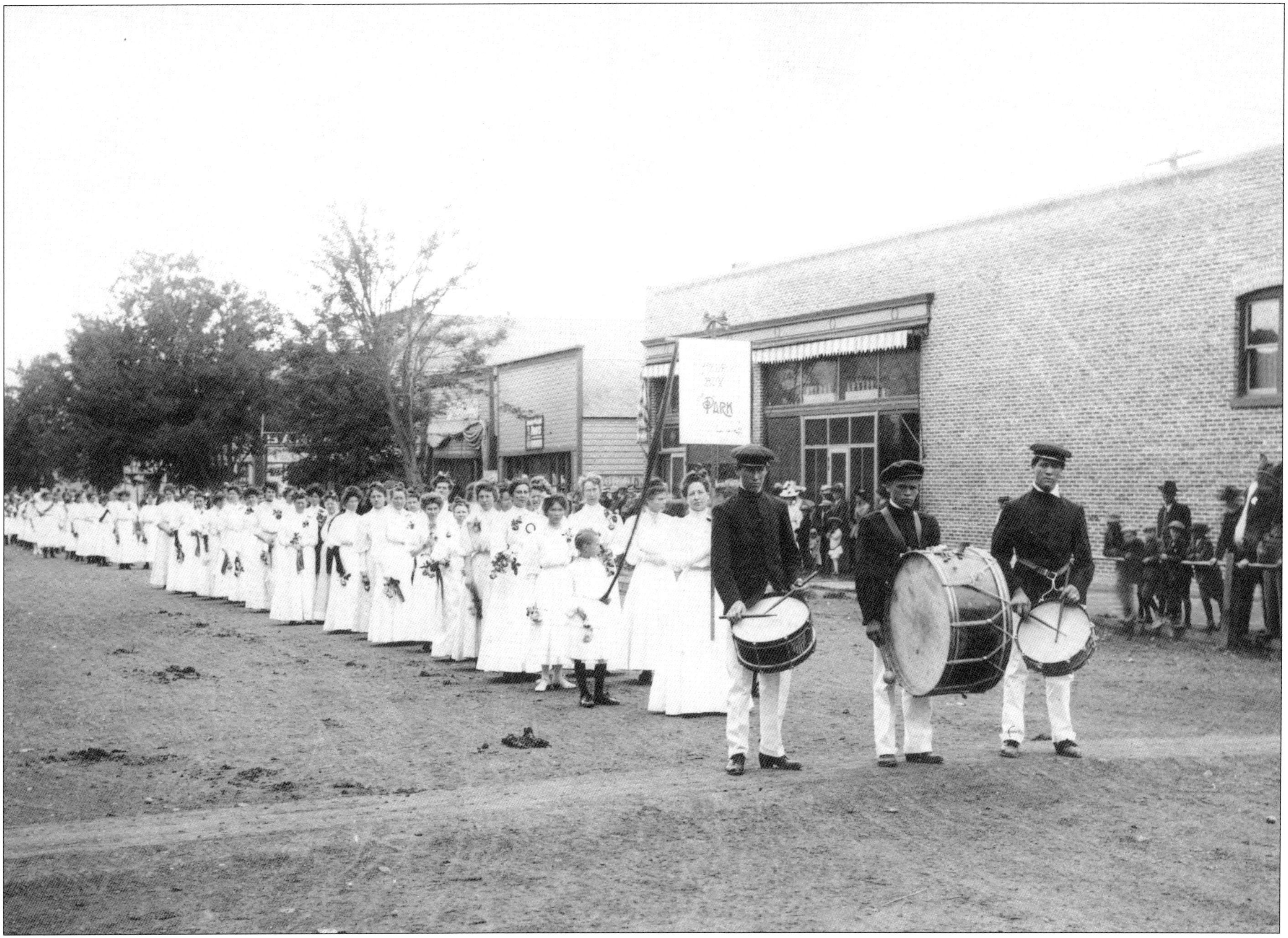

Ford Day Parade, circa 1925.

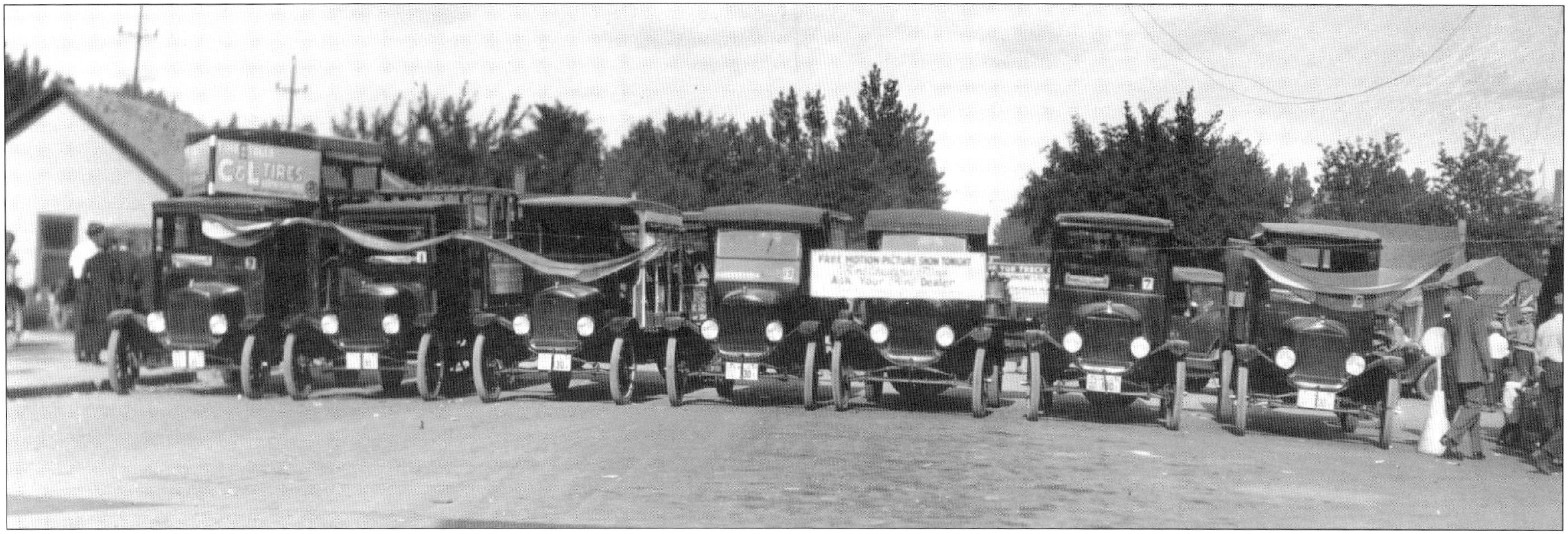

Ford Demonstration, 1925

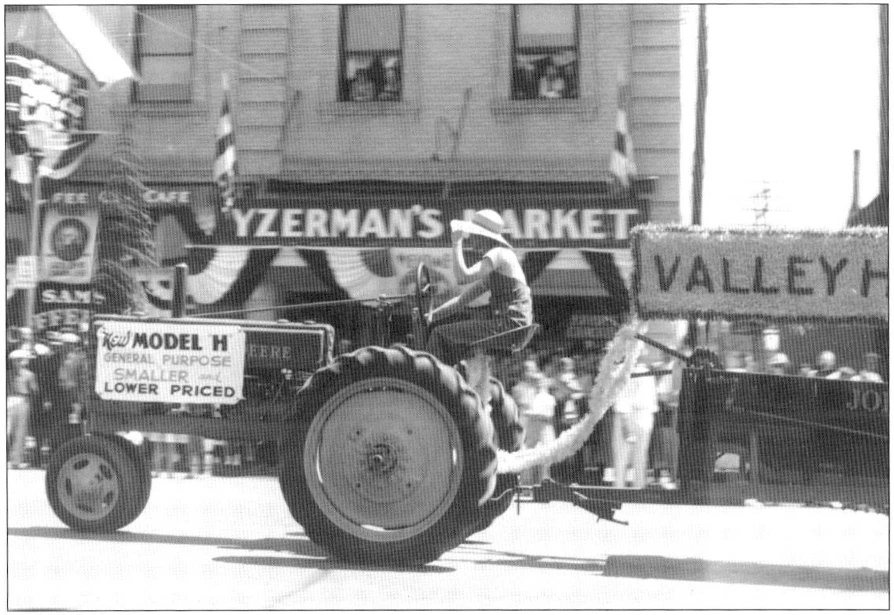

Fern Hiner on a Ford Modcl II Tractor pulling the Valley Hay and Implement float, 1925.

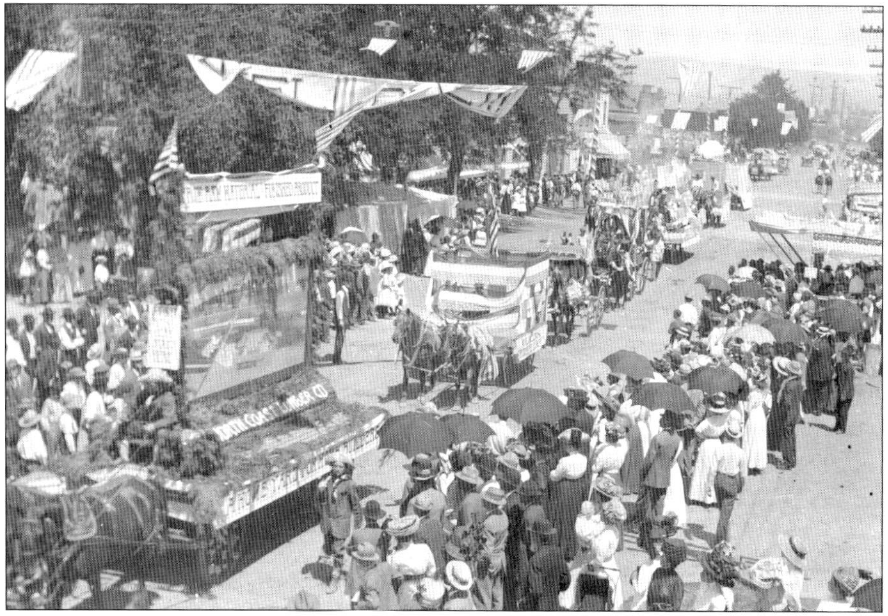

View of a Fourth of July Parade on Sixth Street looking north, circa 1910.

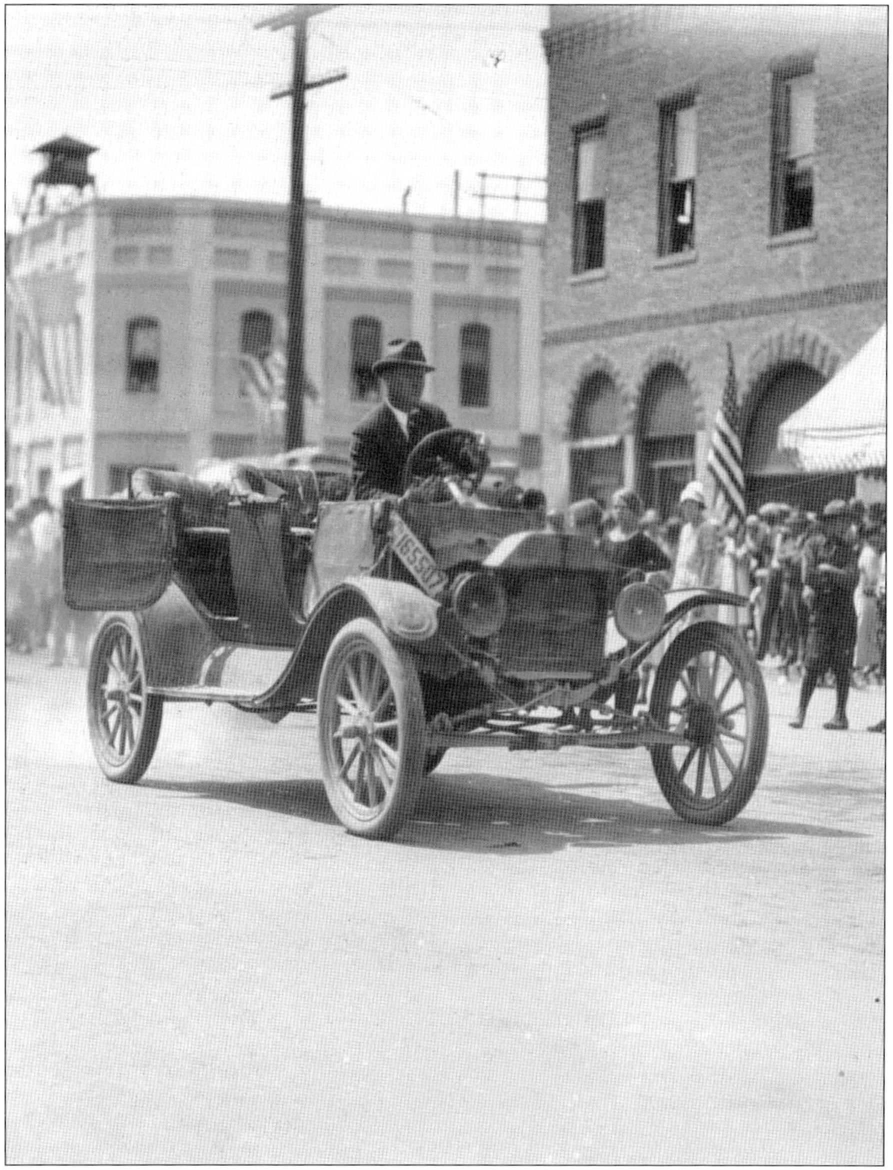

Ford Day Parade, July 4, 1925.

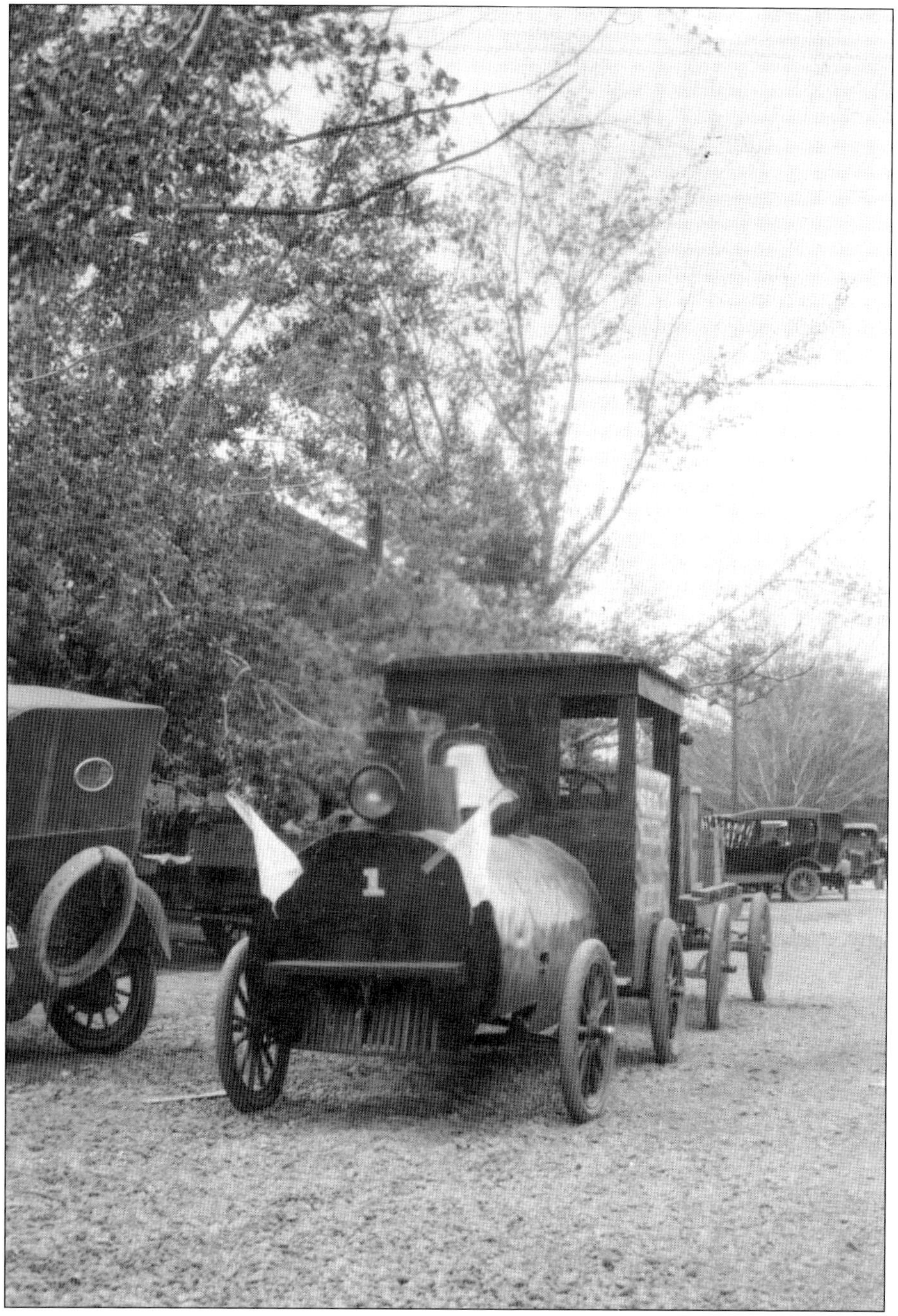

Locomotive made of a Model T used to advertise Ford Day to neighboring communities, circa 1925.

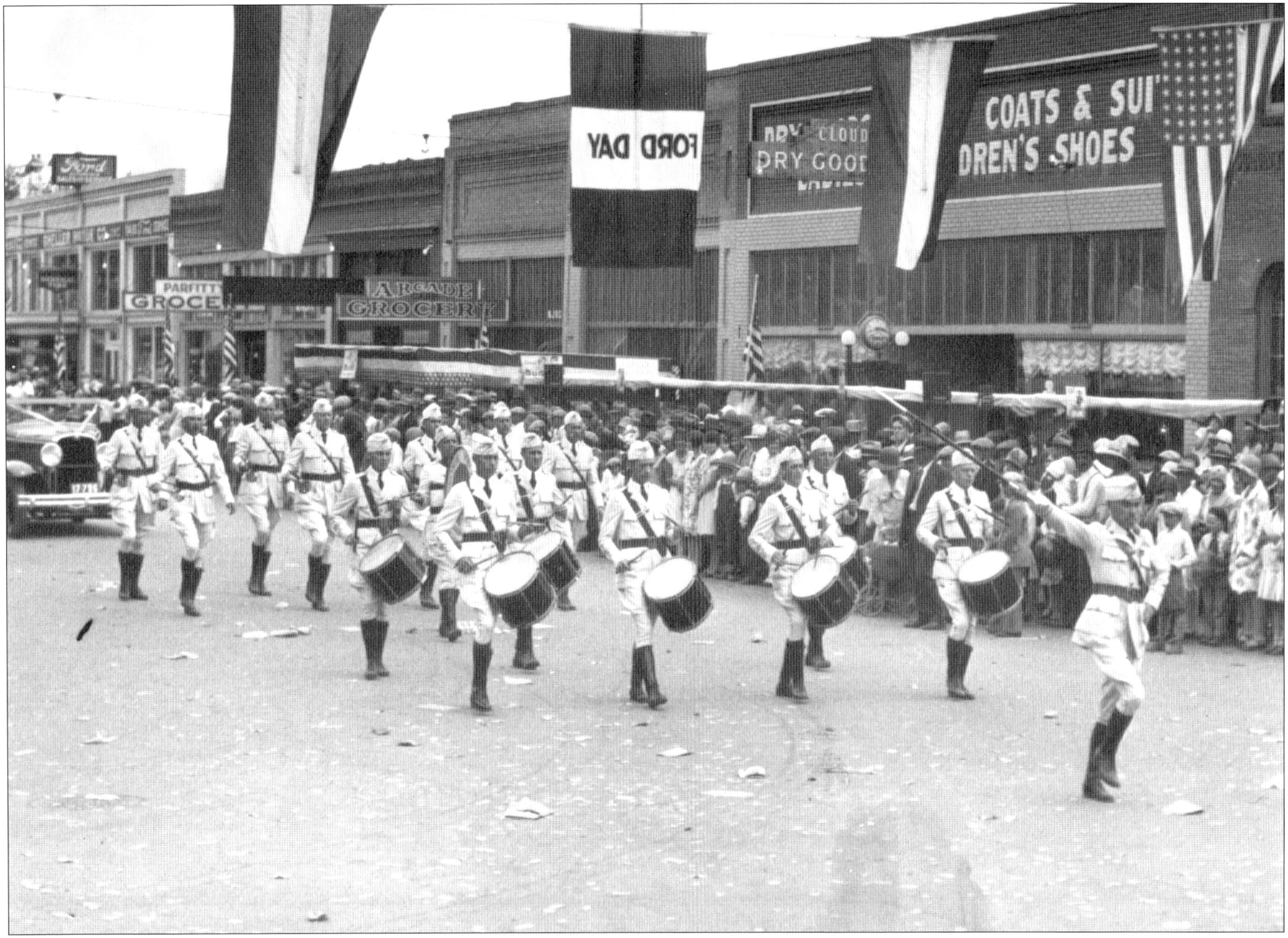

Sunnyside Legion Drum and Bugle Corps, Ford Day Parade, 1928.

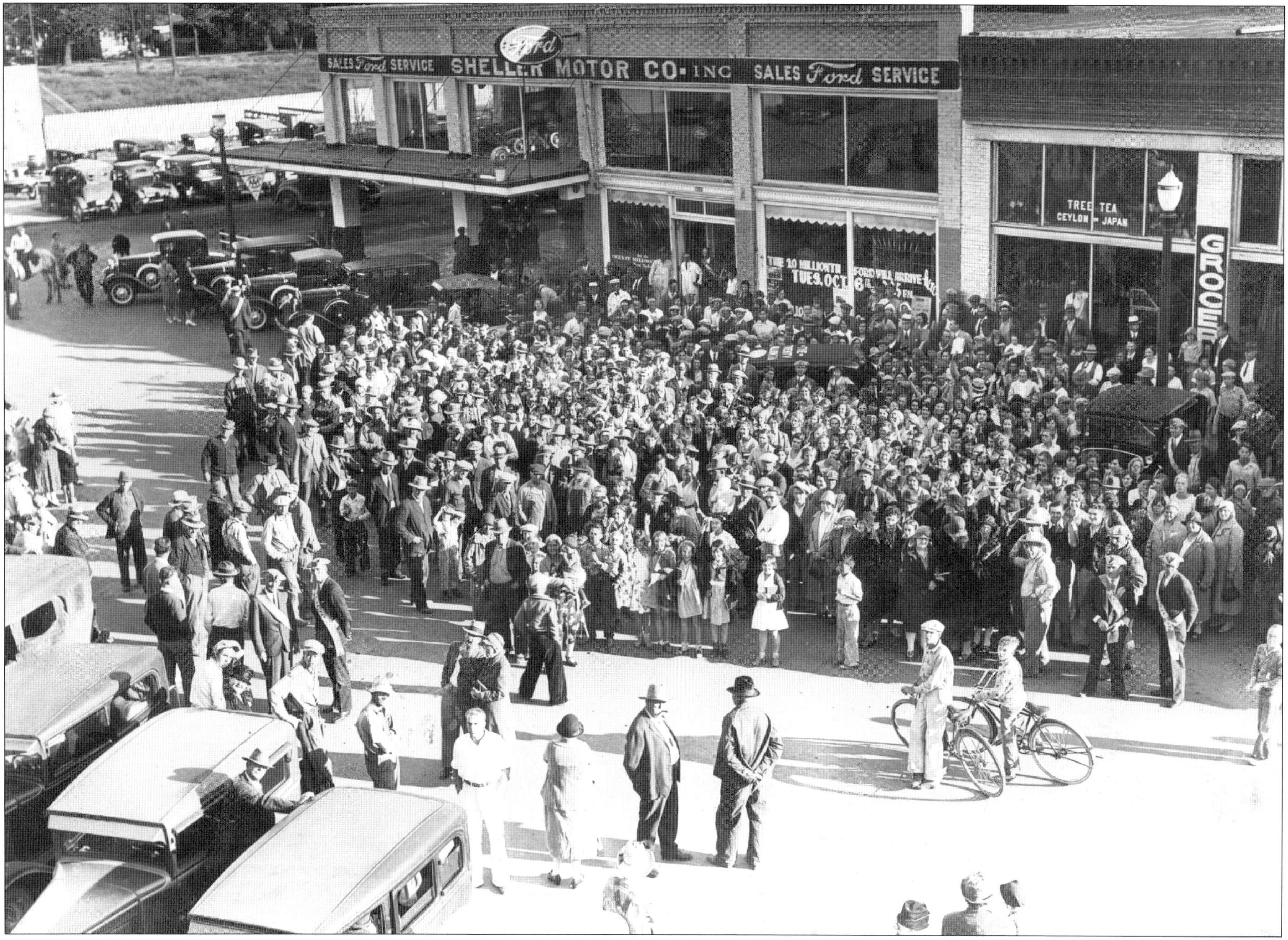

On October 6, 1931, the 20 Millionth Ford Car arrived in Sunnyside as a part of a promotional tour around the country. The car is located in the middle of the crowd with writing on the top.

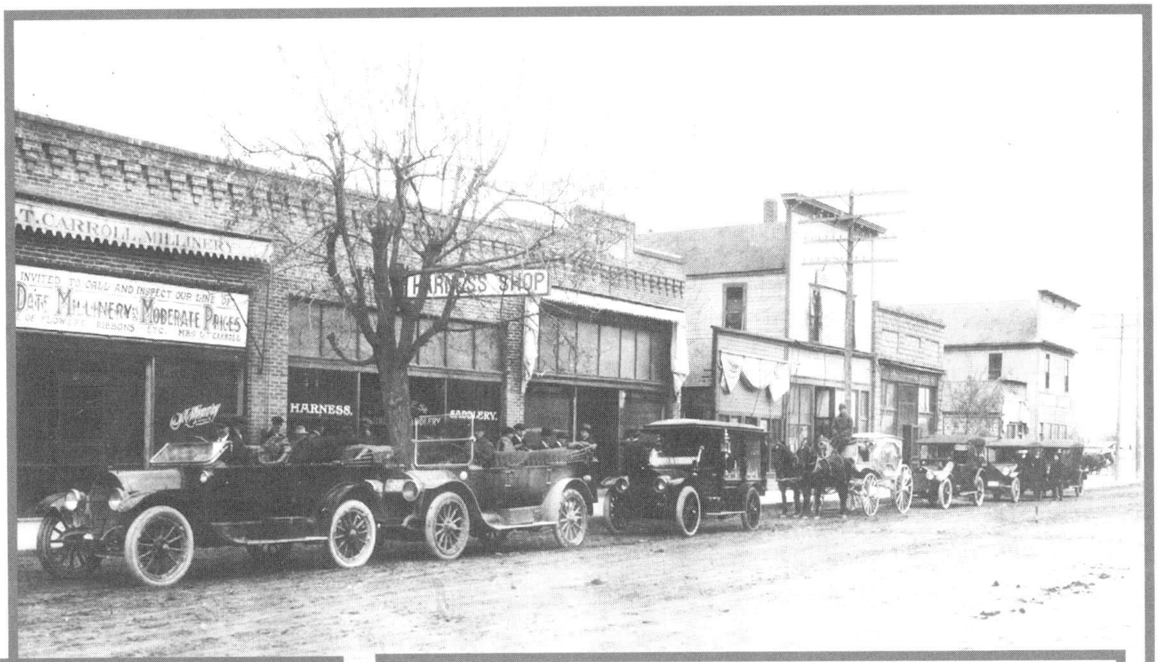

A Stroll Down Memory Lane...

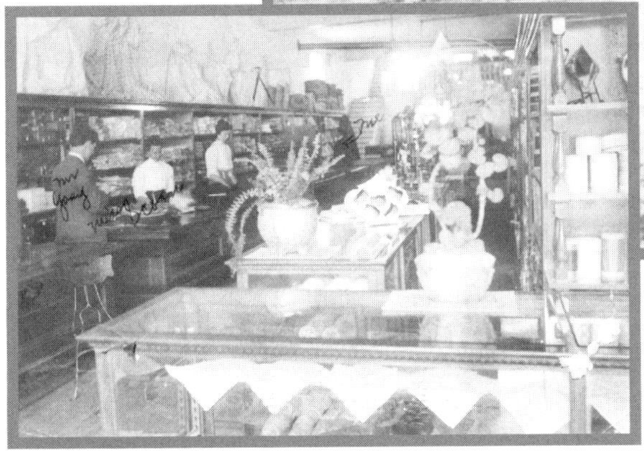

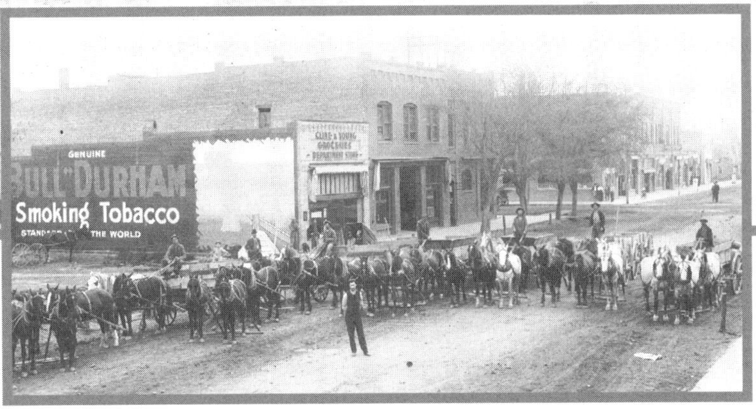

Rediscover Your Roots

Sunnyside Museum

704 South 4th Street, Sunnyside, Washington 98944 • 837-6010

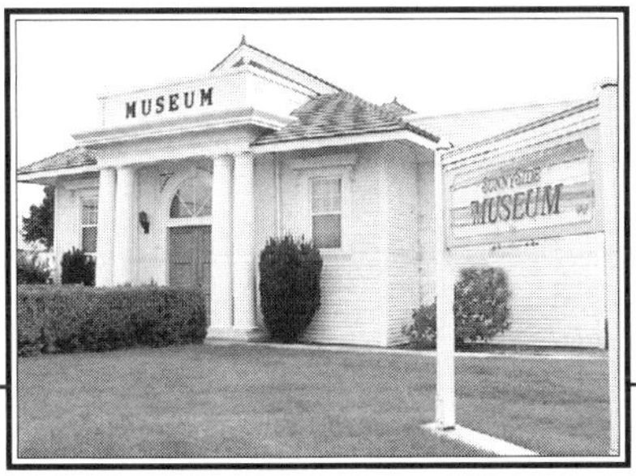

Interested In Donating Copies Or Original Photographs Of Early Sunnyside? Give Us A Call And Help Build Memories At The Sunnyside Museum.

Van de Graaf Ranches, Inc.

"Proud To Be A Part of the Lower Valley since 1959"

1691 Midvale Rd., Sunnyside, Washington, 98944 • 509-837-3151

Dick and Maxine Van de Graaf came to the Valley in 1959 with their young family and began their cattle feeding operation right away.

The family and business have steadily grown with the Valley over the past 40-plus years.

As one of the largest family owned and operated businesses in the Yakima Valley the Van de Graaf's pride themselves on a strong work ethic and community involvement.

They are proud to be a part of the Valley's rich history.

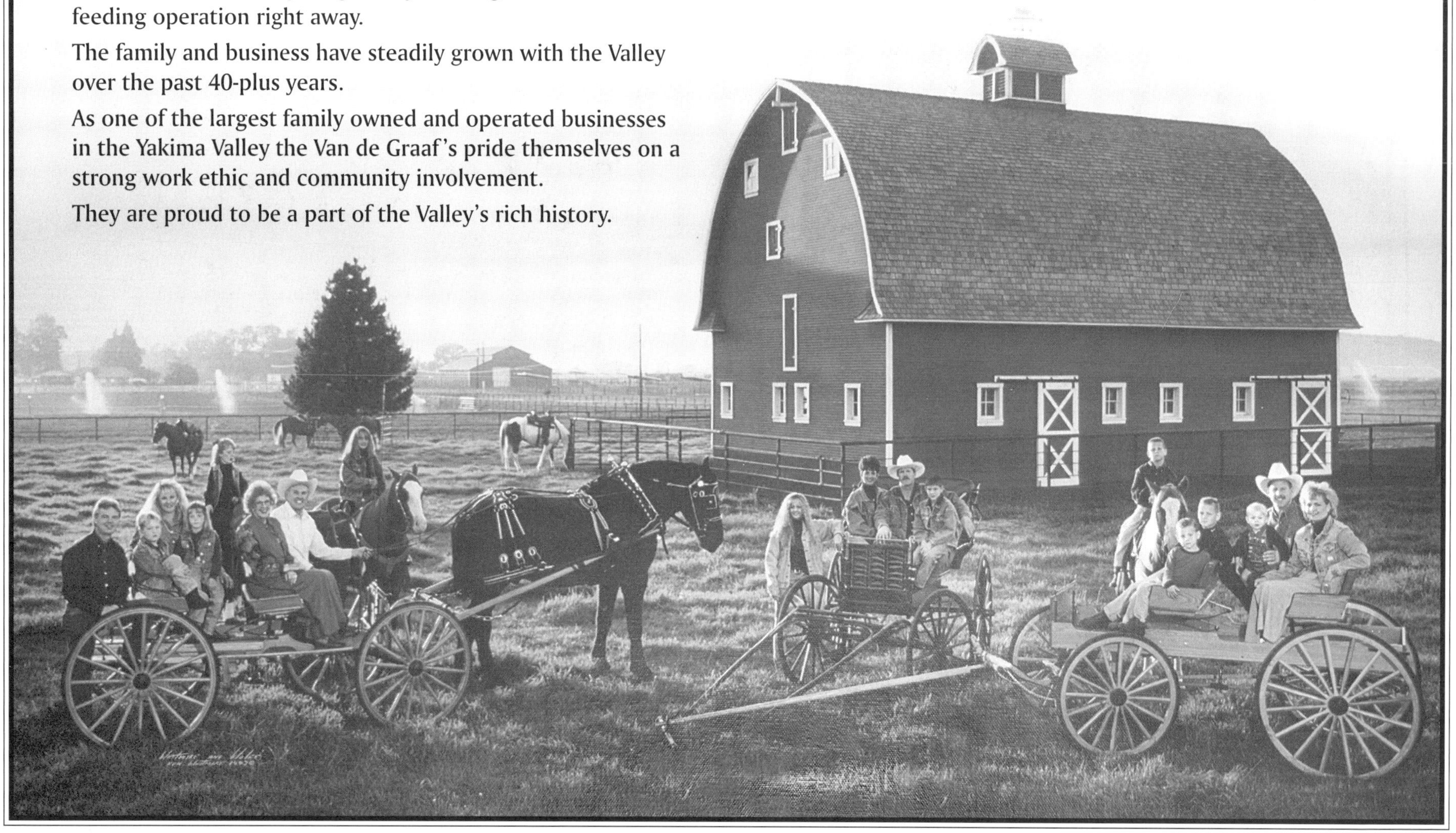